DEVELOPMENT AND VULNERABILITY
IN CLOSE RELATIONSHIPS

The Jean Piaget Symposium Series
Available from LEA

SIGEL, I. E., BRODZINSKY, D. M., & GOLINKOFF, R. M. (Eds.) •
New Directions in Piagetian Theory and Practice

OVERTON, W. F. (Ed.) • The Relationship Between Social and
Cognitive Development

LIBEN, L. S. (Ed.) • Piaget and the Foundations of Knowledge

SCHOLNICK, E. K. (Ed.) • New Trends in Conceptual Representation:
Challenges to Piaget's Theory?

NEIMARK, E. D., DeLISI, R., & NEWMAN, J. L. (Eds.) • Moderators
of Competence

BEARISON, D. J., & ZIMILES, H. (Eds.) • Thought and Emotion:
Developmental Perspectives

LIBEN, L. S. (Ed.) • Development and Learning: Conflict or Congruence?

FORMAN, G., & PUFALL, P. B. (Eds.) • Constructivism in the
Computer Age

OVERTON, W. F. (Ed.) • Reasoning, Necessity, and Logic:
Developmental Perspectives

KEATING, D. P., & ROSEN, H. (Eds.) • Constructivist Perspectives on
Developmental Psychopathology and Atypical Development

CAREY, S., & GELMAN, R. (Eds.) • The Epigenesis of Mind: Essays
on Biology and Cognition

BEILIN, H., & PUFALL, P. (Eds.) • Piaget's Theory: Prospects and
Possibilities

WOZNIAK, R. H., & FISCHER, K. W. (Eds.) • Development
in Context: Acting and Thinking in Specific Environments

OVERTON, W. F., & PALERMO, D. S. (Eds.) • The Nature and
Ontogenesis of Meaning

NOAM, G. G., & FISCHER, K. W. (Eds.) • Development and
Vulnerability in Close Relationships

REED, E. S., TURIEL, E., & BROWN, T. (Eds.) • Values and
Knowledge

DEVELOPMENT AND VULNERABILITY
IN CLOSE RELATIONSHIPS

Edited by

Gil G. Noam
Kurt W. Fischer
Harvard University

 LAWRENCE ERLBAUM ASSOCIATES, PUBLISHERS
1996   Mahwah, New Jersey

Lawrence Erlbaum Associates, Inc., Publishers
10 Industrial Avenue
Mahwah, New Jersey 07430

Library of Congress Cataloging-in-Publication Data

Development and vulnerability in close relationships / edited by Gil
   G. Noam, Kurt W. Fischer.
      p.   cm. — (The Jean Piaget Symposium series)
   Includes bibliographical references and index.
   ISBN 0-8058-1369-1 (c : alk. paper)
   1. Interpersonal relations in children.   2. Attachment behavior in
children.   I. Noam, Gil G.   II. Fischer, Kurt W.   III. Series.
BF723.I646D48   1996
158'.2—dc20   95-41219
                                                CIP

Printed in the United States of America
10 9 8 7 6 5 4 3 2 1

To our parents,
Ernst and *Lotte Noam*
Kurt and *Irmgaard Fischer*
Who nurtured us in our first relationships

Contents

IV: Dynamics and Themes of Relationship in Personality Development

Introduction:
The Foundational Role of Relationships in Human Development

Gil G. Noam
Kurt W. Fischer

How do people develop in their important relationships? How do two people come together to form a new, close relationship? How do relationships affect or determine who we are and who we become? These questions should be central to the study of development, but most researchers, at least in English-language communities, neglect these questions of relationship and focus instead on analyses of individuals, as if people were basically alone, with occasional brushes with other people.

Contrary to this individualist assumption, people are fundamentally social, and relationships are part of the fabric of being human. Social relationships, especially close ones, form an essential foundation for the development of human beings, molding each person's mind and behavior. Many of the most important classic works in social science, including psychology and philosophy, have recognized the foundational role of relationships, analyzing the social foundations of intelligence, morality, language, emotion, culture—all the many parts of being human (Baldwin, 1894; Benedict, 1934; A. Freud, 1936/1955; S. Freud, 1909/1955; Mead, 1934; Sullivan, 1953; Wittgenstein, 1953).

Unfortunately, the middle of the 20th century saw replacement of the centrality of relationships with solipsistic individualism, which reduced the social nature of human development (Chomsky, 1986; Kohlberg, 1969; Piaget, 1983; Skinner, 1938). Each mind contained its own language, its own morality, its own logic, its own reinforcement history; and relationships with other people were at best ancillary. If relationships remained important, it was only as objects of contemplation for individuals considering others' perspectives or as occasional skirmishes between independent individuals gathering data for their cognitive models.

Fortunately, the classical focus on relationships was not entirely lost, however, and tools are available for moving the study of development back to its relational origins. Through fields such as psychoanalysis, philosophy, and anthropology, the relational nature of humanity continued to be recognized, and even some scholars who neglected relationships in their research made efforts to acknowledge their centrality (Kohlberg, 1969, 1978; Piaget, 1977). Now many scholars are reexamining these classic relationship concepts and bringing them back into the study of human development. In this book we aim to present the central concepts and findings about the foundational nature of relationships and to provide a framework for transforming the study of development by bringing relationships to the fore.

TRANSFORMATION OF DEVELOPMENT
THROUGH RELATIONSHIPS

The new relational casting of psychology emphasizes the core nature of relationships in all aspects of human functioning from the very beginning of life and therefore begins with the central questions about people in relationships that we posed at the start of this preface (Bowlby, 1969–1980; Fischer & Watson, 1981; Gilligan, 1982; Maccoby, 1990; Noam, Powers, Kilkenny, & Beedy, 1990; Rogoff, 1990; Schore, 1994; Stem, 1985; Vygotsky, 1978; Wozniak & Fischer, 1993; the various chapters of this book). These questions and the answers proposed for them are transforming the nature of explanation of human activity and experience. The mind does not reside in one person but in relationships and communities, composed of many people's interconnected minds, which mutually support and define each other. Each person grows in important, close relationships in communities and cultures. Those relationships are so central to each person's activity and experience that without them, no scientific explanation can even begin to analyze mind and action.

Not only are relationships at the center of mind and action, but minds are no longer merely brains that happen to be in bodies. People are embedded: Our minds are parts of our bodies, and with our mind/bodies we act, think, and feel jointly with other people as part of a social and physical world (Bronfenbrenner, 1993; Fischer & Granott, in press; Gibson, 1979; Lakoff, 1987; Noam et al., 1990). This ecological perspective has begun to take hold in many arenas of social science and especially in the study of development. Just as species of animals have niches in nature that constitute essential parts of what those animals do and how they live, so we human beings are entwined with our "niches." The people, objects, and events we live with are literally parts of our mind/bodies, affording our actions, thoughts, and feelings, as Gibson (1979) would say. There is no mind without body and world, no mind without other people.

One strand in this return to relationships has been the emphasis on diverse pathways of development, especially how early close relationships mold people's development. This theme is central in psychoanalysis, and attachment theory has built on psychoanalysis to propose ways that early close relationships produce specific pathways for development of personality and cognitive functioning (Ainsworth, Blehar, Waters, & Wall, 1978; Bowlby, 1969–1980; Bretherton, 1985; Schore, 1994; Sroufe, 1984). Attachment theory has helped to transform relational concepts into shapes that can be readily studied in developmental research. Hundreds of studies have examined how early relationships mold children's personalities and competencies. Children develop basic ways of interacting with others, especially in close relationships, which are called *internal working models* in attachment parlance. The attachment framework has thus helped to bring relationships into focus in the study of development. Many of the chapters in this book deal centrally with concepts and research on attachment, seeking to build a comprehensive analysis of how people develop in relationships (see especially Bretherton, chapter 1; Shaver & Clark, chapter 2; Case, chapter 3).

Focusing on the foundational nature of relationships is so transformative that it even changes attachment theory. If relationships are at the center of human action and thought, then attachments influence people not merely through effecting "internal" change by producing working models that guide individuals from the inside. Relationships are more than internal influences on separate individuals. Instead, people actually participate in each other's minds, and their working models take part in their relationships with other people (Fischer & Ayoub, chapter 7, this volume; Fischer & Granott, in press; Noam, 1990), just as objects are actually a part of perceptions and actions in more traditional cognitive domains (e.g., Gibson, 1979). Working models are patterns of living and participating with others, not models that are merely internally imposed on other people. A theme that pervades this book is the need to change concepts like internal working model and internalization to reflect the natural connections between people's constructions of relationships and the real exchanges they experience with the important people in their world.

VULNERABILITIES THROUGH RELATIONSHIPS

Another goal of this book is to bring together clinical and developmental approaches by analyzing the vulnerabilities as well as the strengths that grow from relationships. That is why we deliberately placed the term *vulnerability* in the title of the volume, and that is why we asked contributors to address directly how relationships contribute to risks, problems, and psychopathologies. The relational approaches have tended to focus on the sustaining and productive elements of close relationships (e.g., Belenky et al., 1986; Gilligan, 1982). There is no question that these creative approaches have provided much evidence that close, empathic, and caring relationships enhance self-esteem, produce vitality in the self, and create supports that can increase learning capacities.

We need to be equally sensitive, however, to the fact that close relationships in the family, the peer world, and romantic involvements can be the cause of great suffering and can create serious problems in the course of development. The most extreme example, of course, is maltreatment, including the injuries of physical abuse and the boundary transgressions of sexual abuse. Not only is the child confronted with physical pain or sexual experiences far beyond any ability to understand and cope with them, but in addition the trust placed in close adults is seriously exploited and undermined. Physical maltreatment and sexual abuse are far more prevalent than was believed until recently, and the developmental consequences can be devastating (Cicchetti, 1990; Fischer & Ayoub, 1994; Herman, 1992; Terr, 1990).

Close relationships become risks not only under these extreme conditions but in more mundane events as well. It is the day-to-day conflicts and small abandonments, the chronic sense of not being listened to that often create long-lasting negative effects. We know from research that chronic parental strife is a serious risk factor for most forms of psychopathology, such as behavioral and emotional disorders and symptoms (Rutter, 1990; Werner, 1990). Similarly, the break up of romantic involvements in adolescence can lead to suicidal ideation or attempted suicide (Noam & Borst, 1994). Furthermore, being ostracized in the peer world or chronically bullied by one's "friends" can also lead to serious developmental problems (Selman, 1975).

These are only a few examples of the many hidden and overt injuries in close relationships. It is probable that every person, as part of normative development, experiences various injuries and develops various long-term vulnerabilities in close relationships. For that reason, it is important to begin to reduce the sometimes artificial boundaries of clinical and developmental psychologies. Developmentalists, we believe, need to rewrite the normal course of life to include conflict and vulnerability, periods of regression and fragmentation. These problems exist right next to our capacities for integration, synthesis, and equilibration, sometimes even growing out of the earlier vulnerabilities (Noam, 1993). Similarly, clinicians need to, and have begun to, account for the adaptive nature of psychopathology, including attempts to solve complex problems through the detour of symptom formation. Traditional medical models of mental health need to be supplanted by truly developmental, interpersonal accounts that allow for dynamic interweaving of problems and strengths (Cicchetti, 1990; Fischer & Ayoub, chapter 7, this volume; Noam, 1990).

A DIVERSITY OF RELATIONAL PERSPECTIVES

These broad ideas on an interactionist and relational approach to development and vulnerability have led us to assemble in this volume theorists and researchers from a variety of different paradigms and traditions. Our goal was to create diversity of outlook so as to generate a productive tension between concepts as well as to detect convergence across differing orientations. Although interactions between approaches based in Piaget, social cognition, attachment, psychoanalysis, and gender issues are varied and at times even antagonistic, we have been impressed with the many similarities and mutual research goals.

Most of the theorists in this book, for example, have come to a relational perspective by discovering the power of interaction, the need to view the individual from the beginning of life as part of a relational matrix or an interpersonal field. In addition, Piagetians, attachment researchers, and psychodynamic thinkers all view development as a process of internalization, of taking the relational experiences from the world into the self. This process of internalization produces in the self not just a replica of the external experiences, but a constructed sense of self and relationships, which is afforded by and participates in real-world experiences with other people.

Earlier relationship patterns thus live on in each person through that person's own structuring of relationships and through the contributions of other people to those relationships. The result is a complex set of interactions between past and present. What has been internalized undergoes transformation, but we have learned from attachment theory and other perspectives how conservative the early relationship experiences usually are. Similarly, we have learned from Piaget and especially the social cognitive perspectives, also assembled in this volume, that there is a tremendous transformational power in the categories we use to understand ourselves and the close relationships we live in. These categories are not just "cold" analytical entities, but play a central role in people's day-to-day lives.

Creative analysis of gender differences provides an important example of how categories can have transformative power (e.g., Gilligan, 1982). In analyzing the diverse pathways of women and men, boys and girls in relationships, the findings about girls' and women's development have entered a stage of generalization. What has been learned about girls' development is being used to revisit and revise traditional models of (human) development, which were not capturing male development very well either. A relationship focus represents the experience of many men better than the individualistic focus of earlier theories.

People in close relationships, even adults, are important teachers and therapists to each other, suggesting and demanding new ways of interpreting the world and often helping each other overcome old vulnerabilities. These developmental opportunities in relationships provide one reason for the lifelong motivation for seeking interpersonal bonds and pursuing empathic understanding in close relationships, despite all the risks involved.

ORGANIZATION OF THE BOOK

Our intention in organizing the sections of this book is to form a circle linking all the chapters, but unfortunately the physical shape of a book in its present form cannot be assembled in a circle. All the relational perspectives represented in the book have influenced each other, and no point of view should claim temporal or intellectual antecedence when it comes to the study of relationships. The interconnection of perspectives and concepts should not be represented in a linear fashion, from chapter to chapter, but rather in a fashion that shows continuous connections and new integrations among the themes and chapters. We will have to rely on our readers to participate actively in the goal of theory construction by using each chapter to deepen the exciting search for common principles in a new interpersonal, dynamic developmental psychology.

We could have started the book with any of the perspectives, but we chose the attachment paradigm because of its detailed research on relationships. The attachment framework divides relationship into three types of attachment: secure, anxious insecure, and avoidant insecure. These categories have provided powerful initial tools for reducing people's multitude of experiences with their caregivers to meaningful configurations for the entire life cycle from infancy through adulthood. The need now is for ways to describe not only the continuities of attachment types over time (the so-called conservative nature of attachment) but simultaneously the typical growth or transformation of attachment patterns. Both this need for further developmental analysis and authors' interests in meaning and cognition have led to a common focus on the concept of working models of attachment relationships. Working models are the frames for relationships that people develop in early life and later build upon and transform as they grow. This concept is worth a great deal of further investigation. Are there normative ways in which people update their working models? What roles do new relationships play in working models?

In the first section of the book (Attachment and the Construction of Close Relationships), Bretherton (chapter 1) analyzes these questions for childhood, and Shaver and Clark (chapter 2) for adulthood. Their chapters describe exciting lines of research involving a variety of different methods for measuring attachment and studying its continuities and changes. Case (chapter 3) then outlines in detail a hypothesis for how a working model develops at one early phase of development, using neo-Piagetian categories and a focus on defense mechanisms. This kind of specific analysis of the cognitive and developmental underpinnings of development of attachment relationships is a theme that pervades later chapters of the book as well. Only when researchers and clinicians can reconstruct these developmental transformations will we be able to understand how so many people are able to transfer from dysfunctional relationships to functional ones across the life span (Noam, 1992).

The second section of the book focuses more explicitly on cognitive development and relationships. Edelstein's (chapter 4) important longitudinal research with Icelandic children and adolescents relates cognitive development to attachment relationships as well as depression and anxiety. His findings and theoretical analysis indicate an important link between these different dimensions. Décarie and Ricard (chapter 5) return to Décarie's pathbreaking work on infant development, especially object and person permanence, and provide a Piagetian interpretation of relationships.

Part III deals with construction of vulnerabilities and strengths analyzed in terms of relational perspectives that focus on social cognitive principles of development. Noam (chapter 6) suggests a need to rewrite developmental theories to incorporate conflicts and vulnerabilities not only in early, immature periods but also in later development. For mature developmental positions he describes both typical relationship problems and developmental tools for overcoming personal and interpersonal vulnerabilities, including the inherent power to create strengths in development, a capacity that can develop at any point in life.

In chapter 7, Fischer and Ayoub describe a set of tools for analyzing developmental changes in working models. To show how these tools can be used, they portray in detail a case study of two adults who showed their strengths and vulnerabilities as they constructed an adult love relationship. This man and woman had difficulties with their caregivers during childhood, and then later as adults they met, got to know each other, fell in love, were married, and then developed major relationship difficulties connected with their attachment histories. In chapter 8, Levitt and Selman introduce their notions of personal meanings and friendships in the context of a constructivist approach to risk-taking. Understanding risk-taking behaviors in adolescence requires analyzing how they relate to earlier developments as well as to friendship patterns: how they involve both strengths and vulnerabilities. Each adolescent constructs her or his own personal meaning for risk-taking behavior.

The final section of the book focuses on how particular relationship themes function dynamically to shape development, especially themes defining the nature of close relationships. Gilligan (chapter 9) and Benenson (chapter 10) focus on issues of gender, outlining different perspectives on male–female differences in relationships. Together they describe powerful differences from early in life in how girls and boys typically navigate the complex web of relationships. Gilligan builds on psychodynamic principles of conscious and unconscious knowing, having and losing voice, and how individuals construct their voices and relationships jointly with other people. Development involves movement not only toward better knowing and more effective voicing but also simultaneously toward loss of knowledge and voice – a dynamic interplay of strengths and vulnerabilities. In her chapter, Benenson reviews the extensive evidence that boys and girls approach social interactions differently by the preschool years if not earlier, with boys tending to prefer group interactions organized hierarchically and girls tending to prefer dyadic interactions organized reciprocally.

In chapter 11, the Luborsky's and colleagues address the role of core relationship themes in young children and how they relate to later adult themes, based on their important research on measuring what psychoanalysts call transference of themes between relationships. Their research shows that adults develop basic wishes, conflicts, and understandings about relationships that they bring to interactions in many times and contexts. These themes include not only the three general attachment patterns but also a number of other core relationship themes, which provide tools for a rich analysis of individual meaning systems.

The final chapter of this section could also be the beginning of the book, according to the circular metaphor for organizing the chapters. Blatt and Blass (chapter 12) reconceptualize Erikson (1963) from a relational perspective, developing the relationship focus in his work. Contrary to some stereotypes, Erikson cannot accurately be viewed as focusing only on separation from others and individual identity. It is important to elaborate the relational aspects of his work to show how his framework highlights contributions of relationships to strengths and vulnerabilities in development. Blatt and Blass interweave two developmental trajectories, that of autonomy and separation with that of inclusion and intimacy. Within this framework, Erikson's theory can be viewed as focusing on development of mutuality, from basic trust to intimacy with others, generative care for others, and love and acceptance of humankind in the wisdom of old age – a fitting conclusion to a book on relationships.

Sullivan (1953) described the dialectical tension that people experience in relationships. On the one hand, people need relationships to survive and grow, to develop their potential, to feel whole and integrated in a family and community, and to engage in the cycle of life, from beginning to end. On the other hand, relationships simultaneously threaten and restrict people, limiting individual freedom and competence, engendering mistreatment, control, and engulfment, and leading to loss of self. The tension between closeness and distance, togetherness and aloneness, understanding and confrontation create great dilemmas in most people's lives. At the same time, the continuous search for new solutions is inherent in every relationship as well as underlying the collective effort that this book represents.

With this book, we aim to establish a firm foundation for the role of relationships in human activity and experience and to promote strong research by bringing together in one place most of the best research and theory on relationships. We hope to stimulate a more radical inclusion of relationships in mind, an ecological focus on the ways that relationships constitute action, feeling, and thought. Although relationships can be studied on their own, this book aims to give them their proper place at the center of human mind and action, not as another in a long list of separate domains of human experience. Human development begins with people in relationships.

ACKNOWLEDGMENTS

This book would not have been possible without the creative input of the Governing Board of the Jean Piaget Society: Society for the Study of Knowledge and Development. The book began when we developed a symposium conference for the annual meeting of the Society, and in that endeavor we received energetic intellectual and administrative support from the Society. At the time, the Society Board had decided to move the conference from its traditional symposium site, Philadelphia, to new meeting places. Montreal was chosen as the first new site, and our symposium provided the theme for the conference. The combination of the JPS energy, the city of Montreal, and the topic of Development and Vulnerability in Relationships led to resounding success! We hope this volume reflects some of that excitement.

We especially thank Henry Markovitz for local arrangements in a new city (he made Montreal possible for the Society), William Gray for putting the program together, and several presidents of the Society who helped with the conference—Jack Meacham, Terry Brown, and Michael Chandler, Lawrence Erlbaum Associates editors Judith Amsel and Robin Weisberg, and other Board and Society members too numerous to mention. We also want to thank the students in our Harvard seminar on Development and

Vulnerability in Relationships, who stimulated ideas about framing the topic as well as critiquing old frameworks.

Funding sources and intellectual support that helped sustain our research as well as our efforts on the book itself include the Harvard Graduate School of Education, McLean Hospital, the Consolidated Department of Psychiatry, Harvard Medical School, the MacArthur Network on Early Childhood, and the Spencer Foundation, the Milton Fund of Harvard University, and the Institute for Advanced Study, Berlin.

Most of all, we thank the authors of this volume for their willingness to work with us so generously. All their chapters have been greatly revised to produce an overall unity and intellectual coherence to the volume and, we hope, fulfills some of the promise of the new focus on relationships in human development.

Gil G. Noam
Kurt W. Fischer

REFERENCES

Ainsworth, M. D., Blehar, M., Waters, E., & Wall, S. (1978). *Patterns of attachment: A psychological study of the strange situation.* Hillsdale, NJ: Lawrence Erlbaum Associates.

Baldwin, J. M. (1894). *Mental development in the child and the race.* New York: MacMillan.

Belenky, M. F., Clinchy, B. M., Goldberger, N. R., & Tarule, J. M. (1986). *Women's ways of knowing: The development of self, voice, and mind.* New York: Basic Books.

Benedict, R. (1934). *Patterns of culture.* Boston: Houghton Mifflin.

Bowlby, J. (1969–1980). *Attachment and loss* (3 vols.). New York: Basic Books.

Bretherton, I. (1985). Attachment theory: Retrospect and prospect. In I. Bretherton & E. Waters (Eds.), *Growing points of attachment theory and research. Monographs of the Society for Research in Child Development, 50*(1–2, Serial No. 209), 3–40.

Bronfenbrenner, U. (1993). The ecology of cognitive development. In R. H. Wozniak & K. W. Fischer (Eds.), *Development in context: Acting and thinking in specific environments* (pp. 3–44). Hillsdale, NJ: Lawrence Erlbaum Associates.

Chomsky, N. (1986). *Knowledge of language: Its nature, origin, and use.* Westport, CT: Praeger.

Cicchetti, D. (1990). A historical perspective of developmental psychopathology. In A. M. J. Rolf, D. Cicchetti, K. Neuchterlein, & S. Weintraub (Eds.), *Risk and protective factors in the development of psychopathology* (pp. 2–28). New York: Cambridge University Press.

Erikson, E. (1963). *Childhood and society* (2nd ed.). New York: Norton.

Fischer, K. W., & Ayoub, C. (1994). Affective splitting and dissociation in normal and maltreated children: Developmental pathways for self in relationships. In D. Cicchetti & S. L. Toth (Eds.), *Rochester Symposium on Development and Psychopathology: Vol. 5. Disorders and dysfunctions of the self* (pp. 149–222). Rochester, NY: University of Rochester Press.

Fischer, K. W., & Granott, N. (in press). Beyond one-dimensional change: Parallel, concurrent, socially distributed processes in learning and development. *Human Development.*

Fischer, K.W., & Watson, M. W. (1981). Explaining the Oedipus conflict. In K. W. Fischer (Ed.), *Cognitive development. New Directions for Child Development* (Vol. 12, pp. 79–92). San Francisco: Jossey-Bass.

Freud, A. (1966). *The ego and the mechanisms of defense* (C. Baines, Trans.). New York: International Universities Press. (Original work published 1936)

Freud, S. (1955). Analysis of a phobia in a five-year-old boy (J. A. Strachey, Trans.). *Standard edition of the complete psychological works of Sigmund Freud* (Vol. 10). London: Hogarth Press. (Original work published 1909)

Gibson, J. J. (1979). *The ecological approach to visual perception.* Boston: Houghton-Mifflin.

Gilligan, C. (1982). *In a different voice: Psychological theory and women's development.* Cambridge: MA: Harvard University Press.

Herman. J. (1992). *Trauma and recovery.* New York: Basic Books.

Kohlberg, L. (1969). Stage and sequence: The cognitive developmental approach to socialization. In D. A. Goslin (Ed.), *Handbook of socialization theory and research* (pp. 347–480). Chicago: Rand, McNally.

Kohlberg, L. (1978). Revisions in the theory and practice of moral development. In W. Damon (Ed.) *Moral development. New Directions for Child Development* (Vol. 2, pp. 83–87). San Francisco: Jossey-Bass.

Lakoff, G. (1987). *Women, fire, and dangerous things: What categories reveal about the mind.* Chicago: University of Chicago Press.

Maccoby, E. (1990). Gender and relationships: A developmental account. *American Psychologist, 45,* 513–520.

Mead, G. H. (1934). *Mind, self, and society.* Chicago: University of Chicago Press.

Noam, G. G. (1990). Beyond Freud and Piaget: Biographical worlds — Interpersonal self. In T. E. Wren (Ed.), *The moral domain* (pp. 360–399). Cambridge, MA: MIT Press.

Noam, G. G. (1992). Development as the aim of clinical intervention. *Development and Psychopathology, 4,* 679–696.

Noam, G. G. (1993). "Normative vulnerabilities" of self and their transformations in moral actions. In G. G. Noam & T. E. Wren (Eds.), *The moral self* (pp. 209–238). Cambridge, MA: MIT Press.

Noam, G. G., & Borst, S. (Eds.). (1994). *Children, youth, and suicide: Developmental perspectives. New Directions for Child Development* (Vol. 64). San Francisco: Jossey-Bass.

Noam, G. G., Powers, S. J., Kilkenny, R., & Beedy, J. (1990). The interpersonal self in life-span developmental perspective: Theory, measurement, and longitudinal case analyses. In P. B. Baltes, D. L. Featherman, & R. M. Lerner (Eds.), *Life Span Development and Behavior,* (Vol. 10, pp. 59–104). Hillsdale, NJ: Lawrence Erlbaum Associates.

Piaget, J. (1977). *Études sociologiques* (3rd ed.). Genève: Librairie Droz.

Piaget, J. (1983). Piaget's theory. In P. H. Mussen (Series Ed.) & W. Kessen (Ed), *Handbook of child psychology: Vol. 1. History, theory, and methods* (pp. 103–126). New York: Wiley.

Rogoff, B. (1990). *Apprenticeship in thinking: Cognitive development in social context.* New York: Oxford University Press.

Rutter, M. (1990). Psychosocial resilience and protective mechanisms. In A. M. J. Rolf, D. Cicchetti, K. Neuchterlein, & S. Weintraub (Eds.), *Risk and protective factors in the development of psychopathology* (pp. 181–214). New York: Cambridge University Press.

Schore, A. N. (1994). *Affect regulation and the origin of the self: The neurobiology of emotional development.* Hillsdale, NJ: Lawrence Erlbaum Associates.

Selman, R. L. (1975). Level of social perspective taking and the development of empathy in children. *Child Development, 42,* 79–91.

Skinner, B. F. (1938). *The behavior of organisms.* New York: Appleton-Century-Crofts.

Sroufe, L. A. (1984). The organization of emotional development. In K. R. Scherer & P. Ekman (Eds.), *Approaches to emotion* (pp. 109–128). Hillsdale, NJ: Lawrence Erlbaum Associates.

Stern, D. N. (1985). *The interpersonal world of the infant: A view from psychoanalysis and developmental psychology.* New York: Basic Books.

Sullivan, H. S. (1953). *The interpersonal theory of psychiatry.* New York: Norton.

Terr, L. (1990). *Too scared to cry: Psychic trauma in childhood.* New York: Basic Books.

Vygotsky, L. (1978). *Mind in society: The development of higher psychological processes* (M. Cole, V. John-Steiner, S. Scribner, & E. Souberman, Trans.). Cambridge, MA: Harvard University Press.

Werner, E. (1990). Protective factors and individual resilience. In S. Meisels & J. Shonkoff (Eds.), *Handbook of early childhood intervention.* Cambridge, MA: Cambridge University Press.

Wittgenstein, L. (1953). *Philosophical investigations* (G. E. M Anscombe, Trans.). Oxford, UK: Oxford University Press.

Wozniak, R., & Fischer, K. W. (1993). Development in context: An introduction. In R. Wozniak & K. W. Fischer (Eds.), *Development in context: Acting and thinking in specific environments* (pp. xi–xvi). Hillsdale, NJ: Lawrence Erlbaum Associates.

Attachment and the Construction of Close Relationships

1 Internal Working Models of Attachment Relationships as Related to Resilient Coping

Inge Bretherton
University of Wisconsin, Madison

Adaptive coping in stressful situations turns, in part, on an individual's inner resources. There are at least two ways in which these inner resources are linked to secure attachment relationships. First, the confident knowledge that an attachment figure is available for emotional support when needed tends to increase an individual's ability to consider alternative solutions when faced with difficult and stressful situations (Bowlby, 1969/1982, 1973). Second, a secure relationship with one or more attachment figures affects successful coping more indirectly through the impact of such relationships on the organization and quality of an individual's representational system. Secure relationships, under this view, facilitate the development of well-organized, adequate, flexible internal working models (representations) of self in relation to important others, and thereby also of the world as a reasonably trustworthy place. Insecure attachment relations, under this view, lead to ill-organized working models that are distorted and disrupted by defensive processes that frequently stand in the way of successful coping.

In this chapter, I summarize Bowlby's (1969/1982, 1973, 1980) ideas on child–caregiver patterns in secure and insecure attachment relationships as related to emerging working models of self and attachment figures. I then review relevant attachment research. Next, I elaborate the concept of internal working models in light of recent ideas from the domain of event representation. I also consider how parent–child dialogues about past and future events may significantly shape the organization of internal working models of self in attachment relationships. After examining the role of childhood trauma in the construction of internal working models, I conclude with a brief discussion of internal working models as related to a capacity for resilient as opposed to maladaptive coping.

ATTACHMENT THEORY AND INTERNAL WORKING MODELS

Since the 1980s, attachment researchers have switched their primary focus from the ethological-evolutionary function of attachment as protection- and security-seeking (Bowlby, 1969/1982) to a closer examination of attachment relations from a representational and communication perspective. How individual differences in parent–child attachment communications are translated into attachment representations has been of particular interest (for a review see Bretherton, 1990; see also Grossmann & Grossmann, 1990).

Following Bowlby, attachment theorists refer to mental representation of self, attachment figure, and the world in general as *internal working models*. The concept stems from a small, influential book on the *Nature of Explanation* by Craik (1943). Craik pointed out that many advantages accrue to an organism that carries in its head a model of the environment and its own actions in it. Such an organism is able to react to future situations before they arise and decide on an optimal course of action by mentally weighing alternative courses of action. Although Craik used the expression "imitation world" in his discussion of internal working models, he did not conceive of working models as strict copies, but rather as mental structures that adequately conserve what he called the relation-structure real-world phenomena (i.e., their temporal and causal sequences).

As a psychoanalyst familiar with Freud's (1940) notions about the "inner world" as a stage for experimental mental action, Bowlby was immediately captivated by the metaphor of representation as an internal working model of the world when he came across it in the writings of the neurobiologist Young (1964). He preferred Craik's metaphor of "working model" to other then current metaphors for representation such as "image" or "map," because the term *working* suggested that representation is not a static process and the term *model* suggested that representations parallel the structure of experience such that an individual can operate on the model to create predictions of the future and extrapolations to hypothetical situations.

Whereas Bowlby followed Craik in suggesting that the function of internal working models is planning, decision making, and interpretation, he went vastly beyond Craik in elucidating the intergenerational, developmental, and communicative processes involved in a child's construction of internal working models of the world, and within that larger model, internal working models of attachment figures and the self.

Craik had been interested in how to build intelligent machines by incorporating working models of the physical world into them. Neither development nor emotion played a role in his conceptualizations. As defined by Bowlby (1969/1982, 1973, 1982), however, internal working models of the relational world are dynamic cognitive/affective mental structures whose initial construction precedes the acquisition of language:

> Starting, we may suppose, toward the end of the first year, and probably especially actively during his second and third year when he acquires the powerful and extraordinary gift of language, a child is busy constructing working models of how his mother and other significant persons may be expected to behave, how he himself may be expected to behave, and of how each interacts with all the others. Within the framework of these working models he evaluates his situation and makes his plans. And within the framework of the working models of his mother and himself he evaluates special aspects of his situation and makes his attachment plans. (Bowlby, 1969, p. 354)

To account for the establishment and increasing complexity of a child's internal working models, Bowlby drew on Piaget's (1951) theory of sensorimotor development. Piaget had postulated that, by acting on their environment, infants develop behavioral schemas that are then continuously adapted to new, often more complex circumstances. Piaget also proposed that infants begin to "interiorize" these increasingly complex schemas in the second year of life, a process that allows them to engage in mental instead of physical trial and error.

Analogously, Bowlby suggested that infants develop internal working models of self and caregiver in relationship out of experienced patterns of interpersonal transactions with them. Thus, in relationships where a parent has fairly consistently acknowledged an infant's needs for comfort and protection, and at the same time respected the infant's need for independent exploration of the environment, the child is later likely to develop a complementary internal working model of self as valued and self-reliant. Conversely, if the parent has frequently rejected the infant's bids for comfort or interfered with the infant's exploration, he or she is later likely to construct an internal working model of self as unworthy or incompetent and a complementary working model of the parent as rejecting. Although not explicitly stated in his writings, Bowlby's implicit views on representation seem closely related to Lewin's (1951) concepts of the psychological "life space" and environmental "demand characteristics"; Werner's (1948) notions on physiognomic perception; and Heider's (1958) attribution theory in which interpersonal responsibility and blame, success, and failure are an integral part of representation. What is modeled internally is the appraisal and reappraisal of personal and shared social meanings. Under this view, representation is not a dispassionate mapping of an objective reality. Rather, such factors as the ability or inability to trust others, self-efficacy or self-inefficacy (Bandura, 1982), belief in a benign or malignant world (Epstein, 1991), and hope (Melges & Bowlby, 1969) are an inextricable part of how an individual represents and thereby creates his or her personal present and future reality.

To explain why rejected children place responsibility for their parents' rejecting behavior on themselves, Bowlby (1980) postulated defensive processes that come into play when parents deny or ridicule a child's attachment behaviors, or when the child experiences a traumatic situation, but a parent gives an innocuous explanation, accompanied by a taboo on further discussion (see Cain & Fast, 1972; Laing & Esterson, 1964). In such cases, children tend to go along with what they are told, and defensively exclude their own interpretations of the experience from awareness, leading to the construction of two separate, mutually inconsistent working models of self and attachment figure. One working model, to which the individual has conscious access, justifies parental rejecting behavior by evaluating the self as bad. The second working model indirectly represents the attachment figure as bad and the self as badly treated. This working model is inaccessible to consciousness but influences interpretive processes.

According to Bowlby, such *defensive exclusion* of information (internal or external) from awareness is one manifestation of the more ubiquitous process of *selective exclusion* in which humans continuously engage to focus attention on relevant stimuli. He illustrated his point by reference to experiments on dichotic listening. A person who is exposed to two simultaneous messages via headphones is aware of monitoring only one of these messages. That the message conveyed to the unattended ear is nevertheless processed at a fairly high level becomes evident when the individual's personal name is inserted into the unattended message. When this occurs, the individual immediately alerts to the second message (see reviews of this literature by Dixon, 1971).

Bowlby also proposed that Tulving's (1972) distinction between semantic and episodic (autobiographical) memory might be helpful in explaining the construction of multiple, but dissociated, working models of self and other in attachment relationships. Clinical studies cited here have shown that an individual may defensively exclude anxiety-provoking autobiographical memories from awareness while retaining conscious access only an innocuous and contradictory explanation supplied by parents. However, when only the "innocuous" version of reality is directly accessible to awareness, the unconscious version of the working model is not completely inactivated and is likely to affect the child's thinking and behavior in often puzzling ways.

EMPIRICAL RESEARCH ON ATTACHMENT COMMUNICATIONS

What is the empirical evidence for these ideas? A number of attachment-theoretic studies have supported and extended Bowlby's notions regarding the emergence of internal working models of self in communication with attachment figures. These show that persistent communicative failures in infant–parent relationships can engender distortions in infants' developing internal working models, even when they do not involve the extreme examples noted by Bowlby (1973, 1980, 1985).

It appears that a caregiver's consistent disavowal or discounting of specific infant signals results in the elimination of specific topics from reciprocal, mutually validating communication. The resulting partial, biased, and distorted communication patterns can interfere with the construction of adequate internal working models of self in relation to attachment figures (see also the review of Stern, 1985, for similar ideas). In other words, a lack of open, mutually responsive communication between attachment partners results in a restricted flow of information about attachment issues that affects the partners' subsequent relationship as well as the infant's developing representation of self-in-relation to current and future attachment figures (Bowlby, 1988).

Ainsworth's painstaking observational work with mothers and infants in naturalistic settings (Ainsworth, Blehar, Waters, & Wall, 1978), points to the pathway whereby parent–child communication patterns are translated into internal working models. Together with her colleagues, Ainsworth discovered that mothers who, in the first 3 months of the infants' life, were relatively insensitive to infant signals during feeding (Ainsworth & Bell, 1969), face-to-face interaction (Blehar, Lieberman, & Ainsworth, 1977), close bodily contact (Ainsworth, Bell, Blehar, & Main, 1971), separation-reunion (Stayton & Ainsworth, 1973), and distress episodes (Bell & Ainsworth, 1972), had infants who—during the last quarter of the first year— had less harmonious relationships with their mothers. In addition, these infants behaved differently from sensitively mothered infants in a laboratory procedure known as the Strange Situation (Ainsworth, Bell, & Stayton, 1974; Ainsworth et al., 1978).

The Strange Situation consists of a standard sequence of episodes in a laboratory playroom where mother and baby are joined by an unfamiliar woman. Of special importance are two sequences during which the mother leaves the room and then returns. Infants whose mothers had responded sensitively to their signals during feeding, crying, holding, and face-to-face episodes at home during the first 3 months of life, welcomed their mothers' return after a brief separation in the Strange Situation, then returned to play. These infants were therefore labeled secure (Group B). Insensitively mothered infants, as determined by the home observations, responded in one of two ways. They either avoided the returning mother in the Strange Situation by snubbing her, looking, turning, or walking away, or refusing interaction bids (insecure-avoidant or Group A) or they responded ambivalently when the mother came back (Group C), seeking close bodily contact but accompanied by angry, resistant behavior. At home, the mothers of the avoidant babies provided less affectionate holding during the first 3 months and frequently rejected bids for close bodily contact during the last quarter of the first year. Mothers of ambivalent babies, by contrast, were inconsistently sensitive at home, and were much less likely to reject close bodily contact than mothers of babies in Group A (Ainsworth et al., 1978).

These findings suggest that a mother's sensitivity plays a major role in setting the initial tone of the relationship, although infants themselves assume an active reciprocal role in upholding the emerging transactional patterns as their memory and information-processing abilities increase. For example, in the Strange Situation, infants classified as avoidant tend not to communicate directly with parents after reunion, as if expecting that attachment behaviors will be rejected (Grossmann, Grossmann, & Schwan, 1986). Studies by Matas, Arend, and Sroufe (1978) also provide examples of the bidirectional nature of miscommunications in insecure parent–child dyads. Twenty-four-month-old children previously classified as insecure in the Strange Situation with their mothers, tended to give up easily and whine when faced with a difficult problem-solving task. Their mothers, conversely, tended not to offer help. In clinical samples (Cicchetti & Beeghly, 1987; Lieberman & Pawl, 1990; Radke-Yarrow, Cummings, Kuczynsky, & Chapman, 1985) such mutually maladaptive communication patterns are even more apparent.

Beyond infancy, studies of parents and their preschool children revealed that attachment partners' ability to communicate openly and sensitively *with each other* was closely linked to their ability to communicate coherently *about* attachment relationships with third persons. For example, how a parent discusses attachment relations in his or her family of origin with an interviewer is strikingly correlated with observed communication patterns between that parent and his or her child (Main, Kaplan, & Cassidy, 1985). Main et al. used a structured, open-ended interview to probe for parental recollections of childhood attachment figures, and for thoughts about the significance of attachment relations in general, including their influence on the parent's own development.

In evaluating the interview transcripts, Main (Main et al., 1985; Main & Goldwyn, in press) discovered that parents of 6-year-olds who were classified as secure with them in the Strange Situation in infancy valued both attachment and autonomy, and were at ease in talking about how attachment relations in their family of origin influenced their own development. Interestingly, this was true whether or not the parents recalled a secure childhood, although those recalling secure childhoods were in a majority.

Parents of children who were classified as insecure-avoidant with them in infancy, on the other hand, dismissed and devalued attachment experiences, maintaining that childhood attachments had little effect on their own development as parents. They frequently claimed not to remember any incidents from childhood. Specific memories that emerged despite this denial were likely not to support the generalized (often highly idealized) descriptions of parents.

Parents of children previously classified as insecure-ambivalent seemed highly preoccupied with earlier family attachments, recalling many specific, often conflict-ridden incidents. However, these parents could not integrate these conflictual childhood memories into a coherent overall picture. In summary, both the dismissing and preoccupied groups found it difficult to discuss attachment relationships in an integrated way. By inference, these parents operated with malorganized, internally inconsistent working models, but were unaware of doing so. Finally, parents of children classified as insecure-disorganized in infancy (a new classification proposed by Main & Solomon, 1990) seemed to be struggling with unresolved issues concerning loss of a parent before maturity (see Main & Hesse, 1990). These results have been replicated, even with samples of mothers whose Adult Attachment Interview was conducted prenatally (Fonagy, Steele, & Steele, 1991; Ward et al., 1990).

Correlations between communication style *within* attachment relations and *about* attachment relations were also obtained for children. In her longitudinal study, Main et al. (1985) discovered that 6-year-olds classified as secure with mother in the Strange Situation in infancy gave coherent, elaborated, and open responses to drawings of parent–child separation scenes. In contrast, children earlier judged insecure-avoidant with mother described the pictured children as sad, but could not say what they could have done in response to separation. Children classified as disorganized/disoriented (Main & Hesse, 1990) were often completely silent or gave irrational or bizarre responses (Main et al., 1985; for similar findings see Cassidy, 1988; Slough & Greenberg, 1990).

Inspired by Main et al.'s (1985) findings, Bretherton, Ridgeway, and Cassidy (1990) studied even younger children, using a story completion format. Thirty-seven-month-olds who were able to address the story issues with little hesitation and produce benign resolutions, were classified as secure. Those who produced irrelevant or very bizarre story resolutions (after a separated family is reunited, they have a car crash) or who pointedly avoided the story issue were classified as insecure. It turned out that these classifications of doll-story responses were highly concordant with classifications of an actual separation–reunion procedure. They were also correlated with maternal responses to a structured open-ended interview modeled on the Adult Attachment Interview but probing maternal representations about her own child (Bretherton, Biringen, Ridgeway, Maslin, & Sherman, 1989).

In attachment-theoretic terms, these findings make sense because internal working models of self and attachment figure are thought to guide information processing of attachment-related issues whether in communication with an attachment partner, or a third person (see also Bretherton, 1990, 1991). At the same time, these findings can be taken to reflect intergenerational processes in the transmission of internal working models. During pregnancy, parents tend to have anticipatory working models of themselves as parents, and of their infant (Heinicke, Diskin, Ramsey-Klee, & Given, 1983; Zeanah, Keenen, Stewart, & Anders, 1985). After the infant's birth, these anticipatory working models must be corrected and fine-tuned to fit the particular baby's temperament and needs (see also Stern, 1985), a task that will be difficult if the parents' internal working models of self and infant are severely distorted by defensive exclusion. Parental communications that are not sensitive to infant signals will then interfere with an infant's emerging ability to construct adequate internal working models of interpersonal relations.

Under this view, the converse is likely to happen for secure parents whose internal working model of attachment figures and of self is well adapted to reality and open to revision. Such parents are likely to give the infant helpful and informative feedback, hence facilitating flexible adaptation to new relationships. Furthermore, both partners' internal working models will be easier to update, because there are few defensive impediments to information processing. Bowlby (1973) addressed this issue in his volume on separation:

> Thus the family experience of those who grow up anxious and fearful is found to be characterized not only by uncertainty about parental support but often also by covert yet strongly distorting parental pressures: pressure on the child, for example, to act as caregiver for a parent; *or to adopt, and thereby to confirm, a parent's false models-of self, of child and of the relationship.*

Similarly, the family experience of those who grow up to become relatively stable and self-reliant is characterized not only by unfailing parental support when called upon but also by a steady yet timely encouragement toward increasing autonomy, and *by the frank communication by parents of working models — themselves, of child and of others — that are not only tolerably valid but are open to be questioned and revised* . . . the inheritance of mental health and mental ill health through the medium of family microculture- . . . may well be far more important, than is their inheritance through the medium of genes (pp. 322-323)

The major new insight that Main et al. (1985) brought to this discussion is that the direct intergenerational transmission of relationship patterns, while relatively common, is not inevitable. In Main et al.'s study, most parents who described secure childhoods had children who related to them securely, but some parents with secure children reported abusive or rejecting relationships in their family of origin. What distinguished this group of parents from parents of insecure children was their ability to discuss adverse childhood experiences with emotional openness, coherence, and reflective insight (see also Fonagy et al., in press). They seemed to have come to terms with what had happened to them, and had gained an understanding why their parents had behaved as they did. Unfortunately, we do not know what specific conditions enabled these individuals to break a vicious intergenerational cycle by reconstructing earlier working models, although a supportive relationship with a spouse and/or therapist have been shown to be helpful (for a review of this literature, see Ricks, 1985).

THE CONCEPT OF WORKING MODEL IN LIGHT OF THEORIES OF EVENT REPRESENTATION

The concept of internal working model of self and attachment figures calls for a representational system that can simulate relationship patterns at the mental level, that is, a representational system that operates with interpersonal event structures (agents interacting with other agents and recipients). When Bowlby (1982) first made use of the concept of internal working models, existing academic cognitive theories focused on concept formation and the ability to recall lists of nonsense syllables. Piaget's work on the interiorization of sensorimotor schemas was relevant, but Piaget had applied these ideas only to logico-mathematical development, not to the representation of interpersonal relatedness.

However, theories of event representation, and "scripts" that emerged in the late 1970s (Mandler, 1979; Nelson, 1986; Schank & Abelson, 1977) have provided some helpful if limited conceptual tools to help flesh out the concept of working models. Event representations or scripts are defined as skeletal mental structures that capture the who, where, what, how, and why of routine events, and whose proposed function is much like that proposed for internal working models, to guide communication, interpretation, and action.

However, as originally formulated, script theory did not tell us much about humans' undoubted ability to apply old models to new situations, the ability to extrapolate from familiar to hoped for, feared, or hypothetical situations, and the ability to build working models from verbal descriptions about unfamiliar events. Nor did script theory explain why humans can think of the same situation at several levels of abstraction (Neisser, 1987), or deal satisfactorily with the role of affect in representation.

Fortunately, Schank's reformulation of script theory in terms of a dynamic memory (see Schank, 1982) provides more specific pointers for thinking about the processing of interpersonal experiences and their subsequent organization and manipulation in memory. Schank argued that autobiographical memories are reprocessed, partitioned, summarized, and cross-indexed, resulting in a variety of interlinked and hierarchically organized schema categories that retain aspects of the structure of the experienced event in terms of time, space, movement, causality, motivation, and affect. Some of these schemas organize mini-event representations into coordinated, longer event sequences (such as the "script" of putting a baby to bed), others summarize information derived from similar mini-events (e.g., all infant–mother feeding situations regardless of context), and yet others generalize across related event sequences (e.g., all caregiving routines). Schank's reconceptualization of script theory, then, allows us to think of internal working models as a multiply intercommunicating hierarchical system composed of schema categories that range from being very experience-near to being very general and abstract. Such a system could plausibly furnish the building blocks required for creating working models of hypothetical situations by extrapolation from remembered experiences or to re-create representations from others' verbal communications. Note that although the type of representational system proposed here can perform the function of simulating experienced, anticipated, or feared events, its multilevel organization is far more complex than is suggested by a simplistic interpretation of the metaphor "internal working model."

There remains the vexing question how concepts borrowed from theories of event representation and dynamic memory can help us conceptualize internal working models of self and other in attachment relationships. After all, these theories were, for the most part, designed to model an individual's understanding of mundane routines (such as going to a restaurant) rather than highly charged transactional patterns with particular individuals.

Although developed with a different aim in mind, I maintain that these theories are entirely consonant with the idea that individuals may develop mental models of relationship patterns with specific partners. Indeed, schemas of interaction with particular partners are presumed, under this view, to form the building blocks from which an individual can derive a general perspective on attachment relationships.

Schank's (1982) revision of script theory also suggests a new way of thinking about "split" working models. There is no logical need to postulate that all representational schemas be accessible to awareness. Indeed, Schank's ideas are entirely compatible with the notion that some transactional schemas may only be available as unverbalizable procedural or sensorimotor schemas. Such procedural schemas could form the most experience-near level in a working model consisting of hierarchically organized affective-cognitive schema systems with an unknown number of levels of abstraction, and in which an experience may be encoded in different ways at different levels. In such a representational system it is not useful to think of an individual's working models of self, attachment figures, and the world as neatly segregated constructions. If the system works well, schemas at various levels of abstraction or generality (i.e., of the physical environment, of "human nature," of attachment relationships in general, and of self and other in specific attachment relationships) are all interconnected. Hence, those individuals who do not feel secure in an interpersonal relationship may come to represent the world as a whole a dangerous, untrustworthy place (Epstein, 1991; Guidano & Liotti, 1983).

Importantly, Schank's (1982) theory can also provide some conceptual tools for discussing the role of defensive phenomena in the construction and operation of working models. If we assume that schemas based on an individual's autobiographical memories form the basis for different types of cross-referenced summary schemas at many levels in a variety of linked schema hierarchies, then it is plausible to speculate that defensive processes might selectively interfere in this important cross-referencing task. In individuals who have experienced secure attachments one would expect a fair degree of continuity and coherence between sensorimotor schemas that can only be accessed procedurally and consciously accessible episodic memories or event schemas (see also Crittenden, 1990). In insecure relationships, by contrast, the memory of an anxiety-provoking experience may be defensively excluded from awareness. Yet, other consciously accessible schemas could have been influenced by the excluded information, provided it was initially processed. The converse might also occur. Autobiographical episodes, accessible to consciousness, might be prevented from in-depth processing and cross-referencing, and thereby from proper integration into the individual's working model of the world. Once the lines of communication within the representational system (working model of the world) are partially or completely severed, later input will not be adequately processed because distorted or dissociated schemas now guide the processing of new experience (Bowlby, 1988; Erdelyi, 1985). Alternatively, later traumatic events may lead to the repression of earlier positive attachment experiences (Noam, personal communication, May 1994).

I therefore favor the view that insecure individuals develop working models of self and attachment figure in which some schemas or schema networks may be dissociated from others across and within hierarchical levels, giving rise to contradictory intrapsychic communications. In such a working model, updating of information may occur at one level or branch of a hierarchy, but may then not propagate to others; or schemas of feared or hoped for events may not be clearly tagged as such and hence treated as schemas of actual circumstances. The possible confusions, contradictions, and distortions in the interpretation and conduct of attachment relations that such malfunctioning internal working models could generate are endless. Furthermore, such processes would also interfere with adequate interpersonal communication as indeed confirmed by research based on the Adult Attachment Interview (e.g., Fonagy et al., in press; Main et al., 1985).

There remains the question as to how a representational system consonant with the propositions discussed here develops. With respect to event memory, research has shown that 3-month-old infants remember event sequences over several weeks provided the original learning context is precisely reinstated (e.g., Hayne, Rovee-Collier, & Perris, 1987; Rovee-Collier & Fagan, 1981; Rovee-Collier & Lipsitt, 1981). By the last quarter of the first year, infants give quite unambiguous indications that they remember the sequential structure and emotional significance of past events. Eight-month-olds who have previously had unpleasant experiences with injections cringe in fear while their arm is being disinfected (Izard, 1978). Infants of this age also display anticipatory smiles during peek-a-boo games before a playmate reappears from behind a cloth (Sroufe & Wunsch, 1972) and become apprehensive when they notice a parent get ready to leave. Building on Schank's (1982) ideas, Stern (1985) postulated that infants may register routine interaction sequences as sensorimotor event representations or, more recently, as proto-narrative envelopes (1994). These representations allow infants to make short-term, in-context predictions (expectations). However, such sensorimotor predictions or anticipations do not yet imply a capacity for free recall.

Representation in the sense of recall memory (although still facilitated by the presence of particular objects), can be observed as toddlers' pretend play emerges early in the second year. By the third year, children are able to enact complex sequences of acts that include others (people or dolls) as actors with intentions and feelings (see Bretherton, 1984, for a review). The ability to encode simple events in language develops concurrently (e.g.,

Greenfield & Smith, 1976; Shore, O'Connell, & Bates, 1984). By the fourth year, children's understanding of event schemas can be tapped through simple interview procedures. If provided with appropriate props, 3-year-olds can demonstrate a good grasp of the order in which the action sequences of routine events take place, especially when these sequences are causally related to each other (see also Fivush, Keubli, & Clubb, 1992). Although they are not yet very good at preserving the distinction between memories of specific events and memories of routines, preschoolers can remember specific experiences when they are sufficiently unusual (a visit to the circus). Older preschoolers not only give more detailed accounts of routine events than younger preschoolers, but are more likely to understand the probabilistic structure of familiar events. Instead of merely "running off" a routine script, these older preschoolers often talk about optional components of scripts (what might, but need not necessarily happen; see Fivush et al., 1992; Fivush & Slackman, 1986). Finally, 3- to 4-year-olds benefit more than 5- to 7-year-olds from being interviewed in a warm, empathic style. Hence, impersonal methods of memory elicitation may give a misleading impression of what younger preschoolers are able to remember about a unique event (Goodman, Bottoms, Schwartz-Kenney, & Rudy, 1991).

This rather brief review of the developmental literature on event representation suggests that, in charting the developmental course of memory, we need to examine important distinctions between "sensorimotor" memories dating from the preverbal period and later event memories that can be narrated, between memories available to free recall versus procedural memories that are only available in cued or contextually scaffolded recall, and memories for routine events versus autobiographical memories for specific episodes (see also, Crittenden, 1990).

Less information is available regarding the hypothesized development of hierarchically organized representational schema systems, as implied in Schank (1982), but relevant evidence is available from the literature on social cognition (Edelstein, chapter 4, this volume). Interview studies in which children were asked to describe themselves and others suggest that the concept (internal working model) of self and other develops from very simple structures during the preschool period, couched mainly in terms of actions and value (good or bad, nice or nasty), into considerably more complex, multilayered, differentiated, multiply connected, hierarchies at adolescence (Case, 1988, chapter 3, this volume; Fischer, 1980; Higgins, 1991; Noam, 1992; Selman, 1980; Selman, Schultz, & Yeates, 1991). These findings suggest that working models of self and others should become much more difficult to reorganize and reconstruct after adolescence, an issue that needs to be resolved by research. Note also, that whereas these developmental findings indicate a growing differentiation and hierarchic integration in verbalizable working models of self, they may underestimate the sophistication of young children's ability to understand their own and others' thoughts and feelings at a more implicit level (Bretherton & Beeghly, 1982; Dunn, 1988; Gottmann & Parker, 1986).

THE ROLE OF PARENT-CHILD DIALOGUE

Attachment theorists have maintained that parent–child relationships characterized by emotionally open and sensitive communications are the royal road to the development of adequate and flexible internal working models of self and other (see Bretherton, 1990, for a review).

However, in reflecting on the role that dialogue plays in the construction of internal working models, Bowlby (1973, 1980) and others (e.g., Stern, 1985) have tended to underscore some of the more problematic aspects of translating remembered experiences into language. Indeed, Stern (1985) maintained that language is a double-edged sword. Whereas it makes experience more sharable with others, it can also drive a wedge between an experience as lived and as subsequently narrated. Like other psychoanalysts, Stern dwells on the possible disjunctions between nonverbalized (sensorimotor–affective) memories and narrative representations that are accessible to conscious reflection. Bowlby (1973, 1980) addressed a related issue when he warned that unbearable mental conflict ensues when a child is forbidden to share his or her remembered experience with others and is, instead, provided with false information.

However, in my view, attachment researchers have failed to give sufficient thought to the facilitating or scaffolding role played by parent–child discourse in guiding the child's construction of internal working models through joint talk about past and future. To illustrate my point, I summarize some studies undertaken by researchers interested in the social construction of reality, but not working within an attachment framework. These researchers focus on the transmission of a variety of cultural values and practices, as opposed to in individual or cultural differences in mental health. I submit that their findings have much to contribute to a discussion of attachment at the representational level.

Nelson (1993) reviewed a series of important investigations on parent–child dialogue that illustrate how parental input can facilitate a child's memory productions, and hence by inference the structure of the child's internal working model of self. For example, Engel (1986), reporting on mother–child conversations about the past, identified "pragmatic" and "elaborative" maternal styles of memory talk. When pragmatic mothers conversed about the past with their 18-month-olds, they spoke in very concrete terms. Elaborative mothers, by contrast, presented their children with rich narratives that specified intentions and causes, and invited their children to help co-construct the narrative. By 2 years of age, children of these elaborative mothers had begun to engage in more complex memory talk than the children of pragmatic mothers. In a similar study of mother–child conversations about the past, Fivush and Fromhoff (1988) discovered "elaborative" and "repetitive" maternal styles.

Tessler (1986) discovered analogous style differences in maternal talk about ongoing events, differences that were related to how the children themselves later remembered these events. In Tessler's experimental study, two groups of mothers were given different instructions on how to behave during a museum visit with their 3½-year-old children. The first group of mothers was asked not to volunteer any comments during the museum visit, but merely to answer the child's questions, whereas the second group was asked to behave "as you normally would." One week later, children of the second group of mothers remembered significantly more about their experiences at the museum than children whose mothers had been assigned to the first group. Interestingly, natural style differences emerged also within the second groups of mothers. Following Bruner's (1986) classification of cognitive styles, Tessler designated these styles "paradigmatic" versus "narrative." Paradigmatic mothers focused on naming and describing objects, in contradistinction to narrative mothers who, like Engel's elaborative mothers, talked about intentions, causes, and feelings. Narrative mothers also tended to create connections between the museum experience and the child's own life. Given the findings on mother–child conversations about the past, it is not surprising that when they were later interviewed by an experimenter, children of narrative mothers remembered more about the museum visit than children of paradigmatic mothers. Most notably, no child remembered objects or events that had not been part of a mother–child dialogue. In a second study, Tessler (1991) additionally found that children of narrative mothers remembered more details, regardless of whether the experimenter who interviewed them adopted a pragmatic or narrative style of memory elicitation.

Unfortunately, there are no corresponding studies on how parents prepare their young children for future events, but Nelson was able to draw on her well-known case study of Emily (Nelson, 1989) whose bedtime talk with parents and after-bedtime crib monologues were regularly audiorecorded beginning at 21 months. Nelson reported that, at bedtime, Emily's parents frequently prepared her for events that would happen the next day or a few days hence. In her subsequent crib monologues Emily recalled these planning talks and often embellished them with simple inferences and speculations (e.g., who would bring a book to read at the babysitter's the next day).

This series of findings on mother–child talk about the past, present, and future suggests that parental styles of structuring and guiding conversation help to create the organization and structure of children's memories. Other studies of parent–child communication have focused on discussions of emotions with respect to gender-specific cultural values. Mothers, in conversing with their children about emotions, implicitly convey what sort of responses are and are not considered appropriate or important in general. They also convey what types of responses are expected of each gender (Fivush, 1993). Mothers of 2½- to 3-year-olds who were asked to discuss memorable events with their children often chose to talk about emotionally charged events. In doing so, they mentioned negative emotions to sons more frequently than to daughters, and more readily accepted statements about negative emotions from sons than from daughters. The same was true of fathers. When mothers did discuss anger with daughters, they more often portrayed the resolution of angry situations through re-establishment of social ties. With sons, mothers more frequently accepted anger as an appropriate response, and did not object when sons mentioned retaliation (girls never did). On the basis of these findings, Fivush maintained that, female children much more than male children, will come to understand emotions as an integral part of social relationships. Boys and girls will hence acquire a very different emotional self-concept, although they seem to acquire knowledge appropriate to the self-concept of both genders (otherwise parents would not be able to adopt socialization strategies appropriate to a child of the opposite gender).

More importantly for Fivush's hypotheses about the socialization of memory, there is much evidence that personal storytelling is an important part of the everyday life of families from many cultural backgrounds. In addition to hearing and participating in stories about themselves, children overhear stories told about other people (Miller, Potts, Fung, Hoogstra, & Mintz, 1990). Moreover, parents bring children in contact with cultural products such as storybooks. Miller, Hoogstra, Mintz, Fung, and Williams (1993) illustrated how one 23-month-old child (Kurt) appropriates a well-known story, and comes to terms with some of its disturbing implications by retelling variants of the story to his mother. In the *Tale of Peter Rabbit* Beatrix Potter depicts a young rabbit who disobeys his mother by entering Mr. McGregor's garden, gorges himself, almost gets caught, loses his way while trying to escape, but finally finds his way home to mother and siblings. Over a period of several weeks, Kurt requested many readings of the story, and then used retellings to work through the various disturbing story issues that did not accord with his own experience of rabbit and human families in gardens. Interestingly, once Kurt had worked out his personal concerns about the story his retellings ceased. In terms of the role of parent–child dialogue in the construction of the child's internal working models of self, it is noteworthy that Kurt's mother accepted and supported his attempts to come to grips with the story's challenges to his inner world. We can imagine a different outcome for Kurt if his mother had insisted, instead, that he stick to the "facts" of the story.

TRAUMA AND THE CONSTRUCTION OF INTERNAL WORKING MODELS

Miller et al.'s (1993) study of how one small child comes to terms with upsetting story situations leads me to consider the incorporation of actual traumatic experiences (as opposed to somewhat upsetting stories) into a child's internal working model of self and the world. Although Bowlby (1980, 1985) was deeply concerned with the importance of open parent–child communication about traumatic events for healthy psychological development, I suggest that he failed to take into account the young child's inability to understand some of these events. Children frequently misinterpret what they are told because their background knowledge and/or level of cognitive understanding are insufficient. Even when parents are very sensitive in preparing their children for painful, invasive, and incomprehensible procedures, the children may blame parents for allowing such traumatic things to happen to them (Robertson & Freud, 1956).

However, when parents themselves find it unbearable to talk about events that they believe to be too painful for the children or that they find too anxiety- or guilt-inducing, the psychological danger to children is even greater. To protect their children from unpleasant reality, parents frequently resist hospital staff members' attempts to debrief children about medical procedures or their illnesses, with the result that a number of child cancer victims grow up without much guidance on how to make sense of their early memories of hospital experiences (Steward, 1993). Ignoring these issues does not mean, however, that the children will not think about the meaning of their traumatic experiences or that the children will be able to construct meaningful interpretations of them on their own. Rather, when either parents or medical staff fail to provide age-appropriate preparation and debriefing, hospitalized children try to share their (perhaps horrifying) misconceptions with each other, misconceptions that may continue to haunt them for many years. Among the rampant misinterpretations that Steward (1993) discovered among young patients were comments such as "they stole my blood" (about drawing blood samples) or "the doctor will be able to see the bad thoughts in my head" (about head X-rays).

Alternatively, parents may underestimate a child's pain, become angry in response to the child's resistance or complaints, and hence side with the medical staff instead of offering comforting explanations to the child. In one recent study, Steward et al. (1991) interviewed children about the touching and handling they received during a medical procedure that had been videotaped 6 months earlier. Children's memories tended, on the whole, to be very accurate. However, one subgroup of children did not rate any of the touches or handling they received as painful on follow-up, even though the procedures they had undergone were so invasive that some of them had to be bodily restrained. Yet these same children provided very accurate descriptions of the clinic room and the medical staff. Steward et al. linked children's lack of pain memories to parental coping strategies, citing the responses of one mother who countered her child's protest cries to the procedure by: "If you don't shut up, I'm going to leave you." Steward et al. wondered whether this child simply chose not to report painful experiences for which he was shamed by his mother, or whether he had repressed them. Investigators have tended not to distinguish between these two alternatives (i.e., deliberate suppression and unconscious repression). Yet, whether the child observed by Steward et al. chose not to mention pain he remembered, or whether he had defensively repressed his pain memories, the inability to talk about the experience deprived the child of opportunities to make sense of it through dialogue with a supportive other.

Even greater difficulties arise when children experience catastrophic events. Terr (1983; see also Terr, 1991) studied a group of children between 5 and 14 years of age who were abducted from their school bus, trapped in a buried trailer truck for more than 24 hours, but finally managed to escape through their own efforts. Four years later, memories of the original event were still clearly etched in the children's minds as shown by their ability to visualize the experience in vivid detail. Rather than repressing the memory of the event itself, as adults with posttraumatic stress disorder are wont to do, the children had suppressed or repressed memories of their subsequent symptoms and behaviors. Panic attacks and nightmares, which many children had mentioned shortly after the kidnapping, seemed to have vanished from their memories. Most notably, in terms of their internal working model of self and the world, victims had acquired a frighteningly pessimistic outlook on life (see also Fischer & Ayoub, chapter 7, this volume). Many felt that they would die young or that the world might soon come to an end. Furthermore, many had reinterpreted events prior to the kidnapping as omens that should have warned them or their parents of the impending disaster (opting for guilt and anxiety over helplessness). Dreams of the event were disguised or modified, and half of the children remembered dying in their dreams. In addition, many children engaged in compulsive posttraumatic play of kidnapping.

Terr reported that the children's parents tended to downplay the significance of the kidnapping event. It is not clear, however, to what extent the children could have weathered this kind of assault on their internal working model of the world as a trustworthy place, even if parents could have been emotionally more available to them.

Because parents are guides and partners in a child's construction of internal working models of self and the world, findings on children's difficulties in processing traumatic memories have implications for assisting parents and other supportive adults in helping the child come to terms with what has happened (Steward, 1988), possibly over a prolonged period of time. By making parents aware of what a child is likely to experience or (in the case of disasters) to have experienced, the parents will be better able to give age-appropriate support to child's coping attempts. Parents will also realize that there may be a need to repeatedly discuss the event at subsequent ages as the child becomes better able to understand its significance.

Neither Stern (1985) nor Bowlby (1973, 1980) sufficiently considered the fact that without parental interpretations some events may not be assimilable at all. When children are faced with otherwise incomprehensible trauma, talking with parents may allow them to make sense of their experiences, at least when parents themselves are able to come to terms with their child's experiences. Indeed, even in nontraumatic situations a child needs adult input to make sense of what occurs. This input, if grossly distorted, may have adverse effects, but without it the child may not become a functioning member of human society.

CONCLUSION

Attachment research supports the view that sensitive and emotionally open communication with parents enables children to develop a well-organized working model of self. Emotionally open child–parent communication patterns are believed to affect the very structure and organization of memory, not just its content. Memory structure, according to attachment theory, may become distorted and malorganized by defensive processes as dissociative and repressive phenomena of greater or lesser pervasiveness interfere with the organization of internal working models and hence with an individual's ability to communicate and to adapt to reality. Although this process is bidirectional (both partner's working models are involved), attachment theory highlights the initial importance of the parent's ability to respond to positive and negative child signals with appropriate feedback.

By sensitively scaffolding their children's attempts at producing narrative accounts of the past, parents promote the development of a well functioning internal working model of self, parent, and the social world that is flexibly adaptable to new circumstances. In this sense, the parents' narrative style comes to be reflected in the structure of children's memories (elaborative or narrative versus repetitive, or pragmatic). We cannot yet make predictions about long-lasting effects of elaborative and restricted narrative styles of parent–child dialogue on adult memory structure, but some of these ideas mesh well with attachment theory's notions about the importance of open communication.

The research on trauma, on the other hand, is a useful reminder that some experiences are exceedingly difficult to process, even when a supportive figure is available. Attachment theory suggests that the assimilation of traumatic experiences will be even more difficult if parents themselves engage in defensive exclusion of their children's pain, but we need to acknowledge that there may be limits to a supportive parent's ability to help a child come to terms with extreme stress. It may be necessary to work through the experience time and again as the child's representational capacity grows. We still have much to learn about how defensive processes operate in parent–child dialogues and how these processes disrupt intrapsychic communication within the schema hierarchy that constitutes an individual's working model of self, others, and the world. We also need to discover more about how such processes interfere both with parents' and children's adaptive coping.

REFERENCES

Ainsworth, M. D. S., & Bell, S. M. (1969). Some contemporary patterns in the feeding situation. In A. Ambrose (Ed.), *Stimulation in early infancy* (pp. 133-170). London: Academic Press.

Ainsworth, M. D. S., Bell, S. M., Blehar, M. C., & Main, M. (1971, April). *Physical contact: A study of infant responsiveness and its relation to maternal handling.* Paper presented at the biennial meeting of the Society for Research in Child Development, Minneapolis, Minnesota.

Ainsworth, M. D. S., Bell, S. M., & Stayton, D. (1974). Infant–mother attachment and social development. In M. P. Richards (Ed.), *The introduction of the child into a social world* (pp. 99-135). London: Cambridge University Press.

Ainsworth, M. D. S., Blehar, M. C., Waters, E., & Wall, S. (1978). *Patterns of attachment: A psychological study of the strange situation.* Hillsdale, NJ: Lawrence Erlbaum Associates.

Bandura, A. (1982). Self-efficacy mechanism in human agency. *American Psychologist, 37*, 122-147.

Bell, S. M., & Ainsworth, M. D. S. (1972). Infant crying and maternal responsiveness. *Child Development, 43*, 1171-1190.

Blehar, M. C., Lieberman, A. F., & Ainsworth, M. D. S. (1977). Early face-to-face interaction and its relation to later infant-mother attachment. *Child Development, 48*, 182-194.

Bowlby, J. (1973). *Attachment and loss. Vol. 2: Separation.* New York: Basic Books.

Bowlby, J. (1980). *Attachment and loss, Vol. 3: Loss, sadness and depression.* New York:

Basic Books.

Bowlby, J. (1982). *Attachment and loss. Vol. 1: Attachment* (2nd rev. ed.). New York: Basic Books. (Original work published 1969)

Bowlby, J. (1985). The role of childhood experience in cognitive disturbance. In M. J. Mahoney & A. Freeman (Eds.), *Cognition and psychotherapy* (pp. 181-200). New York: Plenum.

Bowlby, J. (1988). *A secure base*. New York: Basic Books.

Bretherton, I. (1984). Representing the social world in symbolic play: Reality and fantasy. In I. Bretherton (Ed.), *Symbolic play: The development of social understanding* (pp. 3-41). New York: Academic Press.

Bretherton, I. (1990). Open communication and internal working models: Their role in the development of attachment relationships. In R. A. Thompson (Ed.), *Socioemotional development. Nebraska symposium on motivation 1988* (pp. 59-113). Lincoln: University of Nebraska Press.

Bretherton, I. (1991). Pouring new wine into old bottles: The social self as internal working model. In M. Gunnar & L. A. Sroufe (Eds.), *Self processes in development* (pp. 1-41). Hillsdale, NJ: Lawrence Erlbaum Associates.

Bretherton, I., & Beeghly, M. (1982). Talking about internal states: The acquisition of an explicit theory of mind. *Developmental Psychology, 18*, 906-921.

Bretherton, I., Biringen, Z., Ridgeway, D., Maslin, C., & Sherman, M. (1989). Attachment: The parental perspective. *Infant Mental Health Journal, 10*, 203-221.

Bretherton, I., Ridgeway, D., & Cassidy, J. (1990). Assessing internal working models of the attachment relationship: an attachment story completion task for 3-year-olds. In D. Cicchetti, M. Greenberg, & E. M. Cummings (Eds.), *Attachment during the preschool years* (pp. 272-308). Chicago: University of Chicago Press.

Bruner, J. (1986). *Actual minds, possible worlds*. Cambridge, MA: Harvard University Press.

Cain, A. C., & Fast, I. (1972). Children's disturbed reactions to parent suicide. In A. C. Cain (Ed.), *Survivors of suicide* (pp. 93-111). Springfield, IL: C. C. Thomas.

Case, R. (1988). The whole child: Toward an integrative view of young children's cognitive, social and emotional development. In A. D. Pellegrini (Ed.), *Psychological bases of early education* (pp. 155-184). Chichester, England: Wiley.

Cassidy, J. (1988). The self as related to child-mother attachment at six. *Child Development, 59* 121-134.

Cicchetti, D., & Beeghly, M. (1987). Symbolic development in maltreated youngsters: An organizational perspective. *New Directions for Child Development, 36*, 5-29.

Craik, K. (1943). *The nature of explanation*. Cambridge: Cambridge University Press.

Crittenden, P. (1990). Internal representational models of attachment relationships. *Infant Mental Health Journal, 11*, 259-277.

Dixon, N. F. (1971). *Subliminal perception: The nature of a controversy*. London: McGraw-Hill.

Dunn, J. (1988). *The beginnings of social understanding*. Cambridge, MA: Harvard University Press.

Engel, S. (1986). *Learning to reminisce: A developmental study of how young children learn to talk about the past*. Unpublished doctoral dissertation, City University of New York, Graduate Center, New York.

Epstein, S. (1991). Cognitive-experiential self theory: Implications for developmental psychology. In M. R. Gunnar & L. A. Sroufe (Eds.), *Self processes in development: The Minnesota symposia in child psychology* (Vol. 23, pp. 79-123). Hillsdale, NJ: Lawrence Erlbaum Associates.

Erdelyi, H. M. (1985). *Psychoanalysis: Freud's cognitive psychology*. San Francisco: Freeman.

Fischer, K. W. (1980). A theory of cognitive development: The control and construction of hierarchies and skills. *Psychological Review, 87*, 477-531.

Fivush, R. (1993). Emotional content of parent–child conversation about the past. In C. A. Nelson (Ed.), *Memory and affect: The Minnesota symposia in child psychology* (Vol. 26, pp. 39-77). Hillsdale, NJ: Lawrence Erlbaum Associates.

Fivush, R., & Fromhoff, F. A. (1988). Style and structure in mother–child conversations about the past. *Discourse Processes, 8*, 177-204.

Fivush, R., Kuebli, J., & Clubb, P. A. (1992). The structure of events and event representations: A developmental analysis. *Child Development, 63*, 188-207.

Fivush, R., & Slackman, E. (1986). The acquisition and development of scripts. In K. Nelson (Ed.), *Event knowledge: Structure and function in development* (pp. 71-96). Hillsdale, NJ: Lawrence Erlbaum Associates.

Fonagy, P., Steele, M., & Steele, H. (1991). Intergenerational patterns of attachment: Maternal representations during pregnancy and subsequent infant–mother attachments. *Child Development, 62*, 891-905.

Fonagy, P., Steele, M., Steele, H., Leigh, T., Kennedy, R., Mattoon, G., & Target, M. (in press). Attachment, the reflective self, and borderline states: The predictive specificity of the Adult Attachment Interview and pathological emotional development. In S. Goldberg, R. Muir, & J. Kerr (Eds.), *John Bowlby's attachment theory*. Hillsdale, NJ: The Analytic Press.

Freud, S. (1940). An outline of psychoanalysis. In J. Strachey (Ed. and Trans.), *The standard edition of the complete psychological works of Sigmund Freud* (Vol. 23, pp. 137-207). London: Hogarth.

Goodman, G. S., Bottoms, B. L., Schwartz-Kenney, B. M., & Rudy, L. (1991). Children's memories for a stressful event: Improving children's report. *Journal of Narrative and Life History, 1*, 69-99.

Gottmann, J. M., & Parker, J. G. (1986). *Conversations of friends: Speculations on affective development*. Cambridge, England: Cambridge University Press.

Greenfield, P. M., & Smith, J. H. (1976). *The structure of communication in early development*. New York: Academic Press.

Grossman, K. E., & Grossmann, K. (1990). The wider concept of attachment in cross-cultural research. *Human Development, 33*, 31-47.

Grossmann, K. E., Grossmann, K., & Schwan, A. (1986). Capturing the wider view of attachment: A reanalysis of Ainsworth's Strange Situation. In C. E. Izard & P. B. Read (Eds.), *Measuring emotions in infants and children* (Vol. 2, pp. 124-171). New York: Cambridge University Press.

Guidano, V. F., & Liotti, G. (1983). *Cognitive processes and emotional disorders*. New York: Guilford Press.

Hayne, H., Rovee-Collier, C., & Perris, E. E. (1987). Categorization and memory retrieval in 3-month-olds. *Child Development, 58*, 750-767.

Heider, F. (1958). *The psychology of interpersonal relations*. New York: Wiley.

Heinicke, C. M., Diskin, S. D., Ramsey-Klee, D., & Given, K. (1983). Pre-birth parent characteristics and family development in the first year of life. *Child Development, 54*, 194-208.

Higgins, E. T. (1991). Development of self-regulatory and self-evaluative processes: Costs, benefits, and tradeoffs. In M. R. Gunnar & L. A. Sroufe (Eds.), *Self processes in development: The Minnesota symposia on child development* (Vol. 23, pp. 125-165). Hillsdale, NJ: Lawrence Erlbaum Associates.

Izard, C. E. (1978). Emotions as motivations: An evolutionary-developmental perspective. In R. A. Dienstbier (Ed.), *Nebraska symposium on motivation* (pp. 163-200). Lincoln, NE:

University of Nebraska Press.

Laing, R. D., & Esterson, A. (1964). *Sanity, madness and the family*. Harmondsworth, England: Penguin Books.

Lewin, K. (1951). *Field theory in social science* (selected theoretical papers. D. Cartwright, Ed.). New York: Harper & Row.

Lieberman, A. F., & Pawl, J. H. (1990). Disorders of attachment and secure base behavior in the second year of life: Conceptual issues and clinical intervention. In M. T. Greenberg, D. Cicchetti, & E. M. Cummings (Eds.), *Attachment in the preschool years* (pp. 375-397). Chicago: University of Chicago Press.

Main, M., & Goldwyn, R. (in press). Interview-based adult attachment classifications: Related to infant-mother and infant-father attachment. *Developmental Psychology*.

Main, M., & Hesse, E. (1990). The insecure disorganized/disoriented attachment pattern in infancy: Precursors and sequelae. In M. Greenberg, D. Cicchetti, & E. M. Cummings (Eds.), *Attachment during the preschool years: Theory, research, and intervention*. Chicago: University of Chicago Press.

Main, M., Kaplan, K., & Cassidy, J. (1985). Security in infancy, childhood and adulthood: A move to the level of representation. In I. Bretherton & E. Waters (Eds.), *Growing points of attachment theory and research, Monographs of the Society for Research in Child Development, 50*, Serial No. 209 (1-2), 66-104.

Main, M., & Solomon, J. (1990). Procedure for identifying infants as disorganized/disoriented during the Ainsworth Strange situation. In M. Greenberg, D. Cicchetti, & E. M. Cummings (Eds.), *Attachment during the preschool years: Theory, research, and intervention* (pp. 121-160). Chicago: University of Chicago Press.

Mandler, J. H. (1979). Categorical and schematic organization in memory. In C. R. Puff (Ed.), *Memory organization and structure* (pp. 259-299). New York: Academic Press.

Matas, L., Arend, R. A., & Sroufe, L. A. (1978). Continuity and adaptation in the second year: The relationship between quality of attachment and later competence. *Child Development, 49*, 547-556.

Melges, F. T., & Bowlby, J. (1969). Types of hopelessness in psychopathological process. *Archives of General Psychiatry, 20*, 690-699.

Miller, P. J., Hoogstra, L., Mintz, J., Fung, H., & Williams, K. (1993). Troubles in the garden and how they get resolved: The history of a story in one child's life. In C. A. Nelson (Ed.), *Memory and affect: The Minnesota symposia in child psychology* (Vol. 26). Hillsdale, NJ: Lawrence Erlbaum Associates.

Miller, P. J., Potts, R., Fung, H., Hoogstra, L., & Mintz, J. (1990). Narrative practices and the social construction of self in childhood. *American Ethnologist, 17*, 292-311.

Neisser, U. (1987). What is ordinary memory the memory of? In U. Neisser & E. Winograd (Eds.), *Remembering reconsidered* (pp. 356-373). New York: Cambridge University Press.

Nelson, K. (1986). *Event knowledge: Structure and function in development*. Hillsdale, NJ: Lawrence Erlbaum Associates.

Nelson, K. (1989). *Narratives from the crib*. Cambridge, MA: Harvard University Press.

Nelson, K. (1993). Events, narratives, memory: What develops? In C. A. Nelson (Ed.), *Memory and affect: The Minnesota symposia on child psychology* (Vol. 26, pp. 1-24). Hillsdale, NJ: Lawrence Erlbaum Associates.

Noam, G. G. (1992). Development as the aim of intervention. *Development and Psychopathology, 4*, 679-696.

Piaget, J. (1951). *The origins of intelligence in children*. New York: Norton.

Radke-Yarrow, M., Cummings, E. M., Kuczynsky, L., & Chapman, M. (1985). Patterns of attachment in two- and three-year-olds in normal families and families with parental depression. *Child Development, 56*, 884-893.

Ricks, M. H. (1985). The social transmission of parenting: attachment across generations. In I. Bretherton & E. Waters (Eds.), *Growing points of attachment theory and research, Monographs of the Society for Research in Child Development, 50*, Serial No. 209 (1-2), 211-227.

Robertson, J., & Freud, A. (1956). A mother's observation on the tonsillectomy of her four-year-old daughter. *Psychoanalytic Study of the Child, 11*, 410-436.

Rovee-Collier, C. K., & Fagan, C. W. (1981). The retrieval of memory in early infancy. In L. P. Lipsitt (Ed.), *Advances in infancy research* (Vol. 1, pp. 225-254). Norwood, NJ: Ablex.

Rovee-Collier, C. K., & Lipsitt, L. P. (1981). Learning, adaptation, and memory. In P. M. Stratton (Ed.), *Psychobiology of the human newborn* (pp. 147-190). New York: Wiley.

Schank, R. C. (1982). *Dynamic memory: A theory of reminding and learning in computers and people.* Cambridge: Cambridge University Press.

Schank, R. C., & Abelson, R. P.(1977). *Scripts, plans, goals and understanding.* Hillsdale, NJ: Lawrence Erlbaum Associates.

Selman, R. L. (1980). *The growth of interpersonal understanding.* Orlando, FL: Academic Press.

Selman, R. L., Schultz, L. H., & Yeates, K. O. (1991). Interpersonal understanding and action: A development and psychopathology perspective on research an prevention. In D. Cicchetti & S. L. Toth (Eds.), *Models and Integrations: Rochester symposium on developmental psychopathology.* (Vol. 3, pp. 289-329). Rochester, NY: University of Rochester Press.

Shore, C., O'Connell, B., & Bates, E. (1984). First sentences in language and symbolic play. *Developmental Psychology, 20*, 872-880.

Slough, N., & Greenberg, M. (1990). 5-year-olds representations of separation from parents: responses for self and a hypothetical child. In I. Bretherton & M. Watson (Eds.), *Children's perspectives on the family* (pp. 67–84). San Francisco: Jossey-Bass.

Sroufe, L. A., & Wunsch, J. P. (1972). The development of laughter in the first year of life. *Child Development, 43*, 1326-1344.

Stayton, D. J., & Ainsworth, M. D. S. (1973). Individual differences in infant responses to brief everyday separations as related to other infant and maternal behaviors. *Developmental Psychology, 9*, 226-235.

Stern, D. N. (1985). *The interpersonal world of the infant.* New York: Basic Books.

Steward, M. S. (1988). Illness: A crisis for children. In J. Sandoval (Ed.), *Crisis counseling, intervention, and prevention in the schools* (pp. 109-129). Hillsdale, NJ: Lawrence Erlbaum Associates.

Steward, M. S. (1993). Medical procedures: A context for studying memory and emotion. In C. A. Nelson (Ed.), *Memory and affect: The Minnesota symposia on child psychology* (Vol. 26, pp. 171-225). Hillsdale, NJ: Lawrence Erlbaum Associates.

Steward, M. S., Steward, D. S., Farquhar, L., Joyce, N., Reinhart, M., Myers, J. E. B., & Welker, J. (1991). *A visit to the doctor: The accuracy, completeness, and consistency of children's memory.* Manuscript submitted for publication.

Terr, L. (1983). Chowchilla revisited: The effects of psychic trauma four years after a school-bus kidnapping. *American Journal of Psychiatry, 140*, 1543-1550.

Terr, L. (1991). Childhood traumas: An outline and overview. *American Journal of Psychiatry, 148*, 10-20.

Tessler, M. (1986). *Mother-child talk in a museum: The socialization of a memory.* Unpublished manuscript, City University of New York Graduate Center, New York.

Tessler, M. (1991). *Making memories together: The influence of mother-child joint encoding on the development of autobiographical memory style.* Unpublished doctoral dissertation, City University of New York Graduate Center, New York.

Tulving, E. (1972). Episodic and semantic memory. In E. Tulving & W. Donaldson (Eds.), *Organization of memory* (pp. 382-403). New York: Academic Press.

Ward, M. J., Carlson, E. A., Altman, S., Levine, L., Greenberg, R. H., & Kessler, D. B. (1990, April). *Predicting infant-mother attachment from adolescents' prenatal working models of relationships*. Paper presented at the Seventh International Conference on Infant Studies, Montreal, Canada.

Werner, H. (1948). *Comparative psychology of mental development*. New York: International Universities Press.

Young, J. Z. (1964). *A model for the brain*. London: Oxford University Press.

Zeanah, C. H., Keener, M. A., Stewart, L., & Anders, T. F. (1985). Prenatal perception of infant personality: A preliminary investigation. *Journal of the American Academy of Child Psychiatry, 24,* 204-210.

2 Forms of Adult Romantic Attachment and Their Cognitive and Emotional Underpinnings

Phillip R. Shaver
Catherine L. Clark
University of California, Davis

Attachment theory (Ainsworth & Bowlby, 1991) provides a life-span account of affectional bonding in close relationships, although until recently its tenets were examined almost exclusively in studies of infants or young children and their parents, not in studies of adolescent or adult relationships. In the mid-1980s, two distinct lines of research branched off from the large and productive literature on attachment in childhood and began to explore the implications of attachment theory for adults. First, Main, Kaplan, and Cassidy (1985) reported that an Adult Attachment Interview (AAI), which focuses on adults' accounts of their childhood relationships with important attachment figures (usually parents), can be used to predict how those adults' infants and young children will interact with them in laboratory situations (such as the well-known Strange Situation) designed to assess individual differences in the quality of child–parent attachment. In a second independent line of research, Hazan and Shaver (1987) reported that the patterns of attachment discussed by Ainsworth and her collaborators (Ainsworth, Blehar, Waters, & Wall, 1978) — patterns labeled *secure, avoidant*, and *anxious-ambivalent* — could be identified in adults, in the context of romantic relationships. The adult romantic versions of the attachment patterns, which have come to be called *attachment styles* in the social psychological literature (Shaver & Hazan, 1993), are dynamically similar to the infant styles. Infant avoidance, for example, which is marked by physically turning away from attachment figures in times of stress, is marked in the adult romantic context by discomfort with psychological intimacy and reluctance to commit oneself to a long-term intimate relationship.

Research following from the Main et al. conception of adult attachment deals with adult *caregiving* patterns. It focuses primarily on an adult's childhood attachment experiences as predictors of (a) the adult's behavior as a caregiver of his or her own child and (b) the quality of that child's attachment. This resulting body of literature is reviewed by Inge Bretherton (chapter 1, this volume). Here, we concern ourselves with the literature that has developed from Hazan and Shaver's (1987) emphasis on adult romantic attachment, highlighting its cognitive and emotional underpinnings. In attachment theory, as Bretherton (chapter 1, this volume) explains, the cognitive-representational aspects of a person's relational style are viewed as components of "internal working models" — cognitive structures similar to "schemas" in Piagetian psychology and in contemporary cognitive social psychology (e.g., Fiske & Taylor, 1991). When studying adults, it is possible to assess conscious aspects of working models directly, by interview or questionnaire, and unconscious aspects indirectly, by observing their effects on the performance of various communication and social perception tasks. Piagetian schemas are often viewed as cognitive structures consisting primarily of skills and descriptive summaries of knowledge in certain domains (for exceptions see Case, chapter 3, this volume; Fischer & Ayoub, chapter 7, this volume; Fischer, Shaver, & Carnochan, 1990; Noam, chapter 6, this volume). In contrast, internal working models of attachment are portrayed as highly emotional structures, representing not just conditions in the world (i.e., facts) but also powerful affects and self-evaluations. Moreover, working models are thought to include defenses, or rules for defensively excluding certain kinds of thoughts and feelings (Bowlby, 1980; Bretherton, chapter 1, this volume; Main et al., 1985).

DYNAMICS OF THE ATTACHMENT BEHAVIORAL SYSTEM

In our work, we have summarized our own and other researchers' writings about the attachment behavioral system with the help of the flowchart in Fig. 2.1 (e.g., Hazan & Shaver, 1994; Shaver & Clark, 1994; Shaver, Hazan, & Bradshaw, 1988). For good evolutionary reasons the human mind, beginning early in infancy, repeatedly asks the question shown in the flowchart's diamond-shaped box: Is there an attachment figure sufficiently near, attentive, and responsive? If the answer to the question is yes, certain emotions (represented by circles in the flowchart) and observable behaviors (represented by squares) follow naturally. When infants notice that their attachment figure is available, interested, and responsive, they become more playful, less inhibited, visibly happier, and more interested in exploration. When an adolescent or adult falls in love, similar positive

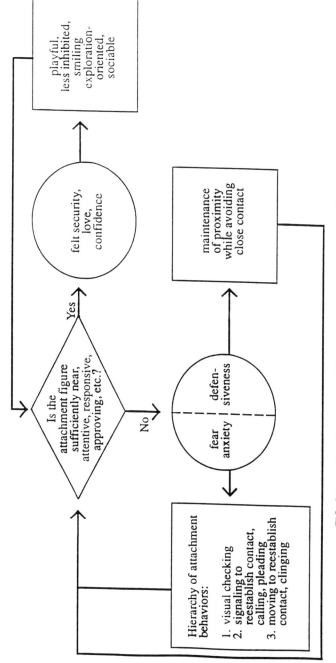

FIG. 2.1. A flowchart model of the dynamics of the attachment behavioral system.

31

emotional effects are evident because the same underlying dynamics are involved.

If the answer to the flowchart's central question is no, fear and anxiety increase sharply and a hierarchy of increasingly intense attachment-related behaviors is enacted — in infancy, visually searching for the attachment figure, calling and pleading to re-establish contact, toddling or running toward this safe haven, and clinging. In the case of adolescent and adult lovers, anxious vigilance is functionally similar to infant vigilance, although it takes more diverse and sophisticated forms.

The third region of Fig. 2.1 (the lower right-hand portion) refers to intimacy-avoidance and detachment. If the innate hierarchy of attachment behaviors repeatedly fails to produce a reduction in anxiety, the mind seems capable of deactivating or suppressing the attachment behavioral system, at least to some extent, and defensively attempting to achieve self-reliance. If unchecked, this eventually leads to the condition Bowlby called *detachment*. We know this state is defensive, as depicted in the figure, rather than arising from a simple erosion of attachment (like a natural fading of memory), because it is quickly replaced by a state of attachment-system activation if an infant comes to believe that his or her temporarily lost or unresponsive attachment figure is once again available and responsive. (As we explain later, a fourth "style" of attachment has now been identified and can be characterized as a *combination* of the activated/anxious and deactivated/avoidant patterns.)

Ainsworth's major contribution to attachment theory was to show that these universal attachment dynamics interact with different caregiving environments to produce important personality differences (e.g., Ainsworth et al., 1978; see Rothbard & Shaver, 1994, for a review of subsequent research). What Ainsworth called secure infants are characterized by all of the processes shown in the upper right-hand portion of the figure. These infants seem to believe, even when their mother is temporarily absent, that she will be accessible and responsive if called upon for help. If upset in mother's absence, securely attached infants cuddle and soothe quickly when she returns. (For convenience, we use the term *mother* to indicate any primary attachment figure, regardless of gender or biological relationship with the infant. We choose this term because, traditionally and in contemporary society, mothers are most likely to function as primary attachment figures.) What Ainsworth called anxious-ambivalent infants are characterized by the processes shown in the lower left-hand portion of the figure. Upon separation from mother, they cry intensely, and upon reunion are difficult to soothe. They throw tantrums and seek contact with their mother while simultaneously rejecting her attempts to offer comfort. Avoidant infants are characterized by the processes shown in the lower right-hand corner of the diagram. They appear prematurely independent and unconcerned about their mother. Often, they do not cry when she departs, and purposefully evade her attempts to seek contact when she returns.

In recent years, an additional category has been added to the typology. The need for this category arose when Main and others noticed a fourth, at first unclassifiable and rather baffling kind of infant, that they eventually called D, for disorganized/disoriented (Carlson, Cicchetti, Barnett, & Braunwald, 1989; Main & Solomon, 1986, 1990). Around the same time, Crittenden (1985) noticed that especially troubled or abusive mothers tend to have infants who exhibit both avoidant and anxious-ambivalent behaviors. She called these infants A/C, following Ainsworth's designation of avoidant infants as Type A and anxious-ambivalent infants as Type C. (Secure infants were labeled Type B.) As soon as the fourth, mixed type was added, it became clear that the four categories form a two-dimensional classification scheme, with the dimensions being anxiety and avoidance (see Fig. 2.2.)

Many studies (reviewed by Bretherton, 1985; Elicker, Englund, & Sroufe, 1992, Rothbard & Shaver, 1994) have shown that the patterns of attachment observable in infancy predict social behavior well into childhood—with teachers and peers, not just with family members—and in a wide variety of situations. In other words, the interactional dynamics of parent–child relationships seem to be lastingly incorporated into children's personalities. What accounts for this cross-age continuity?

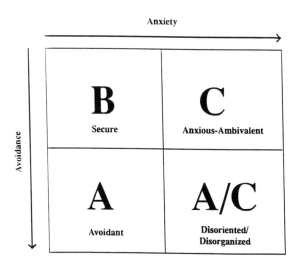

FIG. 2.2.   Diagram of four infant attachment styles defined in terms of two dimensions: anxiety and avoidance.

WORKING MODELS OF SELF
AND RELATIONSHIP PARTNERS

In the first volume of his *Attachment and Loss* trilogy, Bowlby (1969) distinguished between two kinds, or aspects, of attachment working models: "If an individual is to draw up a plan to achieve a set-goal [a temporary goal regarding relations with an attachment figure] not only [must] he have some sort of working model of his environment, but he must have also some working knowledge of his own behavioural skills and potentialities" (p. 112). In a subsequent book, Bowlby (1979) extended this proposition as follows:

> Much influenced by the special role given to feeding and orality in psycho-analytic theorizing is the concept of internal "object," a concept that is in many ways ambiguous. . . . In its place can be put the concept, derived from cognitive psychology and control theory, of an individual developing within himself one or more working models representing principal features of the world about him and of himself as an agent in it. Such working models determine his expectations and forecasts and provide him with tools for constructing plans of action. (p. 117)

In Bowlby's later writings, and in the research field they inspired, these two kinds of working models are called *models of self* and *models of others*. Each kind of model is portrayed as emotionally positive or negative: "Confidence that an attachment figure is likely to be responsive can be seen to turn on at least two variables: (a) whether or not the attachment figure is judged to be the sort of person who in general responds to calls for support or protection [i.e., positive vs. negative models of others]; and (b) whether or not the self is judged to be the sort of person towards whom anyone, and the attachment figure in particular, is likely to respond in a helpful way [i.e., positive vs. negative models of self]" (Bowlby, 1973, p. 238). Bowlby also explained that these two mental structures (models of others and models of self) are often complementary and mutually confirming. "Thus, an unwanted child is likely not only to feel unwanted by his parents but to believe that he or she is essentially unwanted by anyone. Though logically indefensible [certainly a child could be unwanted by parents yet still be loved by others], these crude over-generalizations are the rule. Once adopted, moreover, they are apt never to be seriously questioned" (p. 238). Hence, a child with a negative model of both self and attachment figures can become an adolescent or adult who implicitly distrusts relationship partners, expects them to be cruel, neglectful, or unpredictable, and feels unworthy of anyone's love. On the other hand, a child who is fairly consistently well-treated by attachment figures can grow up feeling that relationship partners are likely to be trustworthy and responsive, and that the self is worthy of love. Although undoubtedly oversimplified, this analysis has proved enormously successful in generating a coherent body of research on adult romantic relationships.

ADULT ROMANTIC ATTACHMENT

In order to extend Ainsworth's typology to the study of adolescent and adult romantic love, Hazan and Shaver (1987, 1990) invented a questionnaire measure of adult attachment styles that distinguishes among the grown-up versions of the three kinds of infants described by Ainsworth et al. (1978) — secure, avoidant, and anxious-ambivalent. This simple, straightforward measure asks respondents to: "think back across all of the important romantic relationships in your life and choose which of the three descriptions below generally fits you best" (the attachment-style labels were not included):

Avoidant: I am somewhat uncomfortable being close to others; I find it difficult to trust them completely, difficult to allow myself to depend on them. I am nervous when anyone gets too close, and often, love partners want me to be more intimate than I feel comfortable being.

Anxious-ambivalent: I find that others are reluctant to get as close as I would like. I often worry that my partner doesn't really love me or won't want to stay with me. I want to get very close to my partner, and this sometimes scares people away.

Secure: I find it relatively easy to get close to others and am comfortable depending on them. I don't often worry about being abandoned or about someone getting too close to me.

The breakdown of attachment styles in Hazan and Shaver's first two studies — 55% secure, 25% avoidant, and 20% anxious-ambivalent — was similar to the breakdown in studies of infants in the United States (Campos, Barrett, Lamb, Goldsmith, & Stenberg, 1983). Similar percentages have been obtained in subsequent adult studies in at least three different industrialized countries (e.g., Collins & Read, 1990; Feeney & Noller, 1990; Mikulincer, Florian, & Tolmacz, 1990).

Studies of adult romantic attachment provided support for Bowlby's notion that mental models of self and other can be positively or negatively charged. Both Collins and Read (1990) and Feeney and Noller (1990) found that adults who score as secure seem to have positive models of both self and others. These adults report having high self-esteem and self-confidence and a generally high regard for others as assessed by measures of trust and altruism. Avoidant adults, as assessed by Hazan and Shaver's measure, seem to display the reverse pattern, having negative models of both self and others. They report significantly lower self-esteem than secure adults and exhibit greater mistrust of others than either the secures or anxious-ambivalents. Anxious-ambivalents seem to harbor evaluatively mixed models. Their model of self appears to be negative — they have relatively low self-esteem, for example — while their model of others is positive in the sense that they view closeness to others as highly desirable.

In the next section, we briefly review some of the major research results amassed to date, concerning the thoughts, feelings, and behavior of romantically avoidant, anxious-ambivalent, and secure adults in relationships with their parents, romantic partners, co-workers, and God. These findings illustrate how positive and negative models of self and others manifest themselves emotionally and behaviorally. (This brief summary is adapted from Shaver & Clark, 1994. For more detailed reviews see Shaver & Hazan, 1993; and Hazan & Shaver, 1994.)

SUMMARY OF RESEARCH ON THREE ADULT ROMANTIC ATTACHMENT STYLES

Adult avoidants describe their parents as rejecting and somewhat cold (Hazan & Hutt, 1993; Hazan & Shaver, 1987; Rothbard & Shaver, 1994), report having poor relationships with parents while attending college (Hazan & Hutt, 1993; Rothbard & Shaver, 1994), and are more likely than secures or anxious-ambivalents to report having a parent with an alcohol problem (Brennan, Shaver, & Tobey, 1991). These findings fit with a large literature on parental predictors of children's avoidant attachment. In their close (or perhaps not so close) relationships, avoidant adults express a general disinterest in seeking and developing intimacy (Shaver & Brennan, 1992; Tidwell, Shaver, Lin, & Reis, 1991), are somewhat pessimistic, and in fact may appear cynical about long-term relationships (Carnelley & Janoff-Bulman, 1992), have a higher break-up rate than secures (Hazan & Shaver, 1987; Kirkpatrick & Davis, 1994; Shaver & Brennan, 1992), and grieve less than secure and anxious-ambivalent adults following a break-up (Simpson, 1990). On the job, avoidants prefer to work alone and use work as an excuse to avoid close relationships (Hazan & Shaver, 1990). Regarding religious beliefs, avoidants are more likely than secures or anxious-ambivalents to be agnostic (failing to commit to either a strong religious or an antireligous position) than secures or anxious-ambivalents and to view God as controlling and distant (Kirkpatrick & Shaver, 1992), suggesting that their models of human attachment figures are used to imagine or apprehend God.

Anxious-ambivalent adults describe their parents as intrusive and unfair, which is perhaps due to inconsistent or unreliable parenting (Hazan & Shaver, 1987; Rothbard & Shaver, 1994). They yearn for romantic relationships and seem desperate to develop intimacy and closeness (Hazan & Hutt, 1993; Kirkpatrick & Hazan, 1994). They are obsessed with romantic partners, suffer from extreme jealousy (Carnelley & Pietromonaco, 1991; Collins, 1993; Hazan & Shaver, 1987), can be argumentative, intrusive, and overcontrolling (Kunce & Shaver, 1994), and report a high break up rate (Hazan & Shaver, 1987; Kirkpatrick & Hazan, 1994; Shaver & Brennan, 1992). They, more than the other two types, tend to break up and then get back together with the same partner (Kirkpatrick & Hazan, 1994). In the workplace, they prefer to work with others but feel unappreciated and misunderstood (perhaps not sufficiently loved) at work. They daydream about success and slack off after receiving praise (Hazan & Shaver, 1990), suggesting that they work more for social recognition than for the value of the job itself. Religious anxious-ambivalents report having more experiences of "speaking in tongues" (babbling hysterically — known technically as "glossolalia") than secures or avoidants, possibly utilizing this behavior as an extreme way to get close to, or cling to, God (Kirkpatrick & Shaver, 1992).

Secure adults describe their parents in generally favorable terms and have good relationships with them while attending college (Hazan & Hutt, 1993; Hazan & Shaver, 1987; Rothbard & Shaver, 1994). They are highly invested in relationships (Collins & Read, 1990; Feeney & Noller, 1990), tend to seek integrative, mutually satisfactory resolutions to conflicts (Pistole, 1989), and tend to have long, stable relationships characterized by trust and friendship (Collins & Read, 1990; Hazan & Shaver, 1987; Kirkpatrick & Davis, 1994; Kirkpatrick & Hazan, 1994). They feel well-liked by coworkers (Hazan & Shaver, 1990) and often adopt parents' religious views and conceptualize God as a warm, trustworthy attachment figure (Kirkpatrick & Shaver, 1990, 1992).

Three sets of studies, which we review next, further highlight differences among the three attachment styles in the realms of cognition, communication, and stress, themes also emphasized in this volume by Fischer and Ayoub (chapter 7) and Bretherton (chapter 1).

Adult Attachment Styles and Cognitive Processes

Various methods have been used to tap cognitive aspects of adults' internal working models. Feeney and Noller (1991), for example, asked subjects to supply an open-ended verbal description of their current steady dating partners. In an analysis of several attachment-related variables, avoidant subjects were notable for having spontaneously mentioned trying to limit their dependence on partners, and trying to limit closeness, affection, and commitment. Anxious-ambivalent subjects did not limit dependence, closeness, affection, or commitment, and indeed spontaneously mentioned what Feeney and Noller called their "unqualified" affection and dependence. Secures generally fell between the two insecure groups, except that they most often mentioned "unqualified closeness." Anxious-ambivalents strongly idealized their partners, avoidants did the opposite, and secures fell in between. Secures mentioned mutuality, couple orientation ("we-ness"), and friendship, whereas avoidants did the opposite, focusing instead on fun and enjoyment. Interestingly, anxious-ambivalents scored lowest on the friendship and fun/enjoyment dimensions, suggesting that their idealization of partners somehow placed their relationships in a category beyond such mundane concerns. Secures reported much more favorable attitudes toward their partners' families than reported by either insecure group. Thus, the models of partners and relationships reflected in subjects' spontaneous, open-ended comments were closely related in theoretically predictable ways to the self-report measure of romantic attachment style.

One potential problem with Feeney and Noller's study is that they had no way of knowing which descriptive elements were simply true of their subjects' relationships and which should be attributed to model-based distortions and projections. This problem was rectified in two subsequent experimental studies, one by Collins (1993) and one by Pietromonaco and Carnelley (1994). Collins provided subjects with written descriptions of potentially negative partner behaviors (e.g., disappearing for a half hour while the couple was attending a party) in a *hypothetical* dating relationship. Subjects explained how they would interpret their partners' behavior, how distressed they would feel, and how they would behave. "As predicted, insecure subjects explained events in ways that reflected fear about the security of their relationships and perceptions of others as unresponsive and rejecting. They also reported greater emotional distress and behavioral intentions that were judged as likely to lead to conflict" (p. 2). In other words, cognitive components of subjects' stable, lifelong, internal working models of others acted as emotion-generating appraisals, which then determined their situation-specific emotional and coping behavior. This fits well with what Fischer et al. (1990) called "the consensus model of emotion" in which emotion-generation is posited to be the result of specific cognitive appraisal processes. (Shaver, Collins, & Clark, 1995, in fact, have argued that internal working models include not only cognitive appraisals, but the resultant emotions and behavioral tendencies as well.)

In a second study, Pietromonaco and Carnelley designed elaborate, realistic descriptions of potential relationship partners who typified particular attachment styles. Subjects' own attachment style, their imagined partner's attachment style, and their gender all contributed significantly to feelings concerning the relationship and assessments of the likelihood that it would eventuate in marriage. Regardless of subjects' own attachment style, they tended to associate good feelings with a secure partner. Interestingly, avoidant men and anxious-ambivalent women — the two groups whose attachment styles seem most congruent with traditional gender-role stereotypes — felt the most negative of all the subject groups toward both themselves and the imagined relationship, a finding consistent with previous studies of gender roles in actual relationships (e.g., Ickes & Barnes, 1978). This happened despite the fact that avoidant men slightly preferred anxious-ambivalent over secure women as imagined marriage partners. The fact that merely imagining a relationship can activate different feelings and expectations among people with different attachment styles indicates the power of internal working models of attachment and their close connection with emotion.

Attachment Styles and Communication

Bretherton (chapter 1, this volume) explains the ways in which children and adults with different *familial* attachment patterns communicate differently. Secure individuals seem to be able to freely access their internal working models and clearly articulate attachment-related thoughts and feelings. Avoidant individuals, in contrast, seem unwilling or unable to recall attachment-related feelings; and anxious-ambivalent individuals seem to have particularly conflictual or confused working models and are enmeshed in and overwhelmed by their feelings in ways that make coherent communication about attachment difficult.

Mikulincer and Nachshon (1991) found that self-reported *romantic* attachment styles relate in similar ways to patterns of self-disclosure in relationships with peers. Secures generally like other people who self-disclose, and they self-disclose appropriately themselves, in proportion to the nature of their relationship with a particular conversation partner. (In other words, they display the kind of reciprocal self-disclosure found by previous researchers to be normative among unacquainted peers.) Anxious-ambivalents also generally like others who disclose, but they themselves disclose too readily and without much concern for their relationship with their conversation partner. In other words, their abundant self-disclosure is sometimes inappropriate. Avoidants tend not to like others who disclose and not to be disclosers themselves.

In order to study the connections between global communication behaviors and attachment security, Kobak and Hazan (1991) asked married couples to engage in a variety of problem-solving and confiding tasks. The wives' attachment security proved to be associated with less rejecting behaviors and increased intimacy of disclosure on their part during the problem-solving task and with their husbands' acceptance of their distress during the confiding task. Husbands' attachment security was associated with less rejecting and more supportive behaviors on the parts of both couple members during problem solving. Husbands' attachment security was also correlated with increased levels of disclosure during the confiding task.

Overall, then, communication patterns differ among adults with different romantic attachment styles in some of the same ways they differ in accordance with attachment patterns measured in other ways and in other contexts (e.g., parenting). Secure adults seem to be able to relate sensitively and with little defensiveness to their own and their partners' feelings. Avoidant adults seem to gate out their own and their partners' feelings, perhaps wishing that feelings (with the possible exception of "fun") did not exist. Anxious-ambivalent adults are open to their attachment-related memories and feelings but are not very good at regulating and describing them. Moreover, they seem preoccupied with their own needs and feelings, to the exclusion of the needs and feelings of others.

Attachment Styles and Coping with Stress

Simpson, Rholes, and Nelligan (1992) observed how couple members coped with an immediately stressful situation. These researchers brought dating couples into the laboratory, placed each partner in a separate room and, unbeknownst to the male partner, told the female partner that later in the study she would undergo a painful and stressful procedure. The partners were then reunited and covertly videotaped. Simpson et al. discovered that the more anxious the female partner became, the more the distinction between secure and avoidant attachment mattered. Avoidant women withdrew from their partner's support as they became more anxious; avoidant men withdrew from supporting their partner as she became more anxious. These results parallel what has been found in studies of infants and their mothers: Avoidant infants are more noticeably avoidant when frightened, and avoidance-engendering mothers withdraw support from their infant when the infant becomes distressed.

In another test of the ways in which people with different attachment styles cope with stressful experiences, Mikulincer, Florian, and Weller (1993) interviewed Israelis immediately following the Scud missile attacks that occurred during the Gulf War. Anxious-ambivalents reported the most intense distress and tended to use what stress researchers call emotion-focused coping techniques (trying to reduce the overwhelming feelings of stress). Avoidants reported more somatization (physical symptoms of stress), hostility, and trauma-related avoidance; they coped with stress by emotionally distancing themselves from thoughts of the threat. Secures used more social support-seeking strategies and fared best in terms of lowered stress levels and subsequent physical health.

The differences between the three attachment types can be characterized in terms of defenses — an important component of internal working models. The avoidant type seems to cope with attachment needs and a variety of threats and stresses by avoidance of emotion, denial of vulnerability, and attempts at repression. Attachment theory helps explain why someone might choose this repressive strategy: He or she had to deny vulnerability and disengage his or her attachment behavioral system in order to live amicably with an attachment figure who disliked close bodily contact or for some other reason was fairly consistently rejecting or neglectful. The anxious-ambivalent person, in contrast, is perpetually vigilant, somewhat histrionic, and anxiety-amplifying rather than anxiety-denying. This pattern emerges, according to attachment theory, when an attachment figure seems unreliable and unlikely to respond unless anxiety and anger are dramatically and insistently experienced and displayed. Notice that both the avoidant and the anxious-ambivalent behavior patterns are defensive, and both are exaggerations of normal "moments" in the general attachment process model outlined in Fig. 2.1. The secure type, in contrast, is relatively undefended, theoretically because no hyperprotection or hypervigilance was required in past dealings with important attachment figures.

BARTHOLOMEW'S FOUR-CATEGORY TYPOLOGY

Just as recent research on infant–caregiver attachment has led to a four-category rather than a three-category attachment-style typology (refer back to Fig. 2.2), a four-category elaboration of Hazan and Shaver's (1987) three-category typology has recently been proposed. Bartholomew (1990; Bartholomew & Horowitz, 1991) was the first to notice that the operational definition of adult avoidance is somewhat different in Main et al.'s (1985) AAI and in Hazan and Shaver's self-report measure of romantic attachment style. In particular, the AAI avoidant is especially high on repression, denial, and invulnerability, whereas the Hazan and Shaver avoidant is characterized by conscious feelings of depression, dissatisfaction, and vulnerability. AAI avoidants are what Bowlby called "compulsively self-reliant" and, according to Main et al., "dismissive" of attachment. The avoidants identified by Hazan and Shaver, in contrast, seem to wish they could maintain close and comfortable romantic relationships, but for some reason feel themselves becoming tense, frightened, or depressed. They are, in Bartholomew's terms, "fearfully avoidant." This distinction, like the avoidant (A) versus avoidant/anxious-ambivalent mix (A/C or D) distinction in the infancy literature, suggests a two-dimensional model of romantic attachment styles (see Fig. 2.3).

One of Bartholomew's key contributions was to incorporate Bowlby's ideas about positive and negative internal working models of self and other, discussed earlier in this chapter, into a two-dimensional structure underlying the four adult attachment patterns. What we earlier called the anxiety dimension when describing the four-fold infant typology (Fig. 2.2), becomes "positive versus negative model of self" in Bartholomew's analysis. What we called the avoidance dimension becomes "positive versus negative model of others" (i.e., of attachment figures). Developmental social-cognitivists have similarly emphasized positive and negative views of self and others in the formation of self-concept. For example, both Noam (1985) and Selman (1980) addressed the ways in which an individual's perspectives on self and others influence behavioral outcomes throughout development.

In line with a passage from Bowlby, quoted earlier, in which he said that the model of self and the model of others tend to be congruent (i.e., both positive or both negative), most people in the "normal" (usually college student) samples studied by social psychologists fall either in the secure cell, indicating positive models of both self and others, or the fearful avoidant

Model of Self

	Positive	Negative
Positive Model of Others	**CELL I** **SECURE** **Comfortable with** **intimacy and autonomy**	**CELL II** **PREOCCUPIED** **Preoccupied with** **relationships**
Negative	**CELL III** **DISMISSING** **Dismissing of intimacy** **Counter-dependent**	**CELL IV** **FEARFUL** **Fearful of intimacy** **Socially avoidant**

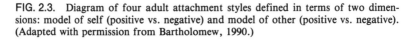

FIG. 2.3.   Diagram of four adult attachment styles defined in terms of two dimensions: model of self (positive vs. negative) and model of other (positive vs. negative). (Adapted with permission from Bartholomew, 1990.)

cell, indicating negative models of both self and others. The other two cells are more complex. Dismissing individuals (more often men than women) manage to maintain a consciously positive image of themselves despite a history of negative interactions with attachment figures. This seems to involve an exceptional degree of self-reliance. Preoccupied (anxious-ambivalent) individuals (more often women than men) manage to view relationships with others as desirable even though previous relationships have helped to create a rather vulnerable, insecure self. Their ambivalence about relationship partners seems to be attributable to the on-again, off-again responsiveness of their primary attachment figures in childhood.

Given this brief overview of the new four-category model of adult attachment, it is possible to connect it with some of the clinical syndromes discussed by other contributors to this volume.

PERSONALITY AND PERSONALITY DISORDERS

Interpersonal Problems

Bartholomew's (1990) four-category attachment typology is closely related to clinically significant personality problems or disorders. This was shown explicitly in two studies by Bartholomew and Horowitz (1991). Research subjects were interviewed to determine their attachment style and they also completed various self-report measures, including a measure of attachment style similar to Hazan and Shaver's (although containing four rather than three categories) and the Inventory of Interpersonal Problems (IIP; Horowitz, Rosenberg, Ureno, Kalehzen, & O'Halloran, 1989). The IIP is a 127-item inventory "designed to assess interpersonal difficulties in a broad cross-section of interpersonal domains" (Bartholomew & Horowitz, 1991, p. 229). It is scored in terms of an eight-section circle, or circumplex, defined by two dimensions: warmth and dominance. The octants are labeled as follows:

1. autocratic (most dominant),
2. expressive,
3. nurturant (most warm),
4. exploitable,
5. subassertive (least dominant),
6. introverted,
7. cold (least warm), and
8. competitive.

The measures were also completed by a friend of each subject.

The interview, self-report, and friend-report measures converged significantly, and the findings of the two studies corresponded well. For each of
the three insecure groups there was a clear pattern of prominent interpersonal problems. Preoccupied subjects were troubled by being overly
expressive, overly nurturant, and too autocratic and competitive; in other
words, their interpersonal difficulties lay mainly in the warm-dominant
quadrant of the circumplex. Interestingly, although their friends tended to
agree with them, the subjects flattered themselves by describing more
difficulty in the expressive and nurturant octants than their friends noted,
and fewer problems in the autocratic and competitive octants than their
friends noted.

Fearful subjects had difficulty due to introversion, lack of assertiveness,
and being exploited—in other words, to low dominance. Their friends
agreed with them but were not quite as extreme in their descriptions as the
fearfuls themselves, suggesting that the fearfuls felt even less assertive and
more exploited than they looked. Dismissing subjects had most difficulty
with coldness, competitiveness, and (to a lesser extent) introversion—in
other words, with extreme lack of warmth. Their friends generally agreed
with them, although placing somewhat more emphasis on introversion than
the dismissings themselves did. Secure subjects were distinctive primarily in
reporting an average degree of difficulty in each octant; in other words,
they were not notable for any single kind of difficulty. They were notable,
however, for agreeing almost perfectly with their friends' descriptions,
suggesting once again a high degree of perceptual accuracy, open communication, and lack of defensiveness.

The two dimensions that define Bartholomew's (1990) typology, self-
model and other-model, are related to other important personality variables. Bartholomew and Horowitz's (1991) subjects completed measures of
distress, self-esteem, and self-acceptance, all of which proved to be related
to the self-model dimension. That is, secure and dismissing subjects were
higher in self-regard and lower in distress (a composite measure of anxiety,
depression, and hostility) than preoccupied and fearful subjects. The
subjects also completed a measure of sociability, and their friends described
them using the same measure. The resulting scores were related to the
other-model dimension; that is, secure and preoccupied subjects were more
sociable, as rated by both themselves and their friends, than dismissing and
fearful subjects.

This pattern of findings suggested to Shaver and Brennan (1992) that
Bartholomew's typology might be similar to Eysenck and Eysenck's (1963)
two-dimensional model of personality, based on the concepts of neuroticism and extraversion. If Bartholomew's self-model dimension were
equivalent to neuroticism and her other-model dimension were equivalent
to extraversion, then people with a secure attachment style would be

nonneurotic extraverts, people with a preoccupied style would be neurotic extraverts, and so on. Shaver and Brennan administered Hazan and Shaver's attachment measure along with the NEO Personality Inventory (Costa & McCrae, 1985), a well-known measure of the so-called "Big Five" personality traits, which include neuroticism and extraversion. Shaver and Brennan then followed up their subjects for 8 months to determine how well the attachment measure, as compared with the entire NEO inventory, predicted relationship developments (e.g., break-ups, increases or decreases in satisfaction, commitment). Secure attachment was significantly correlated with both nonneuroticism and extraversion, and fearful avoidance was significantly correlated with both neuroticism and introversion, but overall, neuroticism and introversion did not fully account for differences among the attachment styles. Moreover, the attachment measures, although brief, predicted relationship outcomes better than the entire NEO-PI over an 8-month period, again suggesting differences in content. Nevertheless, it is worth noting that secures are to an extent nonneurotic extraverts, and fearful avoidants are neurotic introverts. Because approximately 50% of the variance in these traits is attributable to genes (Loehlin, 1992), the Shaver and Brennan study suggests that some of the variability in attachment styles may be due to heritable temperament, not wholly to childrearing features.

Attachment Styles and Models of the Self

Clark, Shaver, and Calverley (1994) pursued the notion of "self-model" in more detail, using a detailed method of self-description designed by Monsour (1985; Harter & Monsour, 1992) and adapted by Calverley, Fischer, and Ayoub (1994) in a study of abused adolescent females (see also Fischer & Ayoub, chapter 7, this volume). In the Clark et al. (1994) study, subjects were asked to provide five adjectives describing themselves in each of several relationships, including relationships with mother, with father, and with a same-gender close friend. They then labeled each adjective as positive, negative, or neutral and transferred all of them to a "bull's-eye" diagram in which the inner circle represented the innermost self and the surrounding middle and outermost circles represented increasingly less central aspects of the self. From the resulting diagrams it was possible to derive a number of scores, such as the number of positive adjectives overall, the number of negative adjectives in the innermost circle, and the number of positive or negative adjectives in the middle and outer circles, the number of adjectives describing self-with-mother that were placed in the innermost circle, and so on.

Most striking were the associations of the adjective measures with the secure and fearful attachment-style ratings. Secure ratings were correlated with more positive ($r = .33$, $p < .01$) and fewer negative self-descriptors overall ($r = -.32$, $p < .01$), while the fearful ratings yielded the opposite pattern — correlations with a lower number of positive ($r = -.29$, $p < .01$) and a higher number of negative adjectives ($r = .33$, $p < .01$). Furthermore, secure ratings were associated with placing most of the positive adjectives in the innermost circle (reflecting the core self), $r = .23$, $p < .05$; fearful ratings showed the opposite pattern, $r = -.29$, $p < .01$. Also, secure ratings were negatively correlated with placing negative adjectives in the inner ($r = -.19$, $p < .05$) and middle circles ($r = -.28$, $p < .01$). Fearful avoidance was also associated with placing fewer father adjectives in the innermost circle ($r = -.32$, $p < .01$) and more father adjectives in the outer circle ($r = .30$, $p < .01$). The pattern was weaker but essentially reversed for the secure ratings ($r = .15$, n.s. and $r = -.22$, $p < .05$, respectively). Thus, the negative self-concepts of the fearful avoidants may be attributable in part to damaging, perhaps abusive, childhood relationships between fearful avoidants and their fathers.

Attachment Styles and Dissociative Disorders

Another striking characteristic of some insecure, mostly fearful avoidant, subjects is dissociation (gaps in memory, experiences of depersonalization and derealization). In studies by Alexander (1993) and Dutton, Saunders, Starzomski, and Bartholomew (1994), adult fearful avoidance has been associated with borderline personality disorder and reports of trauma symptoms thought to be associated with childhood abuse. Several researchers (e.g., DiTomasso & Routh, 1993) argued that dissociative symptoms may be concurrent with diagnoses of posttraumatic stress disorder resulting from extreme abuse. In the AAI, Main, van IJzendoorn, and Hesse (1993) noted several dissociative responses in their D-like (perhaps fearful avoidant) subjects. These responses were described as "lapses in the monitoring of reasoning or discourse when asked to . . . discuss potentially traumatic events — specifically, important deaths and/or abuse experiences" (pp. 3-4). Strikingly, D-like subjects, during the AAI, produce prolonged awkward silences, provide odd associations, occasionally utter extremely tangled and ungrammatical sentences, fail to finish sentences, act as though an important death did not occur (e.g., saying, "She always likes" rather than "liked"—years after "she" died), and seem erroneously to believe that they were somehow responsible for the death of an important loved one (e.g., by failing to concentrate sufficiently during public prayers for the person on the night he or she died). These odd reactions are not unlike some of the behaviors displayed by D children. For example, Main and Hesse (1990) found that 6-year-olds who had previously been classified as disoriented/disorganized at 12 months of age were largely dysfluent —

exhibiting fearful, disorganized, contradictory, and irrational-seeming thought processes, and using violent or bizarre descriptions when narrating interactions between a child and a mother doll in a modified Strange Situation suitable for their age group.

Main et al. (1993) recently developed a self-report inventory that contains two major scales for identifying people who exhibit D-like lapses or errors during the AAI. One scale, Unresolved State of Mind, taps disorganized thinking during the description of attachment-related traumatic experiences, especially loss and abuse. On each of its subscales — Responsibility for Tragedy, Confusion/Disorientation, Lost Memories, Uncontrolled Memories, Feeling Possessed — the means were significantly higher for D-like adults (identified by the AAI) than for members of any other attachment group. The second scale, Unusual Beliefs, was used to assess whether D-like interviewees reported having "unusual ideation regarding space-time relations and/or causality" (p. 10); and in fact, these people did score higher than members of the other attachment groups on three of four Unusual Belief subscales: Astrology, Spiritualism, and Mind-Reading.

Summary

There is now considerable evidence that adult attachment patterns are related — at least at the extremes — to clinically significant psychopathology. Of most concern are extreme fearful avoidants who seem likely to be a product of neglectful, troubled, or abusive relationships during childhood.

PROBLEMS IN THE STUDY OF ADULT ATTACHMENT

Despite considerable progress during the past 5 years in the study of adult romantic attachment and its associated vulnerabilities and pathologies, there are many obstacles and dilemmas confronting future researchers. In this section we briefly describe some of these challenges.

Measurement

Attachment theory is now the basis of some 20 different measures of adult attachment (Shaver & Clark, 1994). It is far from clear that they all converge, even though the researchers who use them all derive their hypotheses from a single theory. More than one paper presented at the 1993 meeting of the Society for Research in Child Development reported that the Hazan and Shaver measure of romantic attachment styles relates weakly, if at all, to attachment classifications derived from the AAI. In some respects this is not surprising. One measure is based on brief self-reports, the other on complex coding of an hour-long interview. One (before being modified by Bartholomew) contained three categories, the other four or more categories. One focuses on a person's own summary of feelings and experiences in romantic relationships; the other, on defensive maneuvers exhibited inadvertently, and perhaps unconsciously, while talking about childhood relationships with parents. The construct validity of one is rooted in studies of romantic relationships, some of which we have summarized in this chapter; the validity of the other is based almost entirely on the attachment classifications of interviewees' children. Nevertheless, the same theoretical reservoir is tapped to explain both sets of findings, and it is difficult to see why, conceptually, the two sets should be totally unrelated.

Only two studies have included both self-report and interview measures of four attachment styles. One of these also included an interview measure of attachment to parents (or in Main's, 1991, terms, "state of mind with respect to attachment," p. 141), which is quite similar to the AAI although coded in terms of Bartholomew's four categories. In the first of these studies (Bartholomew & Horowitz, 1991; Bartholomew, personal communication, May 1995), all three measures converged to a significant degree. That is, when a self-report measure of current attachment style, an interview measure of current attachment style, and a retrospective interview measure of attachment to parents — all based on the same four-category scoring scheme — were compared, they proved to be significantly associated. (Moreover, reports from friends converged with these other measures.) This suggests that failures to find convergence between the AAI and the Hazan and Shaver measure are based in part on a failure to consider their different conceptions of avoidance, which were distinguished clearly by Bartholomew in 1990.

Even if there is significant convergence between self-report and interview measures of adult attachment, however, much work is needed to discover when self-reports are least valid and whether longer self-report measures can substitute for difficult-to-code interviews. These goals are currently being approached by several investigators, including Main and her co-workers.

Attachment Styles and Temperament

Some developmentalists (e.g., Chess & Thomas, 1982; Kagan, 1984) have been tempted, almost from the moment that Ainsworth discovered three stable attachment types, to explain these types in terms of innate temperament.

Attachment theorists have countered this temptation in several ways. First, they have noted that infants often show one attachment pattern with mother and a different one with father. This makes it seem that a particular child can adopt any of the three or four major attachment styles, depending on the parental caregiving environment. Fox, Kimmerly, and Schafer (1991) responded to this observation by showing that, given sufficiently large samples, the behavior of infants observed in separate Strange Situation sessions with mother and with father is somewhat consistent. Unfortunately for their argument, however, adult romantic attachment studies (e.g., Brennan & Shaver, 1995; Collins & Read, 1990; Kirkpatrick & Davis, 1994) indicate that husbands' and wives' attachment styles are not statistically independent. (For example, secure men are slightly more likely than would be expected by chance to be paired with secure women.) To the extent that parental attachment styles are linked with the attachment styles exhibited by their children in the Strange Situation—and this extent is great, 80% (e.g., Fonagy, Steele, & Steele, 1991; Main et al., 1985)—the styles children exhibit in the presence of their mothers and fathers should be about as similar as the styles of the husbands and wives themselves, and this is precisely what Fox et al. found. Thus, their data do not constitute convincing evidence of temperament effects on infant attachment behavior.

A second challenge to temperament theorists is that young children's attachment styles vary systematically in response to changes in parental caregiving environment. For example, in a Minneapolis poverty sample Sroufe and his colleagues (Egelund, Kalkoske, Gottesman, & Erickson, 1990; Erickson, Sroufe, & Egelund, 1985; Sroufe, Carlson, & Shulman, 1993) showed that children's security varied in tandem with their mothers' economic and relationship security. (A recent 4-year study of *adult* attachment styles by Kirkpatrick and Hazan, 1994, found the same thing: a considerable tendency toward stability, modified in a minority of cases by changes attributable to relationship formation and break-up.)

A third criticism of temperament interpretations of attachment style is based on intervention studies. Anisfeld, Caspar, Nozyee, and Cunningham (1990) provided empirical support for Ainsworth's (1967; Ainsworth et al., 1978) claimed that "close physical contact [is] an antecedent to attachment" (Anisfeld et al., 1990). Two days after giving birth, one group of mothers received soft baby-carriers (a cloth device that keeps a baby in physical contact with its mother) and another group of mothers received plastic infant seats (to keep their children at a distance). At 13 months, all infants were tested in the Strange Situation. Infants who had been transported in the soft carriers were more likely to be classified as secure than those who had been carried in the infant seats. (An unusually large number of infants were classified as avoidant in the plastic-seat condition, suggesting that not only does proximity promote attachment, but distance promotes detachment.)

Van den Boom (1990) and Lieberman, Weston, and Pawl (1991) conducted even more stringent tests of the efficacy of interventions, recruiting especially difficult or troubled populations of mothers and infants. van den Boom tested temperamentally difficult babies and provided half of their mothers with sensitivity training. The mothers in the experimental group proved to have more securely attached infants at 12 months than the mothers in the control (no training) group. In the Lieberman et al. (1991) study, anxiously attached, low socioeconomic status, recently immigrated mother–infant dyads were targeted. Half of the anxious dyads received weekly mother–infant psychotherapy and were found to produce more securely attached infants 1 year later than the anxiously attached dyads who did not receive psychotherapy.

Other recent research has shown, however, that measures of negative affectivity/reactivity and attachment security do seem to be related (e.g., Braungart & Stifter, 1991; Izard, Haynes, Chisholm, & Baak, 1991; Teti, Nakagawa, Das, & Wirth, 1991; Vaughn et al., 1992; Wachs & Desai, 1993). Irritability (assessed neonatally) and high heart-rate variability (assessed at 3, 6, and 9 months) have also been linked with insecure attachment measured at 12 to 14 months of age (Calkins & Fox, 1992; Izard, Porges, et al., 1991; van den Boom, 1989). Vaughn et al. pointed out that although quality of attachment and temperament are related, the amount of overlap is modest, accounting for no more than 25% of total variance. Future studies will undoubtedly delineate the overlap and inter-action of temperament and attachment still further, but it seems unlikely that either influence will ever be rendered unimportant.

Continuity and Change

One of the biggest questions concerning the social basis of personality development is: What accounts for continuity and change in attachment styles? As explained earlier, Bowlby (1973) and other attachment re-searchers (e.g., Bretherton, 1990) argued that internal working models are the mechanisms of continuity. These working models are thought to be based in real experience and to determine emotions and guide behavior. They are also considered to be flexible enough to change when the incoming data are highly discrepant from the current conception of self and others. But how much can and do internal working models actually change?

Recent studies and reviews have documented the stability of attachment style over time, in adulthood as well as childhood (e.g., Elicker et al., 1992; Kirkpatrick & Hazan, 1994; Rothbard & Shaver, 1994; Sroufe et al., 1993). Yet studies also show that some children and adults do change (perhaps as many as 25%, depending on age, length of time studied, social conditions, and the particular measures used), so it is important to determine how and why. Sroufe et al. (1993) maintained that changes in attachment style are "lawful." As discussed in our section on temperament, changes in a child's attachment classification from insecure to secure seem to track the mother's improved adjustment, which is sometimes attributable to her formation of a stable romantic partnership. Studies of adults conducted by Hazan, Hutt, and Markus (1991) and Kirkpatrick and Hazan (1994) suggested that, although adult attachment styles are generally stable over periods of several years, some adults' styles do change (or at least are reported to change) in response to important relationship experiences (acquisition of a supportive partner, break-up of an important relationship, success in long-term psychotherapy). These findings must be viewed somewhat cautiously, however, given Sroufe, Egelund, and Kreutzer's (1990) discovery that "poor adaptation and history are not 'erased' by change. Earlier patterns may be reactivated, and early history adds to current circumstances in predicting current adaptation" (cited in Sroufe et al., 1993, pp. 316–317).

The adult studies conducted to date are too brief (3 or 4 years in length) to allow us to decide whether apparent changes in attachment style are temporary or permanent. It seems likely that at least some of the apparent changes will be reversed under stressful conditions, which is the pattern documented by Sroufe et al. in their studies of children. Still, we assume that some of the documented change is real and stable. Main and her collaborators (personal communication, August 1994) identified some secure adults (assessed with the AAI) who seem likely to have been insecure as children, because at least one of their parents was abusive or neglectful. These "earned secures," who are able now to talk undefensively and coherently about their painful childhood experiences, rear children who are secure in their presence when tested in the Strange Situation (see Pearson, Cohn, Cowan, & Cowan, 1994). Hazan et al. (1991) interviewed the 25% of their adult sample who said they had changed attachment styles at some point in their lives. The changes were generally attributable to important close relationships that violated expectations based on previous relationships with attachment figures. Bowlby (1988), in his final book about psychotherapy, argued that a therapist can serve as a model-altering "secure base" for clients, allowing them to explore and reconstruct their internal working models of self and others. Presumably, adolescents and adults, as they gain increasing independence from parents and other childhood attachment figures, can undertake such revisions with the help of friends, lovers, mentors, and counselors other than professional therapists, but the details of these naturally "therapeutic" relationships remain to be studied.

The Complexity of Internal Working Models

One of the thorniest problems of contemporary attachment theory is the vagueness and slipperiness of the working-models construct. Bowlby (e.g., 1988), speaking more as a clinician than a researcher, speculated that there can be conflicting models of a particular person (e.g., mother), that some models may be conscious and others unconscious, and that different models may be evoked by different situations or relationship partners. How can these complexities be measured? Turner and Feldman (1992) showed that adults believe they have exhibited different attachment styles in different romantic relationships, mostly as a function of their partners' behavior. Collins and Read (1990) showed that members of dating couples tend to have attachment styles that match the styles of their partners' opposite-sex parent, suggesting that the salient parent model in a heterosexual romantic relationship is the model of the opposite-sex parent. Intuitively, it would seem that each of us constructs models of all of the important people in our lives. How these are integrated—assuming that they are integrated—to form a single model or system of models corresponding to a particular attachment style is unknown. All of the research reviewed in this chapter assumes that such integration occurs—otherwise a person would not have a single, unified attachment style—but there are few good ideas about how such integration is achieved. (See Collins & Read, 1994, for a start.)

Attachment and Gender

In Hazan and Shaver's (1987) initial adult attachment studies, there were no gender differences in the distribution of attachment styles, a finding similar to the lack of gender differences in studies of infant–caregiver attachment. However, with the advent of Bartholomew's four-category measure (Bartholomew & Horowitz, 1991) and the completion of longitudinal studies using the three-category measure (e.g., Kirkpatrick & Davis, 1994), it has become necessary to take gender into account. Both self-report and interview measures of Bartholomew's four categories yield more male than female dismissing avoidants. The self-report measure of the four categories sometimes turns up more female than male fearful avoidants, and the interview measure sometimes turns up more female than male preoccupieds. All of these differences are compatible with U.S. gender role norms, suggesting that gender role socialization somehow adds to, or interacts with, attachment history to produce different average outcomes for men and women. This matter deserves careful study.

Kirkpatrick and Davis (1994) found that couples consisting of an avoidant male and an anxious-ambivalent (preoccupied) female were more likely to last (albeit unhappily) than couples consisting of an anxious-ambivalent male and an avoidant female. Presumably, the avoidant females rejected their gender role atypical ("weak," "wimpy") partners. Anxious-ambivalent females, on the other hand, being like the media-identified "women who love too much," clung to their gender role-congruent avoidant male partners despite the pain inherent in doing so (Morgan, 1993). This is another way in which gender roles must be taken into account in future studies of adult romantic attachment.

SUMMARY AND CONCLUSION

Attachment theory provides both a general model of cognitive and emotional processes in close relationships and an explanation of the ways in which relatively stable individual differences in personality are created as the normative, biologically universal attachment behavioral system interacts with particular close-relationship environments. The theory is both ethological and cognitive in its origins and emphases. The cognitive portion of the theory asserts that stable individual differences in attachment orientations, or styles, are attributable to working models of self and others that can be characterized, in a general way, as affectively positive or negative. The two dimensions of this set of models—self (positive or negative) and others (positive or negative)—create a typology of four major social types: secure, preoccupied (anxious-ambivalent), fearful avoidant, and dismissing avoidant. Within this typology, secure and fearful individuals appear most different from each other. Secure individuals have generally positive models of themselves and their major relationship partners, and this seems to allow them to think and communicate openly and coherently about feelings. Fearful individuals have generally negative models of themselves and others, in some cases because of a history of abuse or neglect. This is associated with low assertiveness and a propensity for anxiety and depression.

Although many controversies and mysteries remain, the attachment-theoretical approach to close relationships has proven its conceptual value and ability to inspire research for almost 35 years. It includes many valuable insights from psychoanalytic and more recent object relational theories but seems more amenable than these theories to a wide range of empirical tests. As a consequence, whatever is weak or missing in the theory can be identified by researchers and gradually corrected. One of the most challenging areas for elaboration and correction has to do with the fruitful but still-vague notion of internal working models. The nature and development of these models, especially the aspects of the models associated with psychological distress and interpersonal vulnerability, raise a host of questions for future research in cognitive development, developmental psychopathology, psychotherapy, and the social psychology of close relationships. The present volume begins to map some of the important areas of overlap between these fields and reveals a stimulating variety of methods and paradigms for future work.

REFERENCES

Ainsworth, M. D. S. (1967). *Infancy in Uganda: Infant care and the growth of love.* Baltimore: Johns Hopkins University Press.

Ainsworth, M. D. S., Blehar, M. C., Waters, E., & Wall, S. (1978). *Patterns of attachment: Assessed in the strange situation and at home.* Hillsdale, NJ: Lawrence Erlbaum Associates.

Ainsworth, M. D. S., & Bowlby, J. (1991). An ethological approach to personality development. *American Psychologist, 46,* 333-341.

Alexander, P. C. (1993). The differential effects of abuse characteristics and attachment in the prediction of long-term effects of sexual abuse. *Journal of Interpersonal Violence, 8,* 346-362.

Anisfeld, E., Casper, V., Nozyee, M., & Cunningham, N. (1990). Does infant carrying promote attachment? An experimental study of the effects of increased physical contact on the development of attachment. *Child Development, 61,* 1617-1627.

Bartholomew, K. (1990). Avoidance of intimacy: An attachment perspective. *Journal of Social and Personal Relationships, 7,* 147-178.

Bartholomew, K., & Horowitz, L. M. (1991). Attachment styles among young adults: A test of a four-category model. *Journal of Personality and Social Psychology, 61,* 226-244.

Bowlby, J. (1969). *Attachment and loss: Vol. I. Attachment.* Middlesex, England: Penguin Books.

Bowlby, J. (1973). *Attachment and loss: Vol. II. Separation: Anxiety and anger.* New York: Basic Books.

Bowlby, J. (1979). *The making and breaking of affectional bonds.* London: Tavistock.

Bowlby, J. (1980). *Attachment and loss: Vol. III. Loss: Sadness and depression.* New York: Basic Books.

Bowlby, J. (1988). *A secure base: Parent-child attachment and healthy human development.* New York: Basic Books.

Braungart, J. M., & Stifter, C. A. (1991). Regulation of negative reactivity during the strange situation: Temperament and attachment in 12-month-old infants. *Infant Behavior and Development, 14,* 349-364.

Brennan, K. A., & Shaver, P. R. (1995). Dimensions of attachment and the dynamics of romantic relationships. *Personality and Social Psychology Bulletin, 21,* 267-283.

Brennan, K. A., Shaver, P. R., & Tobey, A. E. (1991). Attachment styles, gender, and parental problem drinking. *Journal of Social and Personal Relationships, 8,* 451-466.

Bretherton, I. (1985). Attachment theory: Retrospect and prospect. *Monographs for the Society for Research in Child Development, 50*(1-2), Serial No. 209, 3-35.

Bretherton, I. (1990). Open communication and internal working models: Their role in the development of attachment relationships. In R. A. Thompson (Ed.), *Nebraska symposium on motivation: Vol. 36 Socioemotional development* (pp. 57-113). Lincoln: University of Nebraska Press.

Calkins, S. D., & Fox, N. A. (1992). The relations among infant temperament, security of attachment, and behavioral inhibition at twenty-four months. *Child Development, 63,* 1456-1472.

Calverley, R. M., Fischer, K., & Ayoub, C. (1994). Complex splitting of self-representations in sexually abused adolescent girls. *Development and Psychopathology, 6,* 195-213.

Campos, J. J., Barrett, K., Lamb, M. E., Goldsmith, H. H., & Stenberg, C. (1983). Socioemotional development. In M. M. Haith & J. J. Campos (Eds.), *Handbook of child psychology: Vol. 2. Infancy and psychobiology.* New York: Wiley.

Carlson, V., Cicchetti, D., Barnett, D., & Braunwald, K. (1989). Disorganized/disoriented attachment relationships in maltreated infants. *Developmental Psychology, 25,* 525-531.

Carnelley, K. B., & Janoff-Bulman, R. (1992). Optimism about love relationships: General vs. specific lessons from one's personal experiences. *Journal of Social and Personal Relation-*

ships, 9, 5-20.

Carnelley, K. B., & Pietromonaco, P. R. (1991, June). *Thinking about a romantic relationship: Attachment style and gender influence emotional reactions and perceptions.* Paper presented at the annual meeting of the American Psychological Society, Washington, DC.

Chess, S., & Thomas, A. (1982). Infant bonding: Mystique and reality. *American Journal of Orthopsychiatry, 52,* 213-222.

Clark, C. L., Shaver, P. R., & Calverley, R. M. (1994, August). *Adult attachment styles, remembered childhood abuse, and self-concept structure.* Paper presented at the annual meeting of the American Psychological Association, Los Angeles, CA.

Collins, N. L. (1993). *Attachment style differences in patterns of explanation, emotion, and behavior.* Unpublished manuscript, State University of New York, Buffalo.

Collins, N. L., & Read, S. J. (1990). Adult attachment, working models, and relationship quality in dating couples. *Journal of Personality and Social Psychology, 58,* 644-663.

Collins, N. L., & Read, S. J. (1994). Cognitive representations of attachment: The structure and function of working models. In K. Bartholomew & D. Perlman (Eds.), *Advances in personal relationships* (Vol. 5, pp. 53-90). London, England: Jessica Kingsley.

Costa, P. T., Jr., & McCrae, R. R. (1985). *The NEO Personality Inventory.* Odessa, FL: Psychological Assessment Resources.

Crittenden, P. M. (1985). Social networks, quality of child-rearing, and child development. *Child Development, 56,* 1299-1313.

DiTomasso, M. J., & Routh, D. K. (1993). Recall of abuse in childhood and three measures of dissociation. *Child Abuse and Neglect, 17,* 477-485.

Dutton, D. G., Saunders, K., Starzomski, A., & Bartholomew, K. (1994). Intimacy-anger and insecure attachment as precursors of abuse in intimate relationships. *Journal of Applied Social Psychology, 24,* 1367-1386.

Egelund, B., Kalkoske, M., Gottesman, N., & Erickson, M. (1990). Preschool behavior problems: Stability and factors accounting for change. *Journal of Child Psychology and Psychiatry, 31,* 891-909.

Elicker, J., Englund, M., & Sroufe, L. A. (1992). Predicting peer competence and peer relationships in childhood from early parent-child relationships. In R. Parke & G. Ladd (Eds.), *Family–peer relations: Modes of linkage* (pp. 77-106). Hillsdale, NJ: Lawrence Erlbaum Associates.

Erickson, M., Sroufe, L. A., & Egelund, B. (1985). The relationship of quality of attachment and behavior problems in preschool in a high risk sample. *Monographs of the Society for Research in Child Development, 50*(1-2), Serial No. 209, 147-166.

Eysenck, S. B. G., & Eysenck, H. J. (1963). The validity of questionnaire and rating assessments of extraversion and neuroticism, and their factorial stability. *British Journal of Psychology, 54,* 51-62.

Feeney, J. A., & Noller, P. (1990). Attachment style as a predictor of adult romantic relationships. *Journal of Personality and Social Psychology, 58,* 281-291.

Feeney, J. A., & Noller, P. (1991). Attachment style and verbal descriptions of romantic partners. *Journal of Social and Personal Relationships, 8,* 187-215.

Fischer, K. W., Shaver, P. R., & Carnochan, P. (1990). How emotions develop and how they organise development. *Cognition and Emotion, 4,* 81-127.

Fiske, S. T., & Taylor, S. E. (1991). *Social cognition* (2nd ed.). New York: McGraw-Hill.

Fonagy, P., Steele, H., & Steele, M. (1991). Maternal representations of attachment during pregnancy predict the organization of infant-mother attachment at one year of age. *Child Development, 62,* 891-905.

Fox, N. A., Kimmerly, N., & Schafer, W. (1991). Attachment to mother/attachment to father: A meta-analysis. *Child Development, 62,* 210-225.

Harter, S., & Monsour, A. (1992). Developmental analysis of conflict caused by opposing attributes in the adolescent self-portrait. *Developmental Psychology, 28,* 251-260.

Hazan, C., & Hutt, M. (1993). *Patterns of adaptation: Attachment differences in psychosocial functioning during the first year of college.* Unpublished manuscript, Cornell University, Ithaca, NY.

Hazan, C., & Hutt, M. J., & Markus, H. (1991). *Continuity and change in inner working models of attachment.* Unpublished manuscript, Cornell University, Ithaca, NY.

Hazan, C., & Shaver, P. R. (1987). Romantic love conceptualized as an attachment process. *Journal of Personality and Social Psychology, 52,* 511-524.

Hazan, C., & Shaver, P. R. (1990). Love and work: An attachment-theoretical perspective. *Journal of Personality and Social Psychology, 59,* 270-280.

Hazan, C., & Shaver, P. R. (1994). Attachment as an organizational framework for research on close relationships. *Psychological Inquiry, 5,* 1-22.

Horowitz, L. M., Rosenberg, S. E., Ureno, G., Kalehzan, B. M., & O'Halloran, P. (1989). Psychodynamic formulation, consensual response method, and interpersonal problems. *Journal of Consulting and Clinical Psychology, 57,* 599-606.

Ickes, W., & Barnes, R. D. (1978). Boys and girls together—and alienated: On enacting stereotyped sex roles in mixed-sex dyads. *Journal of Personality and Social Psychology, 36,* 669-683.

Izard, C. E., Haynes, O., Chisholm, G., & Baak, K. (1991). Emotional determinants of infant-mother attachment. *Child Development, 62,* 906-917.

Izard, C. E., Porges, S. W., Simons, R. F., Haynes, O. M., Hyde, C., Parisi, M., & Cohen, B. (1991). Infant cardiac activity: Developmental changes and relations with attachment. *Developmental Psychology, 27,* 432-439.

Kagan, J. (1984). *The nature of the child.* New York: Basic Books.

Kirkpatrick, L. A., & Davis, K. E. (1994). Attachment style, gender, and relationship stability: A longitudinal analysis. *Journal of Personality and Social Psychology, 66,* 502-512.

Kirkpatrick, L. A., & Hazan, C. (1994). Attachment styles and close relationships: A four-year prospective study. *Personal Relationships, 1,* 123-142.

Kirkpatrick, L. A., & Shaver, P. R. (1990). Attachment theory and religion: Childhood attachments, religious beliefs, and conversion. *Journal for the Scientific Study of Religion, 29,* 315-334.

Kirkpatrick, L. A., & Shaver, P. R. (1992). An attachment-theoretical approach to romantic love and religious belief. *Personality and Social Psychology Bulletin, 18,* 266-275.

Kobak, R. R., & Hazan, C. (1991). Attachment in marriage: Effects of security and accuracy of working models. *Journal of Personality and Social Psychology, 60,* 861-869.

Kunce, L. J., & Shaver, P. R. (1994). An attachment-theoretical approach to caregiving in romantic relationships. In K. Bartholomew & D. Perlman (Eds.), *Advances in personal relationships* (Vol. 5, pp. 205-237). London, England: Jessica Kingsley.

Lieberman, A. F., Weston, D. R., Pawl, J. H. (1991). Preventive intervention and outcome with anxiously attached dyads. *Child Development, 62,* 199-209.

Loehlin, J. C. (1992). *Genes and environment in personality development.* Newbury Park, CA: Sage.

Main, M., & Hesse, E. (1990). Parents' unresolved traumatic experiences are related to infant disorganized status: Is frightened and/or frightening parental behavior the linking mechanism? In M. T. Greenberg, D. Cicchetti, & E. M. Cummings (Eds.), *Attachment in the preschool years* (pp. 161-184). Chicago: University of Chicago Press.

Main, M., Kaplan, N., & Cassidy, J. (1985). Security in infancy, childhood, and adulthood: A move to the level of representation. *Monographs of the Society for Research in Child Development, 50,* (1-2), Serial No. 209, 66-104.

Main, M., & Solomon, J. (1986). Discovery of a new, insecure-disorganized/disoriented attachment pattern. In M. Yogman & T. B. Brazelton (Eds.), *Affective development in infancy* (pp. 95-124). Norwood, NJ: Ablex.

Main, M., & Solomon, J. (1990). Procedures for identifying infants as disorganized/

disoriented during the Ainsworth Strange Situation. In M. T. Greenberg, D. Cicchetti, & E. M. Cummings (Eds.), *Attachment in the preschool years* (pp. 121-160). Chicago: University of Chicago Press.

Main, M., van IJzendoorn, M. H., & Hesse, E. (1993). *Unresolved/unclassifiable responses to the Adult Attachment Interview predictable from unresolved states and anomalous beliefs in the Berkeley-Leiden Adult Attachment Questionnaire.* Unpublished manuscript, University of California, Berkeley.

Mikulincer, M., Florian, V., & Tolmacz, R. (1990). Attachment styles and fear of personal death: A case study of affect regulation. *Journal of Personality and Social Psychology, 58,* 273-280.

Mikulincer, M., Florian, V., & Weller, A. (1993). Attachment styles, coping strategies, and posttraumatic psychological distress: The impact of the Gulf War in Israel. *Journal of Personality and Social Psychology, 64,* 817-826.

Mikulincer, M., & Nachshon, O. (1991). Attachment styles and patterns of self-disclosure. *Journal of Personality and Social Psychology, 61,* 321-331.

Monsour, A. (1985). *The dynamics and structure of adolescent self-concept.* Unpublished doctoral dissertation, University of Denver, Denver, CO.

Morgan, H. J. (1993). *Emotional extremes and attachment in conflictual romantic relationships.* Unpublished doctoral dissertation, University of Massachusetts, Amherst.

Noam, G. G. (1985). Stage, phase, and style: The developmental dynamics of the self. In M. W. Berkowitz & F. Oser (Eds.), *Moral education: Theory and application* (pp. 321-346). Hillsdale, NJ: Lawrence Erlbaum Associates.

Pearson, J. L., Cohn, D. A., Cowan, P. A., & Cowan, C. P. (1994). Earned- and continuous-security in adult attachment: Relation to depressive symptomatology and parenting style. *Development and Psychopathology, 6,* 359-373.

Pietromonaco, P. R., & Carnelley, K. B. (1994). Gender and working models of attachment: Consequences for perceptions of self and romantic relationships. *Personal Relationships, 1,* 63-82.

Rothbard, J. C., & Shaver, P. R. (1994). Continuity of attachment across the life course: An attachment-theoretical perspective on personality. In M. B. Sperling & W. H. Berman (Eds.), *Attachment in adults: Theory, assessment, and treatment.* New York: Guilford.

Selman, R. L. (1980). *The growth of interpersonal understanding: Developmental and clinical analyses.* Orlando, FL: Academic Press.

Shaver, P. R., & Brennan, K. A. (1992). Attachment styles and the "big five" personality traits: Their connections with each other and with romantic relationship outcomes. *Personality and Social Psychology Bulletin, 18,* 536-545.

Shaver, P. R., & Clark, C. L. (1994). The psychodynamics of adult romantic attachment. In R. F. Bornstein & J. M. Masling (Eds.), *Empirical perspectives on object relations theory* (pp. 105-156). Washington, DC: American Psychological Association.

Shaver, P. R., Collins, N. L., & Clark, C. L. (1995). Attachment styles and internal working models of self and relationship partners. In G. J. O. Fletcher & J. Fitness (Eds.), *Knowledge structures in close relationships: A social psychological approach.* Hillsdale, NJ: Lawrence Erlbaum Associates.

Shaver, P. R., & Hazan, C. (1993). Adult romantic attachment: Theory and evidence. In D. Perlman & W. H. Jones (Eds.), *Advances in personal relationships* (Vol. 4, pp. 29-70). London, England: Jessica Kingsley.

Shaver, P. R., Hazan, C., & Bradshaw, D. (1988). Love as attachment: The integration of three behavioral systems. In R. J. Sternberg & M. L. Barnes (Eds.), *The psychology of love* (pp. 68-99). New Haven, CT: Yale University Press.

Simpson, J. A. (1990). The influence of attachment style on romantic relationships. *Journal of Personality and Social Psychology, 59,* 971-980.

Simpson, J. A., Rholes, W. S., & Nelligan, J. S. (1992). Support seeking and support giving within couples in an anxiety-provoking situation: The role of attachment styles. *Journal of Personality and Social Psychology, 62*, 434-446.

Sroufe, L. A., Carlson, E., & Shulman, S. (1993). Individuals in relationships: Development from infancy through adolescence. In D. C. Funder, R. D. Parke, C. Tomlinson-Keasey, & K. Widaman (Eds.), *Studying lives through time* (pp. 315-342). Washington, DC: American Psychological Association.

Sroufe, L. A., Egelund, B., & Kreutzer, T. (1990). The fate of early experience following developmental change: Longitudinal approaches to individual adaptation in childhood. *Child Development, 61*, 1363-1373.

Teti, D. M., Nakagawa, M., Das, R., & Wirth, O. (1991). Security of attachment between preschoolers and their mothers: Relations among social interaction, parenting stress, and mothers' sorts of the Attachment Q-Set. *Developmental Psychology, 27*, 440-447.

Tidwell, M., Shaver, P. R., Lin, Y., & Reis, H. T. (1991, April). *Attachment, attractiveness, and daily social interactions*. Paper presented at the annual meeting of the Eastern Psychological Association, New York.

Turner, R. A., & Feldman, S. S. (1992, August). *Stability in attachment across partners*. Paper presented at the International Society for the Study of Close Relationships, Orono, ME.

van den Boom, D. (1989). Neonatal irritability and the development of attachment. In G. A. Kohnstamm, J. E. Bates, & M. K. Rothbart (Eds.), *Temperament in childhood*. New York: Wiley.

Vaughn, B. E., Stevenson-Hinde, J., Waters, E., Kotsaftis, A., Lefever, G. B., Shouldice, A., Trudel, M., & Belsky, J. (1992). Attachment security and temperament in infancy and early childhood: Some conceptual clarifications. *Developmental Psychology, 28*, 463-473.

Wachs, T. D., & Desai, S. (1993). Parent-report measures of toddler temperament and attachment: Their relation to each other and to the social microenvironment. *Infant Behavior and Development, 16*, 391-396.

3 The Role of Psychological Defenses in the Representation and Regulation of Close Personal Relationships Across the Life Span

Robbie Case
Stanford University

Investigations of infant attachment are proving fruitful for understanding the general pattern of close personal relationships across the life span. This line of work began with Bowlby's (1969) general theory of attachment, and Ainsworth's (1973) observation of human infants who had been exposed to brief periods of separation from their mothers in an unfamiliar environment. When separated from their mothers for 2 minutes in a strange situation, virtually all human infants exhibit some form of protest and/or distress. When their mother returns 2 minutes later, however, this universal behavior gives way to marked individual differences. The most common response is to approach the mother eagerly for comfort; then, after a period of reassurance (occasionally mixed with mild aggression on the baby's part), to return to playing with the interesting objects that the novel environment contains. Two other responses are frequently seen as well. In the first, babies actively avoid their mothers, even if they attempt to engage the infants. In the second, babies exhibit prolonged ambivalence: approaching their mothers and soliciting comfort, but then refusing comfort when it is offered and behaving in a "whiny" or "clingy" fashion (Ainsworth, Bell, & Stayton, 1971). Finally, a third (relatively infrequent) response has recently been identified, in which babies freeze or act in a disorganized fashion (Main & Hesse 1990; Main & Solomon, 1980). Due to limitations of space, this final response is not analyzed in this chapter.

Subsequent work by Ainsworth (1983) cast some light on the origins of the first three patterns. When they are in the home, mothers of "avoidant" infants seem uncomfortable if their babies make frequent bids for physical proximity or assistance. They have high standards for their babies and encourage early independence. Mothers of "ambivalent" babies appear anxious about their babies' physical safety, and tend to discourage rather than encourage independence. Finally, mothers of the most "typical" or "normative" babies are somewhere in between. They neither solicit nor discourage physical proximity but respond freely when the baby seeks it out (Ainsworth, 1983).

In cultures whose normative childrearing practices are different from our own, the percentage of children in these three categories differs. In northern Germany, for example, the percentage of children in the avoidant category is considerably higher than in the United States (Grossmann, Grossmann, Spangler, Suess, & Unzner, 1985). In Japan, the percentage of children in this category is considerably lower (Miyake, Chen, & Campos, 1985). The three categories themselves appear to remain quite stable across cultures, however. Individual infants' patterns also remain relatively stable over time (Waters, 1988), and predict their social adjustment at later points in the life cycle. In one of the largest U.S. studies, children's adjustment with their peers at 4 to 5 years of age was shown to be strongly correlated with their earlier attachment status (Sroufe, 1983). As might be expected, avoidant and ambivalent infants had more adjustment difficulties than their peers.

Three distinct patterns of interpersonal behavior have also been identified in adulthood, which appear to map directly on to those that are observed in infancy (see Main, 1992; Shaver & Clark, chapter 2, this volume). Although no studies have yet followed children from infancy through to adulthood, there is a strong similarity in form between the general categories of behavior that are seen in infancy and adulthood (Shaver & Clark, chapter 2, this volume). In addition, it has been shown that adults' reports of their early attachment experience predict their own childrearing behavior. In one study, for example, pregnant mothers were asked about their earliest attachment experiences, and were classified in one of the three attachment categories on the basis of their verbal responses. This classification turned out to be strongly predictive of their infants' attachment status 1 to 2 years later (Main, 1992). The possibility thus exists that an intergenerational cycle may be established. The childrearing behavior of a mother may influence a child's own disposition toward close personal relationships in adulthood. It may also affect the manner in which the children raise their own children, and hence the disposition of these children toward close personal relationships when they are grown (see also Bretherton, chapter 1, this volume).

Of course, the full picture is unlikely to be that simple. There are bound to be many cases where people's stance toward close personal relationships changes in the course of their development, and their relationship with their own children is markedly different from the relationship they had with their parents. Still, even if early attachment experience is only one factor among many that influence close relationships in adulthood, it is interesting to reflect on how such an influence might operate. The most widely accepted suggestion that has been offered to date has utilized Bowlby's (1969) notion of a working model. The basic notion is that babies form a working model of their relationship with their primary caretakers in the first year of life, which then serves as a sort of template that influences and organizes subsequent social relationships of a close personal nature (see Bretherton, 1985, chapter 1, this volume; Main, 1992). In this regard, the working model may be thought of much like a Piagetian structure: An early view of the world to which all subsequent interactions with the world are assimilated, and that changes only gradually as new experience accumulates.

There are several important differences between the notion of a working model and the Piagetian notion of a cognitive structure, however. One of these is that Piagetian structures are energized by "epistemic" emotions such as curiosity, whereas working models are energized by emotions such as love, fear, and anger. A second difference is that Piagetian structures are presumed to misrepresent the world in many ways at early stages of development, and to be plagued by internal conflicts and inconsistencies due to children's low level of cognitive development. By contrast, working models have implicitly been presumed to constitute relatively accurate representations of children's early social world (Stern, 1991). Although inconsistencies in these models have been noted, their source has been placed in the external social world that the models represent, not in the child (Main, 1992). A third difference is that although Piagetian structures are presumed to be related to social behavior in a rather indirect fashion, working models are presumed to be related to this behavior a good deal more directly. In particular, differences in children's working models are presumed to play a major role in generating the different patterns of response that are seen in the strange situation. For avoidant and ambivalent children, these behaviors are seen as *psychological defenses* against the conflicts that their working models contain, and that the strange situation elicits (Bretherton, 1985; Main & Weston, 1982).

My own primary line of work since 1970, has been conducted within the Piagetian tradition (Case, 1985, 1992). It is from this perspective that I have studied children's social and emotional development (Case, 1988, 1991, in press; Case, Hayward, Lewis, & Hurst, 1988), and it is this perspective that I bring to the attachment literature. Because my interests overlap with those of attachment theorists, I have been fascinated with the data and theory that their work has generated. On the other hand, because my theoretical background is different, I have been led to ask a somewhat different set of questions.

The questions that I address in this chapter are as follows:

1. What sort of working model of a relationship can a preverbal infant of 8 to 12 months actually form?
2. What is there about such a model, or about this age range, that makes this the first period at which infants exhibit separation protest in the strange situation?
3. How do the working models of infants in the three major attachment categories differ?
4. How do these differences influence the behavior that infants manifest in the strange situation?
5. How might a psychological defense actually work in a young infant: that is to say, what might be its underlying mechanism?
6. Do infants' working models represent their relationship with their parents accurately, or do they distort this relationship in some fashion?
7. How do psychological defenses, and the working models with which they are associated, change with development?
8. Finally, how might the working models and defensive patterns that are established in infancy relate to the corresponding patterns of thinking and behavior that have been identified in adults?

The answers I propose to these questions are derived from my own particular (neo-Piagetian) view of cognitive and emotional development, which is summarized in the next two sections.

A NEO-PIAGETIAN VIEW OF COGNITIVE DEVELOPMENT

The major assumptions of my theory are drawn from classical Piagetian theory. The first holds that no aspect of reality, whether internal or external, social or physical, can simply be "apprehended" by the human infant. Rather, it must be constructed. The second holds that the constructive processes children have available at different stages of their development are different, and that each has its own distinctive set of properties. The third holds that the constructive processes of later stages are assembled from those of earlier stages, by a process of differentiation and coordination.

Three further assumptions are drawn from the contemporary literature on children's learning and cognition. The first holds that the best way to model children's developing mental processes is as a sequence of increasingly powerful procedures for solving problems, and an increasingly powerful set of conceptual representations, both of which can best be modeled using the formalisms of contemporary cognitive science (not symbolic logic, which was the form of modeling that Piaget employed). The second holds that the content of children's procedural and conceptual knowledge is highly dependent on the sociocultural matrix in which their lives are embedded. The third holds that, even under optimal social conditions, there is a ceiling on the complexity of the structures children can assemble at any age level – due to the existence of systemwide constraints on their information-processing capacity.

My own particular view of these constraints, and the knowledge structures to which they typically lead, is illustrated in Fig. 3.1. What this figure indicates, in schematic form, is the general sort of knowledge structure children typically construct, at each of the classically defined stages of cognitive growth. As may be seen, there are four general levels of such structure, one corresponding to each stage. As may also be seen, progression through any stage takes place in a series of three steps. Prior to their entry into any stage, children possess the ability to activate two different structures but only in isolation, not together. This state is represented in the figure as A (which stands for one structure) or B (which stands for a second structure). As they enter any new stage, children develop the ability to integrate these two structures. This integration is symbolized in the figure, by a solid line connecting the two letters. As they move through the stage, children develop the ability to relate two of these newly integrated entities in a tentative fashion. This tentative connection is symbolized by a dotted line, connecting a pair of A–B units. Finally, at the end of the stage, children become capable of connecting these entities in a fashion that is tightly integrated and coherent. This connection is symbolized by an X in the figure. Transition to the next stage is made possible, at least in part, because these new systems of integrated operations are spontaneously practiced, with the result that the overall structural system becomes consolidated, and can be treated as a single element. The whole complex structure can thus be re-represented as a single unit (e.g., A) in the next cycle of development and can be related to other structures of similar complexity (e.g., B).

A COMPLEMENTARY VIEW OF INFANT EMOTIONS

A full account of children's mental functioning requires an account of the emotions that they experience at different stages of their life, and the effect of these emotions on their cognition. The account that my colleagues and I have developed (Case, Hayward, Lewis, & Hurst, 1988) is based on three basic assumptions. The first is that infant emotion serves two basic biological functions: (a) to differentially energize, and thus to prioritize, the various cognitive and/or behavioral responses in the infant's repertoire; (b) to signal infants' current internal state to the members of their primary

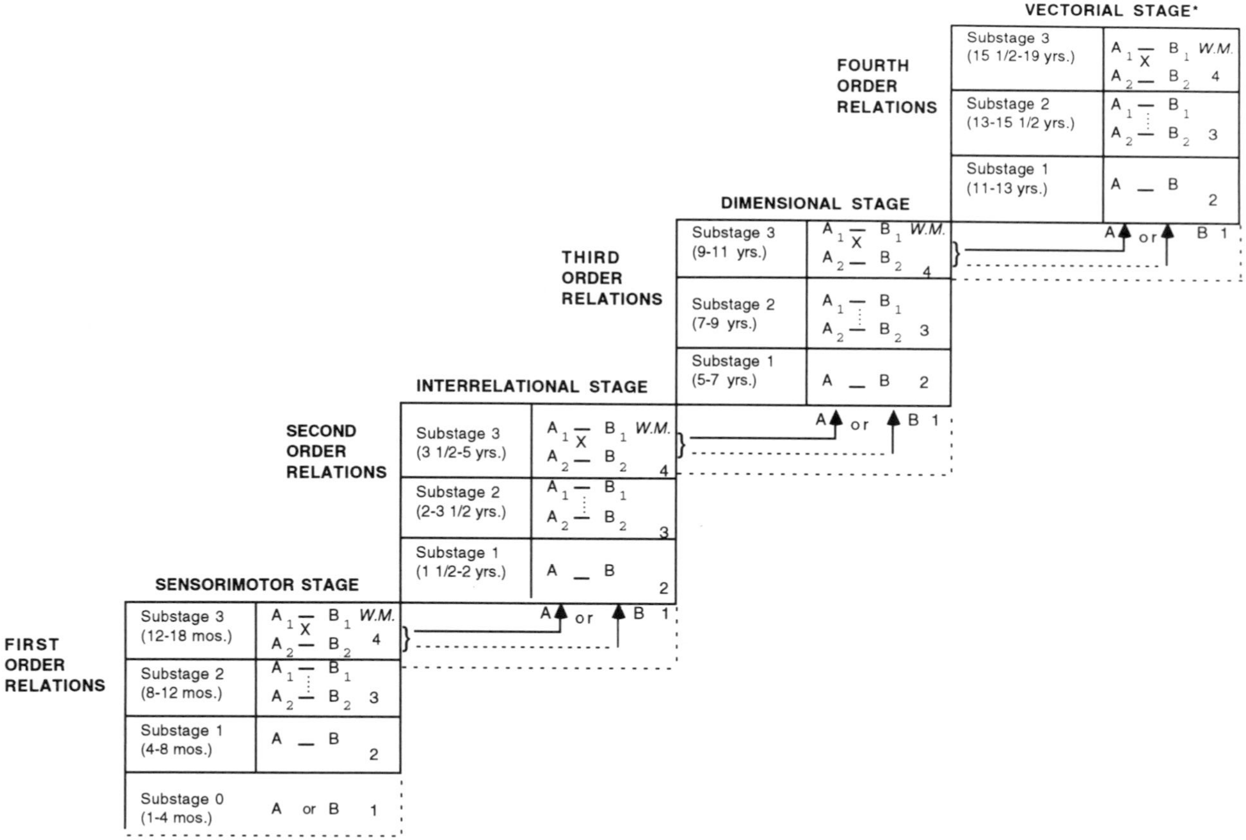

FIG. 3.1. Hypothesized structure of children's knowledge at different stages and substages of development. The letters signify mental units or structures, the straight lines the relationships that are perceived among them. The dotted lines with arrows signify the process that takes place when a group of relationships become sufficiently well consolidated that it can function as a single unit in higher order constructions.

social group. The second assumption is that each of the basic emotions with which infants are endowed is designed to deal with a particular class of life-enhancing or life-threatening situations, and that each emotion is automatically "primed" when the cognitive system detects a situation of this sort. The third assumption—and the one that proves most critical in this chapter—is that pairs of emotions that are designed to energize opposing action tendencies (such as approach vs. avoidance) are internally wired so that the expression of one automatically exerts an inhibitory effect on the other, and vice versa.

In the case of infant attachment, the particular emotions that are most relevant are rather basic ones, such as joy, interest, sadness, fear, and anger. The assumptions that are made about each of these emotions, the situations they are designed to deal with, and their patterns of mutual facilitation and inhibition, are indicated in Fig. 3.2.

ANALYZING THE DEVELOPMENT OF ATTACHMENT WITHIN THIS GENERAL COGNITIVE AND AFFECTIVE FRAMEWORK

Development in the Orienting Stage

During the period from 1 to 4 months, infants' orienting responses become increasingly flexible. They become better at orienting toward two different sensory constellations in succession, and shifting their focus back and forth between the two at will. Because babies can switch their attention back and forth between various aspects of their mother's presence at will, it seems safe to suggest that, by the end of the first major stage, they should have formed an internal perceptual model of their mother that represents her presence in a coherent fashion (Case, 1991). From the point of view of their past development, this model may be thought of as representing the complex network of closely linked sensations and feelings: ones that babies regularly experiences with their mothers, in the context of day-to-day interaction with them. From the point of view of the development that is to take place in the future, this whole complex may be thought of as a single entity, and represented with a single symbol (say B).

Development During Sensorimotor Substage 1 (4–8 months)

Somewhere around the age of 4 months, infants become capable of differentiating and coordinating two sensory–affective representations of the sort that they consolidated earlier. The emergence of this new capability has been demonstrated in a broad range of experimental situations (Lewis,

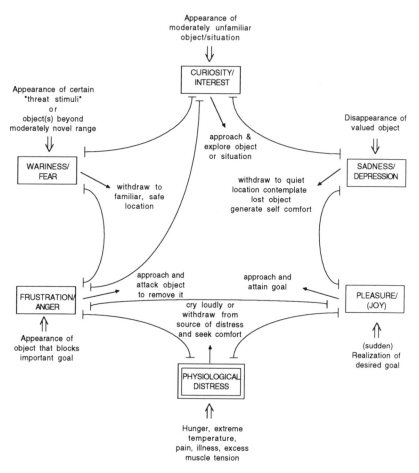

FIG. 3.2.   Five specific emotional states, and one general physiological state. For each state, a typical "elicitor" is indicated with a double arrow, and the motor response that is primed is indicated with a single arrow. Inhibitory connections among states are indicated with blocked lines.

1993; Lewis & Ash, 1992). However, it is also evident in infants' daily life with their primary caretakers in the following behaviors: (a) initiation of conversation (i.e., loud vocalization in the context of some sort of visual contact with mother, followed by a pause, and a close monitoring of the mothers' vocal response), (b) nonverbal requests for assistance (e.g., heightened motor activity, coupled with extensions of both arms in their mothers' direction), and (c) initiation (or reciprocation) of motor play (e.g., reaching out to the mother, grabbing her hair, and tugging; then breaking into laughter if mother responds with a mock cry, or brings her head down against the baby's stomach and tickles it).

Each of the foregoing routines indicates that infants are forming two-component rather than unitary representations of their interactions with their mothers. By the end of the substage, whenever babies generate their part of a pattern in a particular context, they appear to have a clear expectation that their mothers will respond in a complementary fashion. If they do, infants show clear pleasure, even delight. If they do not, babies look sad and turn away (Brazelton, Tronick, Adamson, Als, & Wise, 1975; Trevarthen, 1980). The sort of working models that these behaviors imply are ones that now contain two clear components: actions on infants' part, and reactions on the mothers'. Using the notational conventions of Fig. 3.1, one could let the child's part of the transaction be represented by one symbol (A), the mother's by another (B), and the relationship between the two by a line connecting them $(-)$.

Development During Sensorimotor Substages 2 and 3 (8–18 months)

In the second and third substages of the sensorimotor period, infants first become capable of focusing on two social transactions in sequence (8–12 months), and then in a more integrated and reversible fashion (12–18 months). The changes that take place in their interactions with their mother include the following: In the first of the two substages, when infants are playing with a small object on the ground, and watching its response (A_1-B_1), they may occasionally stop, turn toward their mother when the object does something interesting, and babble loudly in her direction, until she responds (A_2-B_2). This is a new behavior, which mothers treat in the same fashion as infants appear to intend it: as an attempt to translate some aspect of their transaction with an object into sound, and share it with their mother. Alternatively, if infants are watching something that happens to frighten them (A_1-B_1), they may decenter, turn to their mother, and give vent to their distress until she intervenes and rescues them (A_2-B_2).

From the point of view of the internal representations that are involved, the foregoing exchanges indicate that infants' representations of their direct transactions with the inanimate world (A_1-B_1) and their representations of their transactions with their mothers (A_2-B_2) are becoming interleaved, a process that Trevarthen (1980) described as the development of "secondary intersubjectivity." To begin with, this interleaving is rather tentative and implies little more than an association that allows children to change the focus of their attention from one representation to another and back. By the end of the stage, however, the two are sufficiently integrated that the relation between them can be explicitly represented, and babies can move back and forth between the two component transactions at will.

The parallel affective change that takes place is that infants' emotions in one interaction come to influence their emotions in another. As a consequence, babies can actually use an emotion experienced in one context either to heighten or to offset an emotion experienced in another. Emotional heightening occurs if the mother reacts in a positive, empathetic fashion when babies turn away from a happy interaction with a toy, and share this interaction with their mother. Emotional dampening occurs when babies turn away from an interaction that is frightening, or that leads to pain, and seek comfort from their mother (assuming that mother reacts in a fashion that is empathetic and soothing). In either case, the key change that takes place during the period from 8 to 18 months is that the infants' models start to include information regarding the heightening or dampening effect that the mother can have on other interactions.

Now consider the relevance of this developmental sequence for the first two questions that were posed in the introduction. The first question was what a working model at the age of 8 to 12 months might look like. The answer to this question is that the model should contain a rich and highly charged set of representations of at least three sorts: (a) the nature of the transactions that can be initiated with the children's primary caretakers, (b) the nature of the transactions that can be initiated with other social or physical objects, and (c) the way in which these two sorts of interactions can be used to complement or offset each other, both physically and affectively.

The second question was why the period from 8 to 12 months is the first one at which infants exhibit attachment behavior in the strange situation. The answer to this question is that the strange situation does not measure the nature of the infants' relationship with their caregivers, or the infants' apprehension of that relationship, directly. Rather, it measures the extent to which the babies understand how their relationship with their mothers can be used to buffer the potential hazards that may be encountered in other sorts of situations. In short, it measures the security that the maternal relationship offers the babies with regard to the children's anxieties about the external world. Because this sort of information cannot be incorporated in babies' working models until the age of 8 to 12 months, protest in the strange situation is not observed until this time (for supporting evidence, see Lewis, 1993; Lewis & Ash, 1992; Stern, 1983).

ANALYZING INDIVIDUAL DIFFERENCES IN THE STRANGE SITUATION

Separation and Reunion Responses Exhibited by Normative Infants

Within the framework that has been presented, how might the behavior of the normative infant in the strange situation be understood? As the mother puts the baby down on the floor near the toys, the perceptual characteristics of the toys, coupled with their novelty, should arouse the baby's curiosity — because the specific properties of the situation match those that this affect is designed to detect, and toward which it is designed to mobilize a response (see Fig. 3.2). The baby should thus start to explore the toys; that is, the baby should start to execute the various motor actions (A_1, A_2, A_3, etc) that are in his or her repertoire, and to witness the reactions that the toys exhibit (B_1, B_2, B_3, etc).

If one examines Fig. 3.2 closely, however, one will notice that some degree of wariness is also elicited by any novel situation. Although this wariness will be kept in check by the inhibitory effect of the babies strong curiosity, it will cause the babies to keep some sort of cognitive "pointer" active in their working memory, which specifies the mother's physical location. Because such a pointer is present, the babies will notice immediately when their mothers get up and start to walk across the room toward the door. Their wariness will increase as a direct function of the mother's distance from the door. Then, at some point, the balance of curiosity and wariness will shift. The babies' curiosity will then be suppressed by the wariness; they will stop playing and look only toward their mother. Finally, at the point where they realize that their mother is actually leaving them, their wariness will turn to active anxiety or fear. They will then abandon their new toys entirely, and start to follow the mother — signalling their distress and/or protest as they do.

As the door closes, and the babies' access to the mother is shut off, they should experience frustration as well as fear, probably accompanied by considerable physiological distress. As a consequence, they should begin to cry or, as a minimum, exhibit sadness and self-comfort. As with any dynamic system of activating and inhibiting forces, the specifics of their response will depend on the specifics of the situation, and their general physiological and emotional state. When a female research assistant comes in and attempts to engage the baby with a new toy, their interest may possibly be aroused enough to temporarily inhibit their expression of distress. However, equally probably, the female experimenter will be perceived as a barrier to the goal they desire (the mother). The babies will thus push her away, directing their attention to the exit.

After 2 minutes, the mother returns. Immediately on spying the mother, the babies' face should show relief and/or joy because these are the affects that are released by attainment of a goal that has long been sought (again, see Fig. 3.2). Under the influence of this newly dominant affect, the babies should approach their mother and greet her in an emotional fashion, perhaps throwing themselves in her arms to be comforted. As the babies attain the safety of their mother's arms, their joy may abate sufficiently such that the (still active) feelings of frustration and anger may be released from inhibition and expressed. Finally, in a relatively short time, these feelings, too, should abate, and the babies' interest in the toys should be rekindled. The babies should therefore crawl or toddle off to explore them, with no residual effect more severe than a slightly elevated level of wariness.

Separation and Reunion Responses Exhibited by Avoidant Infants

Consider next the behavioral syndrome that is exhibited by avoidant babies in the same situation (cf. Main, 1981; Main & Weston, 1982). Except in severe cases, avoidant infants also appear distressed by their mothers' departure. Indeed, at this point, it is difficult to distinguish their behavior from that of normative children, for the same switch from curiosity-driven to wariness- and fear-driven behavior takes place. When their mothers return, however, avoidant babies display no strong joy or relief. They do not actively approach the mother, or seek any form of contact with her. In fact, if the mother picks them up they usually resist her efforts—either actively or passively—and continue to direct their attention toward the toys or some other aspect of the physical environment.

Before attempting to explain this behavior, it is worthwhile to recall the data that were mentioned at the outset concerning the nature of the relationship that such children have with their mothers in the home. Mothers of such children are more likely than other parents to discourage bids for physical proximity and comfort. They also report a higher baseline level of frustration when their babies violate some behavioral expectation they hold for them, and express more irritation (although not physical aggression) toward their infants when they do so. Finally, they are more likely to react negatively to unsolicited touch by their own infants (or by anyone else), and to be critical of their infants.

If this is the basic relational context in which the infant's life is being lived (and either the mother or the baby, or both, might be contributing to it), how might one explain the resulting behavior that is observed in the reunion situation? Like all other infants, avoidant infants, when they reach the bifocal stage of the sensorimotor period, should become capable of building working models that represent transactions in which they engage with the inanimate world and the relationship of these transactions to those in which they engage with the animate world. In contrast to other babies, however, avoidant babies more often encounter situations in which they turn to their mothers—for rescue, for comfort, or for sharing some positive emotion— but encounter some subtle form of resistance on her part, one that makes it more likely that they will have to deal with the situation that they are encountering on their own. Thus, the working models of avoidant babies are likely to be different from those of normative babies, in the manner indicated in the right-hand panel of Fig. 3.3.

The working model on the right is presumably the one that leads avoidant infants to exhibit more anger and aggression toward their mothers in the home. The question that it raises, however, is why it leads them to exhibit such apparently neutral affect in the strange situation, coupled with a refusal to be comforted by the mother? In order to answer this question, consider the internal sequence of events that is likely to transpire when a working model such as that in Fig. 3.3 is applied in the strange situation, and the mother returns. Babies with such a model will want to maintain some degree of proximity to the mother because physical proximity to her has been associated with safety in the past (recall that the mother has never been abusive or actively mistreated her infant). As these infants do approach, however, or even contemplate approach, they are likely to experience a higher level of negative affect than normative babies. The result is a classic conflict. On the one hand, these babies are a good deal more in need of comfort and reassurance than other babies, due to the nature of their working models, and the degree of uncertainty about maternal availability that this model implies. On the other hand, these babies are likely to be more angry and/or anxious about rejection because they have a history of having their bids for proximity-seeking or thwarted in some fashion.

In the face of this increased need, but increased vulnerability to anxieties about rejection, these babies are likely to be placed in situations of emotional overload, for which some form of defensive behavior (i.e.,

SENSORIMOTOR "WORKING MODEL" OF SECURE BABY		SENSORIMOTOR "WORKING MODEL" OF INSECURE AVOIDANT BABY
1. IF I AM PLAYING WITH TOY AND MOM IS NEARBY TALKING, READING, ETC.	$A_1 - B_1$: $A_2 - B_2$	1. IF I AM PLAYING WITH TOY AND MOM IS NEARBY TALKING, READING, ETC.
2. AND IF I WANT RESCUE OR COMFORT...	$A_2 - B_2$	2. AND IF I WANT RESCUE OR COMFORT...
3. I CAN TURN TO MOM AND GO TO HER, AND SHE WILL PICK ME UP, SAVE ME AND LET ME CUDDLE	$A_2 - B_2$	3. I CAN TURN TO MOM AND APPROACH HER BUT SHE MAY/MAY NOT LET ME GET INTO HER ARMS AND CUDDLE.

FIG. 3.3.   Sensorimotor models constructed by "secure" and avoidant children, of situation where they become upset while they are playing with their toys, and their mother is nearby.

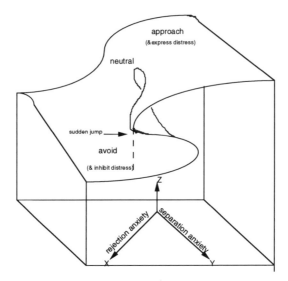

FIG. 3.4. Catastrophe model of avoidant response.

behavior directed toward reducing the arousal and conflict rather than dealing with the external situation) is likely to be exhibited (Case et al., 1988). One response that has served this role since birth is looking away from mother, while maintaining at least some degree of physical proximity (Lewis, 1993; Main & Weston, 1982; Stern, 1983). This response is likely to be augmented at the bifocal stage by active play with the toys that are available, so that the affect induced by the exploration will add to the inhibitory effect on more painful affects. From the perspective of these infants' psychological systems, one could say that looking away from the mother achieves two highly desirable outcomes. First, it protects these babies from the anger and/or fear of rejection that might be experienced if they looked at the mother directly; it does so by diminishing the force of the stimulus that might arouse these feelings (the mother's face) and replacing this stimulus with another one (e.g., a toy), which will arouse an affect that will actively inhibit these feelings (e.g., interest). Second, looking away allows babies to maintain close physical proximity to their mothers, and thus experience the comfort of knowing that her physical presence is nearby.

The foregoing analysis contains implicit answers to the third and fourth questions that were posed at the outset of this chapter. The third question was how the working models of different infants might differ. The answer is that they differ in the information that they represent regarding maternal availability as a buffer for negative events in the rest of the world. The two models also differ in the valence of the feelings that is associated with the maternal relationship as a consequence.

The fourth question was how differences in infants' working models might lead to behavioral differences in the strange situation. The answer here is that they lead to different forms of behavior because the strange situation is one in which the mother's normal presence as a buffer is temporarily disrupted and reinstated. The disruption activates infants' feelings about their mothers as a buffer, and puts the infants' positive and negative feelings in conflict. For normative babies, the positive feelings override the negative ones. Thus, what is observed is immediate approach. For avoidant babies (or normative babies whose original model has been modified, due to a prolonged separation), the balance tilts in the other direction. The most likely behavior is thus one in which the infants avoid direct contact with the mother, while monitoring her presence peripherally, at a distance that feels "safe."

EARLY MECHANISMS OF PSYCHOLOGICAL DEFENSE

The foregoing analysis also suggests an answer to the fifth question, namely, how might a psychological defense work in young infants? As is hopefully apparent, avoidant infants do not "figure out" that they will feel better if they look away from their mothers than if they look directly at her. Rather, the behavior that these infants exhibit emerges as a spontaneous and dynamic synthesis of their existing emotional and behavioral tendencies.

An analogy may be made to the behavior of lower mammals, when approached on their own turf by an intruder of the same species. When this sort of event occurs, such animals appear to experience a mixture of anger and fear. If the threat value of the intruder (size, posture, etc.) is not too high, they will attack. However, once the threat value of the intruder reaches a critical value, they will suddenly flee. In effect, there is a region in the threat continuum where a sharp transition or "cusp" may be identified, and where their behavior switches from "fight" to "flight." Even when they are in flight, however, one can still detect the presence of other feelings and action tendencies (Tinbergen, 1961). As they reach the edge of their own territory, for example, they may slow down and stop, as though pulled by the security this territory offers, and reluctant to leave it. Under certain circumstances, they may possibly "fall into orbit," circling the intruder at a safe distance, but still drawn by the pull of their home base.

Such behavior, and the "cusp" or sudden change in valence from approach to avoidance, is well modeled mathematically by a dynamic system in which a few variables reciprocally support and inhibit each other, in the fashion that was indicated in Fig. 3.2. The branch of this theory that is relevant to this particular case is "catastrophe theory" (Zeeman, 1976). This theory has been applied to human children's behavior by Van der Maas and Molinaar (1992), and has been shown it to be quite general. My proposal as to how infants' avoidant behavior is produced is illustrated in Fig. 3.4. The two basic affects and action tendencies that control children's behavior are anxiety about separation (which energizes a tendency to approach), and anxiety about rejection (which energizes a tendency to avoid). The difference between normative and avoidant children is that they start in different regions of the space, because avoidant children have a higher degree of anxiety about rejection. As a consequence, the experimental situation moves them in the direction of the arrows, and produces avoidance rather than approach. This difference is not an absolute one, however. If normative children are abandoned for a longer period of time, they may also begin to feel rejected, and exhibit avoidance on reunion, rather than approach. By the same token, if avoidant children are abandoned in the security of their own home, their anxiety about rejection may be lower, and they may exhibit approach rather than avoidance on reunion.

To the more general question of how infant defenses operate, the answer I would suggest is as follows. Infants' working models exert an influence on the blend of feelings that they experience in any situation with their primary attachment figures. One of the most difficult conflicts a human being (or any primate, for that matter) can experience is one where they feel intensely angry toward and/or fearful of rejection by, a person to whom they are also very strongly attracted and upon whom they are completely dependent. Psychological defenses in infancy provide a temporary resolution to this conflict, by producing a resolution which "balances" the two major opposing tendencies (i.e., approach and avoidance), and produces a degree of spatial proximity that reflects this balance. This same automatic balancing serves to keep the overall the degree of arousal in the manageable range, because the activation of one group of feelings actively inhibits the intensity of the other. The final behavior is not consciously planned. It results from the fact that the situation elicits a particular blend of emotions and action tendencies, some of which "support" and some of which "inhibit" each other. The various action tendencies interact with each other in a spontaneous manner, as in any dynamic system, in a manner that reflects not just the nature of the tendencies that are involved, but their absolute magnitude (Van der Maas & Molinaar, 1992; Van Geert, 1991). Although the behavior that ultimately emerges cannot always be predicted, it may be seen, at least after the fact, to have obeyed the laws to which any such dynamic system is subject.

THE IMPACT OF PSYCHOLOGICAL DEFENSES ON THE VERIDICALITY OF CHILDREN'S REPRESENTATIONS

The sixth question that I posed at the outset of this chapter was whether the psychological defenses of young infants should be thought of as stemming from some sort of active distortion of reality, or from an accurate representation of a reality that is painful and difficult to face. The answer that I propose to this question is "both." The behavior of normative infants and avoidant infants are both produced by the same mechanism: the dynamic resolution that takes place in a system of mutually supporting and inhibiting affects. Moreover, the behavior is in each case energized by a working model that accurately represents the day-to-day availability of the mother for interaction and/or comfort. Nevertheless, the dynamic synthesis that takes place, in the case of avoidant infants, is one that ultimately leads to the distortion of reality.

In order to explicate this paradox, consider first the case of normative infants. As their external situation changes, infants' internal "coding" or "representation" of their external situations change, and they experience a different affect (anxiety caused by separation). Under the control of this new affect, the previously dominant affect (curiosity elicited by the novel environment) is inhibited, and infants proceed to deal with the new situation in an effective manner. Finally, when the mother returns, the babies display clear evidence of both positive and negative affect, with the former ultimately triumphing over the latter. One could say that, at the sensorimotor level, a reasonable "working through" of the mini-conflict takes place, and a comfortable working relationship is re-established. As soon as this occurs, these babies return to their exploratory activity.

What about infants' representations of the situation in the brief interval when they are alone and distressed prior to the mother's return? One could term the behaviors they engage in at this time, such as staring at the door where their mothers disappeared and comforting themselves by thumb sucking, as *coping mechanisms* because they help babies to cope with the existing situation and the feelings that this situation arouses. No "distortion" is involved. The babies have been abandoned by their mothers in an unfamiliar environment. This is a serious threat, at least potentially, and the babies treat it this way, reacting with an appropriate emotional response and behavior: Babies comfort themselves in the situation to remain calm, and continue to stay prepared for the mother's rearrival. As soon as the opportunity arises, the babies make an immediate beeline toward their mothers, expressing both their relief and joy at her arrival, and their anger or distress at having been abandoned in the first place. In summary, the secure babies' representations of the situation are realistic, appropriate, and coherent, and the feelings that the babies exhibit are appropriate and coherent as well.

Now consider the reunion situation from the perspective of avoidant infants. Cognitively, these babies also "know" that their mothers have abandoned them in a strange environment and that they have returned. However, affectively, these infants cannot experience the full depth of their distress or anger because these feelings are actively inhibited by the fact that they are looking away rather than toward their mothers, and are engaged in visual and/or manual exploration of their physical environment. Although the mechanism generating the behavior is the same, then, the result is different. Rather than experiencing the immense relief mixed with anger that normative babies experience, avoidant babies experience their mothers' re-arrivals as a more neutral event. This is where the distortion occurs. The reality is that these babies do not feel neutral on their mothers' arrival. The affective systems of these babies are highly energized, and what they experience is a mixture of strong positive and negative emotions. However, the subjective experience is the opposite: As far as these babies know, they feel fine, or at least okay (and their mothers are okay, too).

What might the long-term consequences of this sort of experience be, if mini-abandonments or rejections of this sort are typical of the infants' experience during this stage of their lives? What I propose is that this sort of distorted internal experience would become a chronic state. As object-relations theorists have suggested (Winnicott, 1960), these babies would develop a model of the "bad mother," or the "rejecting mother," whom they would hate and do everything they could to avoid. These infants would also develop a model of the "good mother," whom they would experience as "just fine." However, when they reach the age where they can reflect on this experience, these infants should come to regard the latter model as typical, because the avoidant response is such an effective inhibitor of negative affect that they should not be aware of the depth of their negative feelings.

In order to show how this might happen, I turn now to an analysis of how the avoidant response might be transformed at subsequent stages of development.

TRANSFORMATION OF EARLY DEFENSES IN THE COURSE OF SUBSEQUENT ONTOGENESIS

The seventh question I raised at the outset was how psychological defenses, and the working models with which they are associated, might change with development. The simplest way to address this question is to continue with the example of avoidant infants, and to assume that the mothers' relationships with their children remain reasonably stable over the next 10-year period. In actuality, such stability may turn out to be the exception, not the rule. Still, for analytic purposes it makes the task much simpler. The point of this section is not to suggest that avoidant behavior in infancy will always produce a parallel form of behavior at each subsequent stage of development. Rather it is to make a start at providing a model of the sort of developmental pathway that might result under the simplest (i.e., most stable) conditions.

Normative Developments During the Interrelational Stage

Somewhere between the age of 1½ to 2 years, most children pass from the sensorimotor to the interrelational stage. As they do, a major transformation takes place in virtually all aspects of their cognitive functioning. For example, (a) children become capable of communicating in terms of *symbols* rather than simple actions and gestures (Piaget, 1962). They become capable of representing complex *social scripts*, rather than just simple dyadic transactions or events (Nelson & Gruendel, 1978). They become capable of seeing the people around them as performing socially scripted *roles*, rather than simply engaging in idiosyncratic behavior (Fischer, Hand, Watson, Van Parys, & Tucker, 1984). They become capable of identifying and labeling their internal states and the internal states of others (Astington, Olson, & Harris, 1988). They become capable of assigning particular behaviors or internal states to evaluative categories, such as good versus bad, or nice versus mean (Fischer & Elmdorf, 1986; Griffin, 1992).

How might children's working models of their mother be transformed, as these changes take place? Virtually all transactions that children engage in with their mothers, and which were formerly experienced as simple dyadic events, should now be re-represented at the symbolic level, and seen to be part of larger event sequences or "scripts." Children should develop particularly rich representations of maternal scripts that center around such prototypical caregiving functions as protection, nurturance, physical care, and teaching (Goldberg-Reitman, 1992). They should have a good sense of their own place in such scripts, vis-à-vis their siblings and other family members, and of the feelings that these scripts occasion. Finally, they should be able to act out such scripts with dolls, or label and evaluate the feelings that these scripts elicit (Goldberg-Reitman, 1992).

For children whose behavior in the strange situation is normative, the general sense one should get by the time they reach the end of the interrelational stage is that they understand what sorts of roles a mother performs, and that they feel confident of their own mother's ability to perform them. In effect, the security that they felt at the sensorimotor stage should remain, and should be translated into a confidence regarding their ability to solicit the protection, affection, and care that they need, under a wide variety of more complex, symbolic, and/or socially scripted circumstances (Goldberg-Reitman, 1992).

Development of the Avoidant Infant During the Interrelational Stage

How might the working models of avoidant children differ from those of normative children, and what might be their response in the same situation? From a purely cognitive point of view, the expectation would be that avoidant children's new capabilities would undergo a transformation of the same general sort. Much of the content of their models would also be the same. Thus, for example, if they were questioned about maternal behavior in some hypothetical protection situation, as in Goldberg-Reitman's task, they should sound much like normative children: asserting that their mothers would rescue them immediately (which of course they would).

The most obvious place one would expect a difference would be in the content of their scripts relating to nurturance, and in the feelings that these scripts arouse. Thus, when asked about relatively mundane scripts bearing on such matters (e.g., what would a mother do if a child had a runny nose), one might see subtle differences in the content of the response (e.g., "She would blow my nose," for normative infants vs. "She would tell me to wipe it," for avoidant infants; or, in more extreme cases, "She would be downstairs in the kitchen").

The continuity between this sort of working model and that proposed for 12-month-olds will no doubt be apparent. The defining characteristic remains the uncertainty about access to the mother, in situations where some form of mild comfort or physical nurturance is desired. In addition to the continuing difficulties that avoidant infants experience in obtaining physical access to their mothers when they are in need of comfort, they might also experience a new sort of difficulty, namely a difficulty in obtaining more symbolic access. Thus, they may now be less confident about receiving empathic attention when they communicate with their mothers via language or show them things that they have made in their play. They may also be less confident about obtaining sympathy when their feelings are hurt, or approval rather than criticism for their daily behavior. If this is so, then one would expect that their working models would come to reflect this newly emergent aspect of their reality, and that they would experience this new reality as a new source of frustration and/or anxiety.

Just as the threats that such children might experience would now include a number of higher level components, so their defensive behavior might also begin to include a number of higher level components as well. As an illustration, suppose that a group of children was subjected to some mild form of rejection, such as being ignored by their mothers for a 2-minute period while the mothers took care of someone else's baby. Suppose further that the children were carefully observed in this situation, and then interviewed about their feelings afterward, as in a study by Masciuch (1991). From normative children, one might expect coping strategies such as trying to help their mother take care of the baby, or talking with her while she does. In the interview, one might expect responses that were mildly positive about the baby, and negative about the fact that their mothers did not talk to them while they attended to the baby.

By contrast, from avoidant children, one might once again expect a stronger internal response, coupled with an external response that seemed calm, but that dealt with the threat by turning away from the mother and toward the environment. The turning toward the environment would no longer need to be exclusively sensorimotor in nature. It might include engaging in symbolic play, creating an active distraction, or having an imaginary conversation with a friend. Similarly, the "toned-down affect" might be given symbolic expression, after the event. Although they might appear upset at the time, avoidant children might deny having any bad feelings whatever, and say that they had felt just "fine." Yet shortly afterward, they might act out their residual bad feelings via displaced anger toward peers or siblings, and/or verbal denigration of their perceived rival (e.g., "She was just a stupid baby. She couldn't even talk yet.").

For both groups of children, then, there would be a sense in which the underlying avoidant response would be maintained, and another sense in which it would be transformed and elevated to a higher plane. For avoidant children, the core mechanism would remain the turning of attention away from a troubling interpersonal event toward something that would inhibit the response to that event. Higher order responses that were built on this core might include verbal denial, denigration, and displacement. For normative children, the core response would remain one of coping with the situation, and actively expressing any feelings — positive or negative — that were experienced in that situation.

Normative Developments During the Dimensional Stage

Between the ages of 4 and 6, another major transformation takes place in children's functioning. Among the most important new abilities that emerge are as follows: (a) the ability to learn *second-order symbols*, such as those involved in reading, mathematics, music, or religious ritual, rather than just first-order symbols such as those involved in natural language (Mounoud,

1986); (b) the ability to represent familiar scripts as *motivated event sequences* or plans, rather than just familiar action sequences (Nelson & Gruendel, 1978). This enables children to generate narratives that are organized around some internal state, problem, or plan (McKeough, 1992); (c) the ability to engage in *rule-based roles*, rather than the simple behavioral roles of early childhood (Case, in press; Fischer et al., 1984) (this new capability allows children to exhibit appropriate role-based behavior, even in social situations that exert a strong pull on them to act in a different fashion); (d) the ability to view their own *internal states* as objects, which can be subject to control, and brought into line with social roles and categories (Case, in press); and (e) the ability to see dimensions as continuous rather than polar, and their own behavior as being rankable with regard to that of other people, on a variety of such *dimensions* (Case, 1992).

How might children's working model of their mothers be transformed as these changes take place? Virtually all transactions with their mothers that were formerly experienced as simple social scripts should now be seen as being part of more general and motivated event sequences. In the context of any such event sequence, children should be aware of their own feelings as well as those of their mothers, and they should be able to control their own feelings or express them in a socially acceptable fashion when the situation calls for it. Both in this context, and in the context of their life with their peers, they should also have a good sense where their own behavior ranks vis-à-vis that of their peers on a variety of dimensions that their mothers value (e.g., sensitivity, intelligence, strength, physical appearance, etc.).

What changes in children's daily behavior might accompany these changes in the working models? As children begin to understand and share their parents beliefs, feelings and judgments, they should begin to see their parents' daily acts of concern, teaching, and so forth, as relating to these beliefs, feelings and judgments. This should produce less resistance to parental actions, when they do not fit the children's own particular desire of the moment. As a consequence they should also become increasingly adept at dealing with their own feelings in a socially acceptable fashion. When resistance to parental commands does occur, it should be more easy to negotiate at a verbal level. Finally, children should have a reasonable sense of their own position on the dimensions that their parents value, and feel confident of their ability to meet parental expectations. To a considerable degree, therefore, feelings about the self and social behavior in general should become liberated from the tyranny of the moment. Children should be able to execute appropriate roles without their parents having to be present, and they should be able to resist temporary insults to their sense of self (Noam, 1991).

Development of the Avoidant Child, During the Dimensional Stage

What sort of changes might one expect in avoidant children, again assuming that the general dynamics of their family life were unchanged? As children learn to inhibit daily expressions of anger of the sort that occur at the sensorimotor and interrelational stages, there might possibly be less external evidence of the underlying dynamic that differentiates avoidant from normative children. Nevertheless, the dynamic should still be discernable in their interpersonal relationships, their working models, and their defensive structures. As their working models come to include their mothers' desires and aspirations for them, as well as their mothers' dimensional evaluations, they may once again discover a new source of concern, namely that their position on the dimensions that are most valued by their parents are not as high as their parents would like, or expect. (Recall that the mothers of such children tend to be more critical of them, as well as finding their bids for physical closeness more aversive.) Just as the earlier frustrations that they experienced around the home with regard to such issues as physical closeness, empathic attention, and so on, were causes of anxiety and/or aggression, so one might now see the continued development of such feelings around negative dimensional attributions. Moreover, just as the mothers' lack of dependability was incorporated in their earlier working models, so the mothers' lack of dependability with regard to positive dimensional evaluations should now become incorporated into their model of her view of them.

What about the children's reaction when subjected to a potentially stressful situation, such as seeing the efforts of a sibling recurrently praised while their own efforts are criticized? For secure children, the prediction would be that such events would be assimilated to a working model in which maternal attributions are generally positive, and the sense of self is positive also. For avoidant children, the prediction would be that such situations would be assimilated to a working model in which a positive sense of self was a good deal more fragile because it has been achieved at the expense of avoiding the feelings that such situations elicit. In effect, then, avoidant children should once again experience such situations as more threatening.

What sort of higher order form of defense might one observe in response to the higher order threat to children's sense of self that would be experienced in such contexts? Because children can now actively think about feeling states, and attempt to control them, there might possibly be a conscious suppression of feelings of anger or hurt at the time a potential insult to self was experienced, under conditions of mild threat. Under more extreme cases, the avoidant response might be instantaneous, and cause the childrens' attention (or actual physical presence) to wander. The earlier displacement of anger and denigration might now be expressed more subtly as displacement of criticism. Finally engagement in other activities, and/or criticism of others, might be accompanied by rationalization. For example, if children were avoiding intimate contact with their mothers for defensive reasons, and directing attention elsewhere (e.g., to a project undertaken with friends), they might invent reasonable stories to explain this interest, such as wanting to conduct the school project because it was so interesting, or wanting to engage in some activity with friends because it was such fun, and so on. These stories would not be completely incorrect, they would simply omit the central motive. Alternatively, if children were displacing anger in the face of the criticism, and were unaware of this fact, they might experience those with whom conflicts developed as being responsible for initiating them. The result in this case might be some form of "projection" of anger on the person to whom the anger was attributed. Finally, the criticism and/or hurt they feel toward their mothers might be displaced and directed toward their siblings or classmates. Regardless of the particular form that their behavior exhibited, then, there would be a continued distortion of some aspect of their inner world.

Once again, this set of changes would not be expected to take place overnight. However, the changes would be presumed to follow a very similar course to the set of changes that took place at earlier stages, and to be governed by a similar set of mechanisms. Rationalization, projection, and criticism would all emerge in an underlying situation in which an affective distortion had already taken place, and bad feelings had become detached from the situation, and the person that first elicited them.

Normative Developments During the Vectorial Stage

As children move into their adolescent years, another transformation takes place in their mental representations and functioning. This change does not appear to be as universal as the changes that take place at lower stages. Still, for those for whom it does take place, the transformation is a highly significant one, which involves the following components: (a) children's understanding of the world becomes more abstract (Inhelder & Piaget, 1958); (b) third-order (abstract, or poetic) symbolization now appears (Biggs & Collis, 1982; Halford, 1982); (c) roles are viewed in more abstract terms, and seen to include a set of general responsibilities and privileges, not just specific behaviors and standards to judge them by (Fischer et al., 1984; Goldberg-Reitman, 1992); (d) narrative accounts now come to include an explicit and rich set of internal events (i.e., events in the plane of consciousness that extend well beyond simply wants and desires, (McKeough, 1992); (e) finally, external events and behavior are viewed as symptomatic of underlying attitudes, traits, or values, (Marini & Case, 1994).

As children construct these more abstract representations, new defensive structures may once again become available. A full account of these defenses is beyond the scope of this chapter (cf. Case et al., 1988; Cramer, 1991; Vaillant, 1977). As an example, however, one might expect many of childrens' concrete rationalizations to be replaced by more abstract ones, in which a principle or cause is sited as a reason for a particular action, rather than just a person or a situation. Although it serves a defensive function, this sort of behavior may come to have very real rewards in its own right. The net effect, is that early conflicts may be buried under one more layer of social cognition, and concealed by one more layer of psychological defense. Awareness of the original forces that set any particular form of behavior in motion may thus become increasingly difficult to realize, even in a therapeutic context.

In many respects, the high-level social representations and strategies of avoidant adolescents might be little different from those of other teenagers. They may have the same general notions of social roles, responsibility, and privileges, for example, and be interested in the same general set of topics and situations. In the area of close interpersonal relations, however, a distinct difference should still be detectable, because their emotional behavior is likely to retain the same core feature that it did in infancy, namely, a coolness regarding issues of strong affective significance, and a denial of their underlying importance.

This general feature, coupled with the defenses that are associated with it, may lead to a distinctive way of relating to potential romantic partners (see Shaver & Clark, chapter 2, this volume). It may also lead to a distinctive way of responding to an adult attachment interview (Main, 1992). Avoidant interviewees may provide a rather sparse description of their early relationship with their primary caretaker (because this was an area of their life that they disengaged from as often as possible). They may also offer a set of rather negative examples when probed to remember salient events (because these sorts of events were relatively frequent, and characterized by high internal arousal). On the other hand, they may disavow having experienced any negative affect in these events, and provide a generally positive—even romanticised—account of their overall relationship with their primary caretaker (because their developmental history has the properties just described). Finally, they may adapt a rather defensive attitude of dismissiveness toward the whole subject, and exhibit a desire to terminate the interview as quickly as possible (Main, 1992). With this set of feelings and beliefs about their own early childrearing, it would not be surprising if they developed a distinctive (and rather distant) style of parenting themselves. The intergenerational cycle would thus be complete.

SUMMARY AND CONCLUSION

Since the 1970s, investigations of infant attachment have proven remarkably fruitful for improving our understanding of close personal relationships across the life span. One of the reasons that research in this area has been so productive, I believe, is that it has provided a vehicle for investigating a set of general hypotheses in which psychologists have long been interested. For almost 100 years, clinical psychologists have believed that children's relationships with their parents play a vital role in influencing the course of their subsequent social and personality development. However, it was not until Bowbly combined notions from the psychoanalytic tradition with notions from ethology and information theory that it became possible to understand how such influences might operate in a very detailed manner, and it was not until Ainsworth invented the strange situation that it became possible to study these processes experimentally.[1]

Although great strides have been made in understanding infant attachment, and the way in which this attachment influences children's subsequent social and personality development, a number of important questions remain unanswered. The questions I articulated in this chapter all have to do with two core constructs: the notion of a working model, and the notion of a psychological defense. These constructs play a critical role in attachment theory as it is currently formulated. However, at the moment, they are still insufficiently developed: It is by no means clear, for example, just what information an infant's working model of his or her caretaker might actually represent; nor is it clear how a psychological defense might operate, or how such defenses might be transformed in the course of ontogenesis.

In this chapter, I have made a preliminary attempt to answer these questions. To do so, I have drawn on three bodies of theory: neo-Piagetian theory, emotions theory, and dynamic systems theory. The first body of theory is useful in characterizing the general structure of children's working models at any given stage of their development. The second body of theory is useful in analyzing children's affective processes, and the role that they play in influencing both their behavior and their working models. Finally, the third body of theory is useful in explicating the dynamic syntheses that emerge, in contexts where conflicting cues are present and/or some sort of affective threat is experienced.

The account of children's attachment that I have proposed, using these three bodies of theory, is somewhat complex. Its general structure, however, is quite simple. In effect, what I have proposed is that the *content* of children's working models is determined by the relationship that they

---

[1]For the influence of Blatz's (1966) theory of infant security on Ainsworth see Ainsworth (1973).

experience with their primary caretakers, whereas the *form* of these models is determined by their general stage of cognitive development. When a child is separated from his or her mother in a strange situation, the child quite naturally experiences this situation as threatening. When the mother returns, however, two potentially conflicting emotions are elicited: (a) relief that the mother has returned, and a desire to approach and be comforted by her, and (b) distress that she abandoned the child in the first place, coupled with anxiety about her disposition toward him or her now. For the normative baby, the first tendency is more powerful, and the result is approach (or approach mixed with mild aggression). For the avoidant baby, the second tendency is more powerful because it is more strongly facilitated by past experience. The behavior that results is thus a dynamic synthesis: one that allows the goal of each action tendency to be realized in part, while the overall system is maintained in a state of emotional balance.

As children grow older, their capabilities of course become much more sophisticated. Thus, situations in which they are separated from their mothers for a 2-minute interval are no longer threatening. Still, the general problem of whether and how close to approach a love object, under conditions of mild threat or conflict, remains a dilemma throughout the life span. The proposal that I advanced in this chapter is a simple yet classical one: namely that, for many children, the defensive pattern that is observed in the strange situation is a "core" one, around which higher order interpretations and responses to similar situations will be organized. Unless their relationship with their parent is altered in some fundamental respect, I believe, children will simply add a new layer of cognitive and affective structure to this sensorimotor core at each subsequent stage of their development. Although the specific thoughts and feelings that they experience will be transformed, then, the affective core will still have the same basic structure, as will their behavior. Thus, normative personalities will be impelled to seek closer affective contact, reassurance, and resolution in times of interpersonal stress. By contrast, avoidant personalities will seek an affective equilibrium that is equally stable, but which is achieved at the expense of greater physical distance, and decreased interpersonal intimacy, insight, and/or integration.

The details of the model that I have presented are of course highly speculative. Still, my hope is that, as a minimum, the model I have proposed will demonstrate the need for a theoretical account that explicates infants' internal processes in greater detail, and provides an account of how these processes are transformed as they grow older. A more general hope is that — as such models are developed — what will emerge is a new body of theory and data: one that will build on existing theory and data yet transform it, spanning normal and abnormal development in the process, and providing a framework that will be useful in both experimental and clinical settings. In this more general hope, I know, I am joined by all the other authors in this volume.

ACKNOWLEDGMENTS

I am indebted to Mary Main for introducing me to the attachment literature, and for making her infant videotapes and adult interviews available for my inspection. I am also indebted to Dan Stern, Morris Eagle, Marc Lewis, Gil Noam, Tory Higgins, and Sheldon Stryker for their comments on an earlier draft of this chapter.

REFERENCES

Ainsworth, M.D.S. (1973). The development of infant-mother attachment. In B.M. Caldwell & H.W. Riccuti (Eds.), *Review of child development research* (Vol. 3, pp. 1-94). Chicago: University of Chicago Press.

Ainsworth, M.D.S. (1983). Patterns of infant–mother attachment as related to maternal care. In D. Magnusson & V. Allen (Eds.), *Human development: An interactional perspective* (pp. 35-55). New York: Academic Press.

Ainsworth, M.D.S., Bell, S.M., & Stayton, D.J. (1971). Individual differences in strange situation behavior of one year olds. In H.R. Schaffer (Ed.), *The ongoing human social relations* (pp. 17-57). London: Academic Press.

Astington, J.W., Harris, P.L., & Olson, D.R. (1988). *Developing theories of mind.* New York: Cambridge University Press.

Biggs, J., & Collis, K. (1982). *Evaluating the quality of learning: The SOLO taxonomy.* New York: Academic Press.

Blatz, W.E. (1966). *Human security: Some reflections.* Toronto: University of Toronto Press.

Bowlby, J. (1969). *Attachment and loss, Vol. 1: Attachment.* London: Hogarth.

Brazelton, T.B., Tronick, E., Adamson, L., Als, H., & Wise, S. (1975). Early mother infant reciprocity. In *Parent-Infant Interaction, CIBA Foundation Symposium*, No. 33. Amsterdam: Associated Scientific Publishers.

Bretherton, I. (1985). Attachment theory: Retrospect and prospect. In I. Bretherton & E. Waters (Eds.), *Growing points of attachment theory and research. Monographs of the Society for Research in Child Development, 50,* 3-35.

Case, R. (1985). *Intellectual development: Birth to adulthood.* New York: Academic Press.

Case, R. (1988). The whole child: Toward an integrated view of young children's cognitive, social, and emotional development. In A. Pellegrini (Ed.), *The psychological bases for early education,* (pp. 155-184). Chichester, UK: Wiley.

Case, R. (1991). Stages in the development of the young child's first sense of self. *Developmental Review, 11,* 210-230.

Case, R. (Ed.). (1992). *The mind's staircase: Exploring the conceptual underpinnings of children's thought and knowledge.* Hillsdale, NJ: Lawrence Erlbaum Associates.

Case, R. (in press). Stages in the formation of a coherent social identity. In S. Stryker & T. Higgins (Eds.), *Self, Affect, and Society.*

Case, R., Hayward, S., Lewis, M., & Hurst, P. (1988). Toward a neo-Piagetian theory of cognitive and emotional development. *Developmental Review, 8,* 1-51.

Cramer, P. (1991). *The development of defense mechanisms.* New York: Springer-Verlag.

Fischer, K.W., & Elmendorf, D.M. (1986). Becoming a different person: Transformations in personality and social behavior. In M. Perlmutter (Ed.), *Cognitive perspectives on children's social development: The Minnesota symposia on child psychology* (pp. 137-178). Hillsdale, NJ: Lawrence Erlbaum Associates.

Fischer, K.W., Hand, H.H., Watson, M.W., Van Parys, M.M., & Tucker, S.L. (1984). Putting the child into socialization. In L.G. Katz, P.J. Wagemaker, & K. Steiner (Eds.), *Current topics in early childhood education* (Vol. 5, pp. 27-72). Norwood, NJ: Ablex.

Fischer, K.W., Shaver, P.R., & Carnochan, P. (1990). How emotions develop and how they organize development. *Cognition and Emotion, 4*, 81-127.

Goldberg-Reitman, J. (1992). Young girls' understanding of their mothers' role. In R. Case, (Ed.), *The mind's staircase: Exploring the conceptual underpinnings of children's thought and knowledge* (pp. 135-152). Hillsdale, NJ: Lawrence Erlbaum Associates.

Griffin, S. (1992). Children's awareness of their inner world. In R. Case (Ed.), *The mind's staircase: Exploring the conceptual underpinnings of children's thought and knowledge* (pp. 189-206). Hillsdale, NJ: Lawrence Erlbaum Associates.

Grossmann, K., Grossmann, K.F., Spangler, G., Suess, G., & Unzner, L. (1985). Maternal sensitivity and newborns' orientation responses as related to quality of attachment in northern Germany. In I. Bretherton & E. Waters (Eds.), *Growing points of attachment theory and research. Monographs of the Society for Research in Child Development, 50*, 233-256.

Halford, G.H. (1982). *The development of thought.* Hillsdale, N.J. Lawrence Erlbaum.

Indelder, B., & Piaget, J. (1958). *The growth of logical thinking from childhood to adolescence.* New York: Basic Books.

Lewis, M.D. (1993) Early socioemotional predictors of cognitive competency at four years. *Developmental Psychology, 29*, 1036-1045.

Lewis, M.D., & Ash, A.J. (1992). Evidence for a neo-Piagetian stage transition in early cognitive development. *International journal of behavioral development, 15*, 337-358.

Main, M. (1981). Avoidance in the service of attachment: a working paper. In K. Immelmann, G. Barlow, L. Petrinovitch, & M. Main (Eds.), *Behavioral development* (pp. 651-693). New York: Cambridge University Press.

Main, M. (1992). Metacognitive knowledge, metacognitive monitoring, and singular (coherent) vs. multiple (incoherent) models of attachment: Findings and directions for future research. In P. Marris, J. Stevenson-Hinde, & C. Parkes (Eds.), *Attachment across the life cycle.* New York: Routledge.

Main, M., & Hesse, E. (1990). Parents' unresolved traumatic experiences are related to infant disorganized attachment status: Is frightened and/or frightening parental behavior the linking mechanism? In M. T. Greenberg, D. Cicchetti, & E. M. Cummings (Ed.), *Attachment in the preschool years* (pp. 161-182). Chicago: University of Chicago Press.

Main, M., & Solomon, J. (1980). Procedures for identifying infants as disorganized/disoriented during the Ainsworth strange situation. In M.T. Greenberg, D. Cicchetti, & E.M. Cumming (Eds.), *Attachment in the preschool years: Theory, research, and intervention* (pp. 121-160).

Main, M., & Weston, D. (1982). Avoidance of the attachment figure in infancy: Descriptions and interpretations. In C.M. Parks & J. Stevenson-Hinde (Eds.), *The place of attachment in human behavior* (pp. 31-59). London: Tavistock.

Marini, Z., & Case, R. (1994). The development of abstract reasoning about the physical and social world. *Child Development, 65*, 147-159.

Miyake, K., Chen, S., & Campos, J.J. (1985). Infant temperament, mother's mode of interaction, and attachment in Japan: An interim report. In I. Bretherton & E. Waters (Eds.), *Growing points of attachment theory and research. Monographs of the Society for Research in Child Development, 50*, 276-297.

Masciuch, S. (1991). The development of jealousy: A preliminary study. *Exceptionality Education Canada, 1*, 125-137.

McKeough, A. (1992). A neo-structural analysis of children's narrative and its development. In R. Case (Ed.), *The mind's staircase: Exploring the conceptual underpinnings of children's thought and knowledge* (pp. 171-188). Hillsdale, NJ: Lawrence Erlbaum Associates.

Mounoud, P. (1986). Similarities between developmental sequences at different age periods. In I. Levin (Ed.), *Stage and structure: Reopening the debate* (pp. 40-58). Norwood, NJ: Ablex.

Nelson, K., & Greundel, J. (1978). Generalized event representations: Basic building blocks of cognitive development. In M.E. Lamb & A.L. Brown (Eds.), *Advances in developmental psychology* (Vol. 1). Hillsdale, NJ: Lawrence Erlbaum Associates.

Noam, G.G. (1991). Beyond Freud & Piaget: Biographical worlds, interpersonal self. In T. Wren (Ed.), *The moral dimension* (pp. [??]). Cambridge, MA: MIT Press.

Piaget, J. (1962). *Play, dream and imitation in childhood* New York: Norton.

Sroufe, L.A. (1983). Infant–caretaker attachment and patterns of adaptation in preschool: The roots of maladaptation and competence. In M. Perlmutter (Ed.), *Minnesota symposia in child psychology* (Vol. 16, pp. 41-81). Hillsdale, NJ: Lawrence Erlbaum Associates.

Stern, D. (1983). The early development of schemas of self, other, and "self with other." In J.D. Lichtenberg & S. Kaplan (Eds.), *Reflections on self psychology* (pp. 49-85). Hillsdale, NJ: Lawrence Erlbaum Associates.

Stern, D. (1991, April). *Discussion of papers in symposium on normal and abnormal pathways of socioemotional development.* Paper presented at the Society for Research in Child Development, Seattle.

Tinbergen, N. (1961). *The herring gull's world.* New York: Basic Books.

Trevarthen, C. (1980). The foundations of inter-subjectivity: Development of interpersonal and co-operative understanding in infants. In D.R. Olson (Ed.), *The social foundations of language and thought* (pp. 312-342). New York: Norton.

Vaillant, G.E. (1977). *Adaptation to life.* New York: Little Brown.

Van der Maas, H.L.J., & Molinaar, P.C.M. (1992). Stagewise cognitive development: An application of catastrophe theory. *Psychological Review, 89,* 395-417.

Van Geert, P. (1991). A dynamic systems model of cognitive and language growth. *Psychological Review, 98,* 3-53.

Waters, E. (1988). The reliability and stability of individual differences in infant-mother attachment. *Child Development, 47,* 483-494.

Winnicott, D.W. (1960). The theory of the parent–infant relationship. *International Journal of Psychoanalysis, 41,* 585-595.

Zeeman, E.C. (1976). Catastrophe theory. *Scientific American, 234*(4), 65-83.

II | Cognitive Development and Relationships

4 The Social Construction of Cognitive Development

Wolfgang Edelstein
Max Planck Institute for Human Development and Education

Social construction of cognitive development refers to the fact that human beings must develop epistemic consciousness of their worlds, a consciousness that is triggered in social relationships and shaped by two sets of structures that affect both its course and its outcomes. On the one hand, epistemic consciousness is maintained and directed by internal structures and mechanisms of the mind. On the other hand, it depends on external constraint systems that represent the specific nature of experience. Thus, the socialization of cognition consists in the interaction of internal structures of the mind with the representations of experience arising in the specific ecological setting of development.

In Piagetian terms, socialization of cognition is the result of a double process: (a) the exposure of the organism to experience of objects and relations in the environment; (b) the interaction, within the mind, of the functional invariants of the equilibration process and the specific representation of experience alimenting their action. Of these, the former is a difference-producing process, whereas the latter is responsible for the unity of the mind. Only the latter was of interest to Piaget.

The concept of individual differences has been a rather homeless concept in Piagetian theory. My endeavor in this chapter is part of the movement that recently has found the support also of Inhelder (1989), to shift the Piagetian preoccupation with the epistemic subject further to the psychological subject than Jean Piaget himself was interested in doing (see Inhelder & Piaget, 1971). This shift hinges on understanding the constraints imposed on development by experiential reality, in particular the reality of affectively charged relationships. In order to unfold the notion of systematic constraints on development, the argument will capitalize on the theoretically underdefined concept of *décalage*. Within the constructivist perspective, the notion of constraints on development (Edelstein, 1992; Schröder & Edelstein, 1991) provides a legitimate place for intraindividual and interindividual differences in development that derive from differences growing out of the formative experiences of children in socially and/or psychologically different life worlds.

The question of constraints on development that produce individual differences is pursued by asking whether affective dispositions that are related to, or generated by, the quality of the child's close relationships represent developmental risks or vulnerabilities affecting cognitive growth. To illustrate, empirical examples of constraints placed on development by insecure attachment, anxiety, and depression are presented. I hypothesize that these disorders, in part, relate to socialization. They may emerge, for example, in families with less than adequate access to social resources and social opportunities or in families characterized by nonnormative patterns of interaction.

INTERNAL STRUCTURE AND EXTERNAL REALITY

Cognitive socialization implies that there are external factors that impact on cognitive development in ways not specified by structural theory. For Piaget, development is primarily a matter of internal processes that draw for their dynamic on the increasing coordination of schemes in the course of the equilibration of cognitive structures. But once we turn our attention to the construction of the schemes, we necessarily refer to concrete realities that trigger the internal process. Thus, exposure to experiential reality is basic to the internal processing of experience, and for exposure to take place, opportunities for interaction with epistemic objects and with persons are necessary. These opportunities are socially constituted and located in a social world where they are unequally yet nonrandomly distributed. They are part of the system of social inequality, which will inevitably produce variability in development. Piaget paid little attention to this — psychological, behavioral, and social — variability. The universality of the stages and the invariability of the sequences represent the empirical thrust of his psychology. Variability enters the theory from a side entrance. In the guise of décalage, variability in rate of development is supported by well-known examples, such as the extreme cases of rural children in Iran or the island of Réunion mentioned by Piaget as a kind of curiosity (see Dasen, 1977, for an account of cross-cultural research on the Piagetian program). And if we read Piaget closely, in spite of his silence, variability or individual differences in developmental performance is continually present, if unacknowledged, in his protocols. It is represented by variations in age among subjects who perform at identical levels, but also by interindividual differences in performance at identical ages; and, as every researcher in the Piagetian tradition is aware of, it is present in intraindividual differences in performance on different tasks by the same subjects.

Piaget ignored variation in cognitive development because his interest is not on the psychological characteristics of individuals, but on the structure of mind. Unexplained variation is stowed away in the residual category Piaget termed *horizontal décalage*. In order to elucidate the meaning of this term, a specification of the role and the quality of experience in development is required. It represents the subjective side of what, from the objective side, can be construed as an account of cognitive socialization.

As long as socialization is taken to refer to the interaction, with the subject, of a reality that, at some point at least in the history of the subject's becoming a cognizing self, is external to the self, this does not differ from the traditional realist epistemology (which generally relies on an empiricist perspective on development and a black box view of internal process). However, this view is not shared by constructivist psychology. It follows from the constructivist view of the mind's operations as held by Piagetian theory that "experience" is dialectical, deriving from the internal structure of the assimilatory process no less than from the physical and social world of objects and relations that give rise to it. In experience, internal structure and external reality are linked in a relationship of mutual entailment. The development of the epistemic relationship simultaneously represents and produces change in the entailment structure that links subject and object, experience and reality, knower and known.

In spite of his preoccupation with the internal dynamic of mind, Piaget's view is explicitly grounded in a social interactionist conception of epistemic practice (e.g., Piaget, 1952, 1970; Inhelder & Piaget, 1958, chapter 18), and thus, a "co-constructive" epistemology fits both with the structure of schema theory and a more explicit role of constraints on the epistemic process to complement it. In this view, the object of experience has an active role in the epistemic process, and whether directed to physical objects or other subjects this is best defined as a process of epistemic interaction, a process here referred to as co-construction (see Noam, chapter 6, this volume; Youniss, 1980; Youniss & Damon, 1992).

The nature of the epistemic process itself is independent of the ultimate nature of the reality constraints imposed on it. Whether these constraints are grounded in the subject's genetic endowment (and thus a prerequisite to cognitive action) or located in the world of objects in the ecology of a child's experience, or whether they are grounded in the energizing and motivating input from interactions in relationships that serve as supports or holding environments for epistemic interaction, the process characteristics will remain the same. Nevertheless, various constraints imposed on the process will affect development differentially, and in order to explain these differences, these constraint modalities will contribute different explanatory heuristics. Thus, if experience is grounded in interaction, the sociocultural patterns of interaction will produce variations in the quality of experience that in turn will impact on the development of cognition. Patterns of experience modulating cognition may be specific to either the participating individuals (e.g., in the family), or to time and place and culture, or to settings within the social structure. Opportunities for experience, cognitive conflict, and decentration may be culturally divergent, historically specific or socially deprived. Risks and vulnerabilities may prove to be regular characteristics of regimes of experience specific to class or culture, producing, as the case may be, interindividual differences in development.

VARIETIES OF EXPERIENCE

Interindividual differences in development refer to either systemic or idiosyncratic differences in individuals' exposure to experience. Selective experience may refer to (a) the object of knowledge, (b) the mechanisms by which experience is processed, or (c) the outcome of development as a prerequisite of future construction.

The Object of Knowledge.   The socializing power of object experience is constituted by the context of action in which the object is embedded. The context of action confers meaning on the object and invests it with epistemic significance. Take the example of the physical object endowed with the contours of a "house": Depending on the social function or action context, the object grounds different social experiences (see Schütz, 1982). This could be, for example, the representation of "home" tainted by the experience of poverty. If even the meaning of physical objects can be socially constituted, this certainly is the case regarding intrinsically social objects of cognition, specifically persons, relations, and interactions. While cognitive and social-cognitive development have been shown to vary depending on the nature of experience with "natural" and "social" objects (Hollos & Cowan, 1973; Keller, 1992; Schröder & Edelstein, 1991) it has remained a moot question how these experiences constrain construction, and how the constraints are brought to bear on cognitive development. For Hollos (1974), who studied the thinly populated and communicatively impoverished area of rural Norway, it is the density of interaction and communication opportunities that differentially affects epistemic encounters even with physical objects. And, ever since Spitz (1945, 1946) presented his findings on maternal deprivation, a wealth of studies have established the detrimental effects on cognitive development of withholding either emotional attention or stimulation through objects.

However, it is a major step from there to understanding just how the experience of interaction with a significant other induces in the mind of the subject the particular "working model" of object interpretation, that, through positive or negative cathexis either of the epistemic encounter itself, or of the object operated on in the encounter constrains the course of cognitive development. To the present, clinical reconstruction of the subject's history appears to have shed more light on the process than mainstream developmental psychology.

Mechanisms.   In Piaget's constructivist theory, the transactions of the subject of cognition with the internal experience of the object ground cognition. These transactions are effected through assimilation and accommodation that may indeed be constrained by the social selection of effects inherent in the way schemata of objects and schemata of interactions are constructed and put to use. Thus, under the constraints of previous experience, schemata may be disfigured or fixated as a consequence of disequilibrated overassimilation or overaccommodation. Cellérier (1987), in line with recent advances in neuroscience, has analyzed the economy of schema operations using the metaphor of success or failure of schema construction and schema survival. The reinforcement a schema receives through successful operation destines it for survival in development. It seems plausible that the constraining effects of experience at work in the assimilation dynamics of the developing mind may generate differences in the quality, the differentiation, and the rate of growth of the cognitive system.

Outcome.   Elicited by the object and mediated by the mechanism of assimilation, a scheme selected for success under the constraints of previous experience will reach an enduring quality as an outcome of the construction process. Depending on the role and quality of experience, outcomes will therefore differ between individuals. But as every outcome is an antecedent condition of further development, differences in developmental status represent conditions of epigenetic differentiation that reinforce interindividual differences. Whenever there is order or regularity in the constraints imposed by the objects of experience, by the mechanism of functional adaptation processing the impact of the object in schema construction, and finally by the outcomes devolving from these processes, we are headed for experience-related intraindividual and interindividual differences in development.

I have dealt here with objects of experience, mechanism, and outcomes as if they were separate entities. But they are, of course, interlocking aspects of scheme construction and operation, separated only in the analytical approach. I have dealt with the process as a psychological one, with experience treated more or less as a private occurrence. But the prevailing orders of opportunity provide differential exposure to experience, and thus differential constraints on development. And although we may fruitfully use a clinical window to search developmental contexts for the incidence of risk or for signs of individual vulnerability, the more encompassing theoretical perspective is to map the evolving societal structures of the distribution of developmental opportunity, such as the incidence of economic hardship (Elder, 1984) or the renaissance of poverty (Garbarino, 1992). Beyond clinical variations in the trajectories of individual constructions, these patterns generate collective variations in the structures, rates, and outcomes of cognitive growth.

DEVELOPMENTAL VARIATION: A SOCIAL CONSTRUCTION ACCOUNT

Just as developmental research in the structural tradition has not frequently related individual differences in development to variations in exposure to experience, socialization research, typically, has ignored intraindividual change along dimensions of interest to developmentalists, and thus failed to relate development to socialization. In his analyses of the children of the Great Depression (Elder, 1974) and the various follow-up analyses of that seminal study (e.g., Elder & Liker, 1982; Elder, Van Nguyen, & Caspi, 1985), Elder studied the effects of the deprivation of material and psychological resources that, during the Great Depression, affected the lives of families that participated in the Oakland Growth Study (Eichorn, 1981) and in the Berkeley Guidance Study (Macfarlane, 1938). He found that these conditions affected the children differentially depending, in particular, on age, gender, and social class. It turned out, for example, that lower class boys were hit harder, and in different ways than were girls, by economic hardship experienced by the family. In terms of macro–micro relationships, father's loss of job proved to be a "developmental risk," that, conjointly with the effects of restrictive conflict regulation strategies, produced differential vulnerabilities for adolescent sons and adolescent daughters at a given age. Girls were found to be more resilient throughout the life span than were boys; the boys, for example, had more medical trouble in later life than had girls (Elder, 1984). Perhaps, we might hypothesize, girls had a better role model in their mothers, who were coerced into a position of familial leadership by the predicament of the fathers.

Elder's studies bear on the unfolding and patterning of the life course rather than intraindividual development. If we critique developmental theory for ignoring the effects of social structures on the pattern of individual experience, we may critique socialization theory for ignoring developmental processes. Thus, Elder did not follow up on the risks generated by macroevents to investigate developmental effects on the person's competence. Rather, he traced the vicissitudes of the person's biography. But the deep structure of cognitive competence belongs to a different order of phenomena than does frequency of medical trouble, and the ability to cope differs from marital adjustment or incidence of divorce, or from depressive episodes, although, of course, the developmental dimensions are phenomenally or causally related to the life-course events. Elder's data permitted him to trace the effects of the Great Depression, via the family, to individual characteristics of the children, and hence to their consequences for the life course (Elder & Caspi, 1988). We can draw on these studies for a variety of relevant inferences: The social construction of the life span represents the outcome of the interaction of a number of co-occurring factors. This represents the objective opportunity structure available to the individual in his particular group. In the case under study, this is deprivation due to the Great Depression as it hit lower class families. Second, there is the specific context of development and its implications. Hypothetically, the relation might be structured as follows: Sons are in a phase sensitive to the predicament of fathers; daughters are affected by the rise of mothers compensating the demise of fathers. The incidence of risk is defined by this encounter of objective and subjective factors. The vulnerabilities and strengths generated by the encounter extend over the life span. The missing link, at present, is the developmental factor. What we must explain is how the level of identity or ego resilience achieved or interfered with can explain the incidence of marital disturbance or medical risk in the men or the adjustment to life in the women who once were children of the Great Depression.

Through a sociological window, Elder observed the conditions of economic hardship, tracing their effects first on families, then on children across lives. Developmental psychologists have traditionally looked at things from a different perspective. Their object has been the course of development in the context of individual biographies. As a rule, they rely on normative rather than nonnormative events (Baltes & Schaie, 1973). Relevance is constituted by the theoretical relationship that is established between the risk condition and the process of development itself.

For a constructivist theory there are relatively few meaningful choices of external conditions that potentially provide variability in developmental process and outcome. A true linkage must obtain between these conditions and the inner structure of the developmental process, to be described, for example, in terms of assimilation. Patterns of parent–child interaction, or patterns of peer interaction, or exposure to educational experience are among possible candidates, inasmuch as these conditions specify variations in the provision of relevant opportunities to participate in cooperation, confront novelty, seek exploration, differentiate perspectives, take the role of the other, engage in cognitive conflict, and so on. All of these represent activities that, in Piagetian and other constructivist theories, are linked to the dynamics of cognitive processes. But surprisingly few researchers have studied social ecologies, family- and class-related conditions of cognitive socialization from the vantage point of cognitive developmental theory. Hollos (1974; Hollos & Cowan, 1973), mentioned earlier, is a case in point. Lautrey and his coworkers (1980) studied the developmental impact of class-related socialization patterns. Doise and Mugny (1984), Mugny (1985), and Perret-Clermont (1980) observed the influence of peer co-construction on the quality of the achievement in cognitive and social cognitive tasks—the basic paradigm underlying the peer-teaching strategy that Damon (1984), in a much quoted review, described from a cognitive-developmental point of view. Krappmann (1991; Oswald & Krappmann, 1991) and his colleagues observed the naturally occurring patterns of peer interaction in groups and their impact on the development of social-cognitive abilities and dispositions such as helping and cooperation. Of course, cross-cultural research in the Piagetian tradition (Dasen, 1977) has mostly been designed to study interindividual differences in performance on basic Piagetian tasks that can be traced to culture-specific functional requirements specifically operating in a given culture (see Cole, Gay, Glick, & Sharp, 1971; Cole & Scribner, 1974) or historical setting (Damerow, 1994; Radding, 1985).

Social settings represent patterns of interaction that vary depending on the material and affective resources allocated, influencing the meaning of the interaction and thus the participating subjects' cognitive intent, the way they come to cognitively relate to the world. Patterns of early interaction with significant others, through the social, structural, and individual resources allocated to them—such as time for child, stimulus display, intensity of care, and quality of affect—orient the child toward enduring modes of epistemic interchange, and thus generate persistent patterns of psychological and social experience imposed, as it were, on the subject's very ability to construct meaning from social and epistemic encounters, and shape these encounters prior to any given act of cognition.

INTRINSIC CONSTRAINTS AND EXTERNAL CONDITIONS

At the close of this account of the social construction of epistemic variability, the sources of variation must be related to developmental performance. These sources may be classified as producing either "intrinsic" or "external" constraints on development, depending on the more proximal or more distal relationship they entertain with the act of cognition. Intrinsic constraints refer to the conditions represented in the cognitive act by the task and the modalities of processing the task. External constraints represent the cultural, social and personal conditions imposed on cognition prior to the cognitive act (see Fig. 4.1).

This differentiation is pursued a little further here. The major determinant of any given performance within a constructivist account of cognitive development is the competence achieved prior to the spell of performance elicited in a given situation: Other things equal, previous outcomes are the best predictors of actual performance. The performance, however, is

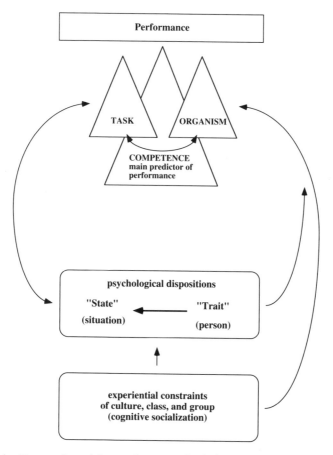

FIG. 4.1. Factors determining performance. Intrinsic constraints internal to the cognitive act in the upper part of the figure; external constraints preceding cognitive act in the lower part of the figure.

modified by the *intrinsic constraints* placed on competence by a given task and by organismic conditions relative to the process characteristics and modalities of the task situation (Schröder, 1989; Schröder & Edelstein, 1991). For example, two different classification tasks that measure the same operational competence in the same logical structure may place different constraints on memory, or appeal to perception in different sensory modalities. Idiosyncratic experience may, of course, interfere with these constraints. A specific learning history may arouse anxiety and inhibit performance on a task. In such cases, external constraints are superimposed on internal ones. Intrinsic constraints are imposed by task characteristics and the process modalities involved in solving the task. They represent variations of task achievement that Piaget, rather unspecifically, subsumed under the notion of décalage. These phenomena are part and parcel of cognitive psychology and much progress has been made in deciphering their effects.

External constraints, in contradistinction, are imposed by experience. They relate to the socialization of the person, his history and biography. Within the task, they bring to life the contexts of exploration and achievement that are characteristic of the person, and represent, beyond the person, the characteristics of the group that shares the experience with her. In summary, exposure to differential experience provides an antecedent condition of cognitive development. With regard to a task, systematic differences may obtain between the experience of rural and urban children, or between lower and middle-class subjects. Required performance may arouse negative affect or stress in a vulnerable group in a test situation; underprivileged subjects may experience anxiety and defense when confronted with a challenge. The meaning of the situation, the cathected context of achievement modifies the act of cognition, imposing what Bowlby has called a working model of reality processing on the construction of objects, persons, and relations.

From a sociological viewpoint, this process has been identified as leading to difference, deficit, or deprivation. The nonrandom distribution of opportunity provides the exploring mind with specific yet regular exposure to experience that is basic to assimilation and construction. Such opportunity structures are ubiquitously provided by the cultural contexts and social ecologies in which children are socialized: the mother–child dyad, the family system, the children's field of interaction with experience in their specific social settings. From a clinical viewpoint, the process is focused on the individual's negative cathexis of the object of experience, neurotic deformation, or the operation of defenses such as repression, regression, or fragmentation (Haan, 1977). What Noam (1988, 1993) calls the encapsulated biography of painful experience or thwarted construction arises to revenant life in the deformed structures of the schemes of assimilation, grinding out, at worst, an impoverished, disequilibrated, or biased representation of reality. This will depend on the maturity of the subject, the history of the disorder, and the context and content of the experience at issue. For Noam, these processes are part and parcel of any present organization of cognition and self. In the microprocesses that determine performance, the subjective history of experience, idiosyncratic or collective, connects the affectional dynamic inherent in the construction activity that, according to Piaget (1981), energizes schema operations, with the act of cognition, the *prise de conscience*. These processes build dispositions affecting later explorations, centrations that fixate the economy of schema activities in assimilation to earlier investments.

Lest this account appear too one-sided, differences in cognitive development as generated by varieties of experience in varieties of epistemic encounters generally represent regimes of difference, not deficit. The normative structure of cognitive achievement imposed on cognitive development historically transforms constraints on development into mechanisms of deficit or failure relative to the success of others who perform to criterion in a world designed to benefit the highly selective optimization of abstract cognitive achievements. This remark has a double edge. On the one hand, it points to the historical process of change imposing a collectively validated norm of achievement on the development of cognition. Conversely, this very process has generated a system of constraints on development that produces risks, vulnerabilities and failures both consecutive to cognitive pressure and stress, and consecutive to deprivation and deficit (Edelstein, 1983).

The historical emergence of such constraint systems provides a starting point for an ecological theory of socialized development accounting for patterns of socializing experience, classes of developmental differences and/or deprivations, and types of developmental outcomes over time that are generated by these differences. Using Bronfenbrenner's theoretical account (Bronfenbrenner & Crouter, 1983), we may identify developmentally effective experience tied to the microsystem of parental bonding and rearing climates as well as sibling interactions that are basic to the intrapsychic system of affective constraints on development. We may identify the opportunity structure of childhood ecologies in the mesosystem, with their privileged classes of physical, social, and cultural objects. Finally, there is the macrosystem of history, culture, and language; of the division of labor and social inequality that determine the meaning of action and the symbolic system that makes up the conscious pattern of a person's life; and of the social relationships in which he or she finds him or herself rooted. None of these systems functions in an isolated way. It is their synergy that across individuals and cohorts generates the developmentally effective patterns of experience that, on the basis of the specific interplay of developmental universals and developmental variations, simultaneously produce individual biographies and collective mentalities.

EMPIRICAL ILLUSTRATIONS

To illustrate the operations of the constraint system on development, we choose the example of external constraints located in the primary socialization matrix and the pattern of relationships with significant others — the attachment pattern between caretaker and child, anxiety arousing and depressogenic stressors — and their influence on cognitive development over time. The examples are taken from our longitudinal study of individual development from childhood to adolescence (Edelstein, Keller, & Schröder, 1990).

Children's attachment to their caretakers has been shown to exert a strong influence on their motivation and ability to explore their environment (Ainsworth, 1990; Bowlby, 1969). The relationship can be construed as follows: Various traditions — both philosophical and psychological — concur that self-respect and feelings of self-worth depend on the recognition of the self by significant others. Conversely, children lacking in a sense of self-worth have been found to experience difficulties constructing adequate models of the world (Bowlby, 1969; Kohut, 1978). In a secure relationship with a caretaker, children experience the recognition of their needs. They feel taken seriously as the persons they are. This provides them with the resilience needed to engage in exploration and brave the unknown. In contradistinction, insecurely attached children will not experience the trust of a caretaker enabling them to sufficiently cathect their selves. They will feel threatened more easily and be less willing to engage in cognitive exchanges with the world. Alternatively, they will be forced into cognitive encounters beyond their capacity and therefore contract an avoidant attitude toward affectivity that again limits their freedom of exploration. Frequently, depression and anxiety will affect their strategies of exploration: depression by limiting the will to explore — a resignation leading to passivity and inaction; anxiety by arousing defenses that interfere with the subject's response to discrepant experience. Thus, insecurity of attachment appears as a risk factor emerging in the system of early relationships that places specific constraints on the cognitive development of the child. We take these constraints to operate on the child's assimilatory activity (Bowlby, 1969; Jacobsen, Edelstein, & Hofmann, 1994). Although insecurity itself represents a risk with which individuals attempt to cope by generating a working model that protects them against confronting novelty, or pushes them toward more confrontations than they can deal with, the anxiety and depression frequently implicated in the insecure child's engagement with the world appear to be elements of such working models. In summary, certain contexts of socialization in the family generate risks including personality dispositions, to which development appears to be vulnerable in highly specific ways. As is seen here, the vulnerability is cumulative, and its effect tends to increase over time rather than decreasing with age or through compensatory experiences.

ATTACHMENT

In the present study, the intraindividual effects of attachment on cognition were observed longitudinally from 7 to 17 years. Attachment was measured at age 7 based on the children's responses to a picture story containing nine pictures that represent a parent–child separation. Subjects were asked what the protagonist child in the story was thinking and feeling during the separation experience, why they felt that way, and what they would do. The children's answers were assessed using a modified version of Kaplan's (1987) method, which is directed at the overall mode of regulating thoughts and feelings about separation (Jacobsen et al., 1994).

As this report focuses on the longitudinal effects of attachment on cognitive development, the cognitive measures need to be described briefly. At age 7, these were a set of Piagetian tasks, assessing conservation of number, substance, weight, area, length, continuous and discontinuous quantity, two-dimensional space, and logical multiplication. With increasing age, age-adequate tasks were added to the battery, and such tasks eliminated that were no longer adequate. Formal operations were assessed by three syllogistic reasoning tasks, as well as by tasks of combinatorial reasoning, multiple compensation, correlation, and the pendulum task. The dependent measures were a composite score based on all concrete and formal reasoning tasks, and a composite score based on the three syllogistic reasoning tasks.

The sample for the study was 89 children, about equally divided as to gender and social class. The children were classified into the four main attachment groups: secure, insecure-avoidant, insecure-ambivalent, and insecure-disorganized. Due to their small number, the insecure-ambivalent children were dropped from the analysis. Data were available for 85 children (see Table 4.1).

Figure 4.2 shows that the three remaining attachment groups differ significantly and consistently from each other in cognitive performance. The secure group outperformed the two insecure groups throughout. Formal operations emerged at about age 12 in the secure group, consolidating over the next 3 years and beyond. The avoidant subjects among the insecure children were considerably less advanced throughout the age span

TABLE 4.1
Distribution of Attachment Groups

Groups	Boys	Girls	Total
B Secure	17	22	39
A Insecure-avoidant	20	9	29
C Insecure-ambivalent	3	1	4
D Insecure-disorganized	7	10	17
Total	47	42	89

Note. No main effects were found for gender or social class. A weak interaction effect obtained for attachment and gender. This effect is due to the fact that the insecure-avoidant pattern is more frequent in boys than in girls.

under study, barely entering full formal operations at age 15, after a long spell of time in the transitional stage. The disorganized group is the most problematic of all. In effect, in some of the tasks, they scarcely advance beyond concrete operations (Fig. 4.3). The age-equivalent developmental discrepancy tends to increase between groups. The differentiation process generally appears to increase with age, gaining momentum at the moment

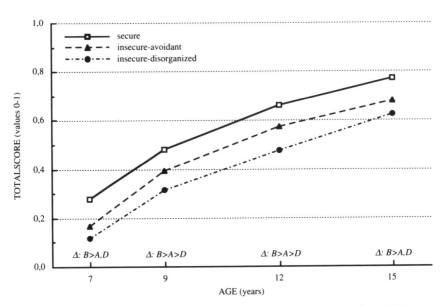

FIG. 4.2.   Developmental course of cognitive competence at ages 7, 9, 12, and 15 in three attachment groups. Scores of 0.2–0.4 represent concrete operations; scores of 0.4–0.6 transitional; scores beyond 0.6 beginning formal operations. Δ = Results of post hoc Duncan tests of group differences at each age level ($p < .05$): B = secure ($n = 39$); A = insecure-avoidant ($n = 29$); D = insecure-disorganized ($n = 17$).

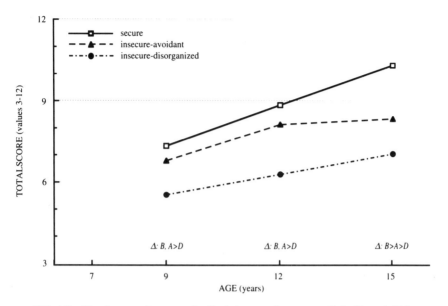

FIG. 4.3.   Developmental course of syllogistic reasoning at ages 7, 9, 12, and 15 in three attachment groups. Scores between 3 and 6 represent preoperational performance; scores between 6 and 9 represent concrete operational performance; scores above 9 represent formal operations. Δ = Results of post hoc Duncan tests of group differences at each age level ($p < .05$): B = secure ($n = 39$); A = insecure-avoidant ($n = 29$); D = insecure-disorganized ($n = 17$).

of transition into formal thought (most clearly evidenced in the developmental pattern of syllogistic reasoning; see Fig. 4.3).

In adolescence, formal thought may indeed represent a challenge to explore multiple possibilities that call upon the individual to leave concrete reference behind. Insecure children may have added difficulties confronting the novelty and stress implied in a venture entirely within the abstract realm of the mind. In line with the theoretical considerations presented here, painful childhood experience with a deficient holding environment may evoke anxiety in the face of the challenge or failure to engage in the cognitive task.

This interpretation is borne out by two additional features, one relative to self, the other relative to object cognition. Previously, I hypothesized that in the anxious and depressive the self was not cathected with positive affect. Some evidence for this is available for the insecure children. On a measure of self-worth, secure children earned significantly better scores: They had better feelings about themselves, and obtained significantly higher self-confidence ratings than both insecure-avoidant and insecure-disorganized children, who were worst off by far. There is evidence in the data that insecure-disorganized children use a disproportionate amount of contradictory responses, and increasingly so with increasing abstractness of task. Thus, contradictory responses attain 80% of all responses by insecure-disorganized children in the abstract syllogistic task, more than double the amount found in the concrete task, and more than four times the amount found among secure children. The insecure children thus show signs of low self-confidence, deficient cognitive regulation, and an abnormal disequilibrium of thought under cognitive stress (Jacobsen et al., 1994).

What is the regime of experience that induces, in the child, the delay in cognitive development and the deficit in cognitive regulation that appear to be typical for the insecure children? Reverting once more to effects tied to objects of experience, mechanisms, and outcomes, we may speculate that the process of accommodation (i.e., reaching out to novel epistemic experience) is adversely affected by an insecurity that curbs exploration. The necessary cathexis of epistemic objects may be withdrawn, and the developmental outcomes are found increasingly deficient.

In the case of insecurity of attachment, then, the regime of experience in the close dyadic relationship of caretaker and child is upset, and with it the basic mechanism of epistemic relations with the world, placing the massive and frequently irrevocable constraints of an unpropitious epistemic working model on cognitive development.

ANXIETY AND DEPRESSION

We are rather well informed about the basic relationship structure that determines attachment and its consequences (Bowlby, 1969; Bretherton, chapter 1, this volume; Shaver & Clark, chapter 2, this volume; Sroufe, 1983). There is little evidence that maladaptive modes of attachment relate to inequalities in the system of opportunities available to families. In contradistinction, anxiety and depression that emerge uniquely in the group of insecurely attached children, are examples of risk factors that, through the social and psychological resources available to families tend to be connected with social class.

Typically, or in a more theoretical perspective normatively, the opportunity structure is biased against the lower class with regard to resources that provide developmental benefits. These resources include workload on parents, time for child, and educational level of mothers, as well as certain patterns of childrearing and intrafamiliar discourse. Interestingly, however, it is mainly atypical or nonnormative conditions *within* social class that specifically explain the emergence of the risk factors of depression and anxiety in children. Families that differ from the relatively low level of educational aspiration characteristic of the lower class are at risk for anxiety. And in this class, a working mother represents a protective factor against depression. On the other hand, children from families that deploy high levels of punitive control strategies are at risk for depression in the middle class. Excessive control may provide the key to the mechanism producing these pathologies. Identical behavioral phenomena may thus acquire contrary meanings depending on their location in the social matrix, and their nonstandard deployment may unleash the developmentally mala-daptive mechanism that generates constraints on accommodation, slowing down the role of cognitive growth and imposing a ceiling on developmental outcome (Edelstein, 1992).

The factors described differentiate families at risk for developmental pathology from nonrisk families. The gender-specific interaction between parents and children in situations of conflict regulation contributes toward the differentiation between the two risk conditions, anxiety and depression (Edelstein, 1992). Specifically, boys in lower class families with punitive fathers are predominantly affected by anxiety. In middle-class children, boys with punitive fathers and girls with overcontrolling mothers are predominantly affected by depression. Again, nonstandard levels of control in close relationships appear to be the key to the pathological condition.

In the longitudinal study mentioned earlier, the developmental trajecto-ries of children who were consistently high on a measure of family anxiety (17%) derived from Sarason's General Anxiety Scale (Sarason, Davidson, Lighthall, Waite, & Ruebush, 1960) were compared with children low on this measure throughout childhood and adolescence. Like the securely and insecurely attached children, these groups differ significantly and cumula-tively in their course of cognitive growth as shown by the developing curve of the composite score of all Piagetian measures included in the study. The difference, at age 15, exceeds 1 standard deviation and equals close to 3 years of developmental time (Fig. 4.4). Again, there are considerable differences in self-confidence between the groups (Schellhas, 1993).

The children in the longitudinal study were also assessed for depression at four measurement occasions between ages 7 and 15 (Hofmann, 1991). Children who were identified as consistently depressed throughout child-hood and adolescence (about 25%) were compared with children either not depressed at all (roughly 50%), or depressed only in adolescence (16%). The results were strikingly similar to those reported for chronically anxious children (Fig. 4.5). Again, the measure of self-worth showed similar differences between the groups.

At this point, one should remember the relationship between attachment, anxiety, and depression. They all derive from the vicissitudes of intimate relationships in childhood. Security of attachment provides a protective factor against the affective disorders represented by the latter. Yet, insecurity of attachment does predict neither anxiety nor depression, nor

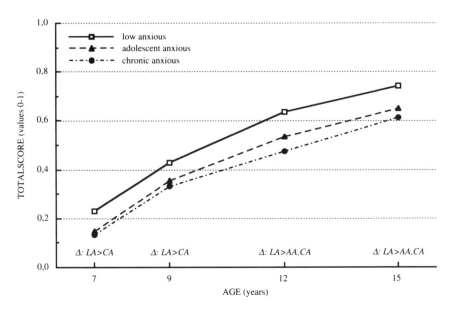

FIG. 4.4.   Developmental course of cognitive competence at ages 7, 9, 12, and 15 by longitudinal patterns of anxiety. Scores of 0.2–0.4 represent concrete operations; scores of 0.4–0.6 transitional; scores beyond 0.6 beginning formal operations. Δ = Results of post hoc Duncan tests of group differences at each age level ($p < .05$): LA = low anxious ($n = 55$); AA = adolescent anxious ($n = 14$); CA = chronic anxious ($n = 16$).

does depression predict anxiety. Anxiety and depression thus represent independent risk factors. Depressives are at risk for anxiety, but not necessarily so. Those who are, suffer additional vulnerability as expressed by increased cognitive delay. Considered alone, depression has the more massive consequences. Perhaps, we may speculate, anxiety leaves the individuals able to continue their efforts at the accommodation and assimilation of novel experience in spite of the impediments it puts in their way. In contradistinction, depression may withdraw the energizing affect altogether and subvert even the attempt to meet the world through the accommodatory activity of the subject's cognitive schemata.

SUMMARY

The developmental vulnerabilities represented by attachment, anxiety, and depression are substantive and quantifiable in terms of age-equivalent years of developmental progress or incremental deprivations. They originate

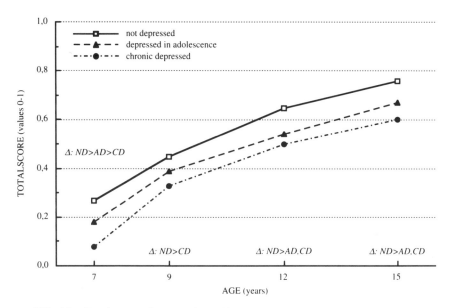

FIG. 4.5. Developmental course of cognitive competence at ages 7, 9, 12, and 15 by longitudinal patterns of depression. Scores of 0.2–0.4 represent concrete operations; scores of 0.4–0.6 transitional; scores beyond 0.6 beginning formal operations. Δ = Results of post hoc Duncan tests of group differences at each age level ($p < .05$): ND = not depressed ($n = 43$); AD = depressed in adolescence ($n = 14$); CD = chronic depressed ($n = 21$).

from different social contexts, some confined to dyadic relationships, others class-specific and collective. They all affect basic processes of cognition.

The findings presented in this chapter show the potential architecture of a theory configuration linking cognitive developmental theory with a psychology of personality and individual differences. On the antecedent side, certain patterns of socializing interaction nested in specific social contexts produce risks for the development of the child's ability for successful epistemic interaction with the world. Vulnerabilities contracted in maladaptive relationships between caregiver and child affect the capacity to explore the world from a secure base and to manage self-confidence in the face of ambiguity and novelty. On the consequent side, we reconstruct the unfolding effects of the developmental vulnerabilities in the course of cognitive growth.

The collective patterns of experience that provide the external conditions or sociostructural determinants of development merit a much closer look than is traditional within structural developmental theory. The cross-cultural near-universality of the basic Piagetian stage structures may have diverted our attention from the individual differences in rate, trajectory, and outcome that obtain in groups exposed to different opportunity structures or different collective standards for the appraisal of their cognitive and social-cognitive worlds. Décalage systems and interindividual differences in intraindividual change provide a royal road toward understanding the dynamics of development under different regimes of experience. For a significant part, however, the dynamic is constituted by children's fate in close relationships that affect their lives from early on.

REFERENCES

Ainsworth, M. D. S. (1990). Considerations regarding theory and assessment relevant to attachment beyond infancy. In M. Greenberg, D. Ciccetti, & M. Cummings (Eds.), *Attachment in the preschool years* (pp. 463-488). Chicago: University of Chicago Press.

Baltes, P. B., & Schaie, K. W. (1973). On life-span developmental research paradigms: Retrospects and prospects. In P. B. Baltes & K. W. Schaie (Eds.), *Life-span developmental psychology: personality and socialization* (pp. 366-395). New York: Academic Press.

Bowlby, J. (1969). *Attachment and loss: Vol. 1: Attachment.* New York: Basic Books.

Bronfenbrenner, U., & Crouter, A. (1983). The evolution of environmental models in developmental research. In P. H. Mussen (Ed.), *Handbook of child psychology* (pp. 357-414). New York: Wiley.

Cellérier, G. (1987). Structures and functions. In B. Inhelder, D. de Caprona, & A. Cornu-Wells (Eds.), *Piaget today* (pp. 15-36). Hillsdale, NJ: Lawrence Erlbaum Associates.

Cole, M., Gay, J., Glick, J. A., & Sharp, D. W. (1971). *The cultural context of learning and thinking.* New York: Basic Books.

Cole, M., & Scribner, S. (1974). *Culture and thought. A psychological introduction.* New York: Wiley.

Damerow, P. (1994). Vorüberlegungen zu einer historischen Epistemologie der Zahlbegriffsentwicklung [Preliminary thoughts about a historical epistemology of the development of the number concept]. In G. Dux (Ed.), *Der Prozess der Geistesgeschichte: Studien zur ontogenetischen und historischen Entwicklungslogik des Geistes* (pp. 248-322). Frankfurt am Main: Suhrkamp.

Damon, W. (1984). Peer education: The untapped potential. *Journal of Applied Developmental Psychology, 5,* 331-343.

Dasen, P. (Ed.). (1977). *Piagetian psychology. Cross-cultural contributions.* New York: Gardner Press.

Doise, W., & Mugny, G. (1984). *The social development of the intellect.* Oxford: Pergamon Press.

Edelstein, W. (1983). Cultural constraints on development and the vicissitudes of progress. In F. S. Kessel & A. W. Siegel (Eds.), *The child and other cultural inventions* (pp. 48-88). New York: Praeger.

Edelstein, W. (1992, September). *Development and socialization. An interactionist account of the dynamics of development under social constraints.* Invited address at the fifth European Conference of Developmental Psychology, Seville.

Edelstein, W., Keller, M., & Schröder, E. (1990). Child development and social structure: A longitudinal study of individual differences. In P. B. Baltes, D. L. Featherman, & R. M. Lerner (Eds), *Life-span development and behavior* (Vol. 10, pp. 152-185). Hillsdale, NJ: Lawrence Erlbaum Associates.

Eichorn, D. H. (1981). Samples and procedures. In D. H. Eichorn, J. A. Clausen, N. Haan, M. P. Honzik, & P. H. Mussen (Eds.), *Present and past in middle life* (pp. 33-51). New York: Academic Press.

Elder, G. H., Jr. (1974). *Children of the Great Depression*. Chicago: University of Chicago Press.

Elder, G. H., Jr. (1984). Families, kin, and the life course: A sociological perspective. In R. D. Parke (Ed.), *Review of child development research: The family* (Vol. 7, pp. 80-136). Chicago: University of Chicago Press.

Elder, G. H., Jr., & Caspi, A. (1988). Human development and social change: an emerging perspective on the life course. In N. Bolger, A. Caspi, G. Downey, & M. Moorehouse (Eds.), *Persons in context: Developmental processes* (pp. 77-113). New York: Cambridge University Press.

Elder, G. H., Jr., & Liker, M. (1982). Hard times in women's lives: Historical influences across 40 years. *American Journal of Sociology, 88*, 241-269.

Elder, G. H., Jr., Van Nguyen, T., & Caspi, A. (1985). Linking family hardship to children's lives. *Child Development, 56*, 361-375.

Garbarino, J. (1992). *Children in danger. Coping with the consequences of community violence*. San Francisco: Jossey Bass.

Haan, N. (1977). *Coping and defending*. New York: Academic Press.

Hofmann, V. (1991). *Die Entwicklung depressiver Reaktionen in Kindheit und Jugend. Eine entwicklungspathologische Längsschnittuntersuchung*. Berlin: Sigma.

Hollos, M. (1974). *Growing up in Flathill*. Oslo: Universitetsforlaget.

Hollos, M., & Cowan, P. A. (1973). Social isolation and cognitive development: Logical operations and role-taking abilities in three Norwegian social settings. *Child Development, 44*, 630-641.

Inhelder, B. (1989). Du sujet épistémique au sujet psychologique [From the epistemic to the psychological subject]. *Bulletin de Psychologie, 42*, 466-467.

Inhelder, B., & Piaget, J. (1958). *The growth of logical thinking from childhood to adolescence*. New York: Basic Books.

Inhelder, B., & Piaget, J. (1971). Closing remarks. In D. R. Green, M. P. Ford, & G. B. Flamer (Eds.), *Measurement and Piaget* (pp. 210-213). New York: McGraw-Hill.

Jacobsen, T., Edelstein, W., & Hofmann, V. (1994). A longitudinal study of the relation between representations of attachment in childhood and cognitive functioning in childhood and adolescence. *Developmental Psychology, 30*, 112-124.

Kaplan, N. (1987). *Individual differences in six-year olds thoughts about separation: Predicted from attachment to mother at age one year*. Unpublished doctoral dissertation, University of California, Berkeley.

Keller, M. (1992, May). *Interpersonal and moral responsibilities in friendship and parent–child relationships*. Paper presented at the invited symposium "Relationships and the development of moral reciprocity", 22nd annual symposium of the Jean Piaget Society, Philadelphia.

Kohut, H. (1978). *The search of the self: Selected writings of Heinz Kohut, 1950-1978* (P. Ornstein, Ed.). New York: International Universities Press.

Krappmann, L. (1991, April). *Peer relationships and social competence: Culture specific performance or universal competence (or both)*? Paper presented at the symposium "Peer relationships and social skills in other cultures" at the SRCD preconference on Peer Relationships, Seattle.

Lautrey, J. (1980). *Classe sociale, milieu familial, intelligence*. Paris: Presses Universitaires de France.

Macfarlane, J. W. (1938). Studies in child guidance. I. Methodology of data collection and organization. *Monographs of the Society for Research in Child Development, 3* (Serial No. 6).

Mugny, G. (Ed.). (1985). *Psychologie sociale du développement cognitif*. Bern: Lang.

Noam, G. G. (1988). A constructivist approach to developmental psychopathology. In E. Nannis & P. Cowan (Eds.), *Developmental psychopathology and its treatment*. San Francisco: Josey Bass.

Noam, G. G. (1993). Normative vulnerabilities of the self and their transformations in moral actions. In G. G. Noam & E. Wren (Eds.), *The Moral Self* (pp. 209-238). Cambridge: MIT Press.

Oswald, H., & Krappmann, L. (1991). Der Beitrag der Gleichaltrigen zur sozialen Entwicklung von Kindern in der Grundschule. In R. Pekrun & H. Fend (Eds.), *Schule und Persönlichkeitsentwicklung* (pp. 201-216). Stuttgart: Enke.

Perret-Clermont, A.-N. (1980). *Social interaction and cognitive development in children*. London: Academic Press.

Piaget, J. (1952). Jean Piaget. In E. G. Boring, H. S. Langfeld, H. Werner, & R. M. Yerkes (Eds.), *A history of psychology in autobiography* (Vol. 4). Worcester, MA: Clark University Press.

Piaget, J. (1970). *Structuralism*. New York: Basic Books.

Piaget, J. (1981). Intelligence and affectivity: Their relationship during child development. In T. A. Brown & C. E. Kaegi (Eds.), *Annual Reviews Monograph*. Palo Alto, CA: Annual Reviews Inc. (Original work published 1962).

Radding, C. M. (1985). *A world made by men*. Chapel Hill: The University of North Carolina Press.

Sarason, S. B., Davidson, K. S., Lighthall, F. F., Waite, R. R., & Ruebush, B. K. (1960). *Anxiety in elementary school children*. New York: Wiley.

Schellhas, B. (1993). *Die Entwicklung der Angstlichkeit in Kindheit und Jugend: Befunde einer Längsschnittstudie über die Bedeutung der Ängstlichkeit für die Entwicklung der Kognition und des Schulerfolgs* Berlin: Sigma.

Schröder, E. (1989). *Vom konkreten zum formalen Denken. Individuelle Entwicklungsverläufe von der Kindheit bis zum Jugendalter*. Bern: Huber.

Schröder, E., & Edelstein, W. (1991). Intrinsic and external constraints on the development of cognitive competence. In M. Chandler & M. Chapman (Eds.), *Criteria for assessment: Controversies in the conceptualization and assessment of children's abilities* (pp. 131-152). Hillsdale, NJ: Lawrence Erlbaum Associates.

Schütz, A. (1982). *Das Problem der Relevanz*. Frankfurt am Main: Suhrkamp.

Spitz, R. A. (1945). Hospitalism: An inquiry into the genesis of psychiatric conditions in early childhood. *Psychoanalytic Study of the Child, 1*, 153-172.

Spitz, R. A. (1946). Hospitalism: A follow-up report on investigation described in volume 1, 1945. *Psychoanalytic Study of the Child, 2*, 113-117.

Sroufe, L. A. (1983). Infant-caregiver attachment and patterns of adaptation in preschool: The roots of maladaptation and competence. In M. Perlmutter (Ed.), *Minnesota symposia on child psychology* (Vol. 16). Hillsdale, NJ: Lawrence Erlbaum Associates.

Youniss, J. (1980). *Parents and peers in social development*. Chicago: University of Chicago Press.

Youniss, J., & Damon, W. (1992). Social construction in Piaget's theory. In H. Beilin & P. Pufall (Eds.), *Piaget's theory* (pp. 267-286). Hillsdale, NJ: Lawrence Erlbaum Associates.

5 Revisiting Piaget Revisited or the Vulnerability of Piaget's Infancy Theory in the 1990s

Thérèse Gouin Décarie
Marcelle Ricard
University of Montreal

When one considers human development, it is clear that no other period offers such intricate close relationships than infancy. Not only is there, at that time, an unparalleled closeness between infant and caretaker, but the numerous behaviors of the infant are themselves of such a fluid nature that it can be extremely difficult to distinguish, within these behaviors, which elements are related mostly to motricity, cognition, or affectivity. The close relationships are not only interpersonal: They are also intrapersonal.

This latter kind of relationship has been our major research interest since the early 1960s. The analysis of the development of the Piagetian notion of object permanence and its link with the Freudian libidinal object was the first scientific endeavor of Gouin Décarie (1965). It was followed by an attempt to assess the relation between the infant's reaction to strangers and his or her level of understanding of causality and object permanence (Gouin Décarie, 1974). More recently, we have been investigating the evolution of social referencing between the ages of 6 and 18 months, in relation to its cognitive prerequisites (Desrochers, Ricard, Gouin Décarie, & Allard, 1994; Ricard, Gouin Décarie, Desrochers, & Rome-Flanders, 1994).

Thus, the analysis of the relationship between the two main aspects of infant's psyche, cognition and affectivity, has become a lifetime research program. Today, this line of research must take into account the fast-growing theories that offer an alternative to Piaget's conception of early development, and in this chapter, we try to evaluate how vulnerable Piaget's key hypotheses about the sensorimotor period have become, now that they have been reassessed by at least three different currents of investigation and theory.

Such a "revisit to Piaget revisited" has more than a purely historical interest. As Beilin (1992) strongly emphasized, Piaget's contribution to developmental psychology is an enduring one: "His theory is still very much a contending presence in the free-for-all that defines current psychological theorizing" (p. 192). Trying to assess today the reassessments of Piaget that span more than two decades seems a timely exercise.

As Halford (1989) pointed out, in the 1960s, when Flavell's (1963) monumental book *The Developmental Psychology of Jean Piaget* appeared, there was a great optimism about the explanatory power of Piaget's theory and observations. At that time, in the United States, behaviorism was losing its grip on developmental psychology, and infancy researchers as well as educational scientists did not question Piaget's basic assumptions, so that studies that tried to validate (more or less successfully) his detailed observations proliferated. This acceptance was so unanimous that, by the end of the decade, Pinard and Laurendeau (1969) could write that "Piaget's difficult system has become enveloped in an aura of prestige irreconcilable with the critical spirit necessary to avoid confusion between hypotheses, opinions, and facts" (p. 121). Soon, the first (and badly needed) reassessments of some of Piaget's main hypotheses relating to infancy began, and they were to expand rapidly in the following years.

Bower played a seminal role in this change. Focusing mainly on what Leslie (1986) would eventually call "objecthood," his works tended to "decorticate" Piaget's object concept, studying not only the aspect of constancy (or permanence), but also how an infant learns to understand that objects retain their identity whatever the spatiotemporal changes they undergo (see Bower 1967, 1974; Bower & Paterson, 1972). *Visually guided reaching* as an indication of the existence of object permanence, was one of Bower's *"chevaux de bataille"* (see Bower, Broughton, & Moore, 1970a, 1970b; Bower & Wishart, 1972). On the ground that very young infants were able to reach toward a visible object, and expected, even in the dark, to find something tangible where they had seen an object, Bower and his coworkers, as well as a number of investigators and theorists after them, concluded to the falsity of Piaget's theory of the gradual and late development of the object concept. An analysis of the importance of visually guided reaching in a Piagetian framework is therefore our first revisit.

In the following decade, Moore and his coworkers (Moore, Borton, & Darby, 1978; Moore & Clark, 1975; Moore & Myers, 1975) carried out a series of ingenious experiments and came to the conclusion that "the development of an understanding that objects are permanent in nature is not mediated by the coordination of action schemes, as Piaget had argued, but rather by the elaboration of rules for determining object identity" (Schuberth, 1983, p. 160). Then, Meltzoff and Moore (1977, 1979) chiseled off another piece of Piaget's theory (whose statue was, by now, toppling on its base) when they found that newborn infants imitated adult facial gestures. They concluded to precocious intermodal matching and the existence of an early kind of representation. A reexamination of *early imitation* is our second revisit.

Among other investigators belonging to this first wave of reevaluation, were Gratch, Butterworth, Bremner, and Harris. Most of their studies focused on the object concept, and within this concept, on one phenomenon characteristic of Stage IV: the "AB error," that is, the fact that the infant, after having successfully retrieved an object hidden at one of two locations, will then return to this same location even when seeing the object disappear at the second location. In a review of these works, Schuberth (1983) noted that, by concentrating exclusively on this AB error and by not taking into sufficient account what comes before and after it in the long sequence of behaviors observed by Piaget, the alternative theories of the evolution of the object concept proposed by these researchers (with the exception of Harris) had a rather limited explanatory power. We believe that this is a very important point, and come back to it later on.

Schuberth's critique, however, no longer applies to the new school of thought that recently emerged in infancy research, and is known as the "Neo-Piagetian" approach.[1] This approach appeared in part as a robust reaction against a second, even more challenging wave of opposition to Piaget's theory. In the first wave, the methods used to test the validity of some of Piaget's hypotheses were not exactly the same but tended to be similar to the observational techniques used by Piaget himself: Although some researchers resorted to emotional reactions, such as surprise, as a cue to the infant's knowledge of the object (e.g., Bower, 1971; Charlesworth, 1969; Lecompte & Gratch, 1972; Ramsay & Campos, 1975), most kept on using direct measures of overt visual and/or motor behaviors during object tracking and search, with only slight manipulations of "natural" situations. In contrast, researchers in the second wave of reassessment of Piaget's hypotheses, a wave that appeared around 1985, used in most instances an entirely new approach, namely, the habituation–dishabituation paradigm. This technique consists in presenting the subjects, first, with a given stimulus to a point where their attention shows a significant decrease (habituation), and then submitting them to a second stimulus that is slightly different (dishabituation); an increase in the level of attention to this new stimulus is taken as a sign of their noticing the difference. Our third and last

---

[1]This new body of theory "must be seen as a hybrid, which rests on a similar set of core assumptions, and which offers an interesting set of potential solutions to the problems posed by the classical Piagetian system, but which introduces new elements into the system that genuinely transforms it, and gives it exciting new possibilities" (Case, 1992, p. 62). See also, in this volume, Fischer, Case, and Noam.

revisit looks at the way these innovative — and quite spectacular — experiments question our conception of Piaget's object concept.

THREE CLASSES OF COGNITIVE ABILITIES

Obviously, the subjects of our three revisits — visually guided reaching, neonatal imitation, and object knowledge — have different degrees of importance for Piaget and his theory. As Pascal would say, they are not *"du même ordre,"* and that is why, before going any further, some distinctions should be made, especially because many of the controversies about the validity of Piaget's theory have been related to age.

One of these distinctions has already been made by Fischer and Bidell (1991), who astutely differentiated between *skills* and *capacities*, adding: "Arguments over the age of acquisition of a capacity are based on the notion that the child can be characterized as either having or not having some fixed capacity regardless of context. The concept of skill recasts this notion in terms of gradually emerging abilities that are context-dependent. Skills are cognitive structures, and constructed *in* and *for* specific contexts" (p. 232).

Such a distinction is extremely enlightening. However, it may prove insufficient, or even misleading, when applied to behaviors as widely different as "visually guided reaching, classification, object permanence or any other tasks" (Fischer & Bidell, 1991, p. 232). We argue — and this *trichotomy* serves as the theoretical framework of our discussion — that one must distinguish between three classes of abilities when assessing the developmental value or meaning of a given cognitive behavior observed in infants.

Few researchers would question that visually guided reaching belongs to the category of infant skills. For Piaget, it is, of course, a cognitive skill, in a way that we try to explicate. But it is always context-dependent, so that it cannot be considered as a true cognitive "capacity." After their detailed description of the development of visually guided reaching, Fischer and Bidell (1991) concluded: "This skill continues to grow for years to come" (p. 215). But there are fixed limits to the growth of this skill — even the visuomanual tricks of a magician have their limits. This is obviously not true of "objecthood," which is a cognitive capacity that becomes very gradually fully independent of context, so that it is what can be called a capacity with limitless potentialities. In a way, objecthood flourishes in the Aristotelian and Kantian discussion on "substance." This also applies to notions such as space, time, or causality.

It does not apply to imitation. Imitation stands somehow in between a cognitive skill and a capacity with limitless potentialities. It is certainly extremely context-bound in the newborn, and it becomes more and more context-free relatively early. The infant can imitate many sounds, many gestures, he or she can imitate a model that is absent, as in deferred imitation, and the actor, in a way, imitates even an absent character that he or she has partially created. But the activity and the notion of imitation has boundaries, and our capacity to imitate and to understand imitation has not evolved through the centuries as our capacity to understand space and time has.

Thus, we consider visually guided reaching as a *cognitive skill*, imitation—but, as we see here, not just any kind of imitation—as a *cognitive capacity*, and object concept as a *cognitive capacity with limitless potentialities*. This last class of cognitive abilities were the really important ones for Piaget, who believed them to be specific to human being. Let us see where the reassessment of Piaget's findings and conceptions relative to these three elements, puts us today.

FIRST REVISIT: VISUALLY GUIDED REACHING

When we talk about "visually guided reaching," we think of manual reaching or, in other terms, of the coordination between prehension and vision. In his observations and discussions concerning the Stage II of sensorimotor intelligence, Piaget (1936/1952) delineated five phases in the development of prehension, from the first phase of impulsive movements and pure reflex, to the fifth and final phase when the child grasps what he or she sees and looks at what he or she grasps, without limitations related to the position of the hand.

Some important points must be stressed here. First, Piaget did not use the word "stage" ("*stade*" in French) in his description of prehension. More cautiously, he saw the five phases as successive moments or steps ("*étapes*") in the progress of prehension.[2] Even if these steps were related in some way to the main stages of sensorimotor intelligence (first step to Stage I; second, third, and fourth steps to Stage II; fifth step announcing Stage III), they were not genuine "stages" in the Piagetian sense, for they did not meet the three minimum criteria required to be characterized as such (Gouin Décarie, 1965; Piaget, 1960): (a) irreversible order of acquisition; (b) integrative

---

[2]The French original reads as follows: "On peut, nous semble-t-il, distinguer cinq étapes dans le progrès de la préhension. Si [. . .] ces étapes ne correspondent pas à des âges définis, leur succession cependant paraît nécessaire (sauf en ce qui concerne peut-être la troisième étape)." Unfortunately, the English translation (Piaget, 1936/1952, p. 89) says: "It seems to us five *stages* may be described in the development of grasping. Even though [. . .] these *stages* do not correspond to definite ages, their sequence nevertheless seems necessary (except perhaps with regard to the third *stage*)."

character of each stage; and (c) the existence, within each stage, of a level of preparation and a level of completion.

One can then ask: If visually guided reaching cannot be described in terms of developmental stages, in what sense can it be a *cognitive* skill for Piaget? The answer to this question depends on our understanding of the notion of "coordination of schemes." The importance of the scheme of prehension in the development of intelligence and the construction of reality in infancy is not related to prehension as such, but to its capacity to enter in a true and efficient coordination with other schemes, and mostly with the scheme of vision. In the fifth step described by Piaget, not only does the infant grasp what he or she sees, but, equally important, looks at what his or her hand is grasping. There lies the cognitive dimension of the skill. There must be a "reciprocal adaptation" between both processes, which are equally important, that is, a "collateral assimilation" of each one by the other through which the object concept is mediated. Piaget (1936/1952) wrote: "Everything that is looked at or sucked tends to be grasped and everything that is grasped tends to be sucked and then to be looked at. This coordination which crowns the acquisition of prehension also indicates an essential progress in objectification . . . [The object] thus acquires a combination of meanings and consequently a consistency" (p. 121).

Unfortunately, this cognitive dimension of visually guided reaching was rarely taken into account by those researchers who used to believe they had disconfirmed Piaget's theory simply because they had observed infants trying to reach an object in the early weeks of life. Today, most researchers agree that a distinction must be made between two types of early reaching: "visually guided reaching," on the one hand, and "visually initiated reaching," on the other. The latter (contrary to Piaget's assertion) would be a primitive eye–hand coordination, that is, "a rudimentary visuo-proprioceptive mapping that is hard-wired and never was (nor will be) conscious" (Bushnell, 1985, p. 150). This visually initiated reaching would exist at birth, whereas visually guided reaching would appear only later, between 3 and 5 months of age.

To go further, one could even ask to what extent these complex sensorimotor acquisitions — visually guided reaching and "manually guided looking" — are crucial to the development of the object concept in a Piagetian perspective. In other words, is this "crowning" achievement in the growth of prehension an essential condition to the development of "objec-thood?"

In a study by Gouin Décarie (1969), 21 thalidomide children suffering from congenital malformations (whose severity varied from simple syn-dactyly to quadruple phocomelia) were administered an object scale and allowed to use whatever means they had to convey their knowledge of the disappearing object (e.g., they could pick up the screen and the object with their mouth or toes). Nineteen subjects reached Stage VI of object concept, even the child with quadruple phocomelia. Two subjects were below Stage VI: One could find the hidden object when it had undergone not more than one invisible displacement (Stage V), and the other, who was mentally retarded, was still in Stage IV.

Fifteen years after their publication, these results have been referred to as raising serious questions about Piaget's theory of object concept, because of the absence of visually guided grasping in these children (Schuberth, 1983). But when Gouin Décarie mentioned her findings to Piaget, expressing her own astonishment that infants unable to fully master prehension had reached such a knowledge of the object, Piaget looked surprised and said: "But the construction of reality by the infant is not a function of one organ or one modality. What an infant cannot achieve through a given 'circuit,' he gets to it by another road." Put otherwise, this statement would mean that the essential factor in the infant's evolution toward a full mastery of the object concept is not visually guided reaching itself, but the process of scheme coordination that it involves, a process that can be efficiently achieved by other sensorimotor actions, experiences, or skills.

This same reply could be addressed to Landau, Spelke, and Gleitman (1984), who studied the development of a very young blind girl. Observing that in spite of her handicap this girl had a knowledge of space (she was able to find a novel pathway between familiar objects), they concluded that, because she could not have gained her spatial knowledge from visual perception, this girl's ability disconfirmed Piaget's description of the acquisition of a notion of space. But very pointedly, when reviewing this study, Fischer and Bidell (1991) stated that its results were fully consistent with Piaget's own observations and predictions, and that the alleged disconfirmation of Piaget's theory of spatial knowledge was due only to a misrepresentation of this theory.

In other words, even though visual perception or visually guided reaching normally intervene and play an important role in the way children build their knowledge of object, space, time, or causality, these skills are not essential to the emergence of cognitive capacities with unlimited potentialities, which rest on various reciprocal adaptations and innumerable cues from other senses.

SECOND REVISIT: NEONATAL IMITATION OF FACIAL GESTURES

Since the 1980s, there has been an accumulation of data and theoretical controversies relative to early imitation. The early imitation of vocal sounds or manual gestures is of secondary importance here. What needs to be "explained away" by Piagetian infancy psychologists is the imitation of tongue protrusion, opening and closing of the mouth, closing of the eyes, or head turning *in the neonate*. For these are all "invisible movements of one's own body," that is, movements that Piaget believed could not be imitated before the infant reached Stage IV (around 8 months of age).

Piaget's (1945/1951) interest was mostly in vocal, not gestural imitation, and this interest stemmed from his theory of language. He saw the word as an internalized deferred imitation of sounds that had become meaningful. For him, the tendency to imitate was innate, but the imitation of sounds and gestures required certain specific cognitive abilities that would develop only gradually. After noticing Lucienne's imitation of the protrusion of the tongue when she was 5 months (Piaget, 1945/1951, observation 18), he considered it, even at that age, to be "pseudo-imitation," or "training under suggestion" ("*dressage*").

It is often forgotten that the first psychologist who analyzed and filmed imitation of the protrusion of the tongue in a systematic fashion, was René Zazzo. His son was 25 days old, and this happened in 1945, the same year Piaget published the last book of his trilogy on infancy, *Play, Dreams and Imitation in Childhood* (1945/1951). At that time, when told of Zazzo's observation, his professor, Wallon, "looked overwhelmed by his student's naïvety" (Zazzo, 1988, p. 6). As to Piaget, he simply did not mention Zazzo, and it took a decade and the replication of Zazzo's initial observation by others on 20 subjects aged 1 to 25 days, to break the silence barrier. Zazzo finally published a paper on neonatal imitation (Zazzo, 1957) 20 years before the study by Meltzoff and Moore (1977). If we insist on this historical aspect, it is only to underscore that, following Zazzo, several French researchers, such as Fontaine (1984a, 1984b), Vinter (1985, 1986) and, for later ages, Nadel (1986, 1988), have been very active in this field.

The first two U.S. reports (Meltzoff & Moore, 1977, 1979) that suggested the existence of imitation of movements invisible on one's own body before the age of 1 month, were not considered at first as valid proof of the phenomenon. They provoked a large number of varied criticisms and were difficult to replicate. The methodological flaws of these original studies were eliminated in a further study by Meltzoff and Moore (1983), and numerous experiments done by other researchers in many countries lead at least to four clear conclusions: (a) The modeling of tongue protrusion increases the rate of tongue protrusion in the neonate. (b) For the imitation of other individual facial gestures, the evidence remains insufficient or still requires validation, as is the case of Meltzoff and Moore's (1989) recent report on the neonatal imitation of head movement. (c) There is a rigorous time frame: the duration of the display must be 60 seconds or more. (d) The movement of the model is important (see Anisfeld, 1991).

Even if all these conclusions are not unanimously endorsed, the evidence for the existence of the imitation of tongue protrusion by the newborn appears very strong today. This casts light on the necessity to reexamine the first and second stages of gestural imitation, as described by Piaget. But does it invalidate all of Piaget's observations on imitation in infancy?

Of course, one must admit that Piaget's theory of language acquisition and the relationship he establishes between internalized imitation and the verbal symbol, are a weak link in his epistemology and have little influence today. It is rather the meaning of neonatal imitation as a *cognitive* process that is important to consider.

In other words, if neonatal imitation of one facial gesture is a valid observation, does it shake the very foundations of Piaget's theory of mental development as a whole? This question, as so many others, cannot be answered without taking into account the sequence of behaviors that follow. For here is a perfect example of the danger of isolating a given behavior without considering its development. What, in fact, happens to neonatal imitation? The majority of investigators who analyzed its developmental course (Heimann, 1989; Jacobson, 1979; Maratos, 1973; Vinter, 1985) concluded that it disappears between 2 and 3 months of age—or, to the latest, at 6 months, according to Fontaine (1984b). In other words, this behavior seems to vanish quite soon, and to reemerge only later, when the infant begins to imitate not only tongue protrusion, but also shutting of the eyes, puffing of the cheeks, opening and closing of the mouth, all these imitations appearing during the second semester of life and tending to solidify with age.

How can this decline of a cognitive ability, which should be characterized, like other similar abilities, by continuous growth, be explained? If a cross-modal matching process and a representational code are at work in neonatal imitation, as suggested by Meltzoff and Moore (1985, 1989), how can these abilities disappear suddenly at 2 or 3 months? Does the complex system underlying these capacities also disappear for several months and then reappear? It seems hard to imagine such fluctuations in basic processes. And if these capacities are innate, why is imitation so context-bound and restricted to the oral area? Why does a cross-modal matching process not allow imitation of eyes closing as well?

In fact, the recent documentation tends to differentiate neonatal imitation of tongue protrusion from its later counterpart, and to see them as two distinct phenomena, early imitation being considered as an innate process that carries different interpretations and labels. Some see it as the result of ethological fixed-action patterns released by sign stimuli (see Anisfeld, 1991), whereas others consider it simply as a stereotyped "facial gesture" (Kaitz, Meschulach-Sarfaty, Auerbach, & Eidelman, 1988). Bjorklund (1987) suggested that early imitation of facial gestures could best be attributed to biologically wired-in mechanisms that do not serve as a basis for more advanced cognitive functioning, but facilitate infant–adult inter-action. According to Anisfeld (1991), instead of being the result of prior modeling, tongue protrusion could be a response released from prior inhibition. Whatever the interpretation, many researchers perceive tongue protrusion by the newborn as a genuine skill, but not a cognitive skill. They see its disappearance as a necessary condition allowing the appearance of a later kind of imitation. This new imitation is not narrowly context-bound, and it grows along with the mental development of the infant, to the point that he or she becomes able to imitate an activity even in the absence of the model and after a delay, and even if he or she has never performed this activity before. This last acquisition is true "deferred" imitation, which differs from the "delayed" imitation observed in young infants by Meltzoff (1985, 1988; Meltzoff & Moore, 1994). Deferred imitation is a cognitive capacity that will develop and flourish in the years to come.

But it will not develop without inherent constraints, as we said before. It is only in the case of what we called "cognitive capacities with limitless potentialities" that these constraints no longer exist. And object knowledge is one of these capacities.

THIRD REVISIT: OBJECT KNOWLEDGE

Among the body of recent research challenging Piaget's views on infancy, the works of Spelke (see Spelke, 1991) and Baillargeon (see Baillargeon & DeVos, 1991) on object knowledge have received wide attention and provoked most interesting discussions.

These authors, through a series of extremely ingenious and well-controlled experiments using the habituation–dishabituation procedure, found that babies as young as 3½ months of age could visually discriminate between some "possible" or "consistent" events on the one hand, and other events that would appear "impossible" or "inconsistent" to anyone under-standing what an object really is. These babies, when confronted with events that violated the physical laws governing the world of objects (e.g., a drawbridge moving freely where a block stood a moment before), reacted with interest—that is, with longer visual fixations—thus demonstrating, Spelke and Baillargeon suggested, that they believed in the continued existence of an occluded object and understood that it kept its very same properties even when it was "out of sight." In other words, infants of that age would possess a cognitive competence far beyond what was attributed to them by Piagetian psychologists. According to Spelke or Baillargeon, the mastery of the object concept, and especially the notion of its permanence, would be extremely precocious.

Needless to say how disturbing and consequential these facts can be, not only to a strict Piagetian, but to anyone studying cognitive development. And that is why, before any major revision takes place, one should hope and wait for further empirical research that will thoroughly confirm and refine these findings. Because most of the available data, up to now, have come from the same laboratories, one obvious way to obtain such confirmation would be to conduct a good number of replication studies, based on the same paradigm. A recent attempt by Lucksinger, Cohen, and Madole (1992) did not support Baillargeon's (1986) conclusions.

However, even if these replications prove positive, which might be the case given the methodological soundness and rigor of Spelke's and Baillargeon's studies, further confirmations will still be needed if we are to admit that the infants' visual dishabituation responses truly reflect a general, genuine knowledge of the object, as claimed by the authors. If infants at that early age do possess such a competence, it should be detectable by some other measures or experimental procedures than habituation. In the 1970s and early 1980s, studies using visual tracking or *visual search* as an index of "object constancy" in young infants failed to establish such a precocious object knowledge: Actually, their findings tended to parallel those obtained from manual search tasks (Moore et al., 1978; Ricard, 1983).

Indeed, would it not be interesting — and perhaps more convincing — in these habituation experiments, to know what exactly the infants were looking at? For example, in Baillargeon and DeVos' (1991) study with the tall carrot, was it the same thing for the subject to keep looking at the second carrot after it had stopped, or to look back at the screen where the "impossible" disappearance had taken place? In other words, if the duration of gross visual fixation in an habituation context is the only behavior through which the 3- or 4-month-olds can show their cognitive mastery of the object, then one is allowed to ask: What kind of knowledge is this?

Baillargeon, as well as Spelke, tended to interpret their findings as indicating a full understanding of the object, and therefore as directly disconfirming the Piagetian theory. In their opinion, because the object concept is there almost at birth, it can no longer be said to develop slowly throughout infancy and to be constructed by the infant through the coordination of his or her own actions and experiences in the environment. What Piaget considered as an acquisition that was not fully achieved till the end of the sensorimotor period, namely object permanence, these authors claimed as occurring right at the beginning. Thus, the development that takes place between 4 and 12–15 months of age, through which an infant becomes more and more efficient at manually searching for hidden objects, is no longer seen as being of a cognitive nature, but rather as a matter of motor and/or problem-solving abilities (Baillargeon, Graber, DeVos, & Black, 1990), or as the result of neurological maturation, as suggested by Diamond (1991), whose theory is also based on "Spelkian" premises.

But as pointed out by neo-Piagetian theorists, these findings, although representing an undeniable breakthrough, should be approached very cautiously, for the abilities they seem to reveal can be easily overestimated (Fischer & Bidell, 1991; Halford, 1989; Montangero, 1991). According to the data provided so far, these abilities seem highly context-dependent, as well as extremely limited and fragile.

As a matter of fact, most of the curves showing the subjects' responses to the test trials reveal not only that the infants dishabituated to the "inconsistent" events, thus demonstrating what the authors concluded is a true object knowledge, but also that these same infants habituated rather quickly to these awkward events. Once they had noticed, by prolonging their first (or second) look at the "impossible" stimulus, that something in it was violating their cognitive expectancies, as the authors put it, almost immediately there was a sudden drop in the duration of their very next look at the same "impossible" event. In other words, it is striking how rapidly these infants admitted, or at least stopped being bewildered, by the impossibility or inconsistency of what they were witnessing. After only one trial, most of the time, they reacted as if the event had become "normal," that is, as if a car rolling through a mouse, or a drawbridge moving freely where a block stood a moment before, were no longer "impossible" events.

How can an object concept, how can the knowledge of the permanence of objects—if it is what these infants really demonstrate—be so easily overcome? How can their reaction to the violation of the expectancies that such a knowledge should imply be so short-lasting? The least one can say is that a knowledge of this kind is far from the "cognitive capacity with limitless potentialities" that a concept of object should be in the Piagetian perspective.

Until satisfactory answers are given to these questions, we have no choice but to resort to more "classical" and economical interpretations of the phenomena brought to light by these experiments. One such interpretation would consider this precocious or innate reaction to "inconsistency" as an instance of the "input systems" studied by Leslie (1986), that is, as a genetically determined mechanism helping the organism to readily cope with the environment. This purely perceptual "module" would provide a basis for the development of further "empirical reasoning," but would not be sufficient in itself to account for such a properly cognitive development.

That sort of explanation would not be incompatible with the views of neo-Piagetians theorists like Halford (1989), Karmiloff-Smith (1991), or Fischer and Bidell (1991), who tried to integrate these early capacities within the wider "epigenetic landscape" of infant cognitive development. Instead of seeing the 4-month-old's dishabituation response as an indication that he or she masters the object concept once and for all, they read it as a first skill, an early step, a precursor, or a promise, we would say, of future yet distinct and more mature competences.

Of course, Piaget himself overlooked these phenomena, and, as Chapman and Chandler (1991) recalled, we now have to take them into account in order to refine our understanding of infancy. But to reject all of the Piagetian theory of object concept on this sole ground would certainly be premature and inappropriate.

AN IMPOSSIBLE REVISIT: PIAGET AND THE SOCIOEMOTIONAL DEVELOPMENT IN INFANCY

One way of establishing a more direct link between our contribution and the general theme of this volume on "development and vulnerability in close relationships," would have been to revisit some of the reevaluations of Piaget's hypotheses regarding socioemotional development during infancy. Unfortunately, this fourth and last revisit could not be undertaken, for the simple reason that there has been no synthetic reassessment of this aspect of his theory. The few neo-Piagetians interested in the sensorimotor period (Case, 1985; Fischer, 1980; Fischer & Camfield, 1986; Fischer, Shaver, & Carnochan, 1990; Halford, 1982; Mounoud, 1986; Pascual-Leone & Johnson, 1991) seldom take into account the socioaffective elements of this period. When they do, their aim is not to reassess Piaget's main assumptions, but rather to reconstruct the whole child (Case, 1988; Halford, 1988). In fact, most authors who worked on the Piagetian theory of socialization started with the preoperational child. Let us try to understand why.

In their recent review of Piaget's writings that form a sketch of his theory of socialization, Youniss and Damon (1992) found their main sources in Piaget's (1932) study of moral judgment, as well as in his 1970 review of his general theory. Thus, these authors (as many others) assumed that one can infer the development of the child's social behavior from his or her reasoning about moral acts, and that there is a direct relationship between what a child thinks about right or wrong and what he or she does in the social environment. It is true that, in this domain, Piaget (1932) himself assumed a close and complex relationship between reasoning and practical activity. But he also believed in a decalage or "time lag" between moral activity itself and "conscious realization" of morality, the former *preceding* the latter (pp. 173-174).

In spite of numerous studies, the link between moral reasoning and moral behavior is still far from being clear. Moreover, moral development is only part and parcel of social development, so that one should seek in works other than *The Moral Judgment of the Child* (Piaget, 1932) a more detailed account of Piaget's position on the affective and social development of the whole individual.

It is in Piaget's lectures at the Sorbonne in 1954 that the clearest, most explicit outline of his hypotheses on both the social and affective developments of the child and their relationship to mental development can be found. Whenever Piaget touched upon this topic in his ensuing works (Piaget, 1945/1951, 1960, 1967, 1968, 1972a, 1972b, 1972c, 1976; Piaget & Inhelder, 1966), he merely reaffirmed this initial stand. The mimeographed report of these lectures, as published by the Centre de Documentation Universitaire (Piaget, 1954), has never been fully translated. What has been translated and beautifully edited by Brown and Kaegi (Piaget, 1954/1981), is part of the version of these lectures as they originally appeared in the *Bulletin de Psychologie*.[3]

In these lectures, Piaget vigorously rejected the hypothesis of a causal relationship between affectivity and cognition, and stressed the functional parallelism of their development:

> If our hypotheses are correct, we shall be able to put intellectual structures and the levels of affective development in parallel, stage by stage. Since structure does not exist without energetics and reciprocally, since every new structure involves a new form of energetic regulation, then, a particular sort of cognitive structure must correspond to every new level of affective conduct. (Piaget, 1954, p. 10, our translation)

Piaget summarized this functional parallelism in a table divided into two main periods and six stages that do not correspond to the six stages of *The Origins of Intelligence in Children* (Piaget, 1936/1952). The first period (that of sensorimotor intelligence and intraindividual feelings) comprises the first three stages: Chronologically, it starts at birth and finishes around 2 years. The second period (that of verbal intelligence and interpersonal feelings), which includes the three remaining stages, begins around the age of 2 years and is not completed before 14 to 15 years. What must be stressed here is that Piaget (1954/1981) was quite explicit: "These [two periods] correspond to nonsocialized and socialized behavior" (p. 15). Even though, at some point, he situated the appearance of the first forms of interpersonal feelings at the end of the sensorimotor period (Piaget, 1954/1981), these

---

[3]The French titles differed from one publication to the other. In the *Bulletin de Psychologie* (Piaget, 1954/1981), the title was: *Les relations entre l'intelligence et l'affectivité dans le développement de l'enfant*. In the mimeographed edition of the Centre de Documentation Universitaire (Piaget, 1954), the title became: *Les relations entre l'affectivité et l'intelligence dans le développement mental de l'enfant*, where, in our opinion, a significant inversion and addition were made. Also, the Sorbonne version (Piaget, 1954) contained some 40 pages which, to our knowledge, were never translated to English.

genuinely social feelings, in his view, could be experienced only with the emergence of language and preoperational thought.

Confronted with such a position, one can easily understand the absence of revision of Piaget's theory on social development in infancy. In the Piagetian perspective, there is simply no social development during the sensorimotor period. There is an *affective* development, an evolution of individualized feelings that unavoidably accompany the infant's sensori-motor actions, but these feelings have no direct influence on intelligence. In other words, there is no "sociocognitive" development.

> During the sensorimotor period preceding language acquisition, we cannot yet speak of the socialization of intelligence. . . . Sensorimotor imitation does not influence intelligence, rather it is a manifestation of intelligence. As for the emotional contacts of the baby with his surroundings (smiles, etc.), these are not interactions which affect the intellect as such. (Piaget, 1967, pp. 155-156, our translation)

Such a theoretical stand offers little leeway in terms of reassessment: one could say that there is no site to revisit, only a ledge. . . . To be fair, this precise aspect of his theory occupies a rather small place in Piaget's *omnia opera*, for he was never interested in social and affective developments per se, but only in the relationship between these dimensions and the formation of intelligence. Still, one can wonder how Piaget, had he be living today, would have integrated within his own framework the accumulation of researches on attachment theory and the growth of the working model (see Bowlby, 1969; Bretherton, chapter 1, this volume), or on infant social cognition (see Cichetti & Beeghly, 1990; Feinman, 1992; Lamb & Sherrod, 1981; Stern, 1985), and especially the few studies on the early ontogenesis of the "theories of mind" (see Bretherton, 1991; Bretherton, McNew, & Beeghly-Smith, 1981; Leslie, 1988; Wellman, 1990, 1993; Wellman & Gelman, 1992).

Surely, because he believed that he was "the only true Piagetian revision-ist" (personal communication, 1970), he would have tried to take into account the infant's close relationships. To do so, he would have had to recontextualize the infant, from a solitary thinking individual mostly fascinated by a world of objects that have to be explored, to an interactive being already using his or her cognitive skills and capacities to adapt to a social world composed of enculturated and communicating human peers and adults (Feldman, 1992).

Thus, Piaget's fate in contemporary infant psychology is somewhat ironic. After a brief period of paradigmatic domination in the early 1960s, his theory became the target of repeated assaults from the discoverers of the "competent infant," who challenged his vision of a gradual, integrated, and rather slow development during the sensorimotor period. Nowadays, as illustrated by the neo-Piagetian current of thought, a new trend seems to emerge, rediscovering the richness and usefulness of Piaget's ideas and perspectives (see Chandler & Chapman, 1991). It is as if a new generation of researchers interested in various aspects of infant development, including the relationships between the infant and his or her human environment, were realizing that the gain in abandoning Piaget would be much smaller than the loss.

ACKNOWLEDGMENTS

Our thanks to Dr. Noam and Dr. Fischer, who were extremely courteous in accepting the subject of this chapter despite its limited relation to the general theme of the symposium.

REFERENCES

Anisfeld, M. (1991). Neonatal imitation. *Developmental Review, 11*, 60-97.

Baillargeon, R. (1986). Representing the existence and the location of hidden objects: Object permanence in 6- and 8-month-old infants. *Cognition, 23*, 21-41.

Baillargeon, R., & DeVos, J. (1991). Object permanence in young infants: Further evidence. *Child Development, 62*, 1227-1246.

Baillargeon, R., Graber, M., DeVos, J., & Black, J. (1990). Why do young infants fail to search for hidden objects? *Cognition, 36*, 255-284.

Beilin, H. (1992). Piaget's enduring contribution to developmental psychology. *Developmental Psychology, 28*, 191-204.

Bjorklund, D.F. (1987). A note on neonatal imitation. *Developmental Review, 7*, 86-92.

Bower, T.G.R. (1967). The development of object permanence: Some studies of existence constancy. *Perception and Psychophysics, 2*, 411-418.

Bower, T.G.R. (1971). The object in the world of the infant. *Scientific American, 225*, 30-38.

Bower, T.G.R. (1974). *Development in infancy*. San Francisco: Freeman.

Bower, T.G.R., Broughton, J.M., & Moore, M.K. (1970a). Demonstration of intention in the reaching behavior of neonate humans. *Nature, 228*, 679-680.

Bower, T.G.R., Broughton, J.M., & Moore, M.K. (1970b). The coordination of visual and tactual input in infants. *Perception and Psychophysics, 8*, 51-53.

Bower, T.G.R., & Paterson, J.G. (1972). Stages in the development of the object concept. *Cognition, 1*, 47-55.

Bower, T.G.R., & Wishart, J.G. (1972). The effects of motor skill on object permanence. *Cognition, 1*, 165-172.

Bowlby, J. (1969). *Attachment and loss: Vol 1. Attachment*. London: Hogarth Press.

Bretherton, I. (1991). Intentional communication and the development of an understanding of mind. In D. Frye, & C. Moore (Eds.), *Children's theories of mind* (pp. 49-76). Hillsdale, NJ: Lawrence Erlbaum Associates.

Bretherton, I., McNew, S., & Beeghly-Smith, M. (1981). Early person knowledge as expressed in gestural and verbal communication: When do infants acquire a "theory of mind?" In M.E. Sherrod & L.R. Sherrod (Eds.), *Infant social cognition* (pp. 333-373). Hillsdale, NJ:

Lawrence Erlbaum Associates.

Bushnell, E.W. (1985). The decline of visually guided reaching during infancy. *Infant Behavior and Development, 8,* 139-155.

Case, R. (1985). *Intellectual development: Birth to adulthood.* New York: Academic Press.

Case, R. (1988). The whole child: Toward an integrated view of young children's cognitive, social and emotional development. In A.D. Pelligrini (Ed.), *Psychological bases for early education* (pp. 155-184). New York: Wiley.

Case, R. (1992). Neo-Piagetian theories of intellectual development. In H. Beilin & P.B. Pufall (Eds.), *Piaget's theory: Prospects and possibilities* (pp. 61-104). Hillsdale, NJ: Lawrence Erlbaum Associates.

Chandler, M., & Chapman, M. (1991). *Criteria for competence.* Hillsdale, NJ: Lawrence Erlbaum Associates.

Chapman, M., & Chandler, M. (1991). Foreword to further debate. In M. Chapman & M. Chandler (Eds.), *Criteria for competence* (pp. 259-265). Hillsdale, NJ: Lawrence Erlbaum Associates.

Charlesworth, W.R. (1969). The role of surprise in cognitive development. In D. Elkind & J.H. Flavell (Eds.), *Studies in cognitive development* (pp. 257-315). London: Oxford University Press.

Cichetti, D., & Beeghly, M. (Eds.). (1990). *The self in transition: Infancy to childhood.* Chicago, IL: University of Chicago Press.

Desrochers, S., Ricard, M., Gouin Décarie, T., & Allard, L. (1994). Developmental synchrony between social referencing and Piagetian sensorimotor causality. *Infant Behavior and Development, 17,* 303-319.

Diamond, A. (1991). Neuropsychological insights into the meaning of object concept development. In S. Carey & R. Gelman (Eds.), *The epigenesis of mind: Essays on biology and cognition* (pp. 67-110). Hillsdale, NJ: Lawrence Erlbaum Associates.

Feinman, S. (Ed.). (1992). *Social referencing and the social construction of reality in infancy.* New York: Plenum Press.

Feldman, C.S. (1992). The new theory of theory of mind. *Human Development, 35,* 107-117.

Fischer, K.W. (1980). A theory of cognitive development: The control and construction of hierarchies of skills. *Psychological Review, 87,* 447-531.

Fischer, K.W., & Bidell, T. (1991). Constraining nativist inferences about cognitive capacities. In S. Carey & R. Gelman (Eds.), *The epigenesis of mind: Essays on biology and cognition* (pp. 199-235). Hillsdale, NJ: Lawrence Erlbaum Associates.

Fischer, K.W., & Camfield, R.L. (1986). The ambiguity of stage and structure in behavior: Person and environment in the development of psychological structure. In I. Levin (Ed.), *Stage and structure: Reopening the debate* (pp. 246-267). New York: Plenum.

Fischer, K.W., Shaver, P.R., & Carnochan, P. (1990). How emotions develop and how they organize development. *Cognition and Emotion, 4,* 81-127.

Flavell, J.H. (1963). *The developmental psychology of Jean Piaget.* Princeton, NJ: Van Nostrand.

Fontaine, R. (1984a). Les imitations précoces: problèmes méthodologiques et théoriques [Early imitations: Methodological and theoretical issues]. *Cahiers de Psychologie Cognitive, 4,* 517-535.

Fontaine, R. (1984b). Imitative skills between birth and six months. *Infant Behavior and Development, 7,* 323-333.

Gouin Décarie, T. (1965). *Intelligence and affectivity in early childhood* (E.P. Brandt & L.W. Brandt, Trans.). New York: International Universities Press. (Original work published 1962)

Gouin Décarie, T. (1969). A study of the mental and emotional development of the thalidomide child. In B.M. Foss (Ed.), *Determinants of infant behavior* (Vol. 4, pp. 167-187). London: Methuen.

Gouin Décarie, T. (Ed.). (1974). *The infant's reaction to strangers* (J. Diamanti, Trans.). New York: International Universities Press. (Original work published 1972)

Halford, G.S. (1982). *The development of thought*. Hillsdale, NJ: Lawrence Erlbaum Associates.

Halford, G.S. (1988). A structure mapping approach to cognitive development. In A. Demetriou (Ed.), *The neo-Piagetian theories of cognitive development: Toward an integration* (pp. 103-136). Amsterdam, North Holland: Elsevier.

Halford, G.S. (1989). Reflections on 25 years of Piagetian cognitive developmental psychology. *Human Development, 32*, 325-357.

Heimann, M. (1989). Neonatal imitation, gaze aversion, and mother-infant interaction. *Infant Behavior and Development, 12*, 495-505.

Jacobson, S.W. (1979). Matching behavior in the young infant. *Child Development, 50*, 425-430.

Karmiloff-Smith, A. (1991). Beyond modularity: Innate constraints and developmental change. In S. Carey & R. Gelman (Eds.), *The epigenesis of mind: Essays on biology and cognition* (pp. 171-197). Hillsdale, NJ: Lawrence Erlbaum Associates.

Kaitz, M., Meschulach-Sarfaty, O., Auerbach, J., & Eidelman, A. (1988). A reexamination of newborns' ability to imitate facial expressions. *Developmental Psychology, 24*, 3-7.

Lamb, M.E., & Sherrod, L.R. (Eds.). (1981). *Infant social cognition*. Hillsdale, NJ: Lawrence Erlbaum Associates.

Landau, B., Spelke, E.S., & Gleitman, H. (1984). Spatial knowledge in a young blind child. *Cognition, 16*, 225-260.

Lecompte, G.K., & Gratch, G. (1972). Violation of a rule as a method of diagnosing infants' level of object concept. *Child Development, 43*, 385-396.

Leslie, A.M. (1986). Getting development off the ground: Modularity and the infant's perception of causality. In P.L.C. van Geert (Ed.), *Theory building in developmental psychology* (pp. 405-437). North-Holland: Elsevier.

Leslie, A.M. (1988). Some implications of pretense mechanisms underlying the child's theory of mind. In J.W. Astington, P.L. Harris, & D.R. Olson (Eds.), *Developing theories of mind* (pp. 19-46). New York: Cambridge University Press.

Lucksinger, K.L., Cohen, L.B., & Madole, K.L. (1992, May). *What infants infer about hidden objects and events*. Poster presented at the International Conference on Infant Studies, Miami, FL.

Maratos, O. (1973). *The origin and development of imitation in the first six months of life*. Paper presented at the meeting of the British Psychological Society, Liverpool, England.

Meltzoff, A.N. (1985). Immediate and deferred imitation in fourteen- and twenty-four-month-old infants. *Child Development, 56*, 62-72.

Meltzoff, A.N. (1988). Infant imitation and memory: Nine-month-olds in immediate and deferred tests. *Child Development, 59*, 217-225.

Meltzoff, A.N., & Moore, M.K. (1977). Imitation of facial and manual gestures by human neonates. *Science, 198*, 75-78.

Meltzoff, A.N., & Moore, M.K. (1979). Interpreting "imitative" responses in early infancy. *Science, 205*, 217-219.

Meltzoff, A.N., & Moore, M.K. (1983). Newborn infants imitate adult facial gestures. *Child Development, 54*, 702-705.

Meltzoff, A.N., & Moore, M.K. (1985). Cognitive foundations and social functions of imitation and intermodal representation in infancy. In J. Mehler & R. Fox (Eds.), *Neonate cognition: Beyond the blooming, buzzing confusion* (pp. 139-156). Hillsdale, NJ: Lawrence Erlbaum Associates.

Meltzoff, A.N., & Moore, M.K. (1989). Imitation in newborn infants: Exploring the range of gestures imitated and the underlying mechanisms. *Developmental Psychology, 25*, 954-962.

Meltzoff, A.N., & Moore, M.K. (1994). Imitation, memory, and the representation of person.

Infant Behavior & Development, 17, 83-99.

Montangero, J. (1991). A constructivist framework for understanding early and late-developing psychological competencies. In M. Chandler & M. Chapman (Eds.), *Criteria for competence* (pp. 111-129). Hillsdale, NJ: Lawrence Erlbaum Associates.

Moore, M.K., Borton, R., & Darby, B. (1978). Visual tracking in young infants: Evidence for object identity or object permanence? *Journal of Experimental Child Psychology, 25,* 183-198.

Moore, M.K., & Clark, D.E. (1975, April). *Piaget's stage IV error: An identity theory interpretation.* Paper presented at the meeting of the Society for Research in Child Development, Denver, CO.

Moore, M.K., & Myers, G.D. (1975, April). *The development of object permanence from visual tracking to total hidings: Two new stages.* Paper presented at the meeting of the Society for Research in Child Development, Denver, CO.

Mounoud, P. (1986). Similarities between developmental sequences at different age periods. In I. Levin (Ed.), *Stage and structure: Reopening the debate* (pp. 40-58). New York: Plenum.

Nadel, J. (1986). *Imitation et communication entre jeunes enfants* [Imitation and communication among infants]. Paris: Presses Universitaires de France.

Nadel, J. (1988). L'imitation immédiate: Introduction [Immediate imitation: An introduction]. *Psychologie Française, 33,* 3-4.

Pascual-Leone, J., & Johnson, J. (1991). The psychological unit and its role in task analysis: A reinterpretation of object permanence. In M. Chandler & M. Chapman (Eds.), *Criteria for competence* (pp. 153-187). Hillsdale, NJ: Lawrence Erlbaum Associates.

Piaget, J. (1932). *The moral judgment of the child* (M. Gabain, Trans.). London: Routledge & Kegan Paul. (Original work published 1932)

Piaget, J. (1951). *Play, dreams, and imitation in childhood* (C. Gattagno & F.M. Hodgson, Trans.). New York: Norton. (Original work published 1945)

Piaget, J. (1952). *The origins of intelligence in children* (M. Cook, Trans.). New York: International Universities Press. (Original work published 1936)

Piaget, J. (1954). *The construction of reality in the child* (M. Cook, Trans.). New York: Basic Books. (Original work published 1937)

Piaget, J. (1954). *Les relations entre l'affectivité et l'intelligence dans le développement mental de l'enfant* [Relationship between intelligence and affectivity in the child's mental development]. Paris: "Les cours de Sorbonne," Centre de documentation universitaire.

Piaget, J. (1960). The general problems of the psychobiological development of the child. In J.M. Tanner & B. Inhelder (Eds.), *Discussions on child development* (pp. 3-27). New York: International Universities Press.

Piaget, J. (1967). *Études sociologiques* [Sociological studies]. Geneva: Droz.

Piaget, J. (1968). Le point de vue de Piaget [Piaget's point of view]. *International Journal of Psychology, 3*(4), 281-299.

Piaget, J. (1970). Piaget's theory. In K. Mussen (Ed.), *Carmichael's child psychology* (pp. 703-732). New York: Wiley.

Piaget, J. (1972a, February 11). Piaget now. Part 1 (Piaget in discussion with B. Hill). *Times Ed. Supp.,* p. 19.

Piaget, J. (1972b, February 18). Piaget now. Part 2 (Piaget in discussion with B. Hill). *Times Ed. Supp.,* p. 19.

Piaget, J. (1972c, February 25). Piaget now. Part 3 (Piaget in discussion with B. Hill). *Times Ed. Supp.,* p. 21.

Piaget, J. (1976). *Le comportement, moteur de l'évolution* [Behavior, the motor of evolution]. Paris: Gallimard.

Piaget, J. (1981). *Intelligence and affectivity: Their relationship during child development* (T.A. Brown & C.E. Kaegi, Ed. & Trans). Palo Alto, CA: Annual Reviews. (Original work published 1954)

Piaget, J., & Inhelder, B. (1966). *La psychologie de l'enfant* [Child psychology]. Paris: Presses universitaires de France.

Pinard, A., & Laurendeau, M. (1969). "Stage" in Piaget's cognitive-developmental theory: Exegesis of a concept. In D. Elkind & J.H. Flavell (Eds.), *Studies in cognitive development* (pp. 121-170). London: Oxford University Press.

Ramsay, D., & Campos, J.J. (1975). Memory by the infant in an object notion task. *Developmental Psychology, 11*, 411-412.

Ricard, M. (1983). L'identité de l'objet chez le jeune enfant [Object identity in infants]. (Monographie 9). *Archives de psychologie, 51*, 261-325.

Ricard, M., Gouin Décarie, T., Desrochers, S., & Rome-Flanders, T. (1994). From cold-blooded cognition to social cognitive development. In A. Vyt, H. Bloch, & M.H. Bornstein (Eds.), *Early child development in the French tradition: Contributions from current research* (pp. 103-117). Hillsdale, NJ: Lawrence Erlbaum Associates.

Schuberth, R.E. (1983). The infant's search for objects: Alternatives to Piaget's theory of object concept development. In L.P. Lipsitt & C.K. Rovee-Collier (Eds.), *Advances in infancy research* (Vol. 2, pp. 137-182). Norwood, NJ: Ablex.

Spelke, E. (1991). Physical knowledge in infancy: Reflections on Piaget's theory. In S. Carey & R. Gelman (Eds.), *The epigenesis of mind: Essays on biology and cognition* (pp. 133-169). Hillsdale, NJ: Lawrence Erlbaum Associates.

Stern, D. (1985). *The interpersonal world of the infant.* New York: Basic Books.

Vinter, A. (1985). *L'imitation chez le nouveau-né: Imitation, représentation et mouvement dans les premiers mois de la vie* [Infant imitation: Imitation, representation, and movement in the first months of life]. Neuchâtel: Delachaux et Niestlé.

Vinter, A. (1986). The role of movement in eliciting early imitations. *Child Development, 57*, 66-71.

Wellman, H.M. (1990). *The child's theory of mind.* Cambridge, MA: MIT Press.

Wellman, H.M. (1993). Early understanding of mind: The normal case. In S. Baron-Cohen, H. Tager-Flusberg, & D. Cohen (Eds.), *Understanding other minds: Perspectives from autism* (pp. 10-39). Oxford: Oxford University Press.

Wellman, H.M., & Gelman, A.S. (1992). Cognitive development: Foundational theories of care domains. *Annual Review of Psychology, 43*, 337-375.

Youniss, J., & Damon, W. (1992). Social construction in Piaget's theory. In H. Beilin & P.B. Pufall (Eds.), *Piaget's theory: Prospects and possibilities* (pp. 267-286). Hillsdale, NJ: Lawrence Erlbaum Associates.

Zazzo, R. (1957). Le problème de l'imitation chez le nouveau-né [The problem of imitation in the newborn]. *Enfance, 10*, 135-142.

Zazzo, R. (1988). Janvier 1945: Découverte de l'imitation néo-natale? [January 1945: The discovery of neonatal imitation?] *Psychologie Française, 33*, 5-9.

III Construction of Vulnerabilities and Strengths in Relationships

6 Reconceptualizing Maturity: The Search for Deeper Meaning

Gil G. Noam
Harvard University

> *A person remains wise as long as he searches for wisdom. As soon as he thinks he has found wisdom, he becomes a fool.*
>
> — Talmud

> *In much wisdom is much grief, and she who increases knowledge, increases sorrow.*
>
> — Ecclesiastes

By means of radical thought, deep intuition, or exemplary actions, men and women throughout the ages challenged the idea that the exemplary life necessitates supporting a flawed world. They were searchers dedicated not only to overcoming the social ills that surrounded them, but to their personal contributions to them. Their critique simultaneously attended to problematic external conditions, and required honest recognition of the self's reluctance hesitations to live a deeper, committed, and — I hesitate to introduce the overused term — *wise life.*

This broadened perspective of self and world has not lost its actuality. It usually occurs as a result of many crises; and it carries no guarantee of ending in a state of equilibrated harmony. Shakespeare's tragic portrayal of old age and declining power is a powerful example. Confronted with the deterioration of his body, the break-up of his kingdom, and the loss of control over his family, Lear realized that his psychological world was shattering. King Lear experienced a devastation never deemed possible to him before, but known to many who try to hand over their world to the next generation. For Lear, loss and aging became synonymous with despondency and destruction. His break-down of family relationships and meaning do not provide us with hope of a new developmental constellation; rather, they expose a hard rhythm of meaning found and meaning lost. Relationships can be severed for the duration and reclaiming insight and love in deeper form does not offer a comforting alternative. Lear's blindness represents an encompassing void: lack of vision, insight, and future. He provides the nightmarish archetype of all who age, the shattering of the foundations of existence without a further chance to reconstitute.

But in its bleakness, Shakespeare's Lear provides us with only one outcome when many are possible. In fact, this story has many counterstories: the freedom that sets in when person and power become less closely identified; the discovery both of what is essential when stifling conventions can be transcended and also of an expanded ability to love despite overwhelming losses.

The German writer–philosopher Lessing has given us such a different, equally timeless story in "Nathan der Weise," for whom adulthood also posed devastating dilemmas. Nathan, a Jew in multicultural Jerusalem, lost his wife and six children in an uprising. Ready to give himself over to hate and revenge, instead he chose the route of mourning, acceptance and life-affirming wisdom. Nathan had to revisit his past, however, when about to lose his much beloved adopted daughter — a daughter of Christians, adopted after the murder of his family. But his principled stance, coupled with his capacity for love, won out for Nathan against the bigoted world that surrounded him. In the classical Greek tradition, Lessing's moral of a universal acceptance of cultural and religious differences goes hand in hand with a paradigm of enlightened self-knowledge and is summarized in Lessing's notion: "Human, learn to recognize yourself, that is the center of wisdom."

King Lear and Nathan the Wise are entirely different accounts, told in different centuries, cultures, and languages. And yet, they present us with two basic experiences about adulthood and aging, two — in this case male — experiential poles that demarcate a developmental space that is further explored in this chapter.

The developmental drama at the endpoint of the life span has engaged many generations of psychologists and psychotherapists. Like none other, Erikson described the life cycle's telos as wisdom in full recognition of human frailty and mortality. In the final stage of the epigenetic cycle, "Integrity versus Despair," he views wisdom as a virtue and an affirmation of the life as it was lived. This positive outlook is now embedded in a more general acceptance of life's continuities, even in the face of one's ultimate departure. Before him, Jung, an early explorer of the transcendent psychological meaning in therapy, provided another adult-developmental focus. The first half of life creates a preoccupation with the external world, on learning about how the world works and gaining some control over it. Only after midlife, Jung observed, do we truly turn to the internal self, the reflection and experience of ever deepening layers of inner meaning. These higher reaches of development are built on a greater commitment to unconscious processes and spirituality and the acknowledgment of the shadow side of one's personality what Jung called the embracing of one's anima and animus. Erikson and Jung thus remind us that aging is accompanied not only by the prevalent losses of abilities and health, significant relationships, and power over institutions, but also by the opportunities for deepened insight, wisdom, freer relationships, and self-acceptance.

The search and struggle described in this chapter are not as precisely located within the last phases of the life span, as they were for Erikson and Jung. Many aged persons do not really care to enter the depth of exploration, and many younger people are drawn to an amazingly profound reflection about life, self, and meaning. Of course, continued life experience and the nearing of death present the person with great opportunities to transcend rigidities of daily living and to evolve playful spontaneity and undefensive reflection. But the burdens of experience, the losses and tragedies and the proven neurobiological decline can all combine to produce premature closure, a preoccupation with times past, and a deadly lack of curiosity. In contrast, special sensitivities and life circumstances can create much earlier in life a deep inner space, integrative reflective capacities and surprising maturity in relationships and social commitments.[1]

Most developmental models, whether they are age or stage related, posit great maturity at the end of the sequence of growth. The lofty ideas used to provide a developmental utopia are aspired by many and achieved by few. We continue to have few convincing definitions of the most evolved forms of development. However, a break-down of the old "typical" forms of adaptation is sufficiently advanced (e.g., changes in gender definitions, parent–child roles, etc.) that the establishment of new, more flexible, inclusive and more generally applicable ideas have to be put forward. Thus, our theoretical foundation is not solid, clinical cases are few, and empirical research is sparse. Creative speculation, however, is quite evolved. We find in most developmental theories an ill-defined, yet generally observed combination of high reflective abilities, impressive perspective-taking and

---

[1]In a very interesting set of studies, Baltes and his colleagues (e.g., Baltes & Smith, 1990) found that wisdom, defined and measured, was the only psychological capacity that did not decline in old age. He and his colleagues claimed that it could also be found in younger and middle aged adults.

deepened sense of commitment. For most theorists, these capacities resolve the basic conflicts and splits that are addressed throughout this book. A picture is painted of tolerance and self-acceptance (e.g., Loevinger, 1976), universal moral imperative (e.g., Kohlberg, 1984), postnarcissistic empathy and wisdom (Kohut, 1977), and a general spiritual dimension in human relationships (e.g., Fowler, 1981; Jung, 1966). To clarify this general point, I turn to Loevinger's (1976) ego development model and introduce the ways she views the highest stages. We could choose most of the existing psychosocial theories of development and, despite their differences, uncover very similar issues.

The most mature stages of ego development, the meaning frames used to understand and orient to self and world, are called the autonomous (I 5) and integrated (I 6) stages. The person has attributes of "courage to cope with conflict," abilities to view reality in complex and multifaceted ways, and to integrate ideas that seem contradictory. Furthermore, the person shows a great degree of tolerance for ambiguity, recognizes interdependence and "will cherish personal ties as among his most precious values" (p. 23). The person expresses his or her feelings vividly, and convincingly, including the manifold sensual experiences.

Similarly, most psychologists who describe complex development, also referred to as "postformal operations," use such attributes as transformational, dynamic, flexible and committed (Basseches, 1984; Perry, 1976). Labouvie-Vief, a creative scholar of adult development, described that "historical change and contextual diversity are valued, resulting in an open flexibility tempered by responsibility and self-reflection" (Labouvie-Vief, Hakim-Larson, & Hobart, 1987). To be fair to Loevinger, Labouvie-Vief, and all the other innovative developmental theorists, we have to know that they do not remain naive to the existence of serious problems even at levels where broad perspective, flexibility, and tolerance are present. But we are not discussing here theorists' complex knowledge about human nature, but their models, definitions and descriptions of development. Being integrated and split, wise and rigid, insightful and simplistic, are typical contradictions, even at complex levels that remain outside most developmental perspectives. We need to end idealizing the self's complexity, the linear movement from limited ability to great capacity, and instead focus on the continued struggles between strengths and weaknesses to the end of life.

Let us consider a more realistic and conflictual person: What if we remind ourselves that even the wisest people with their broad perspectives partake in a highly fragmented social system and their life courses reflect, and internally even enlarge these divisions and contradictions? I believe that we emerge with a deeper picture where vision and ideal, tolerance and perspective are not bereft of their counterparts: loss of courage and nihilism, rigidity of character, lack of creativity, and so on. In fact, we can empirically expect typical tensions between vulnerability and development since many people who have experienced difficult life histories are the ones who are propelled to greater wisdom and deeper meaning. In other words, suffering is frequently the initiator of development, but development is not necessarily the healer of suffering!

SELF-REPRESENTATIONS AND RELATIONSHIPS

In this section, many dimensions of mature self-representations that also span a wide range of developmental domains are addressed. I do not assume that all of them are synchronized, following the same path of development and becoming integrated in each individual. Some people will experience a strong process-orientation but will not frame their struggles in terms of creativity. Others will focus little on their own individuality and be far more interested in political and social commitments. Discussed here are a variety of psychological arenas where the new developmental construction can be expressed. Thus, I describe developmental possibilities that now have a good chance to occur when stimulated, not inevitable outcomes of an inner logic of growth.

Questioning Unity: Contradiction and Process

Researchers have shown that cognitively, the person can now move beyond dualistic, and single abstractions to a dynamic, contradictory, and dialectic constructions of reality (e.g., Commons, Richards, & Armon, 1984; Fischer & Ayoub, chapter 7, this volume; King, Kitchner, Wood, & Davidson, 1989). This understanding also opens to new possibilities for the development of self and personality. Earlier in development the essence of self-representation is organized through an attempt at logic, unity, and a cohesive biographical narrative. Because self and personality even then resist too much unity, overcontrol and rigidity become the way to deal with the constant threat of disunity, experienced as disorganization. This struggle between order and disorder has fundamentally shifted now. Motion and change, Basseches (1984) found in his study of "dialectical thinkers," is viewed as basic to the nature of knowledge. This leads to an affirmation of an everchanging self that coincides with a critique of stagnation in personality development. Not to achieve totality of self or cohesiveness in life plans does not necessarily represent failure anymore. Unity is seen in much more human terms: One can strive for it, but never fully realize it.

Many people I have interviewed remember back and experience themselves as having been too intellectualized and far too preoccupied with consistency and clear life trajectories. These preoccupations are now suspiciously interpreted as too close to a totalitarian attempt by the self to control and punish. Self-unity is further evaluated as an obsessive pursuit of a fragile self. Instead, the self is seen to be continuously in flux, and there is a realization of many possibilities of who the self can be and can become, not just an established identity, created in adolescence and fixed for life. Broughton (1978) labeled this phenomenon as *identity always in crisis*—an intelligent play of words with Erikson's "identity crisis." Crisis, even when painful and disorganizing, now creates less of a threat since the person views it as growth-promoting.

This orientation potentially frees the person from a perspective on life full of possessions, including the idea of possessing the self and significant relationships. The new world view, instead, introduces greater valence of being, not having, a distinction Fromm (1976) so eloquently described in his late work entitled *To Have or to Be*. He criticized the "having" mode of the industrialized world and introduces "being" as the ethically more mature and psychologically healthier style. In his exposé of a "new person" in a humanistic society, he included as essential attributes the transformation of narcissism and greed and the development of mature love based on a sense of continuous evolution of personality. For Fromm, only this idea of being, living in the moment, and recognizing our human potentials and limitations, has a chance of producing freedom and protecting life-negating rigidities. Gaining more flexibility from preoccupations with self, from the limitations imposed by control, achievement, status, and prestige also provides a new rhythm in life, a more detached and simultaneously more vital space in which those painful life themes that have organized biography can be readdressed.

Fromm's ideas regarding a continuously emerging sense of being correspond with my own ideas of development. His perspective, however, becomes developmentally naive when he claims this mode to be preferable for every person, despite the fact that his prescriptions necessitate highly evolved perspectives on human nature and social responsibility. What are the developmental preconditions for people to create such a self-mode? And don't individuals have to go through periods of owning themselves, needing to possess, circumscribe and categorize—essential developmental accomplishments earlier in development? But Fromm presented us with the important conviction that we need to move beyond the illusion that possessing unity and organization produce true identity.

Instead, the representation of continuous evolution of the self, while threatening stability and constancy, often leads to questioning of the very existence of "self." What exists with greater lucidity for the person is a unique set of experiences and a commitment to "being" now subordinated under an even broader, and more developmental category of "becoming."

That sense of process gains greatest prominence, far greater than any static-seeming concept of unity, selfhood or role identity.

Beyond Control: Intuition and Spontaneity

The person derives little satisfaction from playing social roles or following conventions for convention's sake; they are viewed as stifling the potential for self-realization and exploration. Earlier preoccupation with social norms and control (even when they were rejected), are now superseded by the ideals of intuition, spontaneity, and creative expression. The person wants to create an openness to the world and to relationships, highly textured and complex representing simultaneously a return to childhood perceptions, only to "know them for the first time," as T.S. Eliot so poignantly put it. An openness toward new experiencing that changes the self, secretly hoped for all along, now becomes a real possibility. This powerful—and romantic—notion is found throughout the literature on the higher systems of experience and consciousness (e.g., Maslow, 1970, 1982). We find in these writings an idealistic and pure notion of an inherently good potential in human nature that will find its own unique expression. But even when one remains more skeptical about these possibilities we can witness the emergence of the idea that discovery is more important than control and that it can also bring an unknown sense of movement and joy.

A recent extension of this point of view is found in Csikszentmihalyi's (1990) widely acclaimed book *Flow*. This manifesto for a new perception provides a great variety of examples of how a process-focus creates new concentration and excitement of life. Through these examples he makes the case that process (or flow) represents a primary force by which we should live. Similarly to Fromm before him, he points out that this attitude helps overcome our preoccupations with outcome, production, and achievement.

At every point in development we find great tensions between different thoughts, desires, wishes, and passions, but now we find that ambiguity and contradiction of different strivings are accepted as essential ingredients of life. This stance, formulated theoretically sounds like this: I do not have to hold two sides of my self and tolerate the ambivalence that derives from them, but I make the very nature of the different desires and the ambiguity it creates the essence of who I am. Thus, fewer decisions are necessary, less closure is demanded. Earlier, the self felt threatened by the difficulties of making choices, and indecision was seen as the main enemy of the efficient and production-oriented self. But now the need for obsessive achievement is being criticized, if not ridiculed. In work and love the person tries to realize the inner nature of freedom, spontaneity, and nonconformity.

Universality and Uniqueness

The developmental accomplishments are relevant in terms of both universality and uniqueness. As the person can overcome self-preoccupations, she can become engrossed in the world and develop an appreciation of being part of a universal experience and commitment of being human. A number of contributors to adult development have given names to this phenomenon. Erikson, for example, observed a move from a time bound to an "all-human and existential identity," Jung observed a transition from ego absorption to a self-transcending consensus.

Interestingly this view of the self as communal, defined by its participation in universal experiences comes with strengthened recognition that no self is like another self. Every experience lives in the moment and can only be found in the very unique world of one person. Knowing the world becomes less abstract and removed and more personal. This personal, contextual and historic aspect of individual experience appears in many developmental accounts (e.g., Edelstein & Noam, 1982; King et al., 1989; Labouvie-Vief et al., 1987). This tension between "self overcome" and "self found" makes this developmental level especially interesting: We observe extreme relativism, expressed also in tolerance toward others as every person is experienced as different, pursuing his or her specific ideas and ideals; and at the same time we can often observe an unbending commitment towards the universality of human experience and suffering, the need to engage in overarching causes, and the pursuit of basic principles (e.g., of nonviolence). Maybe the person can be so very relativistic because he or she is steeped in basic and general principles such as justice, fairness, empathy.

True Self–False Self

The commitment to one's own experience, both in the moment, in times past, and in future times relates to another important issue: The need to be true to oneself, as well as to ones' relationships and causes. Much written about yet elusive, the true self consists of a set of feelings that indicate cognitive, emotional, moral, or spiritual authenticity. This need for personal truthfulness, of course, is present since childhood, but it now moves to center stage as a conscious, yet not intellectualized preoccupation. The person at this developmental level knows that often what one is and lives ends up revealing the self.

Clinically, Winnicott (1958, 1965) wrote most insightfully about the distinction between true and false self. Despite the fact that he did not present a worked-out framework, and instead shared observations and ideas in a few short papers, the continued use of his ideas demonstrates that he captured a very relevant set of issues. Winnicott anchored the true self in creativity, spontaneity, and a feeling of reality: "The spontaneous gesture is the True Self in action. Only the true self can be creative and only the true self can feel real. Whereas the true self feels real, the existence of a false self results in a feeling unreal or a sense of futility" (p. 148). Winnicott further connected the true self to a sense of aliveness and living in one's body, experiencing the soma. For Winnicott, the true self gets formed extremely early in life. He stated: "The true self appears as soon as there is any mental organization of the individual at all, and it means little more than the summation of sensori-motor aliveness" (p. 149).

Although Winnicott described the true self mostly as an outgrowth of early development, the examples of false self tend to be of later ages. This should not surprise, as Winnicott viewed the false self as socialized, emerging from inept parenting and other environmental influences that create a compliant self. The false self hides the true self creating an intellectualized mind that becomes dissociated from the body. Winnicott wrote:

> The world may observe academic success of a high degree, and may find it hard to believe in the very real distress of the individual concerned, who feels "phoney" the more he or she is successful. When such individuals destroy themselves in one way or another, instead of fulfilling promise, this invariably produces a sense of shock in those who have developed high hopes of the individual. (p. 144)

Falseness does not only alienates the self from itself, but also from the transitional space where play and fantasy reside. In Winnicott's theory, the adult experiences this space through a participation in "culture," where symbols evolve. A consequence of the false self is the inability to enter this space, because of preoccupation, lack of concentration, and the inability to creatively loose oneself. Winnicott's unwavering commitment to the self that remains spontaneous, creative and alive is impressive. It is not hard, however, to detect a romantic, Roussauean ideal of the good inherent forces of the person and the bad influences of socialization. This belief in the child's original vitality, also contributes to locating the true self developmentally so early.

Interestingly, although the development of a true self might be related to very early experiences, the preoccupation with its existence and the program to recapture it, is a relatively late occurrence in development. The great dilemma in later development is that although living a "true life" becomes essential, people can only feel when they are being real and true to themselves, but they do not reflectively know how to be real. In fact, any attempt to get closer to an experience of true self through a process of thinking undermines the very process one pursues. Furthermore, the full recognition of relativity in human experience makes it impossible to have someone else define the true self. If someone else, even a therapist, were to try a definition, it would not be a true self anymore, nor would it create a chance to evolve it.

This represents a crucial difference to other times in development, when will, intellect, and individual decisiveness were seen as superior organizers of the self than emotions, intuitions, and a basic recognition of desires. For that reason, the person can now, as never before develop a "co-equal" relationship between thoughts and feelings. The thoughts become dynamic, human, and deepen to insight, the feelings are taken seriously as signs about the validity of reflection and thinking and often serve as guides toward deeper discoveries. In the process, the very distinction between the cognitive and the emotional domains ceases to be too useful, as the intertwining can become almost complete. In the study of wisdom, related to our topic here, a variety of researchers also stress the essential integration of thought, feeling, and experience (e.g., Fischer & Ayoub, chapter 7, this volume; Pascual Leone, 1989). The powerful abilities to make cognition emotional and feelings reflective has profound implications for the inner experience and the pursuit of a vital, true self.

Before we found a conflict between the person's inner self (often not even recognized any more because one lives too far removed from it) and the social role the self has to play. But now a figure–ground shift is occurring, where living a life true to one's inner nature and self-chosen principles comes first, and social roles need to be in the service of these goals. Living estranged from one's direct and nonintellectualized experiential roots creates enormous suffering to the imprisoned self. Even under the strict rules of self-negation most people retain a sense that important aspect of the personality have gotten lost on the way. But the person has few tools available to remedy the situation, especially because many aspects of the self that need to be found (e.g., feeling vulnerable, open, etc.) are viewed as weaknesses and their pursuit as self-indulgent. This combination of estrangement and rejection of the potential remedies produces the prisonlike tightness of the self discussed before. With interest the person begins to explore the ways the strangled and lonely self feels — for example, like the child once did in an authoritarian family. Pursuing a sense of vitality is not viewed as indulgent any more. Theoretically, at no point in development do we find as clear a need to extend the highly generalized and cognitive ideas of Piaget and introduce a person with an inner, experiential self and a biographical life.

Unconscious Processes

The process-orientation helps people become more tolerant toward those aspects of the self and relationships that remain mysterious and unknown.

Not everything has to be clarified and follows explicit roles. Thus, persons develop new and deeper appreciation of myths, symbols, and dreams as intuitive forms that support our imaginations but defy full understanding. By now it is accepted that the self can only capture some aspects of reality, which further supports the knowledge of the limitation of the controlling self.

The sense of being, so much part of a constructing person, is lost when we classify the categories of knowing without the personal meanings of the individual. Intrapsychically, the limits of our knowledge are experienced as a vast reservoir of experience that is a part of us and even guides us and yet is never fully comprehended by the actor. This appreciation of the depth of human experience makes these people often open toward spiritual meanings and religious interpretations of experience. Rarely preoccupied with the specifics of religious dogma, spirituality for them is a process of discovering deep, and personally important metaphors. Of course spirituality can exist at any point in life—or it can never become part of a person's meaning system—but now everyday life is often framed in moral and spiritual form.

A most important development is the shift from seeing unconscious motivation as an enemy of the self where understanding produces control to a set of processes that should, wherever possible, be joined and seen as an enhancement of life. Thus, strict boundaries between conscious preoccupations and unconscious motivations become far less important and worth fighting for than before. The vision is broader, and it includes the previously hidden, the shameful and irrational as known aspects of the human condition and the self. Another way of putting this issue is that the self is far less defensive and open to experiencing the contradictions between stated desires and the ingeniously elaborated possibilities to undermine them.

As we now turn to the continuous risks and serious vulnerabilities that many people at this developmental position have to endure, an even richer yet torn inner and interpersonal world will emerge.

VULNERABILITY AND RISK

When the strengths combine to produce so many new possibilities in development—flexibility and motion, self-transcendence and deepened relationships and so on—why do we have to deal with risks and vulnerabilities? Wisdom, certainly is and should be almost exclusively described in terms of human strengths, and developmental achievements. For that reason Henry Thoreau could say that "It is characteristic of wisdom not to do desperate things," a statement we would today couch in more technical language: Wisdom represents mostly a "protective factor." To be nominated to a study of wise individuals is as honorable as being sought out for advice by significant decision-makers. Yet, deepened insight and commitments can be deadly dangerous, as we can witness in history from Socrates to Gandhi and from Galileo to Martin Luther King.

From the Bible and early Greeks to the 19th century, philosophers have idealized wisdom and insight, yet have reminded us of the story that its very pursuit led to man's expulsion from paradise. Another, more psychological versions of this idea is the saying that "Man is always the victim of his truths." Into this multifaceted statement we read a great many interpretations. Important for our discussion now is the idea that we are not only the active searchers of truth, but that knowledge finds us, it shapes our outlook and produces realities that are not entirely in our control. Tragedies are built around such an idea. That we can become victims of our truths speaks to the idea that insight can also represent a risk factor. Our truths are liberating but at some other level they can create more complex labyrinths. Are we strong enough to endure the full weight of this truth? What if not?

This section discusses how the new capacities are coupled, like earlier in development, with significant problems, breakdowns, and dysfunctions. Personal and interpersonal vulnerabilities usually do not play the same encompassing role now as earlier in development. But it is the people who have difficult life experiences or traumas to work out, such as migration far from their places of origin, imprisonment in camps, witnessing of war, or the horror of familial abuse, who are often pushed toward these complex forms of development not despite but because of the suffering in their lives. Few therapists have had to deal with this problem as directly and tragically as Victor Frankl. In his famous account of life in a Nazi concentration camp, he told of a moment of special despondency in the group of prisoners and the need to address them:

> Then I spoke of the many opportunities of giving life a meaning. I told my comrades (who lay motionless, although occasionally a sigh could be heard) that human life, under any circumstances, never ceases to have a meaning, and that this infinite meaning of life includes suffering and dying, privation and death. I asked the poor creatures who listened to me attentively in the darkness of the hut to face up to the seriousness of our position. They must not lose hope but should keep their courage in the certainty that the hopelessness of our struggle did not detract from its dignity and its meaning. (Frankl, 1985).

Throughout *Man's Search for Meaning*, Frankl made the convincing argument that the sustaining and developing of meaning, even under the most unimaginable of conditions, is the key to psychological survival. The very traumas, splits, and alienations form the backdrop against which this development can occur, but development does not necessarily heal the internal manifestations of these tragedies. But we know astonishingly little about this dialectic between pain and evolved insight and meaning.

All the strengths described before are now enhanced by an uncanny clarity of vision and a razorlike ability to cut to the essence. What one finds, without the soothing tools of self-deception, is often unbearable despite all the acceptance of self and world. Memories and present experiences can be less bearable than when insight was clouded. Among the many manifestations of serious conflict and problems, I choose four that I have observed most frequently and that represent basic configurations in development: (a) the tension between character rigidity and the newly created process-orientation; (b) the desperation that comes with the lack of creative expression; (c) the tenacity of life themes that now can become more, not less painful; and (d) the loss of meaning in relationship to suicidality. I exemplify the vulnerabilities with clinical experiences, to provide simultaneously a window on the clinical-developmental process.

Character Rigidity and Developmental Process

The idea that character is fixed and cannot be greatly transformed beyond midlife was Freud's conviction and has remained controversial ever since. Freud even went so far as to discourage psychoanalysis for those beyond 40 as he was convinced that their personalities were too set to benefit from treatment. This position has been abandoned by a subsequent generation of analysts and therapists who noticed considerable potential for change during all periods of life. We now know that new developmental potential described in the previous section bears the potential to transform character: to let go, to loosen up, to overcome obsessive and compulsive ruminations and narcissistic ambitions. One paradox of aging lies in this experience: People can become more set in their ways, even "petrified" if unchallenged and at the same time they can gain a broader perspective from which previous rigidity of character can be confronted.

From this new vantage point — again not necessarily a matter of age alone as we find serious rigidity in younger people and great flexibility in older ones — it is especially frustrating to witness one's own character limitations. Not surprisingly, we find greater self-acceptance even of problematic aspects of self, but heightened pain sets in that the overall process-orientation (the self as becoming, rather than being) does not translate to all aspects of one's personality. In contrast to the experienced possibilities of a freer self, the rigidities become ever more difficult to bear. The character limitations, such as excessive stinginess and withholding, chronic preoccupations and narcissistic rage, now stand in direct confrontation with some of the ideals, motivations, and goals that mark this new developmental world. The conflict can create a tremendous despair and a tragic sense of living against one's inner nature, removed from one's creative potential.

The clinical theorists from the diverse psychoanalytic traditions[2] all share in one important distinction that has come to be known as *syntonic* and *dystonic* character development. Syntonic character refers to an acceptance by the person of the basic mode of operating in the world. The sociopath, for example, who generates a whole set of negative responses from people and institutions yet does not think anything to be wrong; or the narcissist who unempathically devalues others, yet thinks it to be their problem to not live up to his or her expectations. What should provide these types with motivation for change? This syntonic style predicts less potential to change than does dystonic character where a discrepancy can be found between how things are and should be (e.g., Vaillant, 1977).

The dystonic character suffers from his or her actions, wants to change at times, recognizes some implication of the self, yet is trapped in a basic mode of adaptation. The question of how some people shift from a syntonic to a dystonic character style has not generated sufficient interest, given how important it is for diagnosis and treatment of all character disorders. When we view character as developing in early childhood and retaining its unbending form throughout life, later entry points into the "character armor" (Reich, 1972) remain unacknowledged or fail to generate a great deal of hope.

The shift is, interestingly, not one of character, but of a way of knowing and evaluating. We can observe an emerging contradiction where consciousness and ideals come to oppose the day-to-day forms of adapting. This, of course, is often the case: Insights can emerge long before behavior and adaptive styles undergo systematic changes. In fact, many people live with this discrepancy for long periods of their lives. But in the case of character disorders or rigid character neurosis it is essential to produce these discrepancies in development as a way to transform character. With new insight, character that was syntonic can become dystonic. The shift leads to

---

[2]For the early psychoanalytic contributors (e.g., Freud, Abraham, Jones, etc.), character was a configuration of behaviors, symptoms, and defenses of early fixations of sexual and aggressive drive (libido). For Wilhelm Reich, these fixations transformed into automatic patterns that become independent of the earlier conflicts. Psychoanalytic ego psychology (Hartmann, Kris, Klein, Erikson, etc.) then freed character from the very close focus on early sexuality, a line of work that culminated in Shapiro's (1965) monograph on neurotic styles, viewed as persistent forms of adaptation and dysfunction. From a developmental point of view, the fixated character traits or neurotic styles are made up of a complex mixture of character traits that reach far back into childhood, and developmental accomplishment that one can expect to change in the course of significant adult development.

a great deal of *inner* suffering, heightening the chances for motivated work toward change.[3]

Essential for the success of such changes is the person's interest in changing. At no time are the chances better than when the natural course of development produces a tension. The entry that now opens provides but an opportunity for a struggle, the conservative forces continue to be extremely resistant to change, but a motivation and new tools for change have now emerged, exemplified by a statement from a patient: "I cannot stand that I always react to any deadline by 'going on strike.' Then I get mad and force myself to do it. There must be other ways."

Paul T. provides us with an example and a chance to discuss these complex issues in greater depth:

> Paul T., a 60-year-old man, at home in the world of business, had undergone a meaningful psychoanalysis in his 30s and again for a year when he turned 50. He was now at a different point in his life, trying to become less preoccupied with professional accomplishment to enjoy a greater and deeper satisfaction in life. He wanted to change his ferociously competitive and critical style that had contributed to his isolation and wanted to become more accepting and giving to others. His children grown, he was trying to create a more loving relationship with his wife. But he was "bouncing" against the limitations of his unbending nature. An impulsive man, somewhat paranoid, and always ready to experience slight, he was known for his explosive outbursts. Although his previous treatments helped him decrease guilt and inhibition, they did not seem to have changed some of his character weaknesses.
>
> His interpersonal relationships, including the one with me, could be described as going from one set of verbal attacks and storming out of the office to another. This behavior was very typical in his life, always related to some sense of injustice or lack of acceptance shown to him by his peers, bosses, and subordinates. But curiously, after each one of these explosions, he was capable of a tremendous amount of perspective and empathy. In fact, he typically experienced a great deal of guilt about how he treated others when he screamed at them, behavior he also used frequently in his home.
>
> Diagnostically, the category of character disorder or even narcissistic personality disorder that he had been given in previous treatments did not quite capture the experience of being with this man who was remarkable in his

---

[3]We know that some aspects of what we traditionally have called *character*, are better called temperament, biological types that are resistant. Kagan's (1989) excellent longitudinal research has demonstrated this point with anxious children. But other aspects of character are better characterized as rigidly established coping and defense styles, which can be changed under the conditions of support and confrontation.

ability to show compassion, to be insightful, and to feel a great deal of remorse. He demonstrated even wisdom and was used by his community as a person to turn to for advice. But he was not able to apply this knowledge sufficiently to the day-to-day adaptations in his life.

Paul T. struggled with a great deal of perspective, and I mean here not only a cognitive ability to understand his own character limitations, but a deep sense of reflection and compassion, at war with impulsivity and chronic anger. The point is that this man has had many experiences that led him to be fearful, fragile toward any of the slights, unable to see that he, in fact, participated in creating the very disappointments that he most wanted to avoid. But in therapy I could not understand nor help him without focusing on the discrepancies between his rigid character and his emerging, process-oriented developmental world. Impulsive actions and explosive nature had to be always viewed in connection to this new perspective about self and human relations.

Paul T. suffered through many disappointments even during the time of his treatment. He was quite capable of tracing his rage and impulsive actions to slights from his childhood: Chronic disappointments in relationship to a distant and accomplished father, who demanded discipline and intellectual rigor from his son. Although he could be sure of his mother's love, it could not compensate for the feelings engendered in relation to the father.

Of course, it was easy to view Paul T.'s frequent rage at me, his belief that I was not truly on his side and did not see him as an equal (despite an age difference of 30 years) as a return to deep earlier hurts and primitive personality problems. But I was more struck by his continual emotional fluctuations between the warm and embracing intelligence that had a very life-affirming and wise side and a depressive, rigid, and self-centered style. Our relationship began to represent the growing capacity to let things rest, to notice how much he interfered with his wish for mutual rather than controlling relationships.

Paul T. had my full collaboration in entering his self-vulnerabilities, in joining him from slight to slight, disappointment to disappointment, rage to rage. Not only did we need to encounter in him the young boy who was so fundamentally insecure and isolated through the reawakened feelings in our relationship. In a continuous point–counterpoint similar to what we hear when we engross ourselves in classical music, the rigid theme was balanced by playfulness and dance. I am convinced, it was not the *return* to past experiences and life themes alone that made him finally become untrapped. In contrast to his earlier treatments, we could now ally ourselves with a new mental set that had emerged in development. Paul T. began to question the very essence of his psychological nature. As he began the process of recovery, the times when his self was at stake at all time decreased. He could keep his eyes on the fact that this self-importance represented a weakness in the new interpretive world in which self-transcendence and principled action independent of what others did to him gained prominence. And the strengthening process-orientation allowed him to avoid long periods of rumination; he could "move on."

This new experience provided me with many entry points, moments to make paradoxical comments, to use humor and metaphor to enlarge our joint space. It was strangely easy sometimes to balance the heavy thoughts that inevitably lead to explosive anger. The importance of a "lightness of being," Kundera's book title Paul T. frequently referred to with pleasure, was already implanted as a concept for some time, but it now became a living orientation from which he could transcend the rigid entrapments of his character.

To be sure, never did Paul T. fully leave the old vulnerabilities behind. A long life had been lived, and important aspects of his personhood had formed. Never did I feel he was undergoing a metamorphosis, nor a flight to heights from which the details of his life's pains ceased to matter. But the new epistemological stance, the love for paradox and process, for a search rather than outcome, evolution rather than emergence proved an essential dimension in his recovery.

I introduced with Paul T. a hopeful clinical example. Before moving to the next topic, however, we need to remind ourselves that many people cannot employ their broadening perspective to the transformation of their rigidities and self-destructive styles. For them, the new development produces more desequilibrium and disillusionment, as they now are more critical without being able to make the necessary changes. Few things in life are harder than dealing with the "almost," a freedom that is so close to realization and yet remains unaccomplished.

Blocked Creative Expression

Creativity, Rollo May (1940) said, requires courage to enter an unknown world, and to confront what existentialists like to call "nothingness." His focus on courage, explored in the physical, moral, and social domains, adds to the dimension of talent and ability. The creative person has to demonstrate strengths to pursue the unknown, to let skills and feelings, thoughts and form, develop a new set of images. We have seen the potential for creativity that comes into existence, when the self is ruled less by convention than by the exploration of deeper connections. The self is seen as having a great deal of depth, and creativity is related to being able to access the many layers freely. Realizing this movement in the self, in relationships, through work and the participation of causes is now one of the central indicators of well-being. Creativity, however, is not measured in terms of specific products but as an expression of the inner self taking the person into ever new, often surprising directions. Sometimes this process is connected to artistic expression, other times to professional contribution, or to intimate relationships. Wherever pursued, it always implies a deepening sense of awareness and curiosity, the most important counterforces to repetition and stagnation.

But knowing about a creative possibility is still removed from developing an inner space and a social context to be creative. Like in the case of character, which can place serious limitations on the ability to live according to the new potentials, the fight for creativity can be devastating, as the person simultaneously can feel so very motivated and so far from realization. Whatever the mode of expression, as painter, writer, thinker, musician, professional, and amateur alike, one senses what life would feel like in the presence of the creative impulse. Courage is only one of the abilities necessary, intuition, knowledge, and a sense of freedom are others.

Sternberg (1988), one of the significant researchers of the creative process stresses the importance in the creative person of going beyond the present knowledge. The creative person always seeks out new ways of expression or understanding. Not every person will have these creative aspirations in development; but the new psychological outlook often breaks down the distinction between personal development and creative expression, thus giving the entire developmental thrust a creative angle. Living potentially closer to ones playful, perceptive, emotional side of personality creates great wishes for a creative experience to leave the established and the given behind, even if only for brief periods.

But many cannot take that step, they remain insecure about their abilities, and fear the loneliness that can accompany a creative search. The path to insight, wisdom, and aesthetic expression is often one of friction or outright rejection: Conventions are broken and established powers retaliate. Following one's creative instincts often means surpassing the parents who did not possess the privilege to pursue their potentials. In fact, patients often describe a lack of courage to pursue their inner voice because of overcommitments to social obligations or to competitive fears.

These complex webs of cultural, familial, and individual factors that have been present all along and put limitations on creative expression are now in full conflict with an inner-psychological world that values creativity more than most other aspects of life. As mentioned before, achievement is inspired less by the power and social standing it might provide, but by standards that cherish exploration, expression, and deepening of insight. This new view on achievement puts a great deal of pressure on the person who continues to feel entrapped and who shies away from creativity. In the midst of this conflict feelings emerge of great regret and lost opportunity. Living a "wrong life" without having the defenses to cover up the depth of this existential dilemma is a cruel experience bestowed on a person at this developmental level.

The lack of creative expression is a lifelong fear and reality in many lives, but at this developmental point it has moved to the very center of existence, experienced almost as vitally as the lack of oxygen or sunlight. Creativity has become essential – the basic life force. Life without it is not worth living. And yet, in many situations the recognition of this essential aspect of living is not coupled with the possibilities of pursuit.

Again, an example brings these ideas closer to the real-life experience in therapy.

Renate R. is a single woman in her mid-30s, self-employed as an architect. She had always excelled in school and found it quite easy to reach professional acknowledgment. Even during difficult economic times when many of her colleagues were out of work, she was building houses. Tied to a family style of not expressing negative feelings nor passions, she lived in this intermediate space of great independence, yet internal acceptance of a world that was not quite hers. Able to form deep and lasting friendships, she remained distant to the idea of a lasting commitment. More can be said about her background, to which I will return, but for now I focus on the issue of creativity.

Renate R. had many talents and architecture, with its continual compromising between her ideas and her clients' wishes and financial abilities, felt too much like a craft or business. Instead, she was drawn to music and poetry, stayed up nights to work on projects that felt far more satisfying to her. Thus, as a central symptom of her treatment emerged this hard-to-define, yet pervasive feeling that she was living removed from an essential expression of self. Not surprisingly, we could find some of the biographical roots of this experience. As a shy girl, she preferred the role of observer, especially of her very flamboyant siblings. When she asserted herself, she tended toward domination of her girlfriends resulting in guilt. Toward her parents she was submissive, yet knowing their limitations she pursued her own life with a certain delight in secrecy.

What was most striking to me in our work was a need for Renate R. to stay in the present. From time to time she entered her past through dreams and reflections, always recovering important memories. But I became convinced that her longing and her isolation were triggered as much by her present epistemological stance as by the evolution of her identity and "archaic internal objects." For her, creativity more than achievement and money became the defining features of her inner self. As I have observed with other clients as well, the world of childhood became part of a much larger search despite a very active and evolving transference. The overarching theme of living a creative life remained the most important issue throughout treatment and the essential indicator of her progress.

At first, I translated her need to stay in the present as a way to avoid revisiting those figures in her life who helped create her inhibitions. But it was only when I experienced in myself the very unsettling feelings of not finding the right words, being silent despite having something to say, and being blocked from expressing strong feelings, could I enter her existential dilemma. In entering this experiential space I learned about the devastating frustrations that one encounters when one begins to live searching for deeper meaning and yet not having invented the words and grammar to give expression. I have only seen a similar, and also deep frustration in children when they can already understand a great deal, but many of their words remain incomprehensible. The puzzled looks on the faces of the adults, despite the child's great efforts to make himself understood represent moments of great discouragement.

As we could jointly experience Renate R.'s and our joint missing language, she gained courage. Each picture and each poem became a manifestation of learning to listen to herself, to discover her own fears, and to begin to listen to others. Only in this context did the relationship to her past become truly relevant to her.

It is too easy to understand the message as biography does not matter, the phenomenology of the present experience is what counts. But that is not what I would like to convey here. It is important to appreciate that when a new perspective emerges about what is most salient about the self, its development and relationships, the past sometimes moves into the background as the person so vehemently creates an urge for present experience. For that reason, therapists have to remain flexible to the essential nature of the past in mental health. As the example shows, the transference, my resistance, her experiences were most strongly tied to our present style of interaction. Although the vulnerability of living without sufficient tools to express a creative desire could be traced to childhood experiences as well, it is important to note that before Renate R. had entered this new way of looking at herself and the world, this conflict was not at the fore. Only now had the core conflict become one of living removed from the creative and intuitive potential of the self. The deepening of the view inside, the use of a creativity as an indicator for a true life, and the continuous search instead of a preoccupation with product were all examples of the complex nature of the self.

Tenacity of Life Themes

We witness a new paradox in development: Framing the self in more universal terms often leads to a decrease of self-preoccupations. The healing of biography becomes synonymous with committing to general causes of suffering (e.g., child abuse, children in war, poverty, oppression, racism). This, of course, is a very productive aspect of recovery not only encountered now; but it has become a typical form of adaptation. With the ability to see the self as an agent of change in a world of suffering and solidarity comes also a deepening of one's sense of unique involvement. Responsibility is not delegated to other people or institutions, the person has to rely heavily on their own resources. At the very moment when the self has become most public, it has also created the greatest private space.

The reason why many people can now be effective leaders is their ability to see things straight in the eye, recognize patterns undefensively and without losing compassion. But this lucid recognition of one's biography, a lack of nostalgic rewriting of life history, can lead to excruciating pain. The lack of defensive perception supports the person's humanity, but also takes away useful buffers and "psychological pain killers." Knowledge and insight can be immensely brutal, and the clarity of vision heightens the suffering.

This stance often comes with acknowledging the fragility of human life and incorporating a sense of mortality in one's own life. Frequently, humor provides a welcome relief from the sharpness of this recognition. Woody Allen, the quintessential worrier about death and dying provides an example with his classic line: "I do not want to gain immortality through my work, I want to gain it through not dying!" But many life experiences do not lend themselves as readily to the distancing relief of humor. Robbed of typical forms of self-deception and self-protection the person with grave traumas and burdensome life history is now reminded with greater clarity and enters the memories with heightened emotional power. How useful, one can argue, were the many defenses that now have lost their power?

The essential attribute of self-empathy is frequently not present in those who are pushed toward the very complex forms of reality constructions. The phenomenon is difficult, but the reason relatively simple: Self-acceptance is not only an accomplishment of later development, but is related to the ways we internalized our first important relationships and how they continue to live with us and in us. For that reason, nagging self-doubts and self-rejection can show their ugly heads long after one had thought them buried. And now with less ability to ward off feelings, process-orientation, and associative thinking, and a willingness to follow unconscious inclinations leads to a renewed wrestling with one's biographical vulnerabilities. The outcome of this struggle is usually unknown, the strengths are fortunately considerable, but the truth — rather than power — orientation, generate a renewed serious struggle for the many who encountered grave adversity. Because the person is often quite forgiving and focused also on the self's contributions, there is less possibility to blame others and to externalize conflicts. I return to this problem and its relationship to suicide, but first I describe Mrs. D., a woman I have seen in therapy for some years.

Mrs. D., a woman in her 50s, grew up in a family where both parents were ambitious and successful professionals. Both parents acted emotionally removed from each other and their two children. They demanded of everyone in the family, even when the children were young to act logically and planfully. Mrs. D. experienced this demand as having to disown her feelings, desires, and even internal potentials. She recalled frequent situations where she had to defend herself against her parents like a defendant in court. Although she was a placid child, she always had a sense that she had transgressed. The family tradition involved to be called to the dining room with her father and mother presiding over a "hearing." They attacked her and demanded better and more logical behavior. The outcome was already known before the hearing had begun: She was at fault.

Trying to reconstruct in therapy whether she was or was not at fault and what the deeper meanings of transgressions were, she could never achieve any sense of certainty. She does know, however, that she "left herself behind," as well as a love for artistic expression, as she began to feel lonelier and uglier, both at home and in school. By adolescence she had become overweight and had begun not only to reject her body, but most of the ways of being in the world. She had become an unhappy young adult, searching for acceptance and comfort and not finding it. This sense of loneliness and self-rejection that she continued to live with throughout her life, was compounded greatly by her father's eroticized relationship with her. The tribunal left the child bewildered and created the roots of self-rejection. Spells of self-doubts escalated throughout treatment to depression and recurrent fantasies about suicide.

Mrs. D. broadened and deepened her perspective in treatment. The transition to the more complex forms of psychological construction are also encountered in a dream, that we tried to decipher for some time.

Mrs. D. and I were driving in a jeep up a very windy road in Greece. The road was surrounded by old olive trees. The higher the road went, the greater the views that opened toward the sea. She loved the freedom, the wind, and the mixture of colors—browns, greens, and blues. Now animals appeared, mostly mules who she liked at first. But she became anxious as the mules expanded in numbers and came closer to the road. I was driving the jeep and she began to take over the steering wheel. The mules were now on the road and she had totally taken over the steering but great fears had taken hold that we were going to crash.

This dream introduced a new phase in our relationship and helped create momentum in Mrs. D.'s development. She was very curious about the many meanings the dream revealed. Greece represented a country of mystery and beauty, stories and eternal truths. She had always envied the tradition in Greek villages to celebrate life by enjoying good food, laughter, and dance. Her family was never capable of similar expressions of joy. Finding the "fountain of direct experience and expression" was a move toward her "true self," from which she had been alienated since early in life.

Mrs. D. was excited about the image of driving up a mountainous road from which the view became more lucid. She created a bridge to the treatment and the deepening of insight and broadening of perspective as we together climbed the mountain. She was, however, disturbed that she was still letting me drive the jeep despite the fact that she wanted to steer herself. Interestingly, she did not want to change places with me, as I expected, and take control. Dreams of being in charge are very frequent at earlier times in development. Now, the goal is more toward jointly moving in time and space. For that reason, I suspect, Mrs. D. complained that the jeep did not allow for joint steering and that she would have to be more ingenious in her dreams to create vehicles that make such collaboration possible. Indeed, her future dreams would introduce many new ways of being in charge together.

The mules, Mrs. D. was convinced, represented her stubbornness and her defenses, those elements in her personality that prevent her from truly enjoying and exploring. These mules, also the stubborn resistors against the family tribunal, remained a powerful theme in the treatment. Whenever she felt free, she had to worry about obstacles in her way. We spent some time over the next weeks to further explore her fears. The mules appeared to Mrs. D. as sexual objects as well, she had seen horses copulating, they reminded her of animal power. Greece now became also a place of Greek dramas and the oracle of Delphi, inevitability of life history in Oedipus Rex and her erotic relationship with her father. In our relationship, she was fearful that we were entering landscapes that would prove dangerous.

We should briefly deal with the issue of defenses from the vantage point of complex development. When the self functioned as prison, the self was aware of the use of defenses, when they broke down much energy was spent re-erecting them. But now, the break-down of defenses is evaluated positively, even when great pain results. Insecurity, vacillation, loss of firmness, and clear identity are accepted in order to abandon alienation, isolation, and a lack of vitality. In Mrs. D.'s case, the forward movement in her ability to see her life with crystal clarity, like a painter meditating on all details of an object, contributed to long stretches of depression and suicidal desperation. Despite a great deal of remembering and re-experiencing, which often leads to a greater ability to "let go," her family trauma became more not less, pronounced. Gone were the times when she was willing to make excuses, to fudge the facts, and to protect her parents. She had learned how to live with the feelings and how to create a language about them, but the new evolved constructions were paid for by less defenses against the original harsh realities in her life.

This is such an important point that I want to address it again using a different language. A strong focus on "being" and "evolving," rather than "having" creates great energy and associative freedom in treatment and in life. But it can also produce a great intensification of suffering. Like a poet, who enters experiences so deeply and uses the self as a musical instrument, is often greeted by insufferable pain as the person is open to so many nuances of experiences. Even after considerable treatment and after overall successful completion of the work, Mrs. D. was left with episodic feelings of self-rejection and self-hostility. This was despite the fact that she had gained considerable freedom of exploration and had found ways to detect and express her experiential self. She was not running away from the extremely difficult experiences in her life. However, exactly this openness of experience intensified her depression and despair. By now these feelings were not neurotic anymore, the self had learned how to bear the intensity of the affect. Mourning and overcoming had led to reduction in symptoms. Paradoxically, Mrs. D. now experienced times in which she was more open towards the vicious attacks and the despairing aspects of her life than she had been when she was able to externalize, seal over, and act out.

Could this paradox in development be involved in a risk for suicide, a preoccupation that periodically befell Mrs. D. as well?

Loss of Meaning and Suicide

Focusing on deeper meaning, trying to create a more socially aware set of commitments, can have its dialectical counterpart: a breakdown of meaning without the solace of creating sufficient life motivation through intimate relationships and institutional affiliations. Döbert and Nunner-Winkler (1994) made similar observations.

> The concept of the meaning of life is connected to the idea of embedding one's biography in more comprehensive social or meaning contexts, transcending the individual. . . . Meaninglessness here no longer consists of the futility of particular actions, but in the absence of good reason for one's existence and conduct of life.

Protection against suicide is provided through strong commitments to relationships and social causes. The person feels responsible not only to the self but to others and often realizes, even in the midst of despair, that suicide is a social act that leaves an entire community vulnerable. Intrapsychically, the person has greater resources containing negative affects as they are viewed as part of a process-orientation in life. But continuity in meaning coupled with a belief in the viability of one's commitments is so important, that its loss creates a great new risk for suicide. Another risk factor is found in the specifics of life history. The movement to complex developmental capacities often stems from social and ethnic marginality and traumatic experiences that hinder the comfortable identification with the existing system. Now that greater perspective, self-awareness, and sensitivities arise, experiences can create a recurrent sense of meaninglessness. Meaning requires a level of flexibility, trust, and involvement with people that is not available to many of these people, and thus, they end up desperately unhappy and disillusioned.

We do not, however, find here as much the depression about being unliked or unloved. Suicidality is often related to a generalized despair about the state of the world, the forms in which we leave the world behind to a next generation. There is a despair that contains perspective and cannot easily be argued with. The forces of the depression might be many but the form it takes is usually one that has a strong component of *Weltschmerz* (loosely translated as pain about the world). This pain is more often than not a motivator toward social action because the self sees itself so much more as a social participant and often knows about the ways institutions work, but for some the pain becomes so great that it interferes with any meaningful activity. This can, of course, be also related to more serious psychopathology, manic depressive illness, psychoses that have been shown to be more prevalent in the gifted and possibly more independent minds found in this development position. But it is rare that people will experience their depression as solely biological.[4]

We began this chapter with an exploration of wisdom, with its emphasis on affirmation of life despite the recognition of severe limitations. Creativity and commitment, love for contradiction and tolerance were part of a larger developmental configuration. Now we have arrived "on the other side": total despair and meaninglessness. This meaninglessness can come in complex forms. The depth of perspective can take another path as well: to produce new resources and to overcome old traumas. Meant is not the creation of a colorful tapestry to cover the critical mirror placed in front of us by many doubting artists, clinicians, and philosophers. Instead, the back and forth between a lack of belief in past and future and the search for new individual and collective strengths, produces unknown possibilities for recovery.

In no time of development are the chances so great to productively re-address long-standing vulnerabilities. The entire constructivist power is

---

[4]They think in multicausal ways and they tend to think in those ways when they try to understand their own symptoms. I have, however, been quite impressed by the ability to have complex minds and to interpret their psychological problems in rather unevolved ways.

geared toward a psychologically healthier life making it less likely than before that old problems become transformed into more complex form. But it is significantly more likely that the person will use the new window to gain different insights into old complexes and destructive internal relationships from the past.

WINDOWS OF POSSIBILITY

Despite powerful loyalties to prevent fundamental change, the person now recognizes with some surprise that new possibilities for change exist. These possibilities are often attributed to the tools of therapy, but more often therapy and psychoanalysis unknowingly tap into these developmental capacities. Sometimes the change will occur with little effort — insight forms unannounced, and spontaneous. In other circumstances a great deal of direct attention and work will be necessary. New interests in others, a strengthening belief in dialogue and joining larger causes will make most people feel less isolated and give them a chance to change the form of their inner object world through new interactions in the social world. Simultaneously, a different kind of inner dialogue, a new valence of feelings and sensitivities, a different experience of time and biography can provide the person with considerably more freedom to move between past, present, and future and to overcome earlier traumas.

A cautionary note is needed here. The turning points and insight I discuss in this chapter are potentials for readdressing problems, not secure paths toward recovery. Even under the best of possibilities, the tension between repetition, rigidity, and disorganization on the one hand and flexibility, exploration, and opening on the other will persist. This will also require the acceptance of vulnerabilities and past experiences — they will not magically disappear. However, retaining a realistic view on recovery, should not prevent us from understanding the new tools of thought, feeling, and action now available to the person. With a new window on the past, the person can begin to pursue unresolved problems, to gain new insight, and to find ways to apply these new tools to overcome traumas and disappointments. That the process of working on past vulnerabilities with new perspective will simultaneously unveil new problems, is part of the difficult dialectic inherent in recovering. In this section, I deal with the naturally occurring process of *developing* resilience, not the clinical uses of these developmental potentials. Table 6.1 can be used as a brief overview and guide of some of the main points in this section.

Fantasy, Reality in a New Space

Past, present, and future are becoming far more intertwined than ever before leading to a greater facility in revisiting old vulnerabilities. Like the

TABLE 6.1
Windows into Change Processes

New temporal relationship	* Past, present, and future become more intertwined and can be more readily accessed. This often leads to greater pain, but also to a possibility to overcome old vulnerabilities through reexperiencing and reframing.
A new "space" for fantasy and reality	* New focus on playfulness, child's intuitions and perceptions leads to a change away from a rigid overenvolvement with "reality." The person can create a protective sphere in which dreams, consciousness, fantasy, etc. create their own life and can infiltrate daily experience.
Reframing biography	* Biography is viewed in process terms, not as a fixed container of early experiences that shape the present. This new view can have a freeing effect from entrapments of the past.
Search for "true self" as compass	* The centrality of authenticity, spontaneity, and vitality all play together to help the person create an inner compass that can guide recovery through the many expected detours and mazes.
New balance of cognition/emotion	* There is not any more a primacy of the cognitive-conceptual, instead truth is viewed as having a strong emotional component that balances the tendency of the complex self toward intellectualizations.
Private self/public self	* Distinctions become far less important than before between private and public self. This leads to more sharing of the inner nature of the self, leading to greater self-knowledge and potential for overcoming of secrets and shame.
Intimacy	* Less preoccupation with self, identity, and boundaries, leads to new freedoms to create intimacy, built on joint explorations, dialogue and a decrease of struggles over autonomy. This, in turn, leads to reduced loneliness and pulls in past relational vulnerabilities into new relationships with potential to transform dysfunctional patterns.
Larger commitments	* The social, moral and spiritual framing of the self often leads to involvements in larger causes. These can help the person become less preoccupied with internal processes and to channel personal experiences and traumas into collective responses.

surrealistic paintings of Magritte, Escher, or Dali, dreams and fantasies can take up a large space in one's conceptions of reality. Having firmed up the differences and boundaries between these spheres in earlier development — conscious and unconscious, fantasy and reality, past and present, and so on — now greater fluidity is allowed, even desired. The surrealists captured the powerful images of this way of experiencing: Dali's objects that take on personalities, speaking back like in the dimly lit room of a child awaking in the middle of the night. Objects live in two worlds simultaneously, for example in Magritte's famous house of night, placed before a sky of day. Or Escher's people being led up and down in a never-ending square of simultaneously climbing and descending stairs. These pictures play with our perceptions, they also represent a fundamental critique of structure, organization, and logic as the most important aspect of human experience.

Not every one converts to surrealism or finds him or herself represented in these pictures. The themes and struggles of this developmental world, however, are represented in a highly private form of constructing the world in which validation of perception and experience through conventions is fundamentally questioned. Many elements of the child's creative, often illogical and magical world reappear, and the images take on symbolic functions: Dali's burning giraffe, for example, set against a dark blue background, represents a child's nightmare and an adult's struggle with the meaninglessness of war. The person now desires to revisit the past, recognizing with existential regret, even despair, that development has consisted not only of gaining greater competency and knowledge but also of losing direct, experiential, and intuitive forms of being and playing.

The yearning of painters, composers, poets, and novelists to recreate that childhood world represents also a desire to break out of the limitations of a complex psychological mind. Orienting to the memories of distant times is not only a vehicle to return to the past, but a metaphor for bringing the strength of childhood experiencing to the "deformed" expert being of the present. This yearning is for a special vitality long lost and can reappear in changed form due to the self's greater integrating capacities. These capacities break down the strict distinctions between past and present and fantasy and reality providing unknown possibilities to create passions long thought lost.

This "living multiplicity" of past and present worlds can bring back a transitional space where reality and nonreality coexist. We know from Winnicott's astute observations how important the development of such a space of imagination is for the child's psychological maturation. Dealing with the loss of the parents in everyday separations by creating transitional objects, the child learns to bear extremely difficult feelings. This intermediate place between reality and fantasy is where pretend play can blossom: engrossing oneself in a world while knowing it is self-created.

Such a space now becomes reinvented and reinhabited on a complex level. The separations are not only from significant primary relationships, but also from systems of thought and institutions. Interestingly, the world one is changing in one's mind is experienced as dangerous and disappointing even when one is successful and holds power because it is defined by functioning and competition: Every winner knows the danger and inevitability of losing. In this space, one does not have to follow the "rules of the game" and can experiment with associative freedom, following images, dreams, and fantasies.

This development has a great deal to do with gaining psychological strengths. We know from psychotherapy and psychoanalysis that the deepening of inner life is often a crucial step in overcoming vulnerabilities. Recovery, in its double meaning, is a way of transforming psychopathology through the recovery of images, memories and dreams. In an earlier stage, one tried to be systematic and orderly. Now the tolerance for playful disorganization plays into this new potential. Giving up linear thinking, the person does not need to follow strict outlines and structures. At first sight, order seems to be the counterforce to disorder but this misunderstanding has contributed to flaws in attempts to recover at previous developmental levels. Now one can notice the paradox — that applying defenses that create systematic order is often in direct opposition to the process of getting better. Recovery is messy, disorderly, and labyrinthine. First one has to join disorganization and find ways to accept it and to learn to explore what it stands for. It is best pursued through flexibility, acceptance of ambiguity, and the ability to entertain the crazy images the self is capable of.

Dreams and fantasies create a disequilibrium that can be health-promoting as they support a new form of creativity and the extension of an expressive transitional space. It is important not to apply logic prematurely and to even postpone the interpretation of dreams in light of the meanings they stand for. This focus on structured meaning creates rationality and order at the expense of spontaneity and emotional experience. Now the messiness of human psychology can be appreciated as part of human creativity and can help depathologize the self.

In the creative space between reality and fantasy many traumatic experiences come up as well, a reason why the search for childhood vitality can be so excruciatingly painful. The vivid memories bring up suffering from a time when one was dependent on the care of others and became traumatized or chronically frustrated. The direct access of dreams and fantasies can create, as we have seen in Mrs. D., considerable despair. In this new space, the suffering can be actively symbolized, through stories, poems, paintings — real or imagined — leading to a productive attempt to express earlier suffering. The dilemma one faces is whether to continue to shut oneself off from a certain sensitivity and intuition or to be more open and in turn, be exposed to painful feelings. The self's new perspective provides greater facility and interest in the path of creating vitality, even when it means times of greater suffering.

Of course, a form of self-healing through pursuit of a self one had left behind has been described by many observers of the so called midlife crisis (e.g., Osherson, 1980; Vaillant, 1977). The commitments of adult life require a specialization of skills and a separation from a great many child and adolescent interests. Now that expertise has been gained the feeling of loss becomes so pronounced in those who feel that they forced themselves and have given up too much. The examples are well known, of the managers who leave their executive suites and turn to art, the English professors who study music, or the businessmen who "break out" and travel with their families around the world. We are often less aware of the years of suffering that have gone into these decisions. Unfortunately, too many people, especially men, translate their yearning for freedom, play, and fantasy into a need to leave their spouses before giving both a chance to inhabit a freer and more creative world together. The excitement found through passion and sexual freedom is often mistakenly viewed as the liberation that comes with a new playfulness and the strengthening of a life of fantasy and exploration. Certainly, sexual exploration can be a guide in that direction, but so often it represents little more than a desperate attempt to avoid the deeper changes in the self. All these attempts, whether successful or not, represent a wish to create a new life space, less focused on adaptation and success and more oriented to the potentially healing world of play, dream, and imagination. The healing begins as the person learns to pay attention to a new set of desires without dismissing them.

Time and Biography

The new psychological space can grow in parallel to the development of a new relationship to time and biography. As we have seen, with greater flexibility to return to one's origins, one replays the flawed moments, the missed opportunities as well as the many choices that created identity. But biography now ceases to be a container of fixed regrets, rigidly held object relations and identity statuses. From the perspective of the present, biography has shifted from an historic accounting to manifesting itself in the present. The past is mostly interesting as it presents itself in the moment to moment experience or in the ways it interferes with a connection to present perception and experience. With this focus the person can also change the perception of the past. Time is not rigidly conserved and need not be guarded in museumlike fashion. The person ceases to be the curator of the family, nation, and culture, treating them as if time had stopped long ago. Instead, the person experiences the past living in the present and the present influencing view of the past.

We cannot overestimate this new time perspective for the process of recovery. Biography, identity, and self are all seen as continuously forming, and for that reason one knows that one can potentially get untrapped at any point in one's psychological evolution. Loewald (1980), the writer whose psychoanalytic perspective is most akin to what I describe here, dealt with this issue around his ideas about transference. He observed in psychoanalysis that the present relationship with the analyst creates as much the experience of the parents as the parent imagos create the form the transference takes. This continued dialectic, which also lives outside of therapy in all intimate relationships, is enormously facilitated by the new ways in which we perceive the past and present to coexist.

With this shift from past to present and present to past many things that seemed so much in the way of inner freedom can be put aside. The person certainly knows that he or she has been harmed and disappointed, arguing for example: "I realized my life consists of many lost opportunities but the essential moments are not only in the past, they also exist in the present and the future. Right now my biography is being written and I have something to do with the script." In a dialectical surprise, the less the person focused on the past, the more possible it is to overcome nostalgic regret or enraged hostility. The causal models where childhood experiences are perceived to have shaped adulthood, so prevalent at the earlier developmental positions, contribute to the very sense of stuckness the person so desperately wants to overcome. It becomes hard to see how one can ever overcome the past, or to "make peace" with it.

The new view where past changes continuously from the point of view of today's experiences and constructions, can be very liberating. A great deal more expectation is generated in the "conversation," "curator," or "causal" models that so easily entrap the person and produce a great sense of disloyalty at all attempts to free the self. Now, the relationship between past and present does not require such stark contrasts. The container of the past that included important relationships does not have to be "thrown over-board." As a consequence, the self need feel less guilty about the work on the past. Continuity is preserved while meanings and affects are fundamentally shifting.

The removal of rigid time barriers and the related possibility to move with greater facility between different "biographical times zones," does not, however, lead to the end of the splitted nature of the self. Many contradictions remain, but the new perspective helps to see the different aspects of one's personality less separated than before and helps one cross the different spheres of the self with greater facility.

A New Inner Compass

Another contribution to recovery comes from the heightened significance attributed to "true self" experiences. As long as the person needed to rule with force to keep the self-organized, he or she often lived against his or her inner nature. I discussed earlier in this chapter Winnicott's astute observation that the false self is compliant, intellectualized, and dissociated from its body. One has to have been close to someone who struggles with these issues to fully know the tremendous suffering that comes from this lack of a basic vitality and authenticity. Everyone certainly has had moments of this experience themselves. The fact that the distinction between "true self" and "false self" has now moved to center stage, means that an "inner compass" becomes available to guide the movement toward health.

This compass is very important because any recovery entails moving through mazes, pursuing false entry points into one's experience and overcoming persistent impasses. These continuous confusions require not only patience and tolerance of ambiguity but also a matrix from which one can intuit and evaluate whether one is moving in the "right" direction. The problem with this point in development has been that too much of the direction-seeking had been delegated to powerful relationships, ideologies or institutions. The self elaborated the strategies of compliance, external validation through achievement, and dissociation through intellectualization. Now these external sources become balanced by a uniquely personal search, often defying convention, past expectations, and solely rational self-evaluations.[5] This focus on one's "true inner nature" can be experienced as dangerous as it can break many traditions that have been so important to one's definition: In the process of overcoming old vulnerabilities, the sense of being true to one's self, not in a rigid and totalitarian sense, but in one that takes one's own experience seriously, is both a process of recovery and an outcome of recovery.

Any process of *developing* resilience involves the search for direction. How else do we know that we are, in fact, making progress, instead of remaining stagnant or deceiving ourselves to think we are getting better? The new compass that helps gaining and regaining direction is not easily defined. Direction-seeking is complicated by the fact that the very nature of the true self is that it avoids certainty, unity, and consistency. Thus, openness to new experiences, to contradiction and inner conflict, becomes so important that direction cannot derive from a prescribed set of rules. Instead, the true self is based on "authenticity," a continuous search for honesty, feeling real, and truthful to some of the basic beliefs and ideals one holds.

Feelings and Mourning

This inner compass accepts feelings as one essential indicator of truth. Feelings are an important way to measure genuineness and authenticity and to distinguish between insights and rationalizations. We know far too little about emotional development at this complex level of development to state with any empirical certainty, whether entirely new types of feelings are now present. We could speculate, for example, that a new sense of exhilaration

---

[5]I realize that Erikson interpreted this unique search for who one is in this world as part of the identity formation of late adolescence. Similarly, Kohlberg and Gilligan (1971) observed a postconventional moral crisis in adolescence. But many aspects of this form of identity are only pursued in adulthood and require rather complex developmental capacities.

emerges when universal justice and human connectedness become insepa-
rable, a state so beautifully given voice in the final chorale, "Ode to Joy" of
Beethoven's Ninth Symphony. But until we have more knowledge in this
domain we are better off concentrating on the balance of emotion and
cognition, which now takes on strikingly new form.

In the earlier developmental positions feelings were often viewed as
messy, unpredictable, and inferior in comparison to more predictable and
controllable thoughts. For that reason emotions often have to be set aside,
suppressed or projected as "female psychology." But there is a major
problem for recovery in this earlier way of handling feelings. Knowledge,
even when it connects to memory, that shuts out emotions is usually not
healing. Most therapists have had the experience of patients who come into
treatment with a fairly good representation of the origins and development
of their problems, but little knowledge of how to move closer to health.[6]

Recovery is strongly related to mourning, an insight we owe to Freud and
all subsequent generations of psychoanalysts. Loss and the incapacity to
mourn appropriately is one core aspect of most types of psychopathology,
not only depression. So often the most knowledgeable patients are the ones
with the greatest problems of entering this world of mourning, a reason why
the treatment of mental health professions can be so complicated. The
struggle in psychotherapy usually consists of finding a path to break
through the defenses erected against these feelings of helplessness and
vulnerability, depression and recognition of loss. The same process is still
extremely difficult for a person in this developmental world. Loss is often
extremely painful, regardless of maturity levels. But now it becomes
possible to ally oneself with a natural movement of feelings, fantasies and
unconscious life. The interpenetrating of thought and feeling, the shifting
back and forth between experience and reflection creates a fertile ground to
tolerate the despair and excruciating pain that mourning entails. In this
respect, the changes in epistemological stance, of thinking about self and
world, can have an essential effect on mental health.

Intimacy and Loneliness

I have oriented on intrapsychic processes until now, experiencing reflecting
and changing inner life. There is good reason for this focus since a
deepening of meaning usually involves a concentrated and consistent view
on one's inner world. However, the importance of relationships continues
to be great and new possibilities for intimacy evolve. The self, firmly
grounded in its uniqueness, can develop deeper forms of intersubjectivity
and dialogue. Less preoccupied with issues of identity and boundaries, the

---

[6]This is also the reason why self-analysis often does not bring about sufficient change.

person can share more of her inner nature. The fear that the self will be taken over, having to submit or to dominate, has subsided, instead the desire is to enter into a meaningful dialogue. Enhanced by more evolved role-taking and empathic abilities, the person can more fully enter the inner reality of another person. This was possible before as well, but we now find considerably less anxiety that entering another person's world will lead to a loss of self.

Similarly, the concern subsides that these interactions will stand in contradiction to one's own ways of organizing the self. Differences in belief, ideology, and cultural heritage are usually viewed as expanding the self. This might be a reason why spiritual thinkers who have evolved great maturity often search out similar people in other religions, such as the influential catholic Merton traveling to the Buddhist Lama and Buber's continued dialogue with Christian theologians. These people, often isolated from the orthodoxy of their own traditions sought intellectual intimacy and common overarching principles. Thus, the person feels less threatened by diversity. At least in theory there is a strong sense that intimacy is based on egalitarian principles, free will, and support.

What are the implications of this new nature of intimacy for recovery? Serious psychological problems often occur through problematic relationships with people who matter most. We do not posses in childhood the possibility to leave destructive environments nor do we really have the capacity to decide whom to love in our families. As impressionable beings we internalize these experiences and people and make them the building blocks of our inner self. In addition, we do not only make others part of our internal world, typical interaction patterns also become generalized. Family and systems therapy has demonstrated how stable and inflexible these patterns can become, especially in dysfunctional families, marriages, and groups. Recovery usually requires involving oneself in relationships, allowing for old experiences and patterns to reemerge and to become part of the new interactions. In fact, on this idea transference in psychotherapy is built; that a new intimacy between therapist and patient creates an environment in which old patterns reappear and can be transformed.

But these transference processes evolve not only in treatment, there they become an explicit tool. The new motivation toward deeper relationships where feelings and thoughts, fantasy and reality are continuously intertwined enhances possibility to revisit past relationships and to restructure one's inner object world. Too much of this process of developing resilience remained inside the self at the previous developmental position. Now there is more potential for searching out others and reflecting about one's past with them. In this respect every relationship becomes somewhat of a peer therapy often not even directly noticed or acknowledged because the person is less preoccupied with differentiating the private and public self. This, in turn, leads to an increased readiness to share previously withheld parts of the self and in the process the person explores "internal foreign territory" and experiments freer relationship patterns. Two simultaneous and contradictory processes occur with great regularity. The basic nature of the self becomes dialogical, leading to a decrease of isolation and loneliness. At the same time, the person can become so keenly aware of the nuances of the unique inner world, that can be accompanied by a new sense of aloneness, a feeling that few others can reach into these depths. How this conflict between sharing a process of experience with others and a certain reclusiveness of self gets worked on is quite dependent on individual differences, specific biographical experiences, etc. The tension will always be present — not resolved at the upper reaches of development. What one can hope for is a greater acceptance of this very basic tension in human existence, which is in itself a healing acknowledgment and a supportive recognition for relationships.

Self-Preoccupations and Commitment to the World

The widening interest in the world is coupled with an experienced personal responsibility to get involved. Personal experiences that have been particularly painful often engage the person to mobilize groups to protect others from a similar fate. This engagement can, of course, occur throughout development but it now becomes almost normative. The high degree of perspective taking, not only with individuals but with the world of universal rights and responsibilities creates a great motivation toward social action, especially on behalf of the unprotected. Causes such as hunger, oppression, the environment, children, and minorities are frequently the arenas of social commitment.

The strength of these commitments, which often takes the form of leadership in groups, derives from a few sources. Gone are the identifications with institutions where one can trust that they will be immune against unjust and arbitrary actions. Too strong are the memories of those moments in history, where institutions became the instruments of power to deny rights and to oppress. One feels more personally called to action, does not hide any more behind the belief that the state or other institutions will take care of the pressing problems of our times. This belief in the individual contribution to social advance and protection of the world can lead to a very individualist perspective and a rejection of all institutional life from a postconventional perspective. But more often institutions are viewed as important vehicles for social change.

The propensity to participate in larger movements or causes can have an healing effect. By engaging in the world one finds expression of some deeply held convictions of the self. It is usually not hard to find a direct link to very basal experiences that continue to be expressed and righted, not only for the self, but for a broader group of beneficiaries. This engagement then makes the person transform the inner preoccupations to involvements in the world. More importantly, what was experienced passively now becomes active and what made one feel isolated and separate has now created the force that joins the person to others. Of course, there is also the danger that the person only lives in the world, avoiding any strong relationship with the self. But it is more typical that the deepening of commitment to a public occurs while the self also becomes more internal and private. What becomes most striking is the accessibility of the private and public self and the willingness to merge these two domains in social involvements.

CONCLUSION

I wanted first to show that high forms of consciousness create their own risks and vulnerabilities, but ended with a rather hopeful note on resilience. The pessimistic reader, who is focused primarily on the repeating nature of human biography, will want to stress remaining entrapments, continued loneliness, alienation, and self rejection throughout life. One can muster much evidence for such continuities of dysfunction and despair. I have been equally impressed by the potentials for transformation inherent throughout development, including the very complex levels. Now the balance has shifted away from rigidity, repetition, and despair and leans more favorably toward greater flexibility, deeper insight, and creative exploration of present. This new balance certainly cannot be equated with living in an equilibrium, since cognitive disorganizations, emotional imbalance, and contradictory actions are still part of the psychological life. Nor, can we speak of necessarily having found fulfillment in work and love. But we can say that it is quite likely that the person has engaged in a new telos that bridges mental health and development: The person will develop a basic growth-orientation of life, in which the past does not necessarily persist, nor is it perceived as the only formative period. This developmental perspective creates more freedom to pursue new experiences in love and work. It also creates a context to explore and experiment and, in turn, produce new windows of opportunities to bring into focus earlier vulnerabilities as well as ways to overcome them, or at least live with them. Broadening the developmental horizon emboldens the self to seek deeper forms of intimacy and greater autonomy. It is this continuous *cycle* we should call development, rather than the stepwise progression from stage to stage. It is precisely this developmental courage, vitality and flexibility, that we should call mental health.

ACKNOWLEDGMENTS

This work was supported by the Alden Trust, the American Suicide Foundation, and was written during a fellowship year at the Institute for Advanced Studies in Berlin. The argument was strengthened through discussions with and comments from Kurt Fischer, Robbie Case, Daniel Stern, Mary Main, and Maryanne Wolf. Editorial assistance was provided by Bracea Molad and Andrew Rhein.

REFERENCES

Baltes, P. B., & Smith, J. (1990). Wisdom-related knowledge: Age/cohort differences in response to life-planning problems. *Developmental Psychology, 26*(3), 494–504.

Basseches, M. (1984). *Dialectical thinking and adult development.* Norwood, NJ: Ablex.

Broughton, J. (1978). *The development of concepts of self, mind, reality, and knowledge. New direction in child development: Social cognition.* San Francisco: Jossey-Bass.

Commons, M. L., Richards, F. A., & Armon, C. (1984). *Beyond formal operations: Late adolescent and adult cognitive development.* New York: Praeger.

Csikszentmihalyi, M. (1990). *Flow: The psychology of optimal experience.* New York: Harper & Row.

Döbert, R., & Nunner-Winkler, G. (1994). Commonsense understandings about suicide as a resource for coping with suicidal impulses. In G. Noam & S. Borst (Eds.), *Children, youth, and suicide: New directions in child development.* San Francisco: Jossey-Bass.

Edelstein, W., & Noam, G. G. (1982). Regulatory structures of the self and post-formal operations in adulthood. *Human Development, 25,* 407–422.

Fischer, K. W., & Ayoub, C. (1994). Affective splitting and dissociation in normal and maltreated children: Developmental pathways for self in relationships. In D. Cicchetti & S. Toth (Eds.), *Rochester symposium on developmental psychopathology: Disorders and dysfunctions of the self* (pp. 1–73). New York: University of Rochester Press.

Fowler, J. W. (1981). *Stages of faith: The psychology of human development and the quest for meaning.* New York: Harper & Row.

Frankl, V. E. (1985). *Man's search for meaning.* New York: Washington Square Press.

Fromm, E. (1976). *To have or to be.* New York: Harper & Row.

Jung, C. G. (1966). *The spirit in man, art, and literature* (R. F. C. Hull, Trans.). Princeton, NJ: Princeton University Press.

Kagan, J. (1989). *Unstable ideas: Temperament, cognition, and self.* Cambridge, MA: Harvard University Press.

King, P., Kitchner, K., Wood, P., & Davidson, M. (1989). Relations across developmental domains: A longitudinal study of intellectual, moral, and ego development. In M. Commons, J. Sinnot, F. Richards, & C. Armon (Eds.), *Adult development* (pp. 57–72). New York: Praeger.

Kohlberg, L. (1984). *Essays on moral development: Vol. 2. The psychology of moral development.* San Francisco: Harper & Row.

Kohlberg, L., & Gilligan, C. (1971). Adolescent as philosopher: The discovery of the self in a post-conventional world. *Daedalus, 100,* 1051–1086.

Klein, M. (1930). *Die Bedeutung der Symbolbildung für die Ichentwicklung.* London: Hogarth Press.

Kohut, H. (1977). *The restoration of the self.* New York: International Universities Press.

Labouvie-Vief, G., Hakim-Larson, J., & Hobart, C. J. (1987). Age, ego and the life span—Development of coping defense processes. *Psychology and Aging, 2*(3), 286-293.

Loevinger, J. (1976). *Ego development.* San Francisco: Jossey-Bass.

Loewald, H. W. (1980). *Papers on psychoanalysis.* New Haven, CT: Yale University Press.

Maslow, A. H. (1976). *Religions, values, and peak experiences.* New York: Penguin.

Maslow, A. H. (1982). *Toward a psychology of being.* New York: Van Nostrand Reinhold.

May, R. (1940). *The springs of creative living.* New York: Abingdon Coxesbury Press.

Osherson, S. (1980). *Holding on or letting go: men and career change at midlife.* New York: The Free Press.

Pascual-Leone, J. (1989). Developmental levels of processing in metaphor interpretation. *Journal of Experimental Child Psychology, 48*(1), 1-31.

Noam, G. G. (1988a). A constructivist approach to developmental psychopathology. In E. Nannis & P. Cowan (Eds.), *Developmental psychopathology and its treatment* (pp. 91-122). San Francisco: Jossey-Bass.

Noam, G. G. (1988b). The self, adult development, and the theory of biography and transformation. In D. K. Lapsley & F. C. Power (Eds.), *Self, ego, and identity-integrative approaches.* New York: Springer-Verlag.

Noam, G. G. (1990). Beyond Freud and Piaget: Biographical worlds—interpersonal self. In T. E. Wren (Ed.), *The moral domain* (pp. 360-399). Cambridge, MA: MIT Press.

Noam, G. G. (1992). Development as the aim of clinical intervention. *Development and Psychopathology, 4,* 679-696.

Noam, G. G. (1993). "Normative vulnerabilities" of self and their transformations in moral actions. In G. G. Noam & T. E. Wren (Eds.), *The moral self* (pp. 209-238). Cambridge: MIT Press.

Noam, G. G. (in press). High risk children and youth: Transforming our understanding of human development. *Human Development.*

Noam, G. G., & Borst, S. (Eds.). (1994a). *Children, youth, and suicide: developmental perspectives.* San Francisco: Jossey-Bass.

Noam, G. G., & Borst, S. (1994b). Developing meaning, losing meaning: Understanding suicidal behavior in the young. In *New directions for child development* (Vol. 64). San Francisco: Jossey-Bass.

Noam, G. G., Recklitis, C., & Paget, K. (1991). Pathways of ego development: Contributions to maladaptation and adjustment. *Development and Psychopathology, 3,* 311-321.

Perry, W. S. (1970). *Forms of intellectual and ethical development in the college years.* New York: Holt Rinehart.

Reich, W. (1972). *Character analysis* (V. R. Carfagno, Trans.). New York: Farrar, Straus & Giroux.

Shapiro, D. (1965). *Neurotic styles.* New York: Basic Books.

Sternberg, R. (Ed.). (1988). *The nature of creativity: Contemporary psychological perspectives.* New York: Cambridge University Press.

Vaillant, G. E. (1977). *Adaptation to life.* Boston: Little Brown.

Winnicott, D. W. (1958). *Collected papers, through paediatrics to psycho-analysis.* London: Tavistock.

Winnicott, D. W. (1965). *The maturational processes and the facilitating environment: studies in the theory of emotional development.* New York: International Universities Press.

7

Analyzing Development of Working Models of Close Relationships: Illustration with a Case of Vulnerability and Violence

Kurt W. Fischer
Catherine Ayoub
Harvard University

How do people develop in their important relationships, and how do two people come together to form a new, close relationship? These two questions should be central to the study of socioemotional development, but no framework or method has been available for analyzing development of people's relationships to answer these questions. Instead, theory and research have focused primarily on continuities across time, such as stability with age in attachment, relationship themes, and relationship models (Ainsworth, Blehar, Waters, & Wall, 1978; Bretherton, Ridgeway, & Cassidy, 1990; Greenberg, Cicchetti, & Cummings, 1990; Horowitz, 1987; Luborsky & Crits-Christoph, 1990; Shaver & Hazan, 1992).

Even scholars who emphasize stability of relationships recognize that people show major developmental changes in their close relationships (Bowlby, 1969; Case, chapter 3, this volume; Gilligan, 1982, chapter 9, this volume; Main & Hesse, 1990; Noam, chapter 6, this volume; Noam, Powers, Kilkenny, & Beedy, 1990; Sroufe & Fleeson, 1986). Indeed, because the changes that occur in relationships during development are so massive, they can easily obscure the continuities (Fischer, Knight, & Van Parys, 1993; van Geert, 1994). Progress in analysis of development and vulnerability in relationships requires a system for analyzing development of relationships and attachments so that both change and continuity can be detected and described.

A key characteristic of relationships is that people follow specific roles with each other, based on cultural norms, individual histories, and joint experiences. For close relationships, attachment theorists typically call these role combinations *working models*[1] (Bowlby, 1969; Bretherton, 1985; Shaver & Hazan, 1992). We have studied development of cultural and individual roles for a number of years and devised methods for describing and predicting their development (Calverley, Fischer, & Ayoub, 1994; Fischer, Hand, Watson, Van Parys, & Tucker, 1984; Kennedy, 1994; Lamborn, Fischer, & Pipp, 1994; Raya, 1993; Watson & Fischer, 1993). In this chapter, we describe these methods through detailed exposition of a couple who fall in love, get married, begin a family, and then develop serious relationship problems.

The system for analyzing change and continuity in working models of relationships analyzes development and use of specific relationship roles by individuals and couples. Development of these roles is molded by both experience in specific close relationships and emotions tied to those relationships, so that the developing roles are constrained to follow socioemotional scripts that are culturally and biologically defined as well as based in individual experience (Fischer, Shaver, & Carnochan, 1990; Frijda, 1988; Lazarus, 1991). Our system for analyzing the development of people's close relationships integrates these components to characterize both (a) individuals' working models of their relationships and (b) couple's coordination of their interactions to form a common working model.

FALLING IN LOVE: A MESHING OF RELATIONSHIP MODELS

To illustrate how to analyze relationship development, we present the case of John Thomas and Susan Jones and describe how they developed models of close relationships and then meshed those models when they met. Our focus is on the working models rather than on the tools used to describe them. The tools and diagrams for representing the models are generally transparent and straightforward, so that a technical presentation of the concepts behind them is not necessary here. The general principles for developmental analysis have been explained in detail elsewhere in presentations of dynamic skill theory (Fischer, 1980; Fischer & Ayoub, 1994; Fischer & Farrar, 1987; Fischer et al., 1990). The cases described here are composites from several real cases, which were combined to protect the subjects' confidentiality.

Susan and John were both in their 30s and very much "in love." They had

---

[1]The word *internal* is often used in addition — internal working models — but it is misleading to call working models *internal*. Like all skills, they are directly linked with context, requiring specific contextual support to function and develop. They are not simply internal! See further discussion later in this chapter.

met a year earlier and had become intrigued with each other. John began to pursue Susan vigorously. He found her beautiful and pure, calling her "my Venus." He sent her flowers every day, dropped in unannounced in her art classroom at a local college, and periodically whisked her away to candle-light dinners and moonlight cruises. After some caution and resistance to his advances, she fell in love with him, too, enjoying all the special attention he gave her and finding that they shared intellect, artistic interests, aesthetics, passion, and much more. Their friends saw them as the perfect couple—intelligent, attractive, charming, and cultured. They decided to get married and remained intensely in love, in the sense that they were obsessed with each other and driven to be together, following a standard emotional script for love (Fischer et al., 1990; Shaver & Hazan, 1992). A year after the wedding, Susan gave birth to a baby girl, whom they named Amy. From her first marriage, Susan also had a 4-year-old son named Peter.

During the next year serious conflicts emerged and grew gradually worse. John acted paternalistic and all-knowledgeable, frequently criticizing his wife and attempting to dictate her activities and how she, Amy, and Peter would dress and act, especially in public. His demands were often excessive, as when he insisted on having sexual intercourse while she was breastfeeding their daughter, despite her objections. At the same time, in public he praised Susan and the children to friends, calling them the perfect wife and children.

Susan enjoyed all the special romantic attention that John had showered on her, and she respected his obvious talents. With his shift to a more controlling, tyrannical approach to their relationship, however, she began to feel betrayed and to withdraw from him. In response to her withdrawal, he alternated between renewed romance and anger. Sometimes he would reassure her that she was his Venus, the perfect woman for him. Sometimes he would become enraged at what he said was her stupidity and lack of gratitude.

The situation deteriorated, with increasingly frequent disputes. John was sometimes violent, hitting his wife, shaking her, or dragging her across the room. Six years after their marriage, Susan separated from him and tried to exclude him from her, Amy's, and Peter's life. Because of the violence and the legal separation, they all became involved with mental health and legal workers, and so we came into contact with them.

DEVELOPMENT OF MODELS OF CLOSE RELATIONSHIPS

An analysis of the development of John's and Susan's models of relation-ships from early childhood illuminates how they formed their working models in childhood, how as adults they came to fall in love, and how their relationship eventually disintegrated. It shows age-related progression through major reorganizations of each one's working models of relationships, followed by a meshing of their models to produce their romance, and then a disintegration of the relationship in ways explainable in terms of their relationship models. The analysis shows both stability and transformation in relationship models and highlights the pervasive effects of emotions in organizing relationships.

People construct their individual working models of close relationships based on the major role relations that they experience in their family and other close affiliations, and gradually they build complex models that connect multiple roles (Edelstein, chapter 4, this volume; Fischer et al., 1984; Gilligan, chapter 9, this volume; Gilligan & Attanucci, 1988; Horowitz, 1987; Luborsky & Crits-Christoph, 1990; Luborsky et al., chapter 11, this volume; Noam, chapter 6, this volume; Noam et al., 1990; Watson & Fischer, 1993). These roles are organized in terms of not only the specific people and their role relationships but also the emotions experienced in the interactions and the contexts in which the interactions occur.

Cognition and emotion flow together in development of relationships. Emotions are not just internal experiences (feelings) but adaptive reactions. People evaluate how a situation relates to their goals and concerns in relationships, and they react emotionally based on that evaluation (Barrett & Campos, 1987; Fischer et al., 1990; Frijda, 1988; Lazarus, 1991). These emotional reactions bias or constrain activity to certain action tendencies or social scripts prescribed by the particular emotion. In this way, emotions mold both immediate activity and long-term development, and these molding effects are especially powerful in close relationships.

Of course, love is one of the central emotions molding relationships, with security of attachment being a major dimension of working models (Ainsworth et al., 1978; Bowlby, 1969; Shaver & Clark, chapter 2, this volume). Attachment theory in its most popular form treats working models as falling simply into three basic types, each based on a different constellation of love and other emotions – secure, ambivalent, or avoidant attachment. We believe that analysis of developing relationships requires descriptions much more differentiated than these three types, including other dimensions of role relationships besides security. Analysis needs as well to include the roles of context and culture in the development of working models of relationships (Fischer & Ayoub, 1994; LeVine & Miller, 1990). These diverse components of working models are all needed to describe the development of John's and Susan's romance and their ensuing troubles.

In characterizing the changes and continuities in development of working models, we start from a different assumption about the nature of developmental pathways. Contrary to the common assumption that development proceeds along a single ladder of stages, we assume that it forms a web of multiple pathways or strands. This developmental web is the norm for the full range of skills, from relationships to logic tasks (Bidell & Fischer, 1992; Fischer et al., 1990). Contrary to the assumptions of many models of the mind, including Piaget's (1957, 1975) and Kohlberg's (1969), people do not have integrated, fundamentally logical minds (Biggs & Collis, 1982; Feldman, 1980; Flavell, 1982; Noam, chapter 6, this volume; Selman & Schultz, 1990). Instead, people's minds are naturally fractionated, even while specific strands can potentially be integrated (Fischer & Ayoub, 1994; Fischer & Pipp, 1984; Noam, Chandler, & LaLonde, in press 1995). The diverse components affecting working models mold the organization of these strands, as becomes evident for John and Susan. Working models of role relationships develop systematically through a series of skill levels, but the skills vary across domains (strands in the web) and do not typically form a unified whole.

One of the central organizers of developing relationships is the positive-negative dimension of emotions, which produces natural affective splitting of development into separate strands. Figure 7.1 shows a developmental web of working models of positive and negative social interactions for many children between ages 1 and 8. Children develop along three emotionally distinct pathways or strands (bold lines in Fig. 7.1) — negative, positive, and

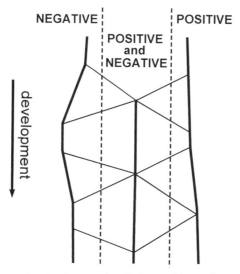

FIG. 7.1. Portion of a developmental web for positive and negative models of interactions. Three strands (domains) of 1- to 8-year-old children's models for social interactions are organized around emotional valence: negative, positive, and negative coordinated with positive (Fischer & Ayoub, 1994). Thick lines mark the main strands, thinner lines mark connections among the strands, and dotted lines mark the approximate separation of the domains.

integration of negative and positive—and they also show many connections between strands (thinner lines). Gradually, they become more able to integrate positive and negative in interactions (e.g., "I'll be nice to you if you're nice to me, but if you're mean to me, I'll be mean back"). At the same time, they also maintain the emotional tendency to split positive and negative interactions, which is retained throughout life. This tendency to split interactions emotionally is pervasive not only in children's interactions but in adults' working models of relationships, and it contributed powerfully to Susan's and John's relationship.

The web in Fig. 7.1 illustrates the general kind of developmental pattern that most working models show, but to be really useful, a web needs to be more specific—representing particular skills and strands, the interactions and feelings of real people. Our analyses describe the development of Susan's and John's working models from early childhood and their development of common working models during their courtship and marriage. Susan and John each organized their working models into two sharply distinct, emotionally split strands, for which distinct emotions and relationship styles were central. The third strand of integration across the emotional split was partly developed for Susan but essentially absent for John. When they met, they meshed their several strands of working models, forming a new joint model that was the basis for their romance and marriage. Understanding the several strands for Susan and John illuminates both how their working models meshed in romance and how the models eventually led to crisis.

Susan Jones: Development of Working Models for Attachment Loss

Susan's mother-to-be was a smart, attractive college student, just 18 years of age. In her first year in college, she fell in love with a charming fellow student, became pregnant with Susan, and dropped out of college. She planned to devote the next years of her life to being a mother and wife. Unfortunately, Susan's father died in an automobile accident before she was born, and her mother had to change her life drastically. Instead of devoting herself to her new family, as she had planned, she decided to continue her schooling.

Baby Susan lived with her mother's parents while her mother went to school, and she grew strongly attached to her grandparents. Around her first birthday, however, her grandfather had a stroke and became disabled. Susan and her mother moved to an aunt's house for several months, but that situation did not prove stable or workable. The following year, after the grandfather had partly recovered from his stroke, they moved back to her grandparents' home. Unfortunately, as a result of the grandfather's disability, the old couple proved unable to cope with their young grand-daughter. Eventually, when Susan was 3 years old, she and her mother moved to an apartment of their own.

The frequent moves and changes in relationships were difficult for Susan. She was cared for occasionally by her mother but more frequently by her grandparents, her aunt, and various other relatives and babysitters. Instead of a few stable close relationships, Susan experienced recurring loss of attachments. By age 4, Susan was both independent and needy, alternating between withdrawal and clinginess. In her play she repeated themes of loss and hypervigilance: Little girls were constantly getting lost or being taken away by monsters.

Susan's working models of relationships at this age involved two prominent domains, shown as two distinct strands in Fig. 7.2. In the domain of disengagement, she felt alone and maintained a detached attitude. In the domain of caring, she felt loved and cared for; but she was constantly in fear of being left alone (shifted to disengagement) — losing her caregiver whom she loved, especially her mother and grandparents. These two domains were sharply split or separated emotionally, as indicated by the double dotted line in Fig. 7.2. Although the domains each had positive and negative aspects for Susan, caring was more positive than disengagement. Much of the time Susan coped by being detached, but when she was able to find a person and situation where she could feel cared for, she wanted to remain there and was anxious about being abandoned or forced to disengage from the relationship. Of course, she generally wanted to have her mother present, not only physically but also emotionally.

Susan gradually developed along the strands in Fig. 7.2. At the simplest level, the initial development of single representations, Susan represented each of the domains in terms of her own basic socioemotional state, with the caregiver's role being assumed as background (as is normal for young children when they focus on themselves). In the caring domain, she was a child loved, ME_{LOVED}, while in the disengaged domain, she was a child alone, ME_{ALONE}. She was clingy because she was afraid of being shifted from a caring relationship to a disengaged one:

$$\begin{bmatrix} \overset{caring}{ME}_{LOVED} \end{bmatrix} > \begin{bmatrix} \overset{disengaged}{ME}_{ALONE} \end{bmatrix} \qquad (1)$$

Susan could also focus on her mother more than herself, and then her dominant working model was whether her mother was present or absent. She feared that her mother would shift from being present in a caring relationship to being gone in a disengaged relationship:

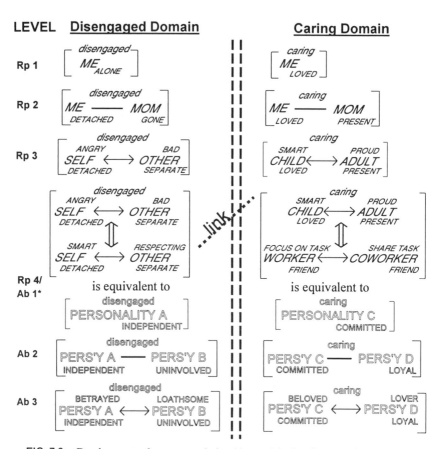

FIG. 7.2. Development of separate relationship models for disengaged and caring domains in attachment loss. *Level Ab 1 marks the emergence of a new kind of skill structure, an abstraction, which grows from the coordination of representational systems. A system of representational systems constitutes a single abstraction, as shown here. *Note.* In the diagrams, square brackets mark skill structures, italicized letters indicate representational sets, outline letters indicate abstract sets, and lines and arrows indicate relations between sets (Fischer & Ayoub, 1994). Numbers attached to the words indicate different but related representations or abstractions. The dotted lines between the domains indicate that the domains are affectively split but not rigidly dissociated. The dotted line marked "link" shows one case of a link across the two domains, involving positive evaluation of being smart. See text for explanation of specific skills.

$$\begin{bmatrix} caring \\ MOM \\ \quad PRESENT \end{bmatrix} > \begin{bmatrix} disengaged \\ MOM \\ \quad GONE \end{bmatrix} \qquad (2)$$

By age 4, Susan could sometimes sustain a more complex relationship model with her mother or grandparent. She related her own roles with those of her mother, coordinating them for each domain into a representational mapping (the second level of representational skills that children develop). She sought to sustain a caring mapping,

$$\begin{bmatrix} & \textit{caring} & \\ \textit{ME} & \text{——} & \textit{MOM} \\ \textit{LOVED} & & \textit{PRESENT} \end{bmatrix} \tag{3}$$

and avoid a disengaged one,

$$\begin{bmatrix} & \textit{disengaged} & \\ \textit{ME} & \text{——} & \textit{MOM} \\ \textit{DETACHED} & & \textit{GONE} \end{bmatrix} \tag{4}$$

Just before Susan's fifth birthday, her mother married a journalist at the local newspaper, and a year later her first brother was born. Joe's birth drastically changed her life, increasing her emotional distance and her feelings of being different. She tried to show her mother that she could help with her brother, but when she was alone with him, she was mean and aggressive, repeatedly taking his toys away and drinking from his bottles herself or keeping him from drinking from them. As he grew older, he started to defend himself and tell his parents what she did, and her hidden anger became more public. She tried to blame Joe, with only minimal success.

As Susan grew older, she developed a working model for a disengaged relationship that combined anger and attributions of badness with the detachment she had developed earlier with her mother. The connection between anger and badness had been present earlier in her relationship with her mother as well, but now with her new capacity for building representational systems (Level Rp 3 in Fig. 7.2), she consolidated anger and badness with detachment and separation in a single working model. Susan used this working model generally across disengaged "close" relationships with her mother, her brother, Joe, and other people:

$$\begin{bmatrix} & \textit{disengaged} & \\ \textit{ANGRY} & & \textit{BAD} \\ \textit{SELF} & \longleftrightarrow & \textit{OTHER} \\ \textit{DETACHED} & & \textit{SEPARATE} \end{bmatrix} \tag{5}$$

When Susan went to school, she excelled academically, and her family was proud of her intelligence. Being smart became a central part of her caring relationships with her mother, stepfather, and brother, and it especially helped her to engage her mother's pride and thus feel loved:

$$\begin{bmatrix} & \textit{caring} & \\ \textit{SMART} & & \textit{PROUD} \\ \textit{CHILD} & \longleftrightarrow & \textit{ADULT} \\ \textit{LOVED} & & \textit{PRESENT} \end{bmatrix} \tag{6}$$

Susan's friendships at school were also based on her academic competence. She formed primarily disengaged relationships with other children, relating around school projects and the other child's respect for Susan's expertise. In this way she developed a different, more positive kind of disengaged working model of relationships, based in another's respect for her intelligence:

$$
\begin{bmatrix}
& \textit{disengaged} & \\
\text{SMART} & & \text{RESPECTING} \\
\textit{SELF} & \longleftrightarrow & \textit{OTHER} \\
\text{DETACHED} & & \text{SEPARATE}
\end{bmatrix} \tag{7}
$$

Because being smart was also central to her working model in the caring domain with her family, Susan began to make important links between her disengaged and caring working models. Although Susan retained a strong tendency to split her disengaged and caring models of relationships (marked by the double dotted lines in Fig. 7.2), she was capable under supportive circumstances of making some links between them. These links were strengthened further by a new kind of working model in the caring domain: In school, she occasionally formed a friendship based on one of the tasks she was involved in, and so she began to develop a working model for friendship founded in sharing specific tasks:

$$
\begin{bmatrix}
& \textit{caring} & \\
\text{FOCUS ON TASK} & & \text{SHARE TASK} \\
\textit{WORKER} & \longleftrightarrow & \textit{COWORKER} \\
\text{FRIEND} & & \text{FRIEND}
\end{bmatrix} \tag{8}
$$

During high school, Susan coordinated several of these concrete working models to form the sophisticated combinations of role relationships that generally become possible at 10 to 15 years of age with the new level of systems of representational systems (Level Rp 4/Ab 1). Susan could combine several concrete working models to form an abstraction (what Inhelder & Piaget, 1955/1958, called "formal operations"), as shown in Fig. 7.2 for both domains. In the disengaged domain, she combined her angry model with her smart one to form an abstract personality role emphasizing her independence. She strived to coordinate detachment, separation, intelligence, and respect, and there was some anger and suspicion as well under the surface.

In the caring domain, she combined her smart/proud model with her task-sharing/friendship one, forming an abstract personality role emphasizing her commitment in caring relationships. She strived to coordinate intelligence, pride, love, connection, task orientation, and friendship, as shown in Fig. 7.2. When she felt secure and not anxious, she could begin to form such a caring relationship of commitment, but she was extremely cautious about extending the commitment beyond a specific task or project. She was concerned about being put in the role of a vulnerable child. In this way she shifted between a committed persona and an independent one, generally preferring independence as safer:

$$\left[\begin{array}{c} \text{disengaged} \\ \text{PERSONALITY A} \\ \text{INDEPENDENT} \end{array} \right] > \left[\begin{array}{c} \text{caring} \\ \text{PERSONALITY C} \\ \text{COMMITTED} \end{array} \right] \qquad (9)$$

In high school and college, Susan continued to excel academically and to base most of her peer relationships in her academic work. Personally she strove to be academically competent, independent, and self-sufficient both emotionally and financially. Most of the time she avoided making commitments to people. When she did make a commitment to a task or person, however, she did so with intensity and total dedication. She believed that commitment required a special kind of loyalty, in which she strove to share her most important beliefs and values with the other person and maintain good faith and trust. Consistent with her general insecurity in close relationships, she tried to avoid any action or statement that could be seen as betrayal. In this way commitment and loyalty were strongly connected for her in a working model at Level Ab 2, an abstract mapping:

$$\left[\begin{array}{c} \text{caring} \\ \text{PERSONALITY C} \hspace{-0.5em}\rule[0.5ex]{2em}{0.4pt}\hspace{-0.5em} \text{PERSONALITY D} \\ \text{COMMITTED} \hspace{6em} \text{LOYAL} \end{array} \right] \qquad (10)$$

During her senior year in college, she developed her first intimate adult relationship. She began to work on a class project with a young man named Larry, and they gradually became close. Larry showered Susan with gifts and praised her femininity, a part of herself that she kept tightly guarded. Larry respected her for her intelligence, thus relating to the talents that were important for both her disengaged and caring models. Larry's respect helped her move from disengaged independence to caring commitment with him. Larry was self-confident and at times arrogant, and he swept her off her feet. He asked her to marry him after graduation, and not knowing her own feelings, she went along with him.

In the meantime, Susan's brother Joe was diagnosed with cancer, but her mother did not inform her of the seriousness of his illness. Blocking out any negative emotions, as she was accustomed to do, she moved ahead with the plans for her wedding. Only 2 weeks before the wedding she learned from a friend at the hospital that her brother was dying. Nevertheless, she was married on schedule, and 3 weeks later while she was on her honeymoon, her brother Joe died. Following her mother's suggestion, she did not return for the funeral but continued on her honeymoon. As evident from this series of events, Susan had a remarkable capacity to remain not only independent but uninvolved emotionally. When she sought independence, she would disengage emotionally to an extreme:

$$\text{(11)}$$

Susan soon became pregnant and had a son, whom she and Larry named Peter. After a year or so, Larry had an affair with another woman, and Susan felt betrayed. She shifted to a disengaged pattern with Larry, and the marriage soon ended. She felt anger and loathing for him but instead of expressing these feelings to him directly, she sabotaged his visits with Peter. She built a sophisticated personality system for disengaging from him, which combined independence and uninvolvement with loathing and a sense of betrayal:

$$\text{(12)}$$

A few years after the divorce, Susan met John. Like Larry, he courted her intensely and swept her off her feet, but Susan felt that he was more of a soulmate than Larry had been. They shared great respect for intellect, an artistic sensibility, many interests, and an exciting sex life. Over the months of their intense courtship, she initially resisted, but eventually they built what she felt was considerable loyalty and trust. John showed an intense love for Susan, and based on it, she constructed a working model that she had never achieved with Larry, combining commitment and loyalty with a strong sense of passionate love:

$$\text{(13)}$$

John Thomas: Development of Working Models
for Hidden Family Violence

Like Susan, John had a difficult childhood, but the difficulties were different for the two of them. Whereas Susan grew up with frequent disruptions of her attachments, John grew up in a family characterized by hidden family violence. His parents made a sharp division between private and public worlds, and in the private world they were tyrannical, especially John's father. Virtually all people in all cultures distinguish private and public spheres, of course, both contextually (home vs. community) and emotionally (e.g., Miyake & Yamazaki, 1995), but John's parents showed a separation so strong that it formed a dissociation, an unconsciously maintained isolation of the two spheres. When family members were operating in one sphere, they had difficulty even thinking or talking about the other sphere. Unfortunately such isolating dissociation is frequent in hidden family violence, in which violent families build a highly positive image in the community, as described elsewhere (Fischer & Ayoub, 1994).

This rigid dissociation is marked in Fig. 7.3 by the double solid lines separating John's private and public domains, which each show independent development of working models of close relationships. Susan had a strong tendency to split disengaged and caring relationships, probably because of her history of loss of attachments after her father's early death. Yet sometimes she could connect parts of the two domains, and often she talked and thought about both of them together. That is why the lines separating her two domains in Fig. 7.2 are not solid: They are partly permeable, like most domains divided by emotional splitting. After early childhood, John showed no such permeability in his dissociation of private and public domains.

When John was 4 years old, he was sitting at the dinner table with his parents and his sister. His father, whose company had just gone bankrupt, sat with stoic silence. His mother glared at her husband, upset that her world of community activities and charity functions was falling apart because of her husband's incompetence. Unknowingly John tried to talk about the life cycle of the turtle, a topic that his mother had proudly asked him to describe at several recent public gatherings to show off his intelligence. His father slapped his face without warning and said in a steely calm voice, "Not one word from any of you! You are all here at my request, and you will speak in this house only when I say you can." Mr. Thomas took pains to emphasize that even his wife stayed in his house only because he allowed it.

This interaction was typical of the tone of young John's household. His father was domineering and at times physically abusive, demanding strict regimentation of his children. John's mother was an active socialite who cared greatly about the appearance and presentation of her children but left their nurturing to a long series of nannies, few of whom remained in the household for long. Most of the positive attention that John received was for his public successes, especially his intellectual performance.

When John began to recite the turtle life cycle at dinner, he was not distinguishing between his family's public and private worlds, inadvertently

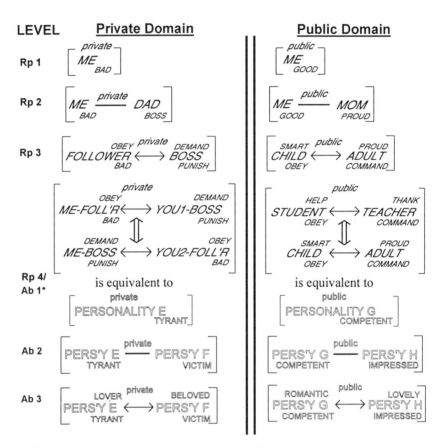

FIG. 7.3. Development of dissociated relationship models for private and public domains in hidden family violence. *Level Ab 1 marks the emergence of a new kind of skill structure, an abstraction, which grows from the coordination of representational systems. A system of representational systems constitutes a single abstraction, as shown here. *Note.* In the diagrams, square brackets mark skill structures, italicized letters indicate representational sets, outline letters indicate abstract sets, and lines and arrows indicate relations between sets (Fischer & Ayoub, 1994). Numbers attached to the words indicate different but related representations or abstractions. The solid lines between the domains indicate a strong dissociation between them. See text for explanation of specific skills.

allowing the domains to be permeable. His mistake was to try to act good in a way that was appropriate for showing off in public, ME_{GOOD}. In the public domain, his mother was proud of his good behavior of showing off his knowledge, and he understood this working model:

$$\left[ME \xrightarrow{\text{public}} MOM \atop {}_{GOOD} \qquad {}_{PROUD} \right] \qquad (14)$$

But his parents did not allow that kind of action in private, where his father was the boss and John was often treated as bad, ME_{BAD}, and expected to submit himself completely to his father's wishes. He needed to distinguish the public working model from this private one:

$$\left[ME_{BAD} \xrightarrow{\ private\ } DAD_{BOSS} \right] \tag{15}$$

During the next couple of years, John had to learn to dissociate these two working models of family relationships. Going beyond knowing when to act on the public model and when on the private, he had to make sure that the private model did not appear in public;:

$$\left[ME_{BAD} \xrightarrow{\ private\ } ADULT_{BOSS} \right] \ \rlap{\big|}{\Big\}} \left[ME_{GOOD} \xrightarrow{\ public\ } ADULT_{PROUD} \right] \tag{16}$$

This form of the working models was more general than the ones specific to mom or dad. In Model 16, the relation of isolating dissociation is marked by the thick line through the symbol for shifting between skills; in Fig. 7.3 this same dissociative process is marked by the solid double lines. With development of isolating dissociation, children build more and more complex working models in each isolated domain, increasing their complexity and sophistication in a manner similar to that for more acceptable social skills (Fischer & Ayoub, 1994). Although hidden family violence may be pathological, it can produce complex, sophisticated working models, as John's development demonstrates.

The next major development in John's working models involved his adding components to the roles and generalizing them further beyond his own family situation. For each domain he began to take on either role in a relationship model, acting sometimes as follower and sometimes as boss, sometimes as child and sometimes as adult:

$$\left[\underset{BAD}{\overset{OBEY}{FOLLOWER}} \xleftrightarrow{\ private\ } \underset{PUNISH}{\overset{DEMAND}{BOSS}} \right] \ \rlap{\big|}{\Big\}} \left[\underset{OBEY}{\overset{SMART}{CHILD}} \xleftrightarrow{\ public\ } \underset{COMMAND}{\overset{PROUD}{ADULT}} \right] \tag{17}$$

In school at age 10, he demonstrated this role switching in his relations with other children, as he began to take on dominant roles in both domains: In the private domain, he became the boss dominating another child, and in the public one he became the adult proud of the other child. He built up these roles especially with a smaller boy named Bruce, who was timid but bright. When John found Bruce alone or away from the teacher's attention, he threatened the smaller boy, hit him, criticized his work, or belittled him. On the other hand, when the teacher was watching, John was especially attentive to Bruce, acting the role of the proud and helpful adult. He helped Bruce finish a routine in gym, worked with him on some arithmetic problems, or asked the teacher if he could sit next to Bruce to protect him from the other boys.

During adolescence, John coordinated several of these concrete working models in each domain to form sophisticated combinations of role relationships at the new level of systems of representational systems, which are shown for Level Rp 4/Ab 1 in Fig. 7.3. He thus formed abstract personalities in each domain. In the private domain, he combined two versions of the boss–follower model, one in which he was boss and one in which he was follower, and thus formed a persona of tyrant–victim (where he sought to be in the dominant tyrant position whenever possible). In the public domain, he combined the proud-adult/smart-child model with that of teacher/student, forming a persona of a competent, helpful person. As part of his dissociation between public and private domains, he shifted sharply between these two personas, just as he had earlier shifted between concrete role relationships for private and public:

$$\left[\begin{array}{c} \text{private} \\ \text{PERSONALITY E} \\ \text{TYRANT} \end{array} \right] \ \text{\ding{}}\ \left[\begin{array}{c} \text{public} \\ \text{PERSONALITY G} \\ \text{COMPETENT} \end{array} \right] \qquad (18)$$

John and his family moved to Chicago when he was 16, and he spent the last 2 years of high school there. Some of his teachers saw him as a highly gifted, charismatic young man, but others felt that he was sneaky and dishonest. He had no close friends and was seen as distant or devious by his peers. He saw himself as a star of the track team and the debate team, and he was often effective at impressing authorities, as evidenced by the teachers who were so impressed with him. He had built a working model in which he used his competence effectively to build relationships with important people by impressing them:

$$\left[\begin{array}{c} \text{public} \\ \text{PERSONALITY G} \text{\textemdash\textemdash} \text{PERSONALITY H} \\ \text{COMPETENT} \qquad\qquad \text{IMPRESSED} \end{array} \right] \qquad (19)$$

In his second year in Chicago, he was accused of involvement in a cheating scandal. Other students strongly implicated him as an organizer of the stealing and circulation of tests. But he avidly and convincingly denied involvement, escaped suspension, and helped to provide evidence against other students. He clearly had mastered his public persona of being competent and impressive with authority figures.

Privately he continued to work to establish himself as dominant in relationships with his peers and siblings, and he became even more skilled at hiding these manipulations from the public eye, as evidenced by his success in covering up his cheating. He constructed a persona in which tyrant and victim roles were more clearly differentiated, so that he could more effectively manipulate them and take on the dominant role himself more of the time.

$$\left[\begin{array}{cc} \text{private} \\ \underset{\text{TYRANT}}{\text{PERSONALITY E}} \text{ ----- } \underset{\text{VICTIM}}{\text{PERSONALITY F}} \end{array} \right] \qquad (20)$$

John attended college, interrupted by service in the U.S. Merchant Marine, and he joined the anti-Vietnam War movement. Although he was an active, public participant in the movement, he was unsuccessful in his efforts to become one of its leaders. In fact, throughout his time in college, the Merchant Marine, and the anti-war movement, he built no major long-term relationships and had no close friends.

In the ensuing years, he gradually established a career as an independent graphics designer and as a literary critic for the local newspaper. He continued to excel at impressing people in authority. His speech was lyrical and full of literary references, and he showed considerable knowledge of the cultural world. He exuded a sense of self-confidence, intellectual superiority, and entitlement. He spoke often of his work with famous actors and artists.

John reported that during these years he had many "great friends" with whom he shared lots of laughter, good times, and intellectually stimulating excursions to dance performances, plays, and other cultural events. Although he had multiple romances, he had no lasting intimate relationships. He talked proudly of dating daughters of famous generals and artists, and he described highly eroticized encounters with beautiful women:

$$\left[\begin{array}{cc} \text{public} \\ \underset{\text{ROMANTIC}}{\text{PERSONALITY G}} \text{ ----- } \underset{\text{LOVELY}}{\text{PERSONALITY H}} \end{array} \right] \qquad (21)$$

Unfortunately, according to him, all the women lacked intellect or artistic interests, and he lost interest in them.

At age 38, John decided that he wanted to settle down, get married, and "have heirs." He met Susan, who was an art instructor at a local college. He began his whirlwind courtship of her, describing her as his beautiful, pure

Venus, sending her flowers every day, surprising her with visits to her classroom, taking her on moonlight cruises and candlelight dinners, and trying to make love to her in the closet in her classroom or on the deck of the cruise ship at night. In this courtship he combined his earlier public models of competent/impressed and romantic/lovely to form a more complex working model that was highly effective in engaging Susan:

$$\begin{bmatrix} \text{ROMANTIC} & ^{\text{public}} & \text{LOVELY} \\ \text{PERSONALITY G} \longleftrightarrow & \text{PERSONALITY H} \\ \text{COMPETENT} & \text{IMPRESSED} \end{bmatrix} \qquad (22)$$

Unfortunately, this complex working model was only for the public domain. As he and Susan became involved and intimate, they began to operate in the private domain, and his dissociated private working model gradually came to the fore. Although it too was complex and sophisticated and had a love relationship at its core, it was founded on the tyrant/victim model that John had been building since early childhood:

$$\begin{bmatrix} \text{LOVER} & ^{\text{private}} & \text{BELOVED} \\ \text{PERSONALITY E} \longleftrightarrow & \text{PERSONALITY F} \\ \text{TYRANT} & \text{VICTIM} \end{bmatrix} \qquad (23)$$

Had John not developed such a powerful dissociation between his public and private models, the presence of love in both models (lover/beloved in the private and romantic/lovely in the public) might have facilitated his linking the two, in the same way that Susan had linked her disengaged and caring models through focusing on her intelligence (Fig. 7.2). Unfortunately John's dissociation prevented that linkage and so made it difficult for him to construct a new private model based on his relationship with Susan.

John and Susan had initially constructed a romantic relationship that successfully combined their working models. Now, however, they were faced with a pressing need to rework their relationship. Description of the joint working model that they co-constructed will help explicate how they fell in love and how the crisis in their relationship emerged.

CO-CONSTRUCTION OF RELATIONSHIP MODELS BY SUSAN AND JOHN

Although Susan and John had different individual working models of close relationships, just as all couples do, they shared strong resonances between their models. Both had a focus on intelligence and competence, both were inclined to energetic courtship, both had a tendency to remain aloof until they felt safe, and both strongly split between more private, involved domains and more public, detached ones. These resonances allowed them to participate in and support each other's working models. It allowed them to fall in love.

Much research and theory on relationships treats working models as if they are a characteristic of an individual. For example, attachment theorists speak of *internal* working models as if people carry a model inside themselves and apply it to others (Bowlby, 1969; Bretherton, 1985), and many psychodynamic theorists talk as if relationship representations, while originating from intimate relationships, come to be so internalized that they function from within the person (Freud, 1936/1966; Greenwald, 1980; Kernberg, 1975; Kohut, 1977; for a creative extension of this work see Blatt & Bass, chapter 12, this volume). We have dropped the word *internal* because it misleadingly minimizes the ecological nature of working models. Other people are literally a part of a person's working models, just as people, objects, and events are a part of all skills (Fischer, Bullock, Rotenberg, & Raya, 1993; Levitt & Selman, chapter 8, this volume; Raya, 1993; Noam, chapter 6, this volume; Rogoff, 1993; Selman & Schultz, 1990). Some classic works such as those of Sullivan (1953), Meade (1934), and Vygotsky (1978) recognized the social-ecological nature of relationships and knowledge more generally. In social conceptions of psychoanalysis, concepts such as projective identification also build on the concept that people jointly construct their social models (Shapiro & Carr, 1991).

This contextual nature of working models explains how Susan and John fell in love with each other, because their working models resonated together, sustaining and providing support for each other. In general, people seek contexts (other people and situations) that support their working models because the models can fully function only with those contexts.

Susan and John supported each other's working models, and in building a close relationship, they co-constructed joint models. Growing from their individual models, the joint models were built separately and became an emergent characteristic of them as a couple (Allport, 1961). Figure 7.4 outlines how their co-constructed models developed in the course of their relationship. Because they were mature adults when they met, their co-constructed models did not begin at the early developmental levels that would be characteristic of children, but instead quickly assumed the sophisticated functioning of abstract persona, similar to the higher levels in the individual working models described in Fig. 7.2 and 7.3.

When Susan and John first met, their relationship was somewhat reserved in the manner of most initial adult relationships in the Northeast of the United States, where they lived. Susan responded to John in terms of her disengaged independent persona (Ab 1 and Ab 2 in Fig. 7.2), and John

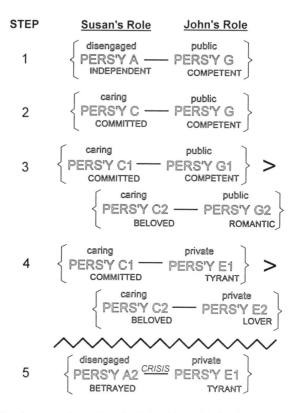

STEP	Susan's Role	John's Role

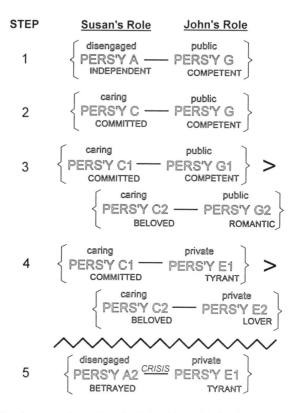

FIG. 7.4.   Development of coordinated relationship models by the couple Susan Jones and John Thomas. *Note.* In the diagrams, pointed brackets are used to indicate that the diagrams represent skills co-constructed in a dyad, not controlled by one individual. The large arrowheads separating two skills at Steps 3 and 4 indicate a shift between the skills, which are both prominent for the couple but are not coordinated yet. The toothed line indicates a major break in the relationship. The word *CRISIS* over the line in Step 5 indicates that the relationship has shifted to be predominantly hostile and contentious.

responded to Susan in terms of his public competent persona (Ab 1 and Ab 2 in Fig. 7.3). Over several interactions they jointly constructed a public, independent relationship based in their individual working models:

$$\left\{ \begin{array}{c} \text{Susan disengaged} \\ \text{PERSONALITY A} \\ \text{INDEPENDENT} \end{array} \quad\mathrel{\rule[0.5ex]{2em}{2pt}}\quad \begin{array}{c} \text{John public} \\ \text{PERSONALITY G} \\ \text{COMPETENT} \end{array} \right\} \tag{24}$$

Note that Susan's role in the joint model is listed on the left and John's on the right. The co-constructed nature of the working model is marked by pointed brackets instead of the flat ones that mark individual working models.

As Susan came to trust John and feel affection for him, she changed her participation from her disengaged persona to her caring one (Levels Ab 1 and Ab 2 in Fig. 7.2). From her perspective, John and she were becoming friends and even soulmates, committed and loyal. John maintained his public persona, trying to impress her with his competence. Their co-constructed relationship transformed from coolly independent to warmly committed, mostly as a result of Susan's shift to her caring persona.

$$\left\{ \begin{array}{cc} \text{Susan caring} & \text{John public} \\ \text{PERSONALITY C} \longrightarrow \text{PERSONALITY G} \\ \text{COMMITTED} & \text{COMPETENT} \end{array} \right\} \qquad (25)$$

John also contributed to the growing closeness by sometimes functioning with his public romantic persona, the one that had led him to so many short-lived, intense romances (Model 21). Susan found his intense courtship highly attractive, and he persisted in his courtship because of his new concern for finding a wife to "make heirs." Together they built two co-constructed models, which they shifted between to fit the needs of the moment.

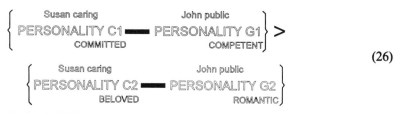

This kind of shifting between working models is a normal part of adult relationships, and often it is transitional to an integration of the two models to form one higher level, more complex model:

The strength of Susan's and John's attraction to each other would normally have led them to build such a sophisticated joint model. Susan would have used her caring model to contribute the beloved/committed component (Level Ab 3 in Fig. 7.2), and John would have used his public model to contribute the romantic/competent component. Unfortunately, John's contribution was only through his public model, and as Susan and he built their (private) life together, he began to shift to his private model. Because of his isolating dissociation between public and private, he was unable to build his private life around his public model.

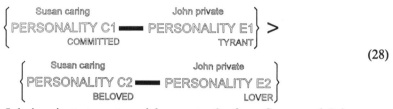

$$(28)$$

As John's private tyrant model came to the fore, Susan and John experienced serious problems. Susan resonated to the lover/beloved part of John's working model (Level Ab 3 in Fig. 7.3), but she did not resonate to the tyrant/victim part. She therefore fought the new co-construction and changed to a different joint model, in which she was no longer caring but disengaged:

$$\left\{ \begin{array}{c} \text{Susan disengaged} \\ \text{PERSONALITY A2} \overset{\textit{CRISIS}}{\rule{2em}{0.4pt}} \text{PERSONALITY E1} \\ \text{BETRAYED} \hspace{4em} \text{TYRANT} \end{array} \right\} \quad (29)$$

John could sometimes respond to Susan's disengagement and sense of betrayal by switching back to his public domain, engaging her in the romantic/beloved models (Models 26 and 28). As they accumulated a history of John's tyrannical, violent actions, however, Susan's attribution of betrayal solidified, and it became ever more difficult for John to accomplish the switch. The sharp dissociation of his public and private domains made it impossible for him to integrate across the domains: He was unable to move beyond his private personas in his intimate family relationships.

In the end, their relationship failed. John lived in the abusive model of hidden family violence, and Susan had the strength to reject that model and disengage from the relationship. The crisis ended their love and their marriage. Feeling totally betrayed (once again), Susan treated John as loathsome (Level Ab 3 in Fig. 7.2). She divorced him and sued for custody of their daughter.

In the public arena of divorce proceedings and custody disputes, John admitted that he had lost his temper with his wife and hit her, but he claimed that she provoked him by "trashing" his work room and "choreographing the whole incident." She stopped being the good wife and mother that she had been before, according to him, and now she was a tyrant and he was the victim in the relationship. He returned to maintaining his public persona of being competent and seeking to impress lawyers, judges, and social workers.

Although this unfortunate outcome makes sense in terms of Susan's and John's working models, it remains a great personal tragedy for both of them and for their children. Perhaps through analyzing how relationships develop and sometimes transform into such tragedies, social scientists may eventually learn ways to help people build joint working models that can overcome the bitter legacies of trauma such as hidden family violence.

CONCLUSION: ANALYZING CHANGE AND CONTINUITY IN DEVELOPMENT OF INDIVIDUAL AND JOINT WORKING MODELS

Close relationships are fundamental to the fabric of human life and culture, yet there have been no tools available for analyzing how relationships develop—neither how individuals come to construct their own models of relationships nor how a couple, family, or small group co-constructs their own joint model of their relationship. The tools we have devised combine role relationships, emotion scripts, and individual experiences with developmental processes to produce a system for analyzing change and continuity in working models of relationships.

Development of working models does not occur along steps in any simple, linear ladder. Indeed, people do not usually have a single working model of close relationships. Instead development of relationships involves movement along several branches in a web. The strands in the web are organized by the context and culture of a person's close relationships as well as the emotions she or he experiences in those relationships. Although strands are separate, they can potentially be integrated, providing links between different aspects of relationships.

Both emotions and experience with close relationships naturally produce affective splitting between strands. In extreme cases, people can actively dissociate strands, keeping them so strongly separated that links between them are virtually impossible. Based on her early history of attachment loss, Susan affectively split the domain of disengagement/independence from that of caring/commitment. Based on his experience with a family that sharply separated a violent private life from a properly positive public life, John went far beyond splitting to actively dissociate his working models for private and public domains.

Through the case of Susan and John, we have shown how the set of dynamic skill tools for depicting developmental webs can be used to analyze both individual development of working models and co-construction of joint models growing out of individual models. Consequently, we have been able to describe three different aspects of relationship development, integrating them into a single account: (a) the enormous changes that occur in relationship models during childhood, (b) the significant changes that occur during formation of new intimate relationships, and (c) the continuities in content and approach that occur across these changes.

The combination of change and continuity is especially evident in the relationship of Susan and John. When they fell in love, Susan and John showed enormous changes as they co-constructed their romantic relationship. The changes in their individual working models were dramatic, and the emergence of a new kind of relationship for each of them was both striking and potentially promising for remolding their lives. Susan built a newly sophisticated working model of a mutual relationship. Her capacity to partly overcome her splitting and to integrate across domains facilitated the development of intimacy and commitment in her and John's relationship. John became committed to a relationship with a woman for the first time in his life. He made major steps toward building a kind of intimate relationship that was new for him and potentially richly satisfying.

At the same time, the negative continuities in their relationships were dramatic, as they continued the separation of their personal lives into two disparate worlds — splitting of disengagement from caring for Susan and dissociation of private from public worlds for John. The continuities of these separations with the traumas of their childhood were evident. Unfortunately, John's dissociation of private and public made it virtually impossible for him to move beyond his family history of hidden family violence. His progress in the relationship ultimately foundered upon his powerful isolating dissociation of public and private and his tendency to create hidden family violence in the private domain. Unfortunately, in this case the troubles from earlier working models undid the promises of the new relationship.

This book reflects the powerful movement in the social sciences toward a more relational approach to human nature: People cannot legitimately be viewed as isolated individuals functioning on their own. Close relationships are essential to human nature. For the centrality of relationships to move beyond argument and affect the nature of scientific research and explanation, we need tools for analyzing how people construct relationships and how they change those constructions during both early development of relationships and formation of new relationships. Through the case of Susan and John, we have shown how a few simple tools focusing on roles and emotions in working models can be used to analyze both individual models and co-constructed dyadic ones. The resulting rich qualitative analysis can both illuminate change and continuity in development of close relationships and move research and theory toward the goal of building a truly relational science of human development.

ACKNOWLEDGMENTS

This chapter is based in part on presentations given at the meetings of the Society for Research in Child Development, March 1993, and the meetings of the Jean Piaget Society, May 1992. Sources of support for the work reported include the MacArthur Foundation Network on Early Childhood, the Spencer Foundation, and Harvard University. We thank Robin Deutsch, Donna Elmendorf, Jane Haltiwanger, Helen Hand, Catherine Kasala, Robert Kintcherff, and Phillip Shaver for their general contributions to the work reported here. We especially thank Gil Noam, Rosemary Calverley, Rebecca Hencke, and Pamela Raya for their contributions to our developmental analyses of emotions in relationships.

REFERENCES

Ainsworth, M. D., Blehar, M., Waters, E., & Wall, S. (1978). *Patterns of attachment: A psychological study of the strange situation.* Hillsdale, NJ: Lawrence Erlbaum Associates.

Allport, F. H. (1961). The contemporary appraisal of an old problem. *Contemporary Psychology, 6,* 195–197.

Barrett, K. C., & Campos, J. J. (1987). Perspectives on emotional development II: A functionalist approach to emotions. In J. Osofsky (Ed.), *Handbook of infant development* (2nd ed., pp. 555–578). New York: Wiley.

Bidell, T. R., & Fischer, K. W. (1992). Beyond the stage debate: Action, structure, and variability in Piagetian theory and research. In R. Sternberg & C. Berg (Ed.), *Intellectual development* (pp. 100–140). New York: Cambridge University Press.

Biggs, J., & Collis, K. (1982). *Evaluating the quality of learning: The SOLO taxonomy (structure of the observed learning outcome).* New York: Academic Press.

Bowlby, J. (1969). *Attachment and loss: Vol. 1. Attachment.* New York: Basic Books.

Bretherton, I. (1985). Attachment theory: Retrospect and prospect. In I. Bretherton & E. Waters (Ed.), *Growing points of attachment theory and research. Monographs of the Society for Research in Child Development, 50*(1–2, Serial No. 209), 3–40.

Bretherton, I., Ridgeway, D., & Cassidy, J. (1990). Assessing internal working models of the attachment relationships: An attachment story completion task for 3-year-olds. In M. T. Greenberg, D. Cicchetti, & E. M. Cummings (Ed.), *Attachment in the preschool years: Theory, research, and intervention* (pp. 273–308). Chicago: University of Chicago Press.

Calverley, R., Fischer, K. W., & Ayoub, C. (1994). Complex splitting of self-representations in sexually abused adolescent girls. *Development and Psychopathology, 6,* 195–213.

Feldman, D. H. (1980). *Beyond universals in cognitive development.* Norwood, NJ: Ablex.

Fischer, K. W. (1980). A theory of cognitive development: The control and construction of hierarchies of skills. *Psychological Review, 87,* 477–531.

Fischer, K. W., & Ayoub, C. (1994). Affective splitting and dissociation in normal and maltreated children: Developmental pathways for self in relationships. In D. Cicchetti & S. L. Toth (Ed.), *Rochester Symposium on development and psychopathology: Vol. 5. Disorders and dysfunctions of the self* (pp. 149–222). Rochester, NY: University of Rochester Press.

Fischer, K. W., Bullock, D., Rotenberg, E. J., & Raya, P. (1993). The dynamics of competence: How context contributes directly to skill. In R. H. Wozniak & K. W. Fischer (Ed.), *Development in context: Acting and thinking in specific environments* (pp. 93–117). Hillsdale, NJ: Lawrence Erlbaum Associates.

Fischer, K. W., & Farrar, M. J. (1987). Generalizations about generalization: How a theory of skill development explains both generality and specificity. *International Journal of Psychology, 22,* 643–677.

Fischer, K. W., Hand, H. H., Watson, M. W., Van Parys, M., & Tucker, J. (1984). Putting the child into socialization: The development of social categories in preschool children. In L. Katz (Ed.), *Current topics in early childhood education* (Vol. 5, pp. 27–72). Norwood NJ: Ablex.

Fischer, K. W., Knight, C. C., & Van Parys, M. (1993). Analyzing diversity in developmental pathways: Methods and concepts. In W. Edelstein & R. Case (Ed.), *Constructivist approaches to development. Contributions to human development* (Vol. 23, pp. 33–56). Basel, Switzerland: S. Karger.

Fischer, K. W., & Pipp, S. L. (1984). Development of the structures of unconscious thought. In K. Bowers & D. Meichenbaum (Ed.), *The unconscious reconsidered* (pp. 88–148). New York: Wiley.

Fischer, K. W., Shaver, P., & Carnochan, P. G. (1990). How emotions develop and how they organize development. *Cognition and Emotion, 4*, 81–127.

Flavell, J. (1982). Structures, stages, and sequences in cognitive development. In W. A. Collins (Ed.), *The concept of development. Minnesota Symposium on Child Psychology* (Vol. 15). Hillsdale, NJ: Lawrence Erlbaum Associates.

Freud, A. (1966). *The ego and the mechanisms of defense* (C. Baines, Trans.). New York: International Universities Press. (Original work published 1936)

Frijda, N. H. (1988). The laws of emotion. *American Psychologist, 43*, 349–358.

Gilligan, C. (1982). *In a different voice: Psychological theory and women's development.* Cambridge, MA: Harvard University Press.

Gilligan, C., & Attanucci, J. (1988). Two moral orientations: Gender differences and similarities. *Merrill-Palmer Quarterly, 34*, 223–237.

Greenberg, M., Cicchetti, D., & Cummings, E. M. (Ed.). (1990). *Attachment in the preschool years: Theory, research, and intervention.* Chicago: University of Chicago Press.

Greenwald, A. G. (1980). The totalitarian ego: Fabrication and revision of personal history. *American Psychologist, 35*, 603–618.

Horowitz, M. J. (1987). *States of mind: Analysis of change in psychotherapy* (2nd ed.). New York: Plenum Press.

Inhelder, B., & Piaget, J. (1958). *The growth of logical thinking from childhood to adolescence* (A. Parsons & S. Seagrim, Trans.). New York: Basic Books. (Original work published 1955).

Kennedy, B. (1994). *The development of self-understanding in adolescents in Korea.* Unpublished doctoral dissertation, Harvard University, Cambridge, MA.

Kernberg, O. (1975). *Borderline conditions and pathological narcissism.* New York: Aronson.

Kohlberg, L. (1969). Stage and sequence: The cognitive developmental approach to socialization. In D. A. Goslin (Ed.), *Handbook of socialization theory and research* (pp. 347–480). Chicago: Rand, McNally.

Kohut, H. (1977). *The restoration of the self.* New York: International Universities Press.

Lamborn, S. D., Fischer, K. W., & Pipp, S. L. (1994). Constructive criticism and social lies: A developmental sequence for understanding honesty and kindness in social interactions. *Developmental Psychology, 30*, 495–508.

Lazarus, R. S. (1991). *Emotion and adaptation.* New York: Oxford University Press.

LeVine, R. A., & Miller, P. M. (1990). Commentary (for section Cross-cultural validity of attachment theory). *Human Development, 33*, 73–80.

Luborsky, L., & Crits-Christoph, P. (1990). *Understanding transference: The CCRT method.* New York: Basic Books.

Main, M., & Hesse, E. (1990). Parents' unresolved traumatic experiences are related to infant disorganized attachment status: Is frightened and/or frightening parental behavior the linking mechanism? In M. T. Greenberg, D. Cicchetti, & E. M. Cummings (Ed.), *Attachment in the preschool years* (pp. 161–182). Chicago: University of Chicago Press.

Meade, G. H. (1934). *Mind, self, and society.* Chicago: University of Chicago Press.

Miyake, K., & Yamazaki, K. (1995). Self-conscious emotions, child rearing, and child psychopathology in Japanese culture. In J. P. Tangney & K. W. Fischer (Ed.), *Self-conscious emotions: The psychology of shame, guilt, embarrassment, and pride* (pp. 488–504). New York: Guilford.

Noam, G. G., Powers, S. J., Kilkenny, R., & Beedy, J. (1990). The interpersonal self in life-span developmental perspective: Theory, measurement, and longitudinal case analyses. In P. B. Baltes, D. L. Featherman, & R. M. Lerner (Eds.), *Life-span development and behavior* (Vol. 10, pp. 59–104). Hillsdale, NJ: Lawrence Erlbaum Associates.

Noam, G. G., Chandler, M., & LaLonde, C. (1995). Clinical-developmental psychology: Constructivism and social cognition in the study of psychological dysfunctions. In D. Cicchetti & D. Cohen (Eds.), *Handbook of developmental psychopathology* (pp. 424–464). New York: Wiley.

Piaget, J. (1957). Logique et équilbre dans les comportements du sujet [Logic and equilibrium in the subject's behavior]. *Études d'Épistémologie Génétique, 2,* 27–118.

Piaget, J. (1975). L'équilibration des structures cognitives: Problème central du développement [Equilibration of cognitive structures: A central problem in development]. *Études d'Épistémologie Génétique, 33.*

Raya, P. (1993). *The relationship between empathic responses in a young neglected child and maternal values, goals, and child-rearing practices: A case study.* Unpublished qualifying paper, Harvard University, Cambridge, MA.

Rogoff, B. (1993). Children's guided participation and participatory appropriation in socio-cultural activity. In R. Wozniak & K. W. Fischer (Ed.), *Development in context: Acting and thinking in specific environments* (pp. 121–154). Hillsdale, NJ: Lawrence Erlbaum Associates.

Selman, R. L., & Schultz, L. H. (1990). *Making a friend in youth.* Chicago: University of Chicago Press.

Shapiro, E. R., & Carr, A. W. (1991). *Lost in familiar places: Creating new connections between the individual and society.* New Haven, CT: Yale University Press.

Shaver, P. R., & Hazan, C. (1992). Adult romantic attachment: Theory and evidence. In D. Perlman & W. Jones (Ed.), *Advances in personal relationships* (Vol. 4). Greenwich, CT: JAI Press.

Sroufe, L. A., & Fleeson, J. (1986). Attachment and the construction of relationships. In W. Hartup & Z. Rubin (Ed.), *The nature and development of relationships* (pp. 51–71). Hillsdale, NJ: Lawrence Erlbaum Associates.

Sullivan, H. S. (1953). *The interpersonal theory of psychiatry.* New York: Norton.

van Geert, P. (1994). *Dynamic systems of development: Change between complexity and chaos.* London: Harvester Wheatsheaf.

Vygotsky, L. (1978). *Mind in society: The development of higher psychological processes* (M. Cole, V. John-Steiner, S. Scribner, & E. Souberman, Trans.). Cambridge, MA: Harvard University Press.

Watson, M. W., & Fischer, K. W. (1993). Structural change in children's understanding of family roles and divorce. In R. R. Cocking & K. A. Renninger (Ed.), *The development and meaning of psychological distance* (pp. 123–140). Hillsdale, NJ: Lawrence Erlbaum Associates.

The Personal Meaning of Risk Behavior:
A Developmental Perspective on Friendship and Fighting in Early Adolescence

8

Mira Z. Levitt
Robert L. Selman
The Judge Baker Children's Center
and *Harvard University*

On Passover, the ceremonial seder involves retelling the story, from a book called the *Haggadah*, of the exodus of the Jews from slavery in Egypt. The *Haggadah* sets the stage for the recounting of the story by assuming the perspective of four representative youths, specifically four sons of unspecified age, who would not be expected to understand the significance of the Passover ceremony, replete with rules, customs, and rituals. Each of the sons, in a different way, approaches the endeavor of understanding the meaning of the risks taken by their ancestors in their flight across the desert to the promised land as spelled out by the Passover ceremony.

The wise son asks: "What is the meaning of the rules, laws, and customs which the Eternal our God has commanded us?" You shall explain to him all the laws of Passover, to the very last detail about the *Afikoman*.

The contrary son asks: "What is the meaning of this service to you?" Saying *you*, he excludes himself, and because he excludes himself from the group, he denied a basic principle. You may therefore tell him plainly: "because of what the Eternal did for me when I came forth from Egypt" I do this. For *me* and not for *him*; had he been there, he would not have been redeemed.

The simple son asks: "What is this?" To him you shall say: "With a strong hand the Eternal brought us out of Egypt, from the house of bondage."

As for the son who does not even know how to ask a question, you must begin for him, as it is written in the Bible, "You shall tell your child on that day: This is done because of that which the Eternal did for me when I came forth out of Egypt."

This introduction implies that the primary purpose of the *Haggadah* is to engage Jews, both young and old alike, in a process by which Passover is made meaningful to them. It is not as simple as this, however. The *Haggadah*, a book rich with human drama and grist for the psychological mill, demonstrates its sophistication by appreciating that the process of meaning making depends at the outset on the definitional relationship between the individual (e.g., each of the sons) and the subject whose meaning is sought (e.g., the risk of flight from an oppressive dominant culture), and its significance to being of the Jewish culture and heritage. Neither the simple son nor the son who does not know how to ask a question inquires about the Passover ceremony in a manner that implies its *relation* to anyone at all. The contrary son, by definition, excludes himself from a connection to the holiday and its associated history by asking about the meaning of the holiday "to you." Only the wise son regards the holiday in relation to his entire people, himself included, but even he may implicitly assume that the meaning of the holiday is identical for all, rather than being personalized for the individual.

Although our focus in this chapter is secular, we are concerned precisely with the notion of a process, as described in the *Haggadah*, of the personal meaning a developing individual (subject) makes with regard to some aspect of the external environment (object). The external object of interest to us is risk-taking behavior (RTB). Although risk-taking may have both positive and negative consequences, our primary interest includes a range of behaviors putting young adolescents, ages 10 to 16, in particular, at physical, social, and emotional risk, such as alcohol and drug abuse, unprotected sexual activity, smoking, dropping out of school, and physical fighting. Through a developmental analysis of a construct we call *personal meaning*, our objective is to understand adolescents' patterns of actual RTB by examining in detail their understanding of risky behaviors *in relation to* the self and the self's personal relationships (i.e., family and friends). This is not meant to imply that the meaning of the risky behavior to particular others or to a larger group would not be taken into consideration, but the ultimate focus would necessarily be on the unique significance of the risky behavior to the individual, as we emphasize, *to me*.

The *Haggadah*'s use of the four sons implies that there exist qualitative differences in the manner in which each individual will ultimately make meaning of the Passover experience. By implication, the wise son's meaning making activity appears to be most adequate, although the ordering of the other three may be arguable (e.g., the comparison of the son who is contrary with the one who is simple). Nevertheless, these qualitative differences herald our view of the crucial developmental differences in the personal meaning process with respect to RTB, detailed in this chapter.

With the analogy to the four sons of the Passover *Haggadah* in mind, we now turn to a more rigorous discussion of the personal meaning construct as a tool by which to understand the serious problem of pre- and early adolescent RTB, and with a wider view toward illuminating the risks and rewards or protective factors of the friendships of this period of life.

There are a number of reasons to focus a study of RTB on the age range of pre- and early adolescence, ages 9 or 10 to about 16. First, although our nation expresses strong interest in the well-being of adolescents per se, it is an obvious corollary that we expect the status of adolescents to be strongly related to the well-being of the adults they will become, adults whose behavioral patterns are likely to promote prosperity or wreak havoc across four or five decades. This presumption of continuity, the notion that adolescence is the "last stop" before the relatively long layover of young adulthood, prompts us to understanding adolescent RTB with an orientation of prevention for the future.

Second, pre- and early adolescence is a fertile ground for the study of certain risky behaviors because, as just discussed, risks are either coming into or heightening in focus throughout this age range (Feldman & Elliott, 1990). Even if an adolescent does not engage in a particular risk, it is likely that he or she knows someone who does.

Third, the reason to focus on the transitions of pre- and early adolescence as the target age range for this discussion of personal meaning concerns the centrality of the developmental nature of the construct. Rather than only trace the ontogenetic unfolding of schemes of personal meaning from childhood to adulthood, our interest is also in the developmental variations in personal meaning among same age adolescents living in different communities, differences that may account, in part, for why some adolescents are more at risk than others. Indeed, the beauty of studying a wide range of adolescents is that (conceptual) heterogeneity will likely yield a portrait of the less mature forms of personal meaning characteristic of younger children, while offering examples of age-appropriate personal meaning and the potential, among a small minority, to represent the highest levels of personal meaning that are theoretically but not necessarily realized by most adults.

Finally, as discussed next, the process by which personal meaning is assessed requires an inclination and capacity for verbalization about the self that makes adolescents the ripest candidates among which to study this construct. Neither children, who lack both heightened self-awareness and sophistication of verbal skills, nor later adolescents and young adults, whose self-awareness has often evolved into closed-over self-consciousness, and whose verbal skills can obscure as well as clarify, are optimal targets for assessment of personal meaning.

PERSONAL MEANING – CONCEPTUAL DEFINITION

All organizational processes require "leadership," an executive function that integrates component processes, plans for the future, and guides organismic expression, much like the service that the frontal lobe provides for the rest of the human organism (Lerner, 1979; Werner, 1948). In the case of RTB, this integrative function is necessary for the synthesis of two psychosocial factors that are presumed to mediate the influence of biological and sociocultural (antecedent) factors on RTB itself. These two psychosocial factors are called *knowledge* and *management*.

Our knowledge component, defined as what the individual knows of a particular "risk" (e.g., of fighting, alcohol consumption, etc.) is divided into the acquisition of factual information and the development of understanding of the nature of risks. We use the term *understanding* of risk in ways that are similar to our earlier theoretical definition of the growth of interpersonal understanding (Selman, 1980). Our focus is on how the growth in the capacity to coordinate the self and others' points of view (perspective coordination) leads to conceptual understanding, in this case of risks (e.g., fighting) and relationships (e.g., friendships).

Our operational definition of psychosocial management is similarly developmental and bifurcated. Because we see risks, both positive and negative, primarily in the context of social relationships, the interpersonal aspect of risk management is conceptualized on the basis of our earlier work on developmental levels of autonomy (interpersonal negotiation) and intimacy (shared experience) functions (see Selman & Schultz, 1990). Intrapersonal management in our model follows developmental lines set out by Vaillant (1977) in his analyses of defense mechanisms.

In the case of early adolescent RTB, the mediation and interpretation of these two component parts into risk-taking choices is performed by the integrative process we call *personal meaning*. Personal meaning is the lens through which knowledge of risks and risk management skills are integrated and focused to effect outcome behavior. Indeed, prevention programs designed to protect youngsters by fostering their psychosocial development may not ensure predictable outcomes because the same set of knowledge and management skills may be differentially processed, interpreted, and utilized by different individuals (Levitt, Selman, & Richmond, 1991).

Just as Freud (1936/1964) described how the ego mediates the effects of the id and superego while maintaining a distinct executive role, in the case of RTB, personal meaning is shaped by knowledge and management, while it simultaneously integrates their effect with other factors to shape their influence on outcome behavior. The substance of personal meaning, the sand from which the lens itself is forged, comprises what might loosely be called *character*. It consists of the psychological makeup and functioning of the individual, broadly defined in terms of the self-concept and interpersonal relationships, and all that goes into their formation. Although the curvature of the lens is defined internally by a certain set of psychological parameters, it is at its conceptual core, an integrative process that takes its shape externally through the synthesis of other factors (see Fig. 8.1).

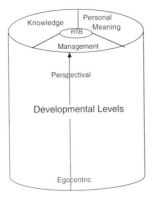

FIG. 8.1.   The developmental psychosocial components of adolescents' RTB.

Functionally, our analysis of the personal meaning of risks refers to an integrative activity by which, through processes of differentiation and integration, an adolescent interprets his or her own behavioral pattern of RTB, taking into account his or her knowledge of and skills used to manage this activity, as a function of his or her own personal configuration of life experience, cultural background, temperamental proclivities, peer culture, family dynamics, school context, and so on.

At the heart of the personal meaning construct in the context of risk is the assumption that an adolescent's understanding of his or her RTB has potential relevance for defining and shaping a sense of who the adolescent is as an individual and as an individual in relation to others. In particular, to the extent that the adolescent views his or her risk choices as statements about him or herself, who he or she wants to be, how he or she wants to relate to others, the values he or she espouses, and so on, these risk experiences have the capacity to be formative and transformative (Lightfoot, 1994), and, we would argue, prophylactic against dangerous risk. However, adolescents do vary in their developmental capacity to conceptualize risk as representative of their own personal and interpersonal lives. Crites (1986, cited in Lightfoot, 1994) suggested that the word *experience* (which we amend to *risk experience*) should be reserved for what is incorporated into one's story, and thus owned, owned up to, appropriated.

The notions of "ownership of experience" and "incorporation of experience into one's story" are the essence of the connective, relational activity encompassed by our construct of personal meaning. The quality of this relational activity has implications for the maturity of personal meaning (see also Noam, 1990). Consider, for example, the difference in the nature of "ownership" between an adolescent boy who describes his use of alcohol (RTB) as "something everybody does" versus the adolescent boy who views his drinking as "something I do to help me calm down in social situations."

Clearly, the second boy is much more aware than the first boy of how drinking relates to who he is and who he would like to be. For the second boy, risk experience is personally and interpersonally defining and transforming.

It may seem obvious that RTB, like any other activity, comes to form and is formed by one's own life circumstances, including personality style, experienced relationships, cultural values, ethnicity, and the like. Clearly, this process of integration is necessarily always at work. However, the significance of the characterization of personal meaning as a developmental process lies in the notion that it is only with the development of the capacity to coordinate points of view that the individual gains perspective on the integrative process (Selman, 1980). In other words, the process of personal meaning implies a developing capacity to appreciate consciously and express explicitly the implicit embeddedness of an individual's pattern of RTB in the complex fabric of one's own life history and social relationships. For example, at the risk of oversimplifying a complex process, it is one thing for an adolescent's abstention from drinking to derive from a pervasive fear of loss of control; it is another thing for that adolescent to be aware that the reason for abstaining is the potential for the abuse/harm of others, or the obverse, the abdication of control to someone else. Throughout daily life, in unexamined fashion, all of us employ the personal meaning process with a range of competency, riding up and down on the personal meaning continuum, as we tune in and out of awareness of the underlying and collateral factors that shape our behavioral choices. From our framework of personal meaning, an early adolescent's growing awareness of the integrated nature of his or her RTB within the complex web of self-concept and social relationships is considered a major preventive factor with regard to negative life outcomes.

Affect and Personal Meaning

As a process by which adolescents understand their own RTBs in relation to their own life stories, personal meaning is a process that is likely to arouse affect in the context of cognition. However, the traditional union of cognition and affect, so frequently pursued by psychologist matchmakers, is not the identified goal or purpose of the personal meaning process. Whereas the inseparability of cognition and affect has been argued before, our emphasis is on the integration of cognition and affect with behavior, as argued by Fischer, Shaver, and Carnochan (1990) and Case (chapter 3, this volume). Echoing the personal meaning construct, this work focuses on the functional relation between a person and the environment, asserting that a representational abstract skill refers not merely to cognitive processes but to feelings that are aroused and the actions taken. Although we would stipulate that the quality of emotional integration must be considered, we agree, with respect to risk-taking, with the position taken by Fischer et al. for the generally adaptive function played by emotion, one that contrasts with a more traditional role for emotion as disrupter of cognition.

For us, the affective charge associated with personal meaning is relevant insofar as it has implications for RTB. In our developmental framework, the significance of personal meaning for actual behavior is that the quality of the connections individuals make between their RTB and their own life experiences figures strongly into how able they are to anticipate the personalized impact of risk-taking on themselves in real-life situations. Personalized connections to one's own life experience that are highly differentiated and well integrated are presumed to enable adolescents to feel the effects of risky behaviors such as drinking alcohol or fist-fighting, as well as simply knowing what they are, in anticipation of the action itself, thereby protecting against it, if warranted. Whereas Lightfoot argued that taking risks and taking possession of experience involves embracing the unforeseen, the un-thought-of, and the new, we would add that an anticipatory capacity for feeling the effects of the contemplated risk enables an adolescent to engage in risks more wisely.

The Conceptual Model

The developmental process of personal meaning and its role vis-à-vis the development of knowledge and management skills comprise the core of our conceptual model of RTB. The model suggests that RTB must be viewed as existing in a transactional relationship with two sets of factors. Antecedent factors, which include biological forces such as temperament, and socio-cultural forces such as family and peer relationships, may or may not be relatively fixed in the life of the individual, but certainly vary across individuals. Psychosocial factors include the trinity of knowledge about risk (both factual knowledge and conceptual understanding), management skills (e.g., intrapersonal and interpersonal negotiation skills), and personal meaning, all three of which are assumed to undergo developmental transformation.

As illustrated in Fig. 8.2, there are two hypothetical pathways between antecedent factors and risk-taking outcome, one "nonstop" (dotted line) and one by way of the psychosocial components (solid line). The nonstop pathway implies that certain biological predispositions and sociocultural factors may operate at such extremes that their influence on risk-taking outcome is virtually automatic, largely independent of the influence of the maturity of the psychosocial components, what we are calling the character development of the individual in question. For example, an extremely impulsive or inhibited temperament, brain anomalies, poverty-stricken,

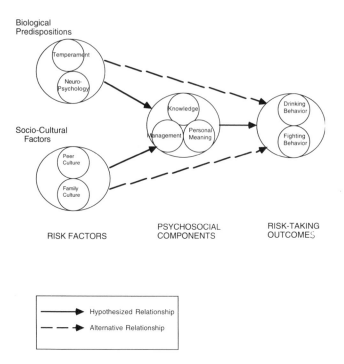

FIG. 8.2.   The conceptual model of RTB (drinking and fighting as example).

drug- and crime-infested neighborhoods, although not wholly determinants of behavior, tend to have predictable directions of influence on risk-taking.

In contrast, the "person-centered" pathway represents the process by which antecedent factors simultaneously influence psychosocial functioning and are mediated psychosocially before their impact on risk behavior is felt. For example, temperamental and neurological factors affect the individual's capacity for absorbing knowledge, whereas sociocultural factors may determine what kinds of knowledge are available to be absorbed. Conversely, the developmental nature of knowledge, management, and personal meaning implies that individuals may understand their own temperament or sociocultural environment as these relate to RTB at different levels of maturity; these developmental differences are assumed to be differentially protective against risk. This mediated effect of personal meaning is presumed to operate at more moderate levels of antecedent forces. Because the two pathways are presumed to coexist, the question posed by the model with respect to these two pathways is not of the either/or variety, but rather, which/when—specifically, which pathway will best describe the nature of influence on RTB under what circumstances (i.e., when). This model suggests that biological and sociocultural factors are each free to take their own pathway, as are different components within the biological or sociocultural realms.

The model also asserts a conceptual interdependence in the growth of knowledge, management skills, and personal meaning. That is, when neither biological nor environmental forces is extreme, the three psychosocial components (knowledge, management, and personal meaning) are presumed to be synchronous in developmental level and reciprocal in their mutual influence. Higher levels of any one component are enabled or anticipated when the remaining two components are themselves in developmental balance. In contrast, low levels of any one component would be expected if both of the other two components were conceptualized at a low level. Age-appropriate developmental balance among the three psychosocial components is assumed to correlate to some degree with risk-resistant behavior.

Why does the developmental process of personal meaning represent more than just old levels of what may generally be referred to as the wine of "ego development" in new bottles (cf. Kaplan, 1987)? First, in contrast to developmental schemes of ego and moral development with which there is some theoretical ancestral kinship (e.g., Kohlberg, 1984; Loevinger, 1976), personal meaning is concerned not only with the psychosocial capacities within the individual that, in theory, are brought to the individual's interactions with the environment. By our definition, personal meaning represents an inherently interactive process involving the manner in which the individual personalizes his or her own pattern of RTB by connecting it to factors in his or her own life (cf. Turner, 1994; Noam, 1990; Noam, chapter 6, this volume).

Second, personal meaning differs from developmental levels in the traditional sense in that the process is not exclusively conceptual. Turiel and his colleagues (Turiel, 1983; Turiel & Smetana, 1984), for example, in their work on conceptions of social conventions, morality, and persons, are careful to point out that their (separate) developmental analyses of social reasoning are confined to each of the conceptual domains, and are not behavioral in nature (although these researchers study the relationship of thought and action). And although Keller and Edelstein (1991) attempted to integrate the structure and content of sociomoral meaning making, their analysis still remains in the social-cognitive domain. Our claim for the developmental analysis of the personal meaning construct is a bit more risky and adventurous; that it is an executive function encompassing conceptual, affective, motivational, and behavioral features. Perhaps the contemporary developmental analysis and empirical work closest to ours is that of Oser and Gmunder (1988/1991) on religious judgment. In that work the researchers focus on developmental variations in the meaning (relationship) of the self to an "Ultimate." Of course one can speculate on how religious beliefs relate to behavior; our focus is directly on the self's connection to the (meaning of the) behavior (and its implications for patterns of actual risk-taking).

Third, although the personal meaning process of connecting risk behavior to life history involves developing abstract conceptual abilities such as self-reflection and perspective coordination, the personalized nature of the material being processed creates a potential for strong affective charge, as noted earlier. This contrasts with conceptual activity as assessed in domains such as moral reasoning, where individuals are concerned exclusively with abstractions such as right and wrong, and the medium for exploration is likely to be a hypothetical situation (Colby & Kohlberg, 1987; Gibbs, Basinger, & Fuller, 1992). Imagine the vista uncovered by asking adolescents to engage in reasoning about the most familiar yet elusive subject of all—the self in relation to one's own actual experience.

Finally, in light of the different nature of what is being measured, we needed to consider the possibility that unlike the models proposed by our own structuralist ancestors, the developmental process of personal meaning would not in fact be captured best by being ordered according to mutually exclusive discrete levels. Indeed, as discussed later, because of the personalized, affectively laden aspects of the process, we suggest that this developmental construct is best represented as a process of natural progress and inevitable regress that may vary (to greater or lesser degrees) with the individual for any given risky behavior.

In summary, the interactive nature of the self in relation to a particular risk, the integration of affective and conceptual processes through personalized study of the self engaged in behavior, and the symbolization of a developmental process according to a relatively fluid rather than relatively discrete set of levels are the three novel hallmarks of the personal meaning process that serve to distinguish it from the historically traditional structural developmental levels from which it evolved. As such, we suggest that personal meaning has the potential to break new ground with regard to both the assessment and the representation of developmental processes. In other words, we think that we may in fact be looking at new wine, one with its own distinct character, in the sense that the nature of the personal meaning process is novel. If so, there is hope that the structural approach to developmental analysis has not exhausted its utility.

RTB in Relation to Early Adolescent Friendship

"Kids fight to prove to their friends they're tough."

"My friend watches me to make sure I don't get in trouble drinking."

"If you grow up together you'll be friends and won't fight with each other."

"Kids get drunk to be cool; their friends are doing it."

These are four adolescent testimonials to the power of friendship to influence children like themselves toward or away from behaviors that we adults believe are risky, in these cases fighting and drinking. No surprise here, certainly not to the parents who worry desperately that their children will get "mixed up with the wrong crowd," one that will steer them in the direction of a range of behaviors that put them at physical, social, and emotional risk, such as alcohol and drug abuse, unprotected sexual activity, dropping out of school, and physical fighting.

Although peer pressure is a commonly recognized force (e.g., Youniss, 1980), its capacity to protect youths from risk is less often acknowledged than its capacity to expose them to it. In fact, it bears emphasizing that, as our childhood reporters assert, friendships can operate proactively to mitigate against risk. But is the role of friends in RTB as simple as "peer pressure?" Does an adolescent's risk-taking fate rest simply with the nature of the crowd one happens to fall into? Just what are the factors and processes that determine whether friendships operate in a risk-promoting or protective fashion? Does friendship operate to effect risky behavior in the same way for all adolescents?

From the perspective of our model, friendship enters into the risk-taking equation under the heading of sociocultural influences. As indicated by the broken pathway, to draw a line directly from friendships to RTB would imply that the number, identity, quality, and so on, of one's friends could directly incline the individual toward or away from risky behavior. In essence, this would be consistent with the mechanism of intense peer pressure, the unilateral expression of the will of the crowd in the outcome behavior of the individual, with virtually no intermediary processing. Specifically, if an adolescent has many persuasive friends who engage in risk, he or she would be more likely to partake than if his or her friends abstain, and vice-versa.

According to the person-centered pathway set forth by our model, however, the line from sociocultural factors to risky behavior may also pass first through the set of three psychosocial components, including personal meaning. This implies that the mere fact of having particular friends or the particular actions of friends may not directly translate into an individual's social behavior. Instead, we contend that the role of friendships in risky behavior may also need to be considered in the context of the personal meaning of that behavior to the individual. In other words, the personal significance of the risky behavior for the self and relationships constructs a framework within which friendships interact to bring about their risk-prone or risk-resistant effect. (Clearly, the individual's general construction of friendships, both developmentally and culturally, is also highly germane to outcome behavior, but this is not our focus here.) In particular, the role of friendship must consider the affective significance of the risky behavior, the manner in and degree to which the individual feels about the behavior. Our task, then becomes to explain the significance of the personal meaning construct as a mediating factor between friendship and risky behavior. Having offered a conceptual definition of personal meaning in relatively abstract terms as it applies to risky behavior, the remainder of this chapter addresses its assessment as a developmental construct with respect to one specific domain of RTB — fighting, and its potential empirical application to the analysis of friendship as a risk or protective factor in the case of two early adolescents involved in the behavior of fighting.

THE ASSESSMENT AND ANALYSIS
OF PERSONAL MEANING

The quest to elucidate the developmental process of personal meaning has entailed the design of an assessment tool through which individuals' personal meaning stories can be maximally brought forth, and the articulation of qualitative transformational processes by which awareness of the integrative activity matures. Personal meaning is assessed through an interview format, the purpose of which is to evaluate the adolescent's capacity for understanding his or her risk choices by personalizing them in the context of the individual's self-concept and relationships. Because personal meaning is assumed to play a synthetic function with regard to the other elements of risky behavior, the interview must also attend to the antecedent factors (of temperament and socioculture), and to the other mediating psychosocial factors (knowledge and management) as these interface with risk choices.

Personal meaning interviews are framed in the context of particular risks (e.g., in the case of this chapter, fighting behavior) and analyzed with respect to three dimensions: valence, thematic orientation, and structural developmental level.

Valence Analysis

For the purposes of understanding the developmental antecedents of risk-prone and risk-resistant behavioral patterns, it is as important to understand why a given adolescent doesn't fight at all, or fights occasionally, or only in certain circumstances, as it is to understand why he or she fights often. Our personal meaning system of analysis incorporates the actual fighting status of the individual in terms of what we call *valence*. Individuals who describe themselves as virtual abstainers from fighting are assigned to a negative valence status, whereas a positive valence denotes the responses of individuals who acknowledge a "greater than zero" pattern of RTB; they admit to fighting on an experimental, occasional, or regular basis. Valence, then, refers primarily to actual risk behavior.

Presumably, these behavioral differences are associated with favorable or unfavorable views of the behavior by the adolescents choosing to engage in or abstain from them. "Fighting only gets you in trouble" is obviously a response consistent with negative valence, whereas "Beating up on people is fun" carries a positive valence. Although an individual who does engage in fighting may indeed disparage the behavior, the essence of the analysis is to understand how the adolescent makes sense out of the reality that he or she does in fact fight, to whatever degree; negative expressions about behaviors in the face of engaging in them (i.e., positive valence) are factored into the structural developmental analysis, discussed later. Less than perfect consistency between actual behavior and expressed attitude toward the behavior may be expected at higher levels of personal meaning, where there is more capacity to gain perspective on one's own behavior, and to consider and reconcile advantages and disadvantages of any behavioral choice. Such gaps between behavior and attitude are likely to be associated with internal conflicts and stresses, the nature of which should be elicited through the personal meaning interview, and probed for its amenability to control through the adolescent's management skills, and for its contribution to the ongoing pattern of RTB.

As straightforward as the valence dimension may appear, its validity has the potential to be obscured if sociocultural factors are not recognized. As a developmental construct, personal meaning is highly individualized in nature, focused on how a particular adolescent understands risk choices in the context of his or her own life. However, part of this unique individual's history is a sociocultural context that shapes the values and exigencies associated with a given risk in similar ways for all members within a group in such a way as to generate a socioculturally determined valence for certain groups. For example, in crime-ridden neighborhoods, physical fighting may become a badge of courage for those whose everyday survival depends on it, whereas groups who do not face this everyday reality would flee to avoid a fight that came their way at any cost. Consider, in fact, the *Haggadah*'s account of the Jews in Egypt who took flight rather than fight the forces of the Pharaoh. This same cultural group, speaking stereotypically — for the sake of argument — might be particularly inclined and eager to engage in fighting of a different variety — not on the mean streets, but say in the Wall Street world of business, where attacks can be no less aggressive and stinging even if not physically violent. Thus, the tendency for fight versus flight may be largely a function of sociocultural context. Again, in the terminology of our model we would say that the valence of fighting could be said to be socioculturally driven. Nevertheless, the capacity to step back and appreciate the influence of one's own sociocultural context on one's own RTB for the purposes of personal meaning making still remains a developmental capacity characteristic of the individual.

Thematic Orientation Analysis

The thematic analysis of personal meaning refers to the content of what, according to an adolescent's own self-analysis, motivates his or her own pattern of RTB. Taken at face value, it is essentially the reason the individual offers to account for his or her behavior choice. It is the actual perspective on people and things one comes with to a risk (e.g., "I don't rock the boat," "If somebody hits me, I hit them back"), as compared to the developing capacity to take perspective regardless of context. This construct would most likely be tapped by a question such as: Why do you engage in risky behavior "X"?

Alongside the valence dimension, thematic orientation represents personal meaning in probably its most categorical, qualitative, obvious, or intuitive sense. The decision regarding what aspect of thematic content, what specific point of view, is most useful to categorize for the purpose of analyzing personal meaning thematically is not so obvious, however. Contents could, for example, be easily categorized on a developmental basis according to the continuum of low-level physicality (associated with concrete, material, irreversible contents) through active and social categories, up through high-level psychological (associated with abstract, hypothetical, reversible contents).

The decision regarding categorization must be considered with regard to a number of potential confounding factors. In particular, one factor concerns again the sociocultural sensitivity in which we seek to embed the construct of personal meaning. We are mindful that thematic contents have cultural meaning which may erroneously be attributed to developmental maturity level, and for that reason reject the developmental categorization of content as previously described per se. With respect to fighting, for example, consider that many inner-city youths report horrendous violence associated with theft of high-priced sneakers. Whereas the essence of the motivational thematic content (i.e., "I fight to get those sneakers") might be considered physicalistic or materialistic (low level) in nature, the culturally derived meaning associated with sneaker ownership in one neighborhood may involve (high level) awareness of features such as power and status that would not necessarily be salient factors in other neighborhoods. Such awareness of the differential significance of sneakers in one's own environment extends beyond analysis of content per se to anticipate the structural developmental analysis described later.

It is important to note that, for our purposes, sociocultural contributions to personal meaning encompass all forms of extradevelopmental variation that influence the interpretation of behavior, including social class, ethnicity, age, and gender, either on the part of the individual engaging in the behavior or an observer. This applies to all forms of behavior, not just risky behavior in the sense addressed in this chapter. Meaningful analyses of thematic content as a function of these factors will necessarily be empirically derived in large part.

At present, for us, because the definition of personal meaning is to be evaluated with respect to its impact on self and relationships, we have chosen to integrate thematic contents into our developmental coding system only with respect to their focus on one or the other of two orientations. Self-oriented responses (integrating valence; $(+/-)$ would include: $(+)$ I'm good at it; $(-)$ I promised myself never to get into a fight. Examples of relationship-oriented responses would be: $(+)$ Everyone looks up to a good fighter; $(-)$ I worry what others will think if I fight. A finer analysis of thematic content will be left for future empirical analysis as a function of age, gender, and especially, ethnic background of our research population.

Structural Developmental Analysis

The developmental analysis of personal meaning represents an attempt to articulate the formal structural qualities that underlie the variety of ways in which children and adolescents think about the personal and interpersonal significance of their own RTB. Whereas the thematic orientation classifies a response with respect to its orientational emphasis toward the self or toward relationships, the structural developmental analysis is concerned with the *qualitative form* of these responses, specifically the quality of the perceived incorporation of risk behavior into one's life story. From this developmental perspective, the structures associated with higher levels of personal meaning are presumed to serve a greater protective function against risk than structures associated with lower levels because they reflect a more differentiated and integrated awareness on the part of the adolescent of the motivations that contribute to risk-taking choices. Risk experience is owned in a manner that speaks to the essentials of the self and relationships.

Table 8.1 offers a series of responses that illustrate the range of developmental maturity of personal meaning, which is to say, the varying degrees of awareness with which risk behavior, in this case fighting, can be understood in relation to the self and relationships. Specifically, the table traces the developmental progression along six levels, from Level 0 (dismissive) through Level 5 (insightful). The responses in the table should be considered with respect to the referential essence of personal meaning:

TABLE 8.1
The Personal Meaning Analysis of "Fighting Behavior." Classification of
Responses Using Developmental Level by Thematic Orientation

Developmental Levels	Orientation to Self Valance		Orientation to Relationship Valence	
	Positive	Negative	Positive	Negative
Dismissive	It's fun beating up on people.	Fighting is stupid.	Fighting is cool.	Only jerks fight.
1 Impersonal rule-based	You have to fight to survive.	Fighting only gets you suspended.	Everyone looks up to someone who can fight; they're tough.	Fighting makes you unpopular.
2 Personal rule-based	I'm a good fighter.	I promised myself never to get into a fight.	Our family is good at fighting; my cousins taught me how.	My girlfriend won't have anything to do with me if I get into fights.
3 Personal need-based isolated	I fight when I'm tense. Any thing will set me off.	I don't fight because I wouldn't respect myself.	If anyone insults my family, I'll fight to defend them.	I worry what others will think of me if I fight.
4 Personal need-based integrated	Part of what allows me to keep calm under pressure is the awareness that I will respond if provoked, and some fear that I'll really lose control of my anger.	Violence is not a part of me, but I might use it as a last resort, rather than sitting on my hostility and having it expressed elsewhere.	I live in a violent neighborhood, and I have to adapt, whether I like it or not, but I don't believe in fighting to solve problems, and it goes against my nature.	I seem to need to keep proving to people that they can't push me around, but I wish there were a better way.
Insightful	I used to tell myself I needed to fight to survive in this neighborhood, but I took a real good look at myself and realized I needed to look cool to cover up.			

What is the meaning of the behavior to me? The basis for the developmental scoring is explained in detail here.

As can be seen in the table, at each developmental level, responses can be classified thematically as either self or relationship oriented. For each orientation, responses can have positive or negative valence, referring to whether the behavior is engaged in or not, and usually whether the attitude toward the behavior is favorable or unfavorable. In considering this summary table, it is important to bear in mind that developmental coding of personal meaning of any risk is based on a series of interviews, not the one- or two-line statements included in the table to illustrate each level. The table entries are intended to represent a quality of meaning that is expressed repeatedly throughout the interview, and that represents a developmental ceiling for the interviewee even in the face of probing for elaboration that has the potential to reveal more sophistication.

Rule-Based Versus Need-Based.   The first developmental differentiation among personal meaning responses is made according to whether they are rule-based or need-based. This broad distinction reflects the two main approaches to meaning making taken by children and adolescents with regard to RTB, defined with regard to (a) the emphasis on self (subject) versus self in relation to RTB (external object), (b) the role of knowledge and management, and (c) general developmental criteria such as increasing differentiation and integration, and greater reliance on internal, nonphysicalistic concerns.

Responses falling under the rule-based approach are governed by the notions of predeterminism and inevitability, resulting from externally imposed behavioral directives. The knowledge component is prominent among these responses, because risk is discussed in a fairly objective, factual manner, applicable to anyone rather than the self in particular. In fact, minimal reference is made to the self at all, the focus at this point being the RTB itself. Similarly, the management component operates in a rather constrained manner under this approach, because outcomes appear to be more preordained than the result of negotiation efforts. Responses from this approach generally involve physical and action-oriented considerations with regard to RTB. There is much more focus on external rather than internal forces, and generally more of a naive objective stance (describing the self's involvement in RTB from the perspective of an observer) than subjective (from the perspective of the self as actor). The thinking that characterizes this approach is typically concrete and undifferentiated in nature, and the reader will find him or herself needing to infer quite a bit about what is meant rather than relying on explicit remarks of the adolescent. Little affect is expected to be aroused by such rule-based thinking.

Need-based responses are distinguished by a shift away from the rather exclusive focus on RTB to a concern with the self in integration with RTB. Integral to these responses is an appreciation that RTB choices have significance for the internal life of the self, in particular, serving or reflecting the psychological needs of the self. (In the case of fighting, for example, this change can be characterized by a "figure–ground shift, represented by a transition in attitude from "I was born to raise hell" to "I'm just fighting to survive.") Accordingly, feelings, motivations, wishes, and other internal processes as well as personal experiences become prominent in these responses in increasingly differentiated fashion. Knowledge about risk is not easily evident in these responses because overt attention has shifted to personalized knowledge about social and psychologically based processes as they pertain to the self, layering over the more impersonal basic informational processes. Management, however, assumes a more active role as the rigidity of rule-based responses is loosened to allow for flexibility in outcome depending on what can be negotiated, though management may apply less to situations focused explicitly on RTB per se, than to identified intrapersonal and interpersonal conflicts of personal significance in general. The quality of thinking, although highly personalized, is at the same time more abstract than before, and is characterized by greater explicit awareness of the subjective nature of experiences associated with RTB. Finally, responses that describe personal need are expected to evoke affect.

Dimensions of Awareness Across Developmental Levels.   Beyond this primary distinction, rule-based responses are further divided into impersonal and personal categories, and need-based responses are broken down into unintegrated and integrated categories, giving rise to Levels 1 through 4. These differentiations reflect the contributions to our developmental analysis of four "awareness dimensions": agency, personalization, self-reflection, and contextualization, each of which is structurally independent of cultural factors. The essence of each awareness dimension is as follows:

Agency: This dimension addresses the manner in which constructs such as causality, control, and responsibility are conceptualized with respect to RTB. Relevant variations of the agency construct include intentionality versus randomness or predetermination, internality versus externality with respect to the self, and the rigidity with which outcomes are effected. The intensity of agency (i.e., the degree to which one experiences a sense of control, responsibility, etc.) may overlap with the more qualitative considerations, but is to be regarded more thematically than as an object of structural analysis. For example, "I swear I will never fight again," may be said with great agentic force, but stem from a rigid and immature (rule based), yet possibly very "functional" world view.

Personalization: Personalized responses convey an appreciation on the part of the adolescent that one's own experience with RTB is unique or, at least, particular to the self. These could include acknowledged differences in one's own pattern of RTB relative to others, differences in the reactions of significant others toward the self's RTB relative to the reactions experienced by others, and particular observations or interactions with RTB that others have not necessarily had (e.g., seeing the consequences of RTB in a friend or relative). In essence, there is an appreciation that "not everyone experiences/has experienced RTB in the way that I have."

Self-reflection: Self-reflection involves the ability to take perspective on one's subjective psychological self, and to identify explicitly internal processes including motivations, personality style, values, and so on, as they relate to RTB. Specifically, RTB is to be understood as fulfilling or being associated with a need or other internal process that is particular to the individual and thereby particularizes the RTB choice.

Contextualization: Contextualization refers to the process of connecting a risk-behavior choice to one's personal background, including temperament, sociocultural influences such as peer group, family make-up and values. It is the explicitly identified psychological need or other internal process associated with the risk-behavior choice that is to be contextualized rather than behavior per se. It is not sufficient for the purposes of contextualization to draw on a personal experience as motivation for a particular behavior choice (e.g., "I'll never drink because I saw my uncle die of liver disease") because no connection of past experience to an internal need state has been explicitly identified.

The emergence of each awareness dimension represents the hallmark differentiating event for each new plateau of personal meaning. The dimensions reconfigure the personal meaning system by introducing new terms by which risk-taking choices can be connected to the individual's own sense of self and relationships with others, including temperament, self-esteem, peer culture, parental values, and so forth. Thus, Level 1 is distinguished from Level 0 by the emergence of responses that reflect an agentic awareness, Level 2 is distinguished from Level 1 by the emergence of personalized responses, Level 3 from Level 2 by the emergence of a reflective capacity, and Level 4 from Level 3 by the emergence of contextualization. Together, the rule-based versus need-based distinction, in synergy with the dimensions, gives rise to the following six levels, described briefly next.

Integration of Dimensional and Developmental Analysis. The four awareness dimensions are distinct constructs in the sense that each one itself helps to define a lens through which personal meaning is analyzed. The dimensions are conceptually hierarchical in that earlier dimensions of awareness are incorporated into later dimensions in necessary but not sufficient fashion. Thus, personalization requires agency if only in the sense that the individual is taking responsibility for his or her actions before he or she can go on to associate those actions with something unique about the self. Self-reflection about internal, psychologically based aspects of the self are not possible without having first recognized the uniqueness of the self. And finally, contextualization can only take place when there is something to put into context, in this system, namely the reflection on a personal need associated with RTB.

Briefly, responses at Level 0 (dismissive) demonstrate undifferentiated, global commentary on the experience of risk-taking. In sharp contrast to the specificity that characterizes mature levels of personal meaning, the diffuse labels or descriptions applied to risky behavior at this level reflect no involvement in the process of personal meaning. None of the four dimensions of awareness comes into play, because there is virtually no identification with the risky behavior as something that the adolescent actively chooses to partake in or not. Nothing is revealed about the self except a style of expression characterized by minimal thoughtfulness or critical evaluation of the activity in question. Hence, as regards the assessment process, the dismissive denotation refers to a failure to take part in the process of examination at the heart of personal meaning; the role of the self is in no way at issue given the global, impressionistic approach to risky behavior. From a behavioral standpoint, the dismissive individual would be likely to engage in risky behaviors and, in general, conduct his life without much cerebral immersion in the process.

At Level 1 (rule-based, impersonal) the thinking about risky behavior takes on a cause-and-effect quality that is more differentiated than Level 0 by virtue of the incipient effort to search for reasons for risk-behavior choices that involve attention to consequences, or at least an appreciation of a significance of risky behavior beyond the immediate subjective experience. Accordingly, the construct of agency emerges as the responses indicate at least implicit personal responsibility for the choice to engage or not engage in the risky behavior. The reasons offered, however, are highly impersonal, as they are rooted in what the adolescent regards as universal truisms about the risky behavior as opposed to anything particular to the self. Personal meaning at this level is virtually synonymous with knowledge about the risky behavior.

Moving to Level 2 (rule-based, personalized), the personalization construct is introduced as responses acknowledge that one may make decisions about risky behavior based on reasoning that pertains primarily or exclusively to the self. However, responses are still characterized as mechanistic and rule-based because of the rigidity and absolutism of the views expressed. Management skills are irrelevant given the fixed nature of the responses. Furthermore, the risky behavior is still discussed largely in terms of a body of knowledge about what the risk entails, consisting mainly of concerns that are physicalistic, associative, and immediate in nature.

At Level 3 (personal need-based, unintegrated), responses are transformed by the integration of the construct of reflection. The cause-and-effect quality of previous levels gives way to an appreciation by the self of the self's internal thoughts, feelings, wishes, and so on, in a way that opens the door to bonafide connections between RTB choices and personal motivation. Responses at this level demonstrate an appreciation that a personal, often subtle psychological need is being satisfied by and is at issue in the risk-taking decision, not simply an automatic, external, or physicalistic response. Flexibility is introduced, with responses about risky behavior no longer presented as virtual fact. This diminishes the knowledge flavoring in responses as noted in previous levels, and introduces the potential role for management skills to address the newly recognized needs of the self. The limitation of this level is that the introspective activity takes place in relatively circumscribed, isolated fashion, with little integration into a larger perspective on the self or relationships.

This further integration occurs at Level 4 (need-based, integrated) and is characterized by the construct of contextualization. In other words, not only do Level 4 responses connect risky behavior to internal states in the moment, but they embed and interweave these connections within a larger framework of personal history data about the self, including biological and sociocultural factors. By this point, the focus on the risky behavior itself, including basic knowledge about it, has receded in favor of a highly personal self-examination. Management skills are so tightly integrated into this self-study as to be not easily recognizable as distinct. The quality of interconnectedness between risky behavior and one's personal history context, defined in terms of the self and relationships, at Level 4 is exceeded at Level 5 (insight) only by the introduction of unconscious material into the weave of the fabric. This is not a feature of the connectedness among risky behavior, self, and relationships that many individuals would be expected to achieve.

Interestingly, the awareness dimensions of agency, personalization, self-reflection, and contextualization bear remarkably similarity to the evolutionary criteria underlying five literary types identified by Rorty (1976). According to her historical analysis of the written record, it is by virtue of increased agency, individuation, self-consciousness, and ownership of experience that literary heroes come over the ages to qualify as "individuals" as defined by a greater connection between the individual and the world that allows for the possibility of mutual transformation. Apparently, our independent empirical analysis of adolescents' meanings of their risk behavior yielded the same, basic conceptual capacities at work toward achieving the goal of integration between an adolescent and his or her world (in this case a world of risk), with the intention of defining and perhaps redefining his or her personal and interpersonal self.

Table 8.2 illustrates that, beyond their thematic contribution, the awareness dimensions themselves undergo developmental transformation as they interact with the developmental levels of personal meaning. The point of entry for each dimension falls along the diagonal, where each appears in least mature form. For example, although the agency dimension heralds Level 1, it continues to be operative through Level 4, but differs structurally across these levels. Within the rule-based category, no real responsibility is assumed by the self for RTB. Rather, behavior is viewed as being governed by external, universally applicable forces or principles, as at the rule-based, impersonal level, or by externally based circumstances that may pertain exclusively to the self, but do not involve personal volition, as at the rule-based, personal level. Personalization enters at the rule-based, personal level, where experience with RTB is conceptualized as particular to the self, if only based on situational factors. This dimension is transformed at the need-based, unintegrated level to consider more internalized, social, and psychological bases for the uniqueness of RTB experience, and to differentiate one's own subjective view of RTB from a more objective view. At the need-based, integrated level of personalization, these subjective and objective views are coordinated, as the adolescent considers the unique factors that support this personalized RTB experience. The reflection dimension presents only within the need-based category where, at the unintegrated level, an observing ego facilitates perspective on internal, subjective, psychological phenomena that motivate RTB, and at the integrated level, it becomes possible to introspect on the basis for the products of introspection from the previous level. Contextualization exists only at the need-based, integrated level, when the self-in-relation to RTB is woven into a fabric of personal context through association with meaningful sociocultural, temperamental, and relational life experiences.

Thus, the developmental levels rely on the awareness dimensions to define a focal maturational achievement characterizing the process of conceptualizing the significance of one's own RTB, and the dimensions rely on the levels to shape their structural evolution. In contrast to more traditional developmental systems such as moral or ego development which are viewed as relatively discrete schemes of construction, each with its own characteristic ways of thinking about a problem, levels of personal meaning can not be sharply drawn, unifocal levels in the same sense. This is because the conceptualization of one's own risk taking behavior, as we have chosen to assess and define it, is a complex, multifaceted process intersecting with everything known or felt about the self and relationships. In effect, the levels of personal meaning symbolize the qualitative differentiation of highly individualized discussions of the meaning of risky behavior. Although the levels trace an empirically derived overall path toward "ultimate personal meaning," these levels of personal meaning are essentially a

TABLE 8.2
Awareness Dimensions

Developmental Levels	Agency	Personalization	Self-Reflection	Contextualization
Dismissive				
Rule-based impersonal	External, physicalistic, lawlike source of influence affecting everybody the same way with respect to RTB. No intentionality or responsibility ascribed.			
Rule-based personal	External source of influence on RTB, more situationally based, applying more particularly to the self. Intentionality and responsibility located external to the self.	Experience with RTB recognized as particular to self, but largely on basis of external, situational factors. Subjectivity of experience acknowledged but not differentiated from objective self.		
Need-based unintegrated	Internally based source of influence on RTB, with specific focus on motivational states, wishes, fears, etc. Responsibility and intentionality now owned by the self.	Subjective nature of RTB experience now perceived in internal, psychologically based terms, and differentiated from objective self.	Observing ego operating, able to take third-person perspective on self's internal motivations, fears, etc., as they bear on RTB choices.	

(Continued)

TABLE 8.2 (*Continued*)
Awareness Dimensions

Developmental Levels	Agency	Personalization	Self-Reflection	Contextualization
Need-based integrated	Responsibility taken not only for internal states underlying RTB, but for understanding the context in which these needs developed.	Uniqueness of RTB experience appreciated as a function of both internal states and background history from which they derive. Simultaneous coordination of subjective and objective experience.	Products of self reflection from previous level become objects of introspection as ground work for contextualization process.	Contributions of agency, personalization and reflection, are integrated into highly differentiated analysis of psychological factors as conduit by which RTB is associated with personal background material. RTB choices are laden with meaning as their relevance to self and relationships is revealed.
Insightful				

heuristic denotation, freeze frames along a continuum to highlight the significance of the contribution of each new dimension in combination with transformations in self in relation to risk, knowledge and management, and standard formal developmental shifts. The dimensions should be viewed as thematic handles by which to grasp hold of a complex constructivist architecture.

In theory, a given response at a given level of personal meaning will represent the contribution of one or more of the dimensions, all operating at the same level of maturity. In reality, however, it is unlikely that all individuals for whom a given dimension is emerging will be synchronized with respect to the developmental status of all the other dimensions at precisely the same point in time. This is why the level terminology should not be misconstrued to imply that individuals fall neatly into one category or another, or that two individuals assigned to the same level are identical in their pattern of personal meaning across risky behaviors.

PERSONAL MEANING—CASE STUDY APPLICATIONS

How do these levels of personal meaning interact with friendship to render it an influence toward or against risk? The following case discussions demonstrate the connection between developmental levels of personal meaning of risky behavior and the role played by friendship as a risk or protective factor. In essence, the manner in which young adolescents understand their own patterns of risky behavior within their own life contexts is assumed to establish parameters that influence the range and nature of the avenues through which friendship can bring to bear its own influence toward or away from risky behavior.

Case 1: Rhonda

Fourteen-year-old Rhonda is discussing the consequences of fighting in her school. "Suspension," she quickly replies, and pauses before continuing, "I've had it before." With minimal prompting she adds, "And, um, makin' you sit down and talk to that person." The interviewer reminds her of the label for this process, namely mediation, and asks Rhonda if she cares for it. "No!" is her immediate response. "If two people don't want to see each other, they don't have to. But if they want to fight, let them fight. Let them get their anger out. Put them in a corner. And let them fight it out. The best thing is to let them fight." When asked how she feels about the teachers and principal who try to stop fights, Rhonda exasperatedly responds, "Eh, let them fight it out, 'cause if they don't let 'em fight it out, they ain't gonna get their anger out. And it's gonna get . . . it's not gonna do nothing but get 'em in trouble." "So what you're saying is, if they keep their anger inside, eventually what will happen?" asks the interviewer. "They's gonna—um, they if they get mad at another person, gonna take that person. They're gonna take all their strength out on that person. And that person like, they'd only did a little bit. But all the person—like—I don't know how to say it. Like I'm supposed to be fighting Camille, ok? But then her boyfriend Mikey got in my face and he was like . . . Don't fight her. And I end up fighting him—And all my anger that I'm mad at her? I'm gonna put it on him. And he's gonna get hurt more."

Rhonda seems to be telling us that, for her, anger is a primary impulse that simply insists on being expressed, and that fighting is therefore inevitable. Preventing a fight in one instance merely achieves a postponement until the next provocation. Because anger doesn't go away until it is expressed, it accumulates so that subsequent provacateurs may receive more than their fair share of expressed anger. Nothing other than physical fighting seems to provide a channel for anger's dissipation.

As it stands, this sample of Rhonda's discussion of fighting represents an example of Level 1, impersonal rule-based personal meaning. Although she actively acknowledges her volitional role in fighting behavior, she believes that fighting is akin to a law of nature, interference with which is unnatural and eventually more problematic. In other parts of the interview, Rhonda observes that she lives in a tough neighborhood where people need to be able to defend themselves, but, consistent with her rigid application of the fighting rule, she denies that her fighting behavior would vary depending on the neighborhood she lived in. She explains the fact that some people do not in fact get into fights in terms of their inability to fight, but seems to regard them as aberrations. "Because, what's the sense of — well, I can't really say, 'What's the sense of living?' See, it's — you gotta have at least a fight in your life. I mean if you don't — I don't know how someone cannot fight. I don't understand." Herein she suggests that fighting actually provides a certain meaning to life, and acknowledges elsewhere that she thinks life must be boring for those who don't fight. Her affective connection to fighting derives mainly from the excitement it provides. Thus, not only does Rhonda think fighting is inevitable, but she thinks it serves the purpose of entertainment, a positive orientation toward fighting to be sure. She cannot break out of her own perspective enough to appreciate that this is her personalized view of fighting, rather than an inherent value that it holds for everyone, and therefore her personal meaning of fighting does not meet the criterion for Level 2. Neither can she step back to reflect upon her life situation, her proclivities toward excitement, and her management of affect long enough to put into context her own need to fight for what sounds like a sense of stimulation in an otherwise unchallenging, dreary existence, and an intolerance for absorbing angry feelings without lashing out.

How does this personal meaning of fighting create a context into which friendship brings to bear a risk-prone or risk-resistant influence? We begin by examining some of the comments that Rhonda makes about friendship in reference to fighting. Rhonda feeds the common view of peer pressure by acknowledging that she and her friends sometimes look to start fights for excitement. Some of her other comments are more provocative. For example, Rhonda explains that fights often get started when someone has been reported to have said something that she doesn't like. When asked by the interviewer if she would believe someone who denied having made the insulting comment, Rhonda replies, "See, all my friends, I can tell when they lie." She goes on to say later that she is prepared to fight friends as easily as nonfriends. Finally, Rhonda offers an interesting insight into the relationship between friendship and fighting, having to do with Robin Hood and Little John. "Well, it's sort of like him and Little John when they fightin'. And then after that, Little John — they fought and Little John beat Ridin — tsk — Robin Hood, and, um, he becomes one of his merry men."

Thus, fighting, in all its inevitability, may ironically promote intimacy. To win at a fight means someone is part of your gang if they so choose.

Given Rhonda's personally meaningful working theory that "the fight must go on," especially when anger is aroused, friendship does not dissuade Rhonda from engaging in fights with a given individual. In contrast to adolescents who consider friendship a relevant factor in whether or not to fight, and for whom friendship therefore acts as a deterrent, Rhonda conducts her fighting according to the principle of equal opportunity. In other words, the power of friendship to impact on RTB in this protective sense (i.e., fights with friends are avoided) is neutralized as a function of Rhonda's personal meaning of fighting. Instead, for Rhonda, friendship seems to play the role of assisting in determining when the situation has occurred necessitating that the bell for a fight should be sounded. By virtue of knowing a person's proclivity to lie, Rhonda can be more confident about whether she has in fact been insulted. Thus, although fighting in general is always going to happen, friendships help to determine the likelihood of only a given fight at a given time. In Rhonda's view, fighting would, ironically, be regarded less as the result of the risk-prone nature of friendship than as the cause of friendships. At this relatively rigid level of personal meaning of fighting, friends could operate at a protective level by being attentive to avoid the kinds of comments that stir Rhonda's rage. The opportunity for peers to influence Rhonda's view of fighting would derive from the experiences she has with them in which it is demonstrated to her that anger can be successfully expressed and exorcised through nonviolent means. In other words, because Rhonda's personal meaning of fighting is virtually synonymous with her knowledge of fighting, her friends must help her learn that her theory of anger is flawed.

Case 2: Gregory

In the course of discussing the reasons why he fights, 11-year-old Gregory is asked what would have to change in his life in order for him not to fight. "Not to go to this school," he replies, discussing an inner-city public school in which he is a fourth grader. Initially he states that he would be less inclined to get into fights in a Catholic school because the punishment would be more severe, but quickly moves from that to say that he gets into fights in his current school because he is angry. When asked how being at this school affects him, he complains about overcrowding and too much homework. In contrast, Gregory talks at length about the advantages of attending a Catholic school. In addition to his perception that there would be less homework assigned, he observes, "It would be like next to a store or something and then I'd be able to get out of school, after school and I'd be

able to go up to like the White Hen and get something to eat or drink . . . "
In musing about the building, which he describes as "big, big, big" he
remarks, "And when they go outside there's a playground in back, so you
can play out back, there are like swings and everything in the back." He
adds that in his own school, there's only a basketball court, and yet no
basketballs are allowed in school because "it's considered dangerous out
there." Finally, he adds that "Catholic schools are like calmer and they don't
have spray paint on the walls and they have like, it's a cleaner school, it's not
like this, and it has a lot of stuff in the rooms, it's not just plastic doors and
stuff like that, they have better doors and everything . . . It doesn't have
floors like this, it has better floors, and it has like floors in the house and
it doesn't have grass stains on each side." "Sounds like a neat place," the
interviewer comments, to which Gregory wistfully replies, "yeah." When
asked if he thinks he will ever be able to go to the Catholic school, Gregory
replies, "No, because I have to stay in this school because my sister grew up
in this school." At one point Gregory is asked to contrast himself with a
student who, he observes, never fights. "Um, he's like an "A" student, and
I'm not an "A" student; sometimes I get "Bs" or "Cs." I get "Bs" or "Cs."
"Does that have anything to do with why he doesn't fight and you do?" He
says, "Yah, because like if I get in trouble and if I did something I'd get in
trouble, I'd just get in trouble . . . I'd get in trouble and they'd take my
good grades off and put bad grades on."

From a developmental perspective, Gregory's personal meaning of
fighting would probably be considered somewhere between Levels 2 and 3.
His discussion of fighting is personalized in the sense that he makes no
claims about the implications of the public school–private school distinction
beyond himself; he does not insist that private school is the route to
nonviolence for everyone. Although his assumption that fighting would
virtually come to an automatic stop in Catholic school could be questioned,
Gregory is able to make the important connection between his behavior and
a particular context, and thereby advances beyond the rigidity of Level 1
that offers fewer options for modification. He also demonstrates the
capacity to reflect on his anger about the conditions of his own school.

In contrast to his initial suggestion that Catholic school would curtail
fighting by imposing stricter punishments, he winds up implying that his
fighting would diminish by virtue of the nurturence (access to White Hen
Pantry), the understanding (not overloading homework), and the respect
for students (reflected in the physical plant and amenities) offered by the
Catholic school. Were he to make his observations about the personal needs
that would be fulfilled for him by the Catholic school in a more explicit
fashion, his personal meaning would be more solidly coded at a Level 3.
From a developmental perspective, the other aspect of his discussion of
fighting that is limited is his view of his own contribution to his fighting

behavior. In contrast to the theoretical leverage into fighting behavior offered by a change in context, Gregory appears to see his own personal course as more narrowly defined. In his mind he is destined to be an average student, and this fate somehow dooms him to get involved in fights. Even the change in schools that would alter his fighting behavior is made somewhat arbitrarily unavailable to him in his view (because his sister went to the public school), as if by decree.

What are the comments Gregory makes about fighting in relation to friendship? Gregory relates the group aspect of friendship to fighting through an elaborate description of how a number of friends would kick a knife among themselves under a set of desks in order to prevent any one person from being caught with it. Groups can also spread rumors associated with fights that draw more and more people into the fight as they too become angry. Despite these apparent ways in which his peer group encourages fighting, Gregory does not feel his fighting behavior would be altered if he had a different set of friends. Gregory notes that he would just walk away from a friend who started trouble with him rather than fight him, and acknowledges that fighting will drive friends away "if they think I fight all the time." Finally, in the course of describing how a peer named Lewis would not fight, Gregory remarks that he and his friend would stick up for Lewis if necessary to prevent him from getting into a fight "because we know he's not a bad student." Lewis is described as an "A" student who "grew up in a good area."

In contrast to Rhonda's view of fighting as inevitable and necessary, Gregory's personal meaning of fighting is more differentiated in a way that alters (increases?) the manner in which friendship may play a risk-prone or risk-resistant role for him. Consider, for example his more differentiated sense of agency. Even the notion that one has choices over whether to fight or not means that the identity of a provocative other (i.e., friend or foe) can be taken into account, and one can consider the implications of fighting for one's future reputation and ability to maintain friendships. This creates an avenue by which friendships can serve a protective function. Gregory claims that he would fight to the same degree even if he had a different set of friends. Yet, given his recognition that he fights because he is angry, and his implicit understanding that he is angry because his needs are not being met in his current school context, it may in fact be the case that friends could have some influence on his fighting through their success or failure to meet his needs that are not met by the school. In other words, because Gregory's personal meaning is at least on the brink of being characterized by being associated with personal needs, friendships may play their risk-prone or risk-resistant roles in particular at this developmental level through their ability to satisfy these needs. Although Gregory indicates that he would be less inclined to fight in a new school context, he also conveys a sense of futile predetermination about the kinds of people who fight and those who don't. In fact, his view of the kinds of kids who fight represents an interesting combination of the role of sociocultural context and some kind of magical predetermination. It also embodies a degree of rigidity that is more characteristic of Level 2 than Level 3. His friend Lewis, for example, seems destined never to have to fight, in part because he is an "A" student (also seemingly a magically predetermined status) and because "he grew up in a good area." Gregory, by contrast, sees himself as locked into an average student status, and as having grown up in a dangerous neighborhood, thereby relegating him to a life of fighting. Interestingly, friendship enters in here in Gregory's view, as a management force to maintain the status quo. By virtue of his status as an "A" student who doesn't get into fights, Lewis is protected by Gregory and his friend from getting into fights. In other words, friendship perpetuates a cycle of nonviolence for some, because friends prevent nonfighters from getting into fights. Kids who are known as fighters, such as Gregory, presumably get no such support.

FINAL CONNECTIONS: A RETURN FROM FIGHTING IN AMERICA TO THE FLIGHT FROM EGYPT

And so, just as prevention programs for risky behavior cannot be effectively designed without an understanding of its developmental antecedents, so too, determination of the effects of friendship on risky behavior requires an understanding of the underlying processes. At the heart of these underlying processes is, we suggest, the personal meaning construct, the process by which adolescents connect their pattern of RTB within the contextual history of their selves and relationships. In essence, this construct yanks from us the luxury of knowing for all adolescents as a group just how risky behavior "works," how to intervene to protect against it in general, or the risk and protective influence of a force such as friendship in particular. If, as we suggest, personal meaning-making is an activity that takes place with characteristically different degrees of maturity, and whose sources of variation also derive systematically from sociocultural (and gender-based) sources, among others, then the answer to the question, "what is the role of friendship in moving the adolescent toward or away from RTB?" is: it depends. Answers, then, about how and/or whether certain friendship relationships have the potential to effect patterns of RTB for a given adolescent or group of adolescents requires knowing something about their developmental maturity and sociocultural background. Teachers, parents, or other concerned adults cannot hope to maximize risk-resistant behavior in youths they care about via friendships or any other vehicle without first reaching out to learn about the role of RTB in these youths' lives. Indeed, this is as it should be, for the spirit of personal meaning is that connections bode well for good health.

To return to our initial focus, the Passover *Haggadah*, we are now in a better position to compare the qualitative differences among the four sons with our developmental levels of personal meaning. In gross terms, the son at the Passover table who does not even know how to ask a meaningful question about the risks taken by the Israelites in their flight from persecution corresponds to Level 0 in the sense that the adolescent who is making personal meaning of the Passover story at Level 0 does not seem to know how or where to begin the process of making meaning of his own risky behavior. At Level 1, a loose analogy can be made to the simple son, who seems to appreciate that something is going on that he should know about, but his approach is generic, in no way related personally to himself. The analogy to the Passover sons breaks down somewhat at Level 2, which is not directly akin to the contrary son's exclusion of the self from the personal meaning process. However, there is a thread of structural similarity that could be considered to overlap with both Levels 2 and 3 by virtue of the fact that, like the contrary son, both Levels 2 and 3 involve an awareness of personalization that is not integrated within a larger process. In other words, like the son who differentiates himself from the group while recognizing the meaning of the Passover holiday for the others, adolescents whose personal meaning is at Level 2 recognize a personalized quality to their RTB, but it is in no way connected to personal needs. Those whose personal meaning is at Level 3 integrate reflective abilities so that risky behavior is integrated with personal needs, but not with more contextualized aspects of their personal history. This leaves us with the wise son who considers the Passover holiday as a member of the larger group. In structural developmental terms, this son would be "wise" and analogized to Level 4 only if his contextualized stance represented a differentiation of his own personalization of Passover and subsequent integration with the larger whole, as opposed to a fused failure to differentiate in the first place. Probing of each son's structure of meaning would be required to make such a differentiation. For our purposes, we assume that the investigators whose data were compiled for the *Haggadah* took appropriate steps to determine that the differentiation was in fact made.

The labels attached by the *Haggadah* to the four sons are certainly more descriptive, more judgmental, more charged than "Level 0, 1, 2, etc." Because we have associated the sons with developmental levels on a structural basis, can these nominal designations be reconciled? Why, for example, is the wise son wise? According to our personal meaning system, the wisdom of this son can be said to derive from the impact that friendship brings to bear on his risky behavior. Just as the wise son of the *Haggadah* steps back from the Passover service to consider what he learns through reading the *Haggadah* as it relates to himself and to himself in relation to his community, the wise confronter of risk can utilize the knowledge or input from his friends in meaningful fashion by stepping back from the risk at hand to consider its significance for him and his close relationships.

By integrating the input of friends with awareness of self and relationships, risky behavior assumes an affective charge that is less accessible to other adolescents for whom knowledge or input about risk is undifferentiated from the meaning of risk due to limitations on their capacity for agency, personalization, reflection, and/or contextualization. Whereas other adolescents receive knowledge or input about risk and possess management skills by which to deal with risk, they lack sufficient perspective on their risky behavior as it relates to themselves to be able to use input from friends to modulate their risky behavior in protective fashion. In contrast, for the wise son who employs a little help from his friends to relate risky behavior to himself, the effects of risk can be anticipated in a visceral way, rendering poor risks less likely to be acted upon. To the wise son—or daughter—a word may be sufficient.

REFERENCES

Colby, A., & Kohlberg, L. (1987). *The measurement of moral judgment: Theoretical foundations and research validation* (Vol. 1) Cambridge: Cambridge University Press.

Feldman, S.S., & Elliott, G.R. (1990). *At the threshold: The developing adolescent.* Cambridge, MA: Harvard University Press.

Fischer, K.W., Shaver, P.R., & Carnochan, P. (1990). How emotions develop and how they organize development. *Cognition and Emotion, 4*(2), 81–127.

Freud, A. (1964). *The ego and the mechanisms of defense.* New York: University Press. (Original work published 1936).

Gibbs, J., Basinger, K.S., & Fuller, D. (1992). *Moral maturity: Measuring the development of sociomoral reflection.* Hillsdale, NJ: Lawrence Erlbaum Associates.

Kaplan, B. (1987). Commentary on "Life-span Developmental Psychology." *Human Development, 10*, 65–87.

Keller, M., & Edelstein, W. (1991). The development of socio-moral meaning making: Domains, categories, and perspective-taking. In W.M. Kurtines, & J.L. Gewirtz, *Handbook of moral behavior and development: Vol. 2. Research* (pp. 89–115). Hillsdale, NJ: Lawrence Erlbaum Associates.

Kohlberg, L. (1984). *The psychology of moral development.* San Francisco: Harper & Row.

Lerner, R.M. (1979). A dynamic interactions concept of individual and social relationship development. In R.L. Burgess & T.L. Huston (Eds.), *Social exchange in developing relationships* (pp. 271–305). New York: Academic Press.

Levitt, M.Z., Selman, R.L., & Richmond, J.L. (1991). The psychosocial foundations of early adolescents' high-risk behavior: Implications for research and practice. *Journal of Research on Adolescence, 1*(4), 349–378.

Lightfoot, C. (1994, June). Literary forms of the hero, and adolescents' narratives of risk-taking. Paper presented 24th annual symposium of the Jean Piaget Society, Chicago.

Loevinger, J. (1976). *Ego development.* San Francisco: Jossey Bass.

Noam, G.G. (1990). Beyond Freud and Piaget: Biographical worlds-interpersonal self. In T.

Wren (Ed), *The moral domains* (pp. 360–399). Cambridge, MA: MIT Press.

Oser, F., & Gmunder, P. (1991). *Religious judgment: A developmental approach.* Birmingham, AL: Religious Education Press. (Original work published 1988).

Rorty, A. (1976). *The identities of persons.* Berkeley: University of California Press.

Selman, R.L. (1980). *The growth of interpersonal understanding.* New York: Academic Press.

Selman, R.L., & Schultz, L.H. (1990). *Making a friend in youth: Developmental theory and pair therapy.* Chicago: University of Chicago Press.

Smetana, J.G. (1983). Social-cognitive development: Domain distinctions and coordinations. *Child Development, 55,* 1767–1776.

Turiel, E. (1983). *The development of social knowledge: Morality and convention.* Cambridge, England: Cambridge University Press.

Turiel, E., & Smetana, J.G. (1984). Social knowledge and action: The coordination of domains. In W.M. Kurtines, & J.L. Gewirtz (Eds.), *Morality and moral development.* New York: Wiley.

Turner, M. (1994). Design for a theory of meaning. In W. Overton & D. Palermo (Eds.), *The nature and ontogenesis of meaning.* (pp. 91–109). Hillsdale, NJ: Lawrence Erlbaum Associates.

Vaillant, G. (1977). *Adaptation to life.* Boston: Little, Brown.

Werner, H. (1948). *Comparative psychology of mental development.* New York: International Universities Press.

Youniss, J. (1980). *Parents and peers in social development.* Chicago: University of Chicago Press.

IV Dynamics and Themes of Relationship in Personality Development

9 The Centrality of Relationship in Human Development: A Puzzle, Some Evidence, and a Theory

Carol Gilligan
Harvard University

> *There are certain risks—including, here, the risk of becoming unable to risk—that we cannot close off without a loss of human value, suspended as we are between beast and god, with a kind of beauty available to neither.*
>
> —Nussbaum (1986)

A PUZZLE

In the second half of the 19th century, psychiatrists treating young women observed that girls "are more liable to suffer in adolescence," and that the girls who suffer include those who seem most psychologically vital, "typically energetic and passionate, 'exhibiting more than usual force and decision of character, of strong resolution, fearless of danger, bold riders, having plenty of what is termed nerve' " (Showalter, 1985, pp. 130, 132). Maudsley and Skey made these observations in England in the 1860s and 1870s. Shortly thereafter, Freud and Breuer (1895/1974) recorded similar impressions in Vienna:

> Adolescents who are later to become hysterical are for the most part lively, gifted, and full of intellectual interests before they fall ill. Their energy of will is often remarkable. They include girls who get out of bed at night so as secretly to carry out some study that their parents have forbidden for fear of their overworking. (p. 321)

237

Countering the generally held impression that hysteria was a sign of mental degeneracy, Breuer concluded, "the capacity for forming sound judgments is certainly not more abundant in [there girls] than in other people, but it is rare to find in them simple, dull intellectual inertia or stupidity" (p. 321).

Freud expanded this characterization. Describing the character of his patient, Fraulein Elisabeth von R., he observed "the features which one meets with so frequently in hysterical people":

> her giftedness, her ambition, her moral sensibility, her excessive demand for love which, to begin with, found satisfaction in her family, and the independence of her nature which went beyond the feminine ideal and found expression in a considerable amount of obstinacy, pugnacity and reserve. (Freud & Breuer, 1895/1974, p. 231)

Like other hysterical young women, Elisabeth suffered from a physical and a psychological paralysis: The pains in her legs made it difficult for her to take even a single step forward; her nature was frozen; she found it painful to stand alone.

This clinical picture of gifted young women suffering psychologically in adolescence persists throughout the 20th century. In 1926, Horney observed girls' difficulties in adolescence and attributed them to a revival of Oedipal conflicts and rivalries, leading to tensions around sexuality and conflicts in relationships with their mothers. In 1944, Deutsch focused on femininity and advised young women to develop an "as if" personality—to wear their femininity like a cloak. Thompson (1964) described girls' loss of vitality in adolescence, and Miller (1991) tied the constriction of girls' sense of self to a narrowing of relationship at that time.

Fine and Zane's (1989) research on high school dropouts provides a corollary to these clinical observations. In a study of adolescents who drop out of a large, urban high school, the girls who dropped out—at the time of leaving school—were among the brightest and the least depressed. The association of psychological vitality with risk for girls in adolescence thus extends through time, across culture, and to both ends of the social class spectrum.

Research on psychological development leads beyond these observations to reveal a startling pattern of developmental asymmetry: Boys are more psychologically at risk than girls throughout the years of childhood, and then girls—stronger and more psychologically resilient than boys in childhood—are suddenly at high risk in adolescence (Peterson, 1988). Throughout childhood, boys are more liable than girls to suffer from episodes of depression, to attempt suicide, to develop learning disorders, to show various forms of out-of-control and out-of-touch behavior. Boys who are having psychological problems in adolescence generally have a history of psychological trouble reaching back into early childhood, whereas girls who experience psychological difficulty in adolescence often have been doing well, or even extremely well up to that time (Achenbach, 1982; Rutter & Garmezy, 1983; Schonert-Reichl & Offer, 1992). Summarizing a growing and complex body of evidence, Machoian (1995) reported that adolescence

is a time when across lines of race and class, girls' suicide attempts rise and peak [at ages 13 and 14]; girls' depression rises, eating disorders emerge, many Latina girls and White girls experience a plummet in their sense of self-worth, and many African American girls experience disconnection from their schools. (p. 43)

In early adolescence, "girls' depression and related suicide attempts rapidly rise, outnumbering boys' by ratios of 3:1 to 9:1" (Machoian, 1995, p. 2; see also Allgood-Merton, Lewinsohn, & Hops, 1990; Angold & Rutter, 1992; Block, 1990; Demitrack, Putnam, Brewerton, Brandt, & Gold, 1990; Greenberg-Lake, 1991; Harris, Blum, & Resnick, 1991; Minnesota Women's Fund, 1990; Peterson, Sarigiani, & Kennedy, 1991; Robinson & Ward, 1991; Rodin, Silberstein, & Striegel-Moore, 1985; Steiner-Adair, 1986, 1991; Whitaker et al., 1990).

Epidemiological studies confirm this developmental asymmetry. Elder and Caspi (1990), investigating the relationship between life stress and psychological illness, discovered that when families are under stress (from economic depression, marital conflict, or the disruption of war), the children most likely to suffer psychologically are boys in childhood and girls at adolescence. Seligman (1991), reflecting on the epidemiology of depression, concluded that "whatever causes the huge difference in depression in adulthood, with women twice as vulnerable as men, it does not have its roots in childhood. Something must happen at or shortly after puberty that causes a flip-flop—and hits girls very hard indeed" (pp. 149–150).

These clinical observations, research findings, and epidemiological data pose a puzzle that has sat in the psychological literature for more than 100 years. Why are boys at greater psychological risk than girls during childhood? What accounts for girls' greater psychological resilience and strength? What happens to girls at adolescence? What explains the sudden drop in resilience, the sudden onset of trouble, and the association between vitality and risk? Girls' problems at adolescence are readily attributed to nature or nurture, to hormones or socialization. Until recently, however, girls' strengths have been of little interest to psychologists and the difference between women's and men's developmental histories, despite the clear implications for prevention and treatment, have not aroused much curiosity.

SOME EVIDENCE

Describing the process of involuntary memory, Proust (1913/1992) captured the difficulty of psychological inquiry:

> It is a labour in vain to attempt to recapture [our own past]. The past is hidden
> somewhere outside the realm, beyond the reach of intellect, in some material
> object (in the sensation which that material object will give us) of which we
> have no inkling. And it depends on chance whether or not we come upon this
> object before we ourselves must die. (p. 51)

In the first of the six volumes of *In Search of Lost Time*, Proust focused on
the process of recollection. A man, going to bed early, reflects on the
process of falling asleep and remembers going to bed early as a young boy
and longing for his mother to come and kiss him goodnight. This memory
of early childhood remains an isolated memory until, one day, he is offered
a *petite madeleine* and the taste of the madeleine suddenly reverses a
long-standing process of dissociation:

> The sight of the little madeleine had recalled nothing to my mind before I
> tasted it; perhaps because I had so often seen such things in the meantime,
> without tasting them, on the trays in pastry-cooks' windows, that their image
> had dissociated itself from those Combray days to take its place among others
> more recent; perhaps because of those memories so long abandoned and put
> out of mind, nothing now survived, everything was scattered; the shapes of
> things . . . were either obliterated or had been so long dormant as to have lost
> the power of expansion which would have allowed them to resume their place
> in my consciousness. But when from a long-distant past nothing subsists, after
> the people are dead, after the things are broken and scattered, taste and smell
> alone, more fragile but more enduring, more immaterial, more persistent,
> more faithful, remain poised a long time, like souls, remembering, waiting,
> hoping, amid the ruins of all the rest; and bear unflinchingly, in the tiny and
> almost impalpable drop of their essence, the vast structure of recollection.
> (p. 54)

I begin with Proust as a way of introducing a 10-year research into
women's psychology and girls' development, because the nature of memory
and the process of recollection became central in this work. As the taste of
the madeleine led Proust's narrator back into the lost time of his childhood,
I found that the sounds of girls' voices recalled the years just before
adolescence and carried a vast structure of recollection for myself and other
women. Crossing and recrossing the terrain between childhood and adolescence in the company of girls and other women, Brown, Rogers, and I
began to map the psychology of what had been an undiscovered country or

lost time. At the edge of adolescence, we heard the onset of dissociative processes, which placed this time in development "beyond the reach of intellect" (Gilligan, Brown, & Rogers, 1990; see also Gilligan, Rogers, & Noel, 1992). The sounds of girls' voices carried a different psychological organization—a different relationship between inner and outer worlds. But then these sounds became dissociated from the scenes of childhood and different voices and images eclipsed a past that then became hard to find. Catching a glimpse of the eclipse provided the first entry into this psychological process.

The Harvard research project on women's psychology and girls' development began in Fall 1981 with a series of studies that focused on adolescent girls. Over the next 5 years, my colleagues and I interviewed girls at the Emma Willard School for girls, and girls and boys in a coeducational independent school, in urban and suburban public schools, and in Boys' and Girls' Clubs in three ethnically different Boston neighborhoods (see Gilligan, 1987a; Gilligan, Johnston, & Muller, 1988; Gilligan, Lyons, & Hanmer, 1990; Gilligan, Ward, & Taylor, 1988).

My strongest impression in interviewing adolescent girls was of moments when the conversation would suddenly drop into a different reality, and a girl would suddenly know what she had seemed not to know: It was as if the psychological world had suddenly become transparent. Or as if the girl was composing a picture that otherwise lay scattered in fragments—thoughts, feelings, impressions, experiences, knowledge, memories. At such times, I discovered a wealth of psychological experience and a depth of psychological understanding that I found at once familiar and surprising: girls' knowledge of the human world.

Pressed to write a paper about this research, I titled it, *The Willing Suspension of Disbelief: Conflicts of Female Adolescence* (Gilligan, 1986) and then wondered about the word *willing*. Listening to girls speak of themselves, their relationships, their responses to conflicts and their construction of conflicts, their hopes and their fears, I often had the sense that they were living in what they knew to be a fictional world, and living in that world as if it was real. At moments in interviews when I sensed an absence, I would ask girls where they were in relation to what they were saying: "Do you really feel that way?" I would say, or "Do you believe that?" or "Is that true?" In response to my questions, girls often entered the conversation at a different level, telling me what they "really" felt, what they "really" thought, what was "really" going on, what they knew. This underreality caught my attention, and I followed its appearance and its eclipse in girls' conversation (Gilligan, 1987a, 1990a, 1990b).

In 1986, Brown and I began a 5-year longitudinal, cross-sectional study of roughly 100 girls attending the Laurel School for girls in Cleveland (Brown & Gilligan, 1992; Gilligan, Brown, & Rogers, 1990; Rogers, Brown,

& Tappan, 1993). At the time we started our yearly interviewing, the girls were 6, 9, 11, 14, and 16 years of age. In the course of the research, the amplification and clarification of girls' voices in the world of the school led to a series of retreats with women psychologists and teachers, and at this point we explicitly joined our study of girls' development with an exploration of women's psychology (Brown & Gilligan, 1992; see also Gilligan, 1990a; Gilligan & Rogers, 1992; Gilligan et al., 1992; Rogers, 1993; Dorney, 1991). Girls' voices, carrying the sounds of an inner world that had become dissociated, opened a vast storehouse of recollection for women, encouraging memory and leading to the discovery of what many women had forgotten: their clear voices, their resilience, their strength, their courage (Brown & Gilligan, 1992; Gilligan, 1990b; Gilligan et al., 1992; Rogers, 1993).

Eight-year-old Diana, when asked about a time when she was not listened to, says that when she tried to speak at dinner, her brother and sister interrupted her, "stealing" her mother's attention. Diana's response was to bring a whistle to dinner, and when she was interrupted, she blew the whistle. Mother, brother, and sister suddenly stopped talking and turned to her, at which point she said, "in a nice voice, 'that's much nicer' " (Brown & Gilligan, 1992, p. 43).

Karen, also 8, tells of the time when she walked out of her classroom on the third day when her teacher did not call on her to do a hard problem. She knew that people seeing her standing in the hall would think that she had gotten into trouble, but Karen also knew that she was not in trouble: "I just couldn't take it," she said. Asked if her teacher knew why she left, Karen responded: "She didn't listen, but I told her, so I guess she knew" (p. 44).

Karen gives voice to her inner world, saying that she lost her temper, she didn't want people to make fun of her, she doesn't do this very often, she wanted to have a chance to do a hard problem, she felt bad because the teacher always called on someone else, she wanted the teacher to have chosen her. At the same time, she carefully observes her teacher, making a fine distinction between her teacher knowing (registering what Karen has told her) and her teacher listening (responding or being moved by Karen).

It was difficult at first to hear girls openly naming relational realities without immediately covering their voices with the labels that in time they would come to affix themselves, calling honesty "stupid" and outspokenness "unfeeling" or "thoughtless" or "selfish" or "rude." Girls' frank naming of relational violations brought a clarity to their daily living. They read the relational climate, and they dressed for the weather. Seeing the grounds for their feelings and actions, they acted directly, without hesitation, blowing the whistle on interruption, leaving when their presence was ignored. Keeping an eye on relationships and turning their ear to the conversation, girls were remarkably sure-footed in the human world.

Eight-year-old Jessie, gives a stark illustration of girls' full voicing of relational realities. She had gone to her friend's house to play, only to find that her friend was playing with another friend and they did not include her. Jessie went up to her friend and whispered in her ear that this was making her feel bad, that this wasn't any fun for her, just sitting there, that if they didn't play with her, she would go home. When her interviewer asks what happened, Jessie says, "She said, 'just go home' " (Brown & Gilligan, 1992, p. 54).

Eight-year-old Lily writes a book called *A Friend*, which she dedicates "to my friends." In the first chapter, "Making Friends," Lily writes, "Making friends is easy with some people and hard with others, and you have to be careful because anything can happen and you will have to cope with it." The second chapter is called, "Fights." Lily writes: "When you and a friend get into a fight, don't worry because it is normal. Everyone gets into fights, right?" Chapter 3 is "Race":

> When you want a new friend, do not judge people by race. Indians, English, Asians, anybody. Pretend you were from Afghanistan, and a year ago you moved to America. You have been living in America for a year but you only have a few friends, but the point of making friends has nothing to do with race.

In the fourth chapter, "The End of Friendship," Lily observes, "In a real relationship there is usually no end of friendship. Hey, it's up to you and your friend to keep your friendship together."

Lily moved to America from Afghanistan; she is trying to make new friends. Her book expresses her longing for a friend but also provides a candid assessment of the realities of friendship: Making friends is sometimes easy, sometimes difficult; fights are normal in relationships, racism interferes with making friends in America, in real relationship, there is usually no end of friendship. But Lily's semi-rhetorical question ("Everyone gets into fights, right?"), carries the edge of a doubt that grows among girls as they reach adolescence: Is girls' experience common knowledge, is what a girl knows through her experience true?

The phrases "I don't know" and "you know," along with "I mean," and "I don't care," began to punctuate girls' conversation, signaling an exploration of reality and relationship and also the onset of dissociative processes. Machoian (1995), studying the sudden rise in girls' suicide attempts at the beginning of adolescence, summarized this powerful link between girls' questions about love and relationships and girls' questions about truth and reality:

> girls' questions about love and relationships appear to be embedded in a search for truth, honesty and reality—and their suicidality holds existential

questions: What is truth? What is love? For girls, these questions are about relationship. (p. 55)

In our longitudinal research we observed girls at the edge of adolescence beginning not to know what they know, beginning to lose relationship, beginning not to care about the honesty in relationship which in another sense they cared about passionately. Dissociation was a brilliant but costly solution to a difficult psychological problem which girls were facing: how to hold different realities and different relationships simultaneously, how to keep vital parts of themselves both alive and out of relationship. The cost was the "honesty in relationships" that many girls said they wanted.

At 11, Jessie feels it is essential for her to conceal her feelings from her friends. If they know she is angry at them, they will retaliate by excluding her and she will find herself alone. Asked about a time when she wanted to say something but didn't, Jessie reveals the strength of her feelings and also the pull toward dissociation. Strong feelings come out of her mouth against her will, at the same time as she is trying to separate her "bad" feelings from herself and to keep the bad parts of herself out of her relationships. On a simple level, Jessie is trying to hide her anger from her friends. On a somewhat more complicated level, she is trying to hide her sadness at the seeming breakdown of these friendships; she no longer feels free to tell her friends what is on her mind and in her heart. What Jessie wanted to say was that she was angry at her friends; she tells her story about anger in the second person:

> When you are really mad at somebody and you want to say something really bad, but you can't, you just can't. It's like it comes out of your mouth and you forget what you are going to say. (Brown & Gilligan, 1992, p. 59)

In Jessie's narrative, anger, the "it," has become separated from herself, the "I," and attached to a second person, the "you" who can't say what you want, who wants to say something really bad ("I hate you"). A paradox is apparent: To make and maintain relationships, Jessie is keeping vital parts of herself out of relationship. The person speaking in relationship is a second person, whose feelings, now once removed, have become truly disturbing.

Hearing girls articulate these psychological processes led to the discovery of a developmental impasse: If girls say what is on their minds or in their hearts, if they speak freely and reveal what they see and hear and know through experience, they are in danger of losing their relationships, but if they do not say what they are feeling and thinking, they will lose relationship and be out of connection with other people. Either way, they will lose relationship and be all alone.

The process of development, the onrush of adolescence, was rapidly covering this moment of insight. Yet girls, in paradoxically giving up relationship for the sake of having relationships or silencing themselves in order to be with other people, were also experiencing confusion, because in one sense they knew what was happening—they were describing what was happening—and in another sense they did not know. Girls' development raised fundamental questions about relationship and about relationships, about truth and reality. More practically, the onset of dissociative processes and the extent to which these processes seemed "normal" raised questions as to whether the paradoxical loss of relationship for the sake of relationships was in fact necessary or inevitable or healthy or good. Because it seemed, in the intensity of many girls' feelings, not only essential, but also adaptive, developmental. Girls were becoming psychologically attuned to the societal and the cultural worlds in which they were living. Miller (1976, 1988) wrote extensively about the psychological costs of this attunement, and formulated the paradoxical giving up of relationship in the struggle for relationships as central to women's psychological suffering.

A healthy resistance or fight for relationship signaled psychological vitality in girls. Vibrant girls, sensing themselves in danger of losing their strong voices and honest relationships, would stand their ground, courageously speak their minds and hearts, show creativity in attempting to find a way around or through the impasse, affirm their experience, dramatize the conflict, join with others, and find help (Brown & Gilligan, 1992; Gilligan, Rogers & Noel, 1992). But girls' outspokenness often made trouble. Jessie describes her fears of finding herself left out by her friends, overwhelmed and alone:

> When you're mad at somebody, sometimes they get really mad, and it really terrifies you because you feel like they are going to tell somebody and they are going to get almost the whole class on her side and it would be one against, I don't know, ten. (Brown & Gilligan, 1992, pp. 59–60)

Asked how she feels, Jessie says, "I don't feel very good. I feel like I'm making this whole fight, that it is really turning out to be a mess."

Twelve-year-old Ritu also says that if her friends know that she is angry at them, they will all get mad at her. Although she lives in a different city and goes to a public school, her image of radical isolation is the same as Jessie's:

> You just don't want everyone to know that you're mad because then they'll all get mad at you, and you wouldn't want them all to be mad at you because then—a big group of people who are mad at you, and you, one, lone.

Ritu's voice carries her feelings. When she is telling me a story about two girls in a photograph that we are looking at together, she observes that the girls look angry and says that they are "really mad." In her story, one girl shuts herself up in her room and "won't open her door"; when she does, she "says nothing." I ask about the anger: What happens to it? Where is it? Where is it in her body? Ritu immediately knows: "In the pit of her stomach and in her throat, like she's going to scream." Later, I ask about sadness; sadness, she says, hesitating for just a moment, is "in — the heart. Her heart will feel sad, like it is breaking."

Ritu feels her feelings in her body, but she also has learned how to separate herself and her voice from her body, holding herself in and raising her voice so that it covers rather than conveys what she feels and knows. Only the tightness in her throat carries the signs of Ritu's anger as she goes up to her friends and says, in a high voice, "So hi, what's up?" When I ask Ritu if her friends can tell that she is mad, she says, "Not really, but sometimes." When I ask if she can tell with her best friend, she says, "Umm, sometimes I can and sometimes I can't." With her mother, however, there is no equivocation: "I can with my mom; I've seen her all my life."

When Ritu senses that her mother is angry at her, she asks her mother, "Mom, are you mad at me?" When she hears her mother say, in a high falling voice, "Nooo," she listens further and hears the sounds of feelings held in; "Cause then she just goes 'Hhhaaa' (sound of letting out breath). So . . . . " The implication is clear. I ask Ritu, what do you say? Again, she speaks to her mom, trying to bring the emotional reality into the relationship: "Mom [with emphasis]; it seems like you're mad at me." And again, she listens, hearing in her mother's voice the suppression or covering of the anger she is picking up: "She says, she goes [high, thin voice] 'No, I'm not mad at you, okay?' " Ritu has hit an impasse. "So okay," she says, shrugging it off. Then what? I ask. She says, "Just sort of forget about it."

Ritu cannot give voice to what is unvoiced in the relationship, without placing herself in the position of knowing better than her mother what her mother feels, or saying what cannot be spoken by her mother and going out on a relational limb. When she says what in one sense she knows, she is contradicted, and she takes in the voice of contradiction. Taking in that voice, she takes in further evidence that the feelings that she was picking up are real. Do you think your mother is angry when she says [high voice] "I'm not angry," I ask Ritu. "Sometimes," she says. "Or do you believe her?" Ritu says, "Sometimes I do and sometimes I don't." Does your mother know when you are mad but acting nice? I ask further. And Ritu says, "No." With her mother, as with her friends, she covers her feelings. "So only you know?" I say. "Yup."

Girls' resilience lies in their resistance to not knowing or forgetting what they know. This resistance is grounded in girls' ability to stay in connection with the psychological world and also in their sense of what is of value, what is loving and truthful. The relational problem that girls experience —

the problem of cruelty and false relationship—is real; it is not just a girls' problem. Strong feelings, openness to others, and an intense desire for relationship heighten girls' vulnerability in relationships. When adolescence brings an intensification of sexual desires and feelings in a world where girls and women are sexual objects and women's sexuality is subject to Puritanical reprisals, when girls' emotional and cognitive grasp reaches further and more deeply into psychological realities that generally remain unspoken and unacknowledged, girls discover that it is not safe for them to voice their desires, to show their feelings, to reveal their knowledge, to see the implications of their experience, to know or to say what others are experiencing. It seems easier, in many ways, for girls to cover their experience and not know what they know, and because this covering coincides with the historical covering of women's and girls' experiences and voices, it is easily dissociated, set apart from consciousness, forgotten (Gilligan, 1990a, 1990b; Gilligan, Rogers, & Tolman, 1991; Rogers, 1995).

Girls who stay out in the open in adolescence or become outspoken at that time often get into trouble and become known as "troublemakers," or "loud-mouthed girls" (Fordham, 1991; see also Gilligan, 1990a). In a study of cultural differences and adolescent development in girls attending an urban high school, it was the African-American girls—the girls found most likely to retain a sense of personal self-worth—who completed the sentence stem, "What gets me into trouble is . . . " by writing, "my big mouth" (Greenberg-Lake Associates, 1991; Taylor, Gilligan, & Sullivan, in press). Girls' desire for relationships and the economic and political consequences of outspokenness, however, combine to create internal and external pressures on girls to become more silent, secretive, hidden, and closed.

When girls' preadolescent strength and resilience give way to increasing uncertainty, a hesitancy in speaking, a tendency to doubt themselves and to dismiss their experience as irrelevant almost before they have said it, or before it can be dismissed by others, girls take the strong and resilient and vital parts of themselves into an underworld for safekeeping. Making connection with this underworld is like making contact with a political resistance (Gilligan, 1990a).

A double standard of evaluation then becomes evident. The growth of self-consciousness and reflective thought, the intensification of sexual feelings and the deepening of emotions or in short, the cognitive and emotional growth of adolescence is accompanied by a loss of resilience and a diminishment of voice and relationship or by open conflict and trouble (Gilligan, Brown, & Rogers, 1990; Rogers, Brown, & Tappan, 1993). To the extent that girls see that you can't have voice without relationship and you can't have relationship without voice, they see the psychological problem of a patriarchal and imperial social order. Girls' psychological development— the development of voice and relationship—is in conflict with the regeneration of patriarchy, and this conflict is played out paradoxically as a tension between relationship and relationships or a trade-off between voice and relationships.

bell hooks (1984), describing her experience growing up a Black girl in a southern Black community, named her intense confusion and deep anxiety:

> I was never taught absolute silence. I was taught that it was important to speak but to talk a talk that was itself a silence. Taught to speak and beware of the betrayal of too much heard speech, I experienced intense confusion and deep anxiety in my efforts to speak and write. (p. 208)

Anne Frank, at 15—a Jew in hiding in Nazi-occupied Holland—named her experience of inner and outer contradiction. In her diary, she wrote that she had the reputation, "little bundle of contradictions" and that this is not for nothing. But, "What does contradiction mean? Like so many words it can be interpreted in two ways: it can mean two things, contradiction from without and contradiction from within" (Frank, 1944/1989, p. 697).

Contradiction from without is "the ordinary"—the consequence of an outspokenness that leads others to find her unpleasant: "the ordinary not giving in easily, always knowing best, getting in the last word, **enfin**, all the unpleasant qualities for which I am renowned."

Contradiction from within, however, is more painful, more difficult, more confusing because it is secret and hidden, "Nobody knows about [it], that's my own secret . . . . I have, as it were, a dual personality."

As Anne described the two Annes that compose this duality, her confusion and anxiety become apparent. One Anne is cheerful, exuberant, sexual, vibrant—this is the Anne whom she called bad, the Anne, she said, whom others find insufferable. The good Anne is better, deeper, purer, but she never speaks or appears in public. She sits alone in silence, serious and frozen:

> I'm awfully scared that everyone who knows me as I always am will discover that I have another side, a finer and better side. I'm afraid they will laugh at me, think I'm ridiculous, sentimental, not take me in earnest . . . . The deeper Anne is too frail for it. Sometimes, if I really compel the good Anne to take the stage for a quarter of an hour, she simply shrivels up as soon as she has to speak, and lets Anne no. 1 take over, and before I realize it, she has disappeared. (Frank, 1944/1989, pp. 697–698)

This split between a sexual and a pure Anne reflects the cultural division of women into whores and Madonnas—a division that Freud (1910/1963) traced to men's unresolved Oedipal problems or difficulty in separating their lovers from their mothers. Klein (1921/1977) believed that the origins of this splitting of women into the good and the bad lay in the relationship between infant and mother, and she located this splitting in a pre-Oedipal, archaic, psychic interior. Anne Frank at 15 described an interior splitting of herself into a good and bad Anne, but this division is laced with confusion because the good Anne is silent, paralyzed, immobile, whereas the bad Anne is lively, vivacious, vital. Anne experienced a problem of relationship that has political and cultural as well as psychological dimensions. She is in hiding psychologically as well as politically, and she cannot see how to bring herself safely out into the open:

> I never utter my real feelings . . . . If I'm to be quite honest, then I must admit that it does hurt me . . . . If I'm watched to that extent, I start by getting snappy, then unhappy, and finally I twist my heart round again so that the bad is on the outside and the good is on the inside and keep on trying to find a way of becoming what I would so like to be and what I could be if — there weren't any other people living in the world. (p. 699)

A THEORY

But human excellence grows like a vine tree

fed by the green dew, raised up

among wise men and just,

to the liquid sky . . . .

We have all kinds of needs for those we love,

most of all in hardships,

but joy, too, strains

to track down eyes that it can trust.

> —Pindar (translated by Nussbaum)

This soil is bad for certain kinds of flowers.

> —Toni Morrison (*The Bluest Eye*, 1970)

The study of girls' psychological development brings the account of psychological development into a political and cultural arena. The relational crisis that girls experience and describe at the edge of adolescence is rooted psychologically in the regeneration of patriarchy: If the inner world of girls and women remains connected with the outer world, both inner and outer worlds will change. The disconnection from women and the dissociation of vital parts of the inner world are essential to patriarchal societies and cultures. These disconnections and dissociations become part of the psychology of both women and men.

The psychological crisis of girls' adolescence, then, seems analogous to the crisis of boys' early childhood. As the study of girls uncovered the structure of this crisis and clarified the dynamics of resistance, it gave words to what was formerly inarticulate and without cultural language. The difference in timing becomes psychologically illuminating. Because girls' initiation into a patriarchal social order tends to occur later than boys' initiation, girls say what for boys often remains inarticulate and inchoate: They are losing connection, they cannot say what they are feeling and thinking, and they are losing relationship and finding themselves psychologically alone. The division between inner and outer worlds creates a psychological instability and heightens the risk of being thrown off balance in times of stress. The desire for relationship creates vulnerability and signals vitality, but it also leads directly into the relational impasse. The power of a close and resonant relationship at such moments of potential impasse is clear.

Early childhood for boys and adolescence for girls are times of psychological crisis, because at these times in development, voice and relationship come into dramatic tension. How wide or how narrow will these channels of connection remain? The Oedipus Complex that Freud formulated as the turning point in boys' psychological development is a crisis of relationship, although Freud did not conceive it in these terms. Young boys come under pressure from without and within to give up close relationship and to cover their vulnerability—to separate their inner world, their self, from the outer world of relationships. The tension between desire and necessity, between the needs of the psyche and the requisites of civilization, forces a compromise between voice and relationships. Freud saw this "compromise formation" as the price of civilization. It signified a definitive taking into the psyche of the outer world, setting the connection between inner and outer worlds and thus establishing the structure of character, but also the structure of neurotic suffering. The Oedipus Complex or relational crisis of boys' early childhood pressures young boys to take into themselves the structure or moral order of a patriarchal civilization: to identify with fathers or with the law of the father, to internalize a patriarchal voice. The superhero play of young boys reflects boys' awareness on some level of a developmental potential; Oedipus of the Oedipus Complex is eventually Oedipus Rex (Apter, personal communication, 1993; Gilligan, 1990a).

To see the relational crisis of boys' early childhood and girls' adolescence as an initiation highlights the break in relationship and exposes the psychological wound or scar. This is the mark of psychological entry into a patriarchal society or culture. At these points of crisis or impasse in psychological development, where vulnerability is intensified and psychological health is at stake, the joining of inner and outer worlds raises a political as well as a psychological question: What if the equation of civilization with patriarchy were broken? What if boys did not psychologically disconnect from women and dissociate themselves from vital parts of relationship? What if girls becoming young women did not dissociate from themselves?

It is in these terms that girls' resistance takes on its full implication. If boys in early childhood resist the break between inner and outer worlds, they are resisting an initiation into masculinity or manhood as it is defined and established in cultures that value or valorize heroism, honor, war, and competition—the culture of warriors, the economy of capitalism. To be a real boy or man in such cultures means to be able to be hurt without feeling hurt, to separate without feeling sadness or loss, and then to inflict hurt and separation on others. What is at stake is boy's manhood, boys' masculinity, their birthright in a patriarchal social order. But this conception of manhood places boys and men psychologically and often physically at risk, because it impedes their capacity to feel their own and other people's hurt, to know their own and other's sadness.

The study of girls elucidates the development of the human capacity for psychological connection: the ability to be in touch with the human world by feeling feelings, picking up resonances, noticing edges, registering psychological changes, responding to relational breaks. Within a culture or civilization that is rooted psychologically in the experiences of powerful men who in gaining power have made radical separations, experiences of connection are for the most part without cultural representation or language. Girls' development reveals how a break in relationship when compounded by a fracturing of experience and reality, leaves feelings of isolation and confusion, a kind of psychological and epistemological alienation. To want relationships or to have close relationships under these conditions means to risk both relationship and reality. The fears surrounding closeness and love and need to protect vulnerability can be understood in these terms.

Debold (1994) observed that if the psychological initiation into patriarchy occurs in early childhood for boys and at adolescence for girls, then the social construction of reality or what Foucault called "the power/ knowledge structure" is taken in at the level of concrete operations for boys and at a formal operational level for girls. The developmental asymmetry carries an important difference: Boys are taking in as a concrete reality (the way things are) what girls are taking in as an interpretive framework (the way things are said to be). This is why girls and women are more likely to see into the gap between psychological experience and a socially constructed reality and to catch sight of the cultural edge. If reality is more questionable to women, dissociative processes are also closer to the surface, and women's knowing and not knowing may consequently be more responsive to changes in the psychological and political climate. Shifts in relational resonances or societal arrangements have led to sudden remembering, or knowing what formerly no one had seemed to know (see Gilligan, 1982; Herman, 1992). The control of women then becomes essential on a psychological and intellectual as well as a sexual level, if the cultural inheritance of a patriarchal social order is to be preserved and carried forward.

Girls' psychological development in patriarchy involves a process of eclipse that is even more total for boys. Because girls at adolescence are more articulate, more psychologically developed than boys in early childhood, more experienced, more firmly rooted in life and relationships, girls reveal through their resistance and resilience (the insistence of their voices in relationship) a process that otherwise is said not to be happening—which otherwise is inconceivable: the covering of a world known through experience by a socially constructed and institutionalized reality. This is why research on girls and women often takes on the character of cross-cultural investigation; it is also why, for more than a century, tapping into women's psychology and girls' development has been at once so psychologically illuminating and so deeply unsettling. The power and also the danger of the talking cure, the *methode clinique*, and the voice-centered, relational method lies in the fact that these methods give voice to a break in relationship that creates psychological risk and signifies a psychological and a cultural problem (Breuer & Freud, 1974; Gilligan, 1982; Gilligan, Brown, & Rogers, 1990; Luborsky et al., chapter 11, this volume; Piaget, 1920). Cultural differences, like psychological differences, will affect the dimensions of this problem (Greenberg-Lake Associates, 1991; Martin-Baro, 1994; Taylor et al., in press).

When Winnicott (1958) observed that the human infant is a member of a couple, he led others to notice that infants were being studied out of relationship. The condition of nonrelation in psychological research and psychoanalysis or therapy was generally mistaken for objectivity or neutrality. Perhaps the psychological construction of infancy—the view of the infant as incapable of relationship—was an artifact of a research methodology that reflected a cultural bias toward separation. In any event, when researchers began studying infants with mothers, they saw a relational reality that previously had been unimagined. The psychological world of early childhood is a relational or interpersonal world; infants desire relationship, find pleasure in human connection, are able to make and maintain relationship (Benenson, chapter 10, this volume; Stern, 1985; Trevarthen, 1979). This insight revolutionized the social construction of the human infant and changed the understanding of psychological development, up to a point.

Because the infant studies also laid the ground for a further discovery, there was a gap between women's psychological experience and the prevailing construction of psychological reality. Women were experiencing relationships with infants during the time when psychologists, including women psychologists, were saying that infants were incapable of relationships. The research of Murray and Trevarthen on mother–infant communication makes this point clear. Through an ingenious technology involving the use of dual, life-sized video monitors (so that infant and mother, rather than facing one another, see one another on a large screen), they were able to interrupt the synchrony of interaction between mothers and their 2-month-old babies by quickly rewinding and replaying either the mother's or the baby's tape. Although mother and infant continued to take in the sounds and the images of relationship (cooing, babbling, baby-talking, smiling), they were actually no longer in relationship; their responses were no longer connected or occurring in relationship with one another. Instantly, both infants and mothers picked up on and responded to the break in relationship.

Voice is a barometer of relationship because it connects the inner and the outer world. Loss of voice is a prime symptom of loss of relationship, a measure of relational deprivation (Bretherton, chapter 1, this volume; Bowlby, 1958; Freud & Breuer, 1895/1974; Gilligan, 1982; Noam, chapter 6, this volume). Following the relational break in the Murray and Trevarthen study, mothers and infants continued to take in pleasant or pleasurable sounds and images, but these images and sounds of relationship were disturbing because they were disconnected from the experience of relationship. The infants responded initially with confusion and puzzlement, and then with distress. The mother's voices carried the disconnection; their emotional tone lessened and the mothers began to objectify their baby and to use an objectifying language, as they stepped back from the interaction and tried to understand what had happened, what was wrong:

> When the mother, unaware that she was to view a replay, was presented with a video sequence of her infant recorded during a normal, live interaction a few minutes previously, her baby-talk systematically changed. Its affective tone was reduced, and she spoke of her infant as behaving in an odd way. Her utterances revealed that she felt her infant was strangely unaware and avoidant. Several mothers said that there must be something 'wrong' in their own behavior that was disturbing to the infant. (Murray & Trevarthen, 1985, pp. 193-194)

The relational crisis of boys' early childhood and girls' adolescence signals a break in relationship. The crisis involves puzzlement and confusion, distress, a change in voice and language—the signs of relational distress. Early childhood and adolescence are the times in development when boys and girls, respectively, tend to experience a disparity between the experience of relationship (responsive connection) and the sounds and images of relationships. What is at stake in these periods of crisis are the basic human capacities for emotional communication and responsive relationship, and the willingness to risk relationship.

In the years when infants were said to be locked up in a primary narcissism or egocentrism, to be incapable of relationship, to be in a state of merger or fusion with others, women were in relationship with infants. In these relationships, women were experiencing and responding to what was said not to be happening, it was as if women's experience was not happening, or was not real. This gap between what women know through experience and what for years was socially constructed as reality explains why so many women have experienced difficulty in saying what they wanted to say or being listened to or heard, or believing that what they know through experience is true.

Research on girls' development makes it clear how the development of relational capacities (mutuality, responsive relationship, emotional communication) through the years of childhood leads to a vast storehouse of psychological experience and knowledge. This experience-based or empirical knowing of the human world may be at odds with the official knowledge of psychology, because it is culled from daily living rather than from the structures of interpretation. As girls struggle at adolescence to know relationship and also reality anew in light of the changes of that time, they may find themselves at the edge of a psychological chasm or silence, where their experience of relationship and truth drops off and they pick up the sounds and images of a different construction of relationships and reality.

Adolescent girls stand midway between the infants and the mothers in the Murray and Trevarthen studies. Like the infants, they respond initially with puzzlement and confusion to the seeming failure of their relational strategies, and then they experience distress when they feel helpless and powerless to affect the relationship. Miller, Jordan, Kaplan, Stiver, and Surrey described these processes in their clinical work with women in therapy (Miller, 1988; Jordan, Kaplan, Miller, Stiver, & Surrey, 1991). When faces are smiling and the affect seems pleasant — when the sounds and the images of relationship are present — but there is an absence of connection, the break in relationship becomes especially confusing when it is said not to be happening, or when the absence of connection is called love (Gilligan, 1984, 1987b). Girls' voices carry this the problem into the human world, where it can be silenced or re-sounded. Like some of the mothers in the Murray and Trevarthen experiments, girls also have a tendency to pick up the distress in the other and to search for the source of the problem within themselves. In this way, girls begin a pattern that is socially and culturally encouraged: to take responsibility for the relationship, to search for ways to mend and repair structurally introduced breaks in connection. Girls and women then struggle to make and maintain relationships within a world where disconnection is built in at a structural level (Gilligan, 1982; Miller, 1976).

Girls' resistance — girls' naming of relational realities — leads then to a complex dynamic. Girls' courage in speaking and girls' fight for relationship, once ordinary, becomes extraordinary or heroic (Gilligan, 1990a; Rogers, 1993). When girls' healthy resistance or psychological resilience begins to jeopardize girls' relationships because it exposes the existing structure of relationships, then girls' strength or vitality leads girls into a political resistance or struggle. Then girls may experience contradiction from without and within, as an outer conflict leads to an inner division or psychological dissociation. Girls then are under internal and external pressure not to know what they know, not to feel what they feel, not to say what is on their minds and in their hearts, not to care about the human world or at least not in the way that they do.

This dynamic of resistance, whereby a healthy resistance turns into a political resistance and then comes to be dissociated or forgotten, plays out in somewhat different ways for boys in early childhood and for girls in adolescence. It explains the association between psychological vitality and psychological risk, and also the power of a talking cure. The heightened risk that affects boys in early childhood and girls at adolescence can be explained then as a function of a relational crisis that arises from the joining of psychological development with the structures of a patriarchal social order.

Like the inclusion of mothers in the studies of infancy, the inclusion of girls in the study of psychological development has led to a process of remembering. With this inclusion, the centrality of relationship in human development becomes clear. But closeness and vulnerability, the condition of relationship, are in tension with the regeneration of patriarchal social order, because patriarchy depends on a disconnection from women and also on the establishment of hierarchy among men. One resonant or confiding relationship remains the best protection against psychological illness under these conditions — providing a kind of psychological safe house in the face of the relational break: a place where it remains safe to speak freely, a space that is resonant to the inner voice, a relationship in which one can speak and be heard. But this solution in the form of a hidden relationship or secret resonance leaves unaddressed the cost of maintaining a public discourse or story about human nature, human development, the human condition, or human experience that is to varying degrees out of relationship and out of touch with what people know or can know through experience.

EPILOGUE

In *History After Lacan*, Brennan (1993) spoke of the separate or autonomous ego as a "psychotic fantasy," which arose from the joining of the Cartesian self with capitalism in the 17th century, initiating what Lacan called "the ego's era." Brennan called it "a social psychosis," because the foundational fantasy of the ego's omnipotence and control was socially constructed as reality, wrapping the imperial "I" in a cultural cocoon. At the end of the 20th century, this "I" is emerging into a newly constructed reality:

> To allow that my feelings physically enter you, or yours me, to think that we both had the same thought at the same time because it was literally in the air, is to think in a way that really puts the subject in question. In some ways, the truly interesting thing is that this questioning has begun. (Brennan, 1993, p. 43)

To know connection on a psychological level as real or even possible, to experience relationship as a kind of psychological breathing or ongoing process of exchange means to question on the basis of experience a social construction of reality that has held patriarchy and imperialism to be necessary if not natural. The power of psychology as a human science to change the human world becomes clear. When a process of dissociation which has been incorporated into a cultural framework yields to an associative process of remembering, then people can know what they know and act on the basis of experience and evidence.

At the end of *The Fragility of Goodness*, Nussbaum (1986) turned to Euripides' play, *Hecuba*. It is a terrible drama of vulnerability overwhelmed. Hecuba, the wife of Priam, has entrusted her young son, Polydorous, to the Thracian king, Polymestor, for safekeeping in war. Polymestor is a man whom she holds in a relationship of guest-friendship, which is one of the deepest and closest of human bonds. After Troy has been sacked, Priam slain, her power gone, her other children killed, Hecuba discovers that Polymestor has betrayed her. He has slain Polydorous for the money he brought with him and left his body unburied on the shore. Of all Hecuba's griefs, this is the one that shatters her. Turning to revenge, she invites Polymestor and his children into the private women's quarters of the camp and then kills the children and puts out Polymestor's eyes.

Nussbaum asked the psychological question: How can we understand this astonishing and sudden reversal of character? Hecuba was a woman known for "her openness, her civic concern and loyalty, her generosity toward the needy and the suppliant, her moderation and fairness, her love and concern for her children." The war and her series of losses would explain her heightened susceptibility to shock. But Nussbaum observed that Euripides' invites us to think more deeply about "the nature of good character, its connection with a child's trusting simplicity, its vulnerability to disease when trust is violated" (p. 398).

When Hecuba discovers that the dead child is her son, she instantly grasps what she could not have imagined: "Untrustworthy, untrustworthy, new, new, are the things I see" (p. 408). She had not imagined the possibility of nonrelation in a relationship of the deepest trust and friendship. Hecuba's character rested on a foundation of trust, vulnerability, and close relationship. Polymestor's betrayal destroyed her world.

Afterward, Hecuba makes her world over in the image of the possibility of nonrelation. It is "a world of splendid security and splendid isolation. It is thoroughly self-contained, looking directly at nobody, risking the light of no eyes. It is buried, private, dark" (Nussbaum, 1986, p. 413).

In their studies of "interactive mismatch and repair" between infants and their mothers, Tronick and Gianino (1986) found that trust comes not from the goodness of the attachment or of the mother per se, but rather from the ability of infant and mother to mend the inevitable breaks in their relationship—to connect with one another following periods of disconnection. In their clinical work with women in psychotherapy, Miller and Stiver, Jordan and Surrey (see Jordan et al., 1991) found that it is the ability to have an effect on the relationship—to affect the relationship—which rebuilds trust after violation. Summarizing the research on emotions and emotional communications in infants, Tronick (1989) wrote:

> Infant emotions and emotional communications are far more organized than previously thought. Infants display a variety of discrete affective expressions that are appropriate to the nature of events and their context. They also appreciate the emotional meaning of the affective displays of caretakers. The emotional expressions of the infant and the caretaker function to allow them to mutually regulate their interactions. Indeed, it appears that a major determinant of children's development is related to the operation of this communication system. (p. 112)

In our research with girls we followed the development of these relational capacities and found that the ability to speak in relationship, to keep the inner world in the outer world, and to create and maintain resonant and responsive relationships are the grounds of girls' psychological strength and resilience. When girls' relationships or communication systems are jeopardized, girls are at risk. Ironically, the very strengths that allow girls to make and then to maintain connection with others begin at adolescence to jeopardize girls' relationships.

Following girls' development through childhood and into adolescence, we witnessed the breakdown of relationship and emotional communication systems on a societal and cultural level. As it was played out by girls in their relationships—in various scenarios of untrustworthiness and betrayal—it also was played out with girls on an interpersonal and a political level. Girls' resistance and the resonances that girls' voices set off in women and men resounded experiences that lay buried in memory, creating an opening—a potential for change. Psychological development and cultural regeneration are involved in a two-way process, each holding the potential to affect the other, and conflict or the outbreak of crisis often carries the seeds of change.

The essence of human development is that psychological growth takes place in relationship. Relationship brings the oxygen of experience into the psyche. The zen of development that makes the process of growth essentially dramatic is that the openness to experience which creates the possibility for psychological growth also creates the potential for being psychologically wounded.

We have come now to the end of the age of modernism—the end of the ego's era. After a century of unparalleled violence, at a time when violence has become appalling, we appreciate again the fragility of humans. We understand better why closeness and vulnerability create the conditions for psychological growth. And we also know more fully the costs of their violation.

REFERENCES

Achenbach, T. (1982). *Developmental psychopathology.* New York: Wiley.

Allgood-Merton, B., Lewinsohn, P., & Hops, H. (1990). Sex differences and adolescent depression. *Journal of Abnormal Psychology, 99*, 55–63.

Angold, A., & Rutter, M. (1992). Effects of age and pubertal status on a large clinical sample. *Development and Psychopathology, 4*, 5–28.

Block, J. (1990). Ego resilience through time: Anticedents and ramifications. In *Resilience and psychological health.* Symposium of the Boston Psychoanalytic Society, Boston, MA.

Bowlby, J. (1958). *Maternal care and mental health.* Report prepared on behalf of the World Health Organization as a contribution to the United Nations Programme for the welfare of homeless children.

Brennan, T. (1993). *History after Lacan.* New York: Routledge.

Brown, L. M., & Gilligan, C. (1992). *Meeting at the crossroads: Women's psychology and girls' development.* Cambridge, MA: Harvard University Press.

Debold, E. (1994). *Toward an understanding of gender differences in psychological distress: A Foucauldian integration of Freud, Gilligan, and cognitive development theory.* Unpublished qualifying paper, Harvard Graduate School of Education, Cambridge, MA.

Demitrack, M., Putnam, F., Brewerton, T., Brandt, H., & Gold, P. (1990). Relation of clinical variables to dissociative phenomena in eating disorders. *The American Journal of Psychiatry, 1479*, 1184–1188.

Deutsch, H. (1944). *Psychology of women.* New York: Grune & Stratten.

Dorney, J. (1991). *Courage to act in a small way: Clues toward community and change among women teaching girls.* Unpublished doctoral dissertation, Harvard Graduate School of Education, Cambridge, MA.

Elder, G., & Caspi, A. (1990). Studying lives in a changing society: Sociological and personalogical explorations. In A. I. Rabin, R. Zucker, R. Emmons, & S. Frank (Eds.),

Studying persons and lives (pp. 226–228). New York: Springer.

Fine, M., & Zane, N. (1989). Bein' wrapped too tight: When low-income women drop out of high school. In L. Weis, E. Farrar, & H. Petrie (Eds.), *Dropouts from school*. New York: SUNY Press.

Fordham, S. (1991). Racelessness in private schools: Should we deconstruct the racial and cultural identity of African-American adolescents? *Teachers College Record, 92*(3), 470–480.

Frank, A. (1989). *The diary of Anne Frank: The critical edition*. New York: Doubleday. (Original work published 1944)

Freud, S. (1963). Contributions to the psychology of love. *Sexuality and the psychology of love* (pp. 49–86). New York: Collier Books. (Original work published 1910)

Freud, S., & Breuer, J. (1974). *Studies on hysteria*. London: Penguin. (Original work published 1895)

Gilligan, C. (1982). *In a different voice: Psychological theory and women's development*. Cambridge, MA: Harvard University Press.

Gilligan, C. (1984). The conquistador and the dark continent: Reflections on the psychology of love. *Daedalus, 113*(3), 75–95.

Gilligan, C. (1986). *The willing suspension of disbelief: Conflicts of female adolescence*. Paper presented at the Laurie Chair Seminar on Women's Psychological Development: Adolescence, New Brunswick, NJ.

Gilligan, C. (1987a). Adolescent development reconsidered. In C. Irwin (Ed.), *New directions for child development: Adolescent social behavior and health* (pp. 63–92). San Francisco: Jossey-Bass.

Gilligan, C. (1987b, February). *Oedipus and psyche: Two stories about love*. Paper presented at the Complex femininity: Changing views of women in psychoanalytic thought conference, Haverford College, Haverford, PA.

Gilligan, C. (1990a). Joining the resistance: Psychology, politics, girls, & women. *Michigan Quarterly Review, 29*(4), 501–536.

Gilligan, C. (1990b). Teaching Shakespeare's sister: Notes from the underground of female adolescence. In C. Gilligan, N. Lyons, & T. Hanmer (Eds.), *Making connections: The relational worlds of adolescent girls at the Emma Willard School*. Cambridge, MA: Harvard University Press.

Gilligan, C., Brown, L., & Rogers, A. (1990). Psyche embedded: A place for body, relationships and culture in personality theory. In A. Rabin, R. Zucker, R. Emmons, & S. Frank (Eds.), *Studying persons and lives* (pp. 86–147). New York: Springer.

Gilligan, C., Johnston, D., & Miller, B. (1988). *Moral voice, adolescent development and secondary education: A study at the Green River School* (working paper). Cambridge, MA: Harvard Graduate School of Education, Project on Women's Psychology and Girls' Development.

Gilligan, C., Lyons, N., & Hanmer, T. (Eds.). (1990). *Making connections: The relational worlds of adolescent girls at Emma Willard school*. Cambridge, MA: Harvard University Press.

Gilligan, C., & Rogers, A. (1992). *Strengthening healthy resistance and courage in girls; a prevention project and a developmental study* (working paper). Cambridge, MA: Harvard Graduate School of Education, Project on Women's Psychology and Girls' Development.

Gilligan, C., Rogers, A., & Noel, N. (1992). *Cartography of a lost time: Women, girls and relationships*. Paper presented at the Lilly Endowment Conference on Youth and Caring, Daytona Beach, FL, and at the Cambridge Hospital-Stone Center Conference, Learning from Women, Boston, MA.

Gilligan, C., Rogers, A., & Tolman, D. (Eds.). (1991). *Women, girls and psychotherapy: Reframing resistance*. Binghamton, NY: Haworth Press.

Gilligan, C., Ward, J., & Taylor, J. (Eds.). (1988). *Mapping the moral domain: A contribution of women's thinking to psychological theory and education.* Cambridge, MA: Harvard University Press.

Greenberg-Lake Analysis Group Inc. (1991). *Shortchanging girls, Shortchanging America: A nationwide poll to assess self-esteem, educational experiences, interest in math and science, and career aspirations of girls and boys ages 9–15.* Washington, DC: American Association of University Women.

Harris, L., Blum, R., & Resnick, M. (1991). Teen females in Minnesota: A portrait of quiet disturbance. *Women and Therapy, 11*(3–4), 119–135.

Herman, J. (1992). *Trauma and recovery.* New York: Basic Books.

hooks, b. (1984). *Feminist theory from margin to center.* Boston: South End Press.

Horney, K. (1926). The flight from womanhood. *International Journal of Psychoanalysis, 7,* 324–339.

Jordan, J., Kaplan, A., Miller, J. B., Stiver, I., & Surrey, J. (1991). *Women's growth in connection: Writings from the Stone Center.* New York: Guilford Press.

Klein, M. (1977). *Love, guilt, reparation and other works, 1921–1945.* New York: Dell. (Original work published 1921)

Machoian, L. (1995). *Love, hope and resistance: A relational perspective on girls' suicidality.* Unpublished qualifying paper, Harvard Graduate School of Education, Cambridge, MA.

Martin-Baro, I. (1994). *Writings for a liberation psychology.* Cambridge, MA: Harvard University Press.

Miller, J.B. (1976). *Toward a new psychology of women.* Boston: Beacon.

Miller, J.B. (1988). *Connections, disconnections, and violations* (working paper no. 33). Wellesley, MA: The Stone Center.

Miller, J.B. (1991). The development of women's sense of self. In J. Jordan, A. Kaplan, J.B. Miller, I. Stiver, & J. Surrey (Eds.), *Women's growth in connection: Writings from the Stone Center.* New York: Guilford Press.

Minnesota Women's Fund. (1990). *Reflections of risk: Growing up female in Minnesota, a report on the health and well-bineg of adolescent girls in Minnesota.* Minneapolis: University of Minnesota, Adolescent Health Program.

Morrison, T. (1970). *The bluest eye.* New York: Washington Square Press.

Murray, L., & Trevarthen, C. (1985). Emotional regulation of interactions between 2-month-olds and their mothers. In T. Field & N. Fox (Eds.), *Social perception in infants.* Norwood, NJ: Ablex.

Nussbaum, M. (1986). *The fragility of goodness.* Cambridge: Cambridge University Press.

Peterson, A. (1988). Adolescent development. *Annual review of psychology, 39,* 583–607.

Peterson, A., Sarigiani, P., & Kennedy, R. (1991). Adolescent depression: Why more girls? *Journal of Youth and Adolescence, 20,* 247–271.

Proust, M. (1992). *In search of lost time.* New York: Modern Library. (Original work published 1913)

Robinson, T., & Ward, J. (1991). "A belief in self far greater than anyone's disbelief": Cultivating resistance among African-American female adolescents. In C. Gilligan, A. Rogers, & D. Tolman (Eds.), *Women, girls and psychotherapy: Reframing resistance.* New York: Haworth Press.

Rodin, J., Silberstein, L., & Striegel-Moore, R. (1985). Women and weight: A normative discontent. In T. Sonderegger (Ed.), *Nebraska symposium on motivation, 1984: Psychology and gender* (pp. 267–307). Lincoln: University of Nebraska Press.

Rogers, A. (1993). Voice, play, and a practice of ordinary courage in girls' and women's lives. *Harvard Educational Review, 63*(3), 265–295.

Rogers, A. (1995). *Exiled voices: Dissociation and repression in women's narratives of trauma* (working paper). Wellesley, MA: The Stone Center.

Rogers, A., Brown, L. M., & Tappan, M. (1993). Interpreting loss in ego development in girls: Regression or resistance? In R. Josselson & A. Lieblich (Eds.), *The narrative study of lives*

(Vol. 2). Newbury Park, CA: Sage.

Rutter, M., & Garmezy, N. (1983). Developmental psychopathology. In P. H. Mussen (Series Ed.) & E. M. Hetherington (Vol. Ed.), *Handbook of child psychology: Vol. 4. Socialization, personality and social development* (4th ed., pp. 7775–9111). New York: Wiley.

Schonert-Reichl, K., & Offer, D. (1992). Gender differences in adolescent symptoms. In B. Lahey & A. Kazdin (Eds.), *Advances in clinical child psychology* (Vol.14, pp. 27–60).

Seligman, M.E. (1991). *Learned optimism.* New York: Random House.

Showalter, E. (1985). *The female malady.* New York: Penguin Books.

Steiner-Adair, C. (1986). The body-politic: Normal female adolescent development and the development of eating disorders. *Journal of the American Academy of Psychoanalysis, 14,* 95–114.

Steiner-Adair, C. (1991). When the body speaks: Girls, eating disorders, and psychotherapy. In C. Gilligan, A. Rogers, & D. Tolman (Eds.), *Women, girls, and psychotherapy: Reframing resistance* (pp. 253–266). New York: Haworth Press.

Stern, D. (1985). *The interpersonal world of the infant.* New York: Basic Books.

Taylor, J., Gilligan, C., & Sullivan, A. (in press). *Between voice and silence: Women and girls, race and relationship.* Cambridge, MA: Harvard University Press.

Thompson, C. (1964). *Interpersonal psychoanalysis.* New York: Basic Books.

Trevarthen, C. (1979). Communication and cooperation in early infancy: A description of primary intersubjectivity. In M.M. Bullowa (Ed.), *Before speech: The beginning of interpersonal communication.* New York: Cambridge University Press.

Tronick, E. (1989). Emotions and emotional communication in infants. *American Psychologist, 44*(2), 112–119.

Tronick, E., & Gianino, A. (1986). Interactive mismatch and repair. *Zero-to-Three, 6*(3), 1–6.

Whitaker, A., Johnson, J., Shaffer, D., Rappoport, J., Kalikow, K., Walsh, B., Davies, M., Braiman, S., & Dolinsky, A. (1990). Uncommon troubles in young people: Prevalence estimates of selected psychiatric disorders in a non-referred adolescent population. *Archives of General Psychiatry, 47,* 487–496.

Winnicott, D. (1958). *Collected papers, through paediatrics to psycho-analysis.* London: Tavistock.

10 Gender Differences in the Development of Relationships

Joyce F. Benenson
McGill University

Social scientists from many fields generally describe women as being more relational than men. That men may also be relational is rarely discussed. Yet, research on children's same-gender friendships suggests that both girls and boys form important relationships. Furthermore, the types of relationships formed by boys and girls in childhood are believed to endure into adulthood. This chapter was designed, therefore, to challenge conceptions of gender differences as differing in degree of relationality and propose instead an analysis that examines the differences in content of the relationships formed by females and males.

More explicitly, it is proposed that people with a feminine style of interaction are more likely than those with a masculine style to relate to one another through mutual empathy, whereas people with a masculine style are more likely than those with a feminine style to relate to one another through mutual assertion. It is necessary to use the term *feminine* and *masculine styles*, because there are people of each biologically determined sex who utilize the style of interaction of the other sex. It is hypothesized that there are at least these two styles of interaction — empathy and assertiveness, both of which form the basis of important relationships.

In the literature to date, only empathy has been accepted as the basis of a relationship. Because exchange of assertion has not been seen as an important foundation of a relationship, it has been virtually ignored. Nevertheless, from the current perspective, assertion is considered a powerful means of relating to others that deserves as much consideration as empathy as the basis of a relationship. To understand more fully the qualities that differentiate feminine and masculine styles of relationships, it is suggested that a careful analysis must be conducted of the content of the relationships.

CONCEPTUALIZATION OF GENDER DIFFERENCES

It is proposed that gender differences in social interaction be conceptualized as relative experience with specific contents of interaction. More explicitly, people with a more feminine style of interaction generally appear to be relatively more experienced than those with a masculine style in relating to others through mutual expressions of empathy. In contrast, people with a more masculine style generally appear to be relatively more experienced in relating to others through mutual expressions of assertion. Nevertheless, in the current perspective, sharing of another's difficulties, as empathy is usually defined, is not considered to be the only basis for a relationship. Rather, both people who base their relationship on empathy and people who base their relationship on assertion are considered to be relational.

This perspective contrasts sharply with the accounts of social scientists from a variety of fields who generally concur in describing women as more relational than men. Specifically, in 1966, Bakan wrote a compelling and influential account of gender differences in which women were described as communal and men as agentic. A host of other theoreticians, clinicians, and researchers have arrived at many analogous descriptions of the differences between men and women. For example, women compared with men have been described as interpersonal versus individualistic (Block, 1973), expressive versus instrumental (Hall & Halberstadt, 1980; Parsons, Bales, & Shils, 1953), connected versus separate (Lyons, 1988), and interdependent versus autonomous (Johnston, 1988). More recently, Tannen (1991) described women as concerned with connection and men with status.

Interestingly, the terms used by social scientists to characterize the differences between males and females bear a strong resemblance to the two major psychoanalytic explanations of gender differences in development in which, again, females are considered more relational than males. The two main psychoanalytic theories, the Freudian and object relational accounts of development, differ in their beliefs about the extent to which an individual is motivated to be a part of relationships and by the extent to which an individual's personality is influenced by early relationships (e.g., Greenberg & Mitchell, 1983; see also Blatt & Blass, chapter 12, this volume; Luborsky et al., chapter 11, this volume). The Freudian perspective suggests that development is motivated by an individual's biologically based drives of sexuality and aggression that conflict with familial and societal bonds. In this model, people are not considered fundamentally relational, but rather desirous of attaining their own individual goals. Their personalities are considered to be shaped as much by their own inner drives and cognitive processes as by their relationships with others. In contrast, the object relational perspective suggests that development is strongly shaped by an individual's empathic relationships with others. Relationships are the building blocks of personality and differences in the quality of empathy in the relationship largely account for individual differences in development. As with the more recent literature in the social sciences on gender differences, it is likely that Freudian psychoanalysts are focusing more on development of masculinity and object relational theorists more on development of femininity.

In fact, much of the theorizing by feminist object relational clinicians stems from the belief that Freud's depiction of and emphasis on the importance of the resolution of the Oedipal conflict for future development was correct for males but not females. The ideas that during the years 3 to 5, boys desire to have close relationships with their mothers, feel competitive with their fathers, fear their father's physically aggressive retaliation, learn to identify with their fathers, and decrease the intensity of their ties to their mothers are well accepted by clinicians. However, Freud's lack of emphasis on the pre-Oedipal years and awkward depiction of girls' development during the Oedipal years is not accepted by many clinicians, and his neglect of the years before age 3 is considered a major weakness of his theory (e.g., Fast, 1984; Horney, 1926).

In response to these purported shortcomings of Freudian theory, feminist object relational theorists emphasize children's early, pre-Oedipal relationships with mothers, especially the importance of empathy in mother's relationships with their children. Furthermore, these theorists add that unlike for boys, a girl's tie with her mother is ongoing, continuing throughout the Oedipal period, and perhaps, for the majority of the girl's life. However, there is marked disagreement among feminist object relational theorists over the quality of girls' versus boys' relationships with their mothers. For example, some theorists believe mothers have healthier ties with their daughters (e.g., Jordan, Kaplan, Miller, Stiver, & Surrey, 1991); in contrast, other theorists suggest that mothers have healthier ties with their sons (e.g., Eichenbaum & Orbach, 1988); and many state that generally mothers help with relational needs but harm autonomous ones, whereas fathers do the opposite (e.g., Chodorow 1978, 1989). Nevertheless, most agree that the future socioemotional development of girls is predicated upon the mutual empathy that develops between mother and daughter.

Importantly, boys are generally excluded from this account of mutual empathy, at least after they complete the Oedipal stage, at the age of 5 or 6. Because empathy is believed to constitute the basis of all relationships, males are therefore considered nonrelational after this age. Specifically, according to Chodorow, because of a boy's need to develop a masculine gender identity, he must renounce his tie to his first caregiver, his mother, and to all other females, and instead identify with his father and other males. Because the mother is viewed as relational and the father as autonomous, a boy's personality is relatively quickly transformed from a relational to an autonomous one, a personality the boy maintains for the remainder of his life. In marked contrast, because a girl's first relationship is with her mother and there is no need to renounce this tie in order to develop a feminine gender identity, a girl remains relational.

Thus, this account assumes that boys are not relational after the age of 5. Empirical research with children between 6 and 10 years of age is inconsistent with this view. For example, studies of children in middle childhood have shown that males engage in much same-sex peer interaction (e.g., Thorne, 1986).

Within the current framework, the interactions of boys, which often involve mutual physical assertion, are accepted as relational. Those people with a more masculine style are considered to form relationships through mutual assertiveness. Consequently, it is possible to shift the focus of conceptualization of gender differences from degree of "relationality" to content of the relationship.

In marked contrast to feminist object relational clinicians and theorists, ethological researchers have focused on the construct of physical assertion as a basic motivation in human development. Ethological researchers emphasize the importance of expression and regulation of assertiveness for the survival and continuation of the species. Males of many species are known to form dominance hierarchies in which members are ranked according to physical toughness. This is thought to allow control of intragroup aggression, such that only males who are similar in strength, and hence will not inflict too much harm on one another, will fight. Furthermore, the formation of a dominance hierarchy may promote organization of males in a way that enhances chances of survival in intergroup fighting and results in the formation of strong bonds between group members. These bonds ensure that members of a group can control any individual within the group who breaks the rules of the dominance hierarchy and that members of a group can work together to protect the livelihood of the group. Human males and females in early childhood and males in adolescence have been found to form dominance hierarchies based on physical toughness in which there are stable, linear, and rigid relations between all dyads. Often the females are found at the bottom of this toughness hierarchy, and even when they are not, females are found to engage in less assertive behavior than males with other group members (Omark, Strayer, & Freedman, 1980; Savin-Williams, 1976, 1979; Strayer, 1980; Strayer, & Strayer, 1976, 1980).

Expression of physical assertion is considered an essential facet of males' development, therefore, and should not be neglected in the study of relationships. In fact, empirical research with young boys and their fathers by MacDonald and Parke (1984) and Parke et al. (1989) found that fathers' and son's capacities to engage in long bouts of physical wrestling were strongly related to sons' socioemotional competence. Thus, quality of forceful, assertive interaction between fathers and sons may be especially important for boys' development. Mothers and daughters or even mothers and sons rarely engage in a similar form of mutual physical assertion. Hence, just as the importance of mutual empathy is emphasized by feminist object relational clinicians for females' but not males' development, the importance of mutual assertion is emphasized by ethological theorists for males' but not females' development.

Given the work of feminist object relational clinicians combined with the empirical observations of ethologists, it is reasonable to hypothesize that many females and males may emphasize different qualities in their relationships with others of the same gender. This view is in accordance with the perspective of Gilligan, Ward, Taylor, and Bardige (1988) that both females and males form important relationships but that often the qualities of these relationships vary by gender. Thus, Gilligan (1988) suggested that relationships have different meanings for the two genders, such that females are concerned with inclusion and exclusion and caring and males are interested in dominance and submission and justice. Furthermore, Gilligan and Wiggins (1988; Gilligan, chapter 9, this volume) proposed a developmental model in which these two views of relationships derive from young girls' experiences with empathic relationships with mothers or other women and young boys' early relationships with assertive authority figures such as their fathers or other men. Finally, McClelland (1985) advocated a model in which many females and males differ in their responses to natural incentives, such that females derive more pleasure from exchange and males from impact. In both Gilligan et al.'s and McClelland's accounts, the content of young girls' relationships with other females differs substantially from the content of young boys' relationships with other males.

The evidence in support of this new perspective is seen most easily in research with children. Because children interact in smaller spaces and are less self-conscious, their relationships are easier to study than those of adults. Research with children has demonstrated gender differences in preferences for different toys and activities (for reviews, see Huston, 1983, 1987; Paley, 1984). Girls generally exhibit preferences for play with dolls and dress-up in which family scenes are enacted, whereas boys generally prefer play with guns, cars, and trucks in which superheroes are created. Further, in a review of the literature, Maccoby (1990) suggested that gender differences are also quite pronounced in styles of social interaction. She described boys as assertive, self-centered, and unidirectional, and girls as relational, collaborative, and reciprocal. Again, however, girls may not be more relational than boys, but the content of the relationships of boys and girls may simply differ.

DEVELOPMENTAL TRAJECTORIES

It is likely that feminine and masculine styles of interaction develop during childhood. The research with children examines children of each biological sex. No attempts are made to distinguish girls who develop masculine styles of interaction from girls who develop feminine styles or boys who develop feminine styles of interaction from boys who develop masculine styles. It is likely that more clarity will result when style of interaction is separated from biological state. Nevertheless, evidence exists using children categorized simply by biological sex that two different ways of forming relationships may have their beginnings early in life.

Temperamental factors that may predispose many females and males to exhibit and elicit specific types of responses may begin the two paths that generally differentiate the different styles of interaction. Already at birth, there is evidence that males prefer physically assertive behavior and that females prefer a more gentle style of interaction. With development, these initially small differences are likely to be magnified by the responses of adults in the child's environment. Boys and girls with more masculine styles of interaction engage in more physically and verbally assertive exchanges than girls and boys with more feminine styles of interaction. In contrast, girls and boys with more feminine styles of interaction engage in behavior that consists of more empathic exchanges than boys and girls with more masculine styles. When the child enters into peer relationships – which are typically segregated by sex until adolescence, these differences in style of interaction diverge further. Careful analysis of the evidence from research with children of differing ages lends support to this hypothesis. Table 10.1 presents some of the gender differences that have been found.

Newborns

In the first few months of life, males and females are strikingly similar. However, a few intriguing sex differences have been found. First, males have been found to engage in more gross motor activity or physical assertion than females. Furthermore, there is some suggestive evidence that level of testosterone, which is generally higher in males than females, may cause the greater physical assertion found in newborn males as compared with females, both for humans and other mammalian species (e.g., Money & Ehrhardt, 1972; Moss, 1967; Parke & Slaby, 1983). In addition, results from other studies with newborns indicate that females are generally more responsive than males to others' efforts to respond with empathy to their emotional distress (Haviland & Malatesta, 1981; Osofsky & O'Connell, 1977). Finally, in the first year of life, males have generally been found to be more irritable than females (Moss, 1967).

There is also some evidence that suggests that female newborns may exhibit some behaviors that form the rudimentary foundations of empathy more than males. More precisely, in the auditory modality, newborn females have been found to be more sensitive than males to others' emotional distress, specifically to the sound of another infant's crying but not to a similar nonhuman noise (Sagi & Hoffman, 1976; Simner, 1971). Further, in the visual domain, newborn females were found to engage in eye contact more than males (Hittelman & Dickes, 1979).

In turn, very young boys and girls are treated by adults as if they do differ in physical assertion and toughness (for reviews, see Huston, 1983; Maccoby & Jacklin, 1974; Malatesta, Culver, Tesman, & Shepard, 1989). Boys are handled in a more physically rough manner and stimulated more than girls. In addition, boys are expected to be physically tougher than girls. In contrast, girls are handled more gently and are expected to be more sensitive to external stimulation than boys. Girls are also offered more help than boys. Also, fathers and sons are known to enjoy longer bouts of physically assertive play than fathers and daughters or mothers and infants of either sex. In addition, mothers have been found to express more positive affect toward daughters than sons. In general, parents who have developed their own sex-typed styles of interaction have been shown to interact more with same- versus cross-sex infants. Furthermore, fathers have consistently been found to treat their sons and daughters more differently than mothers. Thus, parents and fathers in particular emphasize sex-typed styles of interaction with their children of the same sex.

1 Year of Age

At 1 year old, children have not been found to differ on the basis of their sex in their security of attachment as measured in the Strange Situation, with the exception of the extreme "D" category in which there are more boys than girls (Carlson, Cicchetti, Barnett, & Braunwald, 1989). Nevertheless, an important finding has been overlooked in the research on early relationships. Several researchers of human infants have found that at 1 year of age, males generally move farther away from their primary caregivers than females (Goldberg & Lewis, 1969; Kagan, 1971; Mahler, Pine, & Bergman, 1975). One possible interpretation of this gender difference is that males are more securely attached than females. An alternative interpretation, how-

TABLE 10.1
Some Sex Differences in Developmental Trajectories

Age	Characteristic	Gender Difference	References
Newborns			
	Gross motor activity	Males higher	Money and Ehrhardt (1972) Moss (1967) Parke and Slaby(1983)
	Responsiveness to adults' attempts to soothe	Females higher	Haviland and Malatesta (1981) Osofsky and O'Connell (1977)
	Responsiveness to other newborns' crying	Females higher	Sagi and Hoffman (1976) Simner (1971)
	Irritability	Males higher	Moss (1967)
	Eye contact	Females higher	Hittelman and Dickes (1979)
1 year			
	Security of attachment	No difference	Carlson et al. (1989)
	Exploration	Males higher	Goldberg and Lewis (1969) Kagan (1971) Mahler et al. (1975)
	Inhibition	Females higher	Robinson et al. (1992)
	Empathy	Females higher	Zahn-Waxler, Robinson, and Emde (1992) Zahn-Waxler, Radke-Yarrow, et al. (1992)
2 Years			
	Verbal & physical Assertiveness	Males higher	Maccoby Jacklin (1974) Parke and Slaby (1983)
	Dominance hierarchy Status	Males higher	Omark et al. (1980) Strayer (1980) Strayer and Strayer (1976, 1980)
	Empathy	Females higher	Hoffman (1977)
	Fearfulness	Females higher	Dunham et al. (1991) Bowlby (1969)

Age period	Characteristic	Sex difference	References
3 to 5 years	Doll play	Females higher	Huston (1983, 1987)
	Family scenes		Paley (1984)
	Guns, transportation vehicles	Males higher	Huston (1983, 1987)
	Superheroes		Paley (1984)
	Dyadic interaction	Females higher	Benenson (1993)
			Parker (1986)
	Nurture	Females higher	Whiting and Edwards (1988)
	Fearfulness	Females higher	Whiting and Edwards (1988)
	Exploration	Males higher	Whiting and Edwards (1988)
	Rough-and-tumble play	Males higher	Maccoby and Jacklin (1974)
	Verbal and physical assertiveness		Parke and Slaby (1983)
			Whiting and Edwards (1988)
	Expression of vulnerability	Females higher	Benenson and Del Bianco (1994)
Middle childhood	Group size	Males higher	Benenson (1990)
			Belle (1989)
			Best (1983)
			Sutton-Smith (1979)
			Thorne (1986)
	Concern with physical prowess of peers	Males higher	Benenson (1990)
	Concern with niceness of peers	Females higher	Benenson (1990)
	Games involving physical assertion	Males higher	Sutton-Smith (1979)
			Thorne (1986)
	Distance from home or school	Males higher	Sutton-Smith (1979)
Adolescence and young adulthood	Concern with justice	Males higher	Gilligan et al. (1988)
	Concern with caring	Females higher	Gilligan et al. (1988)

ever, is that females and males relate to caregivers in different ways, with daughters more than sons sharing empathy with mothers.

A final interpretation is that females may perceive external danger or internal distress more quickly than males, without being less securely attached. That is, males may explore further than females, not because they are more securely attached, but because of different systems that organize behavior, such as the fear system in combination with the exploration system. These other systems are believed to be independent of the attachment system (Bowlby, 1969).

Researchers of the quality of attachments formed between parents and children have not found any evidence that females are less securely attached than males (e.g., Carlson et al., 1989). Therefore, it is more probable that one of the other two interpretations is more accurate. That is, females may look to a caregiver for empathy more readily than males, either because sharing empathy with a caregiver is more important for females' than males' relationships or because females have a lower threshold than males for the perception of distress or danger. In fact, there are several studies that support both these interpretations. Specifically, in support of the hypothesis that females enjoy expression of empathy more than males, Zahn-Waxler and her colleagues (Zahn-Waxler, Radke-Yarrow, Wagner, & Chapman, 1992; Zahn-Waxler, Robinson, & Emde, 1992) found that at 14 and 20 months of age, females are more empathic than males toward their mothers in realistic situations where empathy would be expected. In contrast, the results of several studies support the interpretation that females as compared with males have a lower threshold for perception of external danger or internal distress. Specifically, Robinson, Kagan, Reznick, and Corley (1992) found evidence that at 14, 20, and 24 months, females were more inhibited than males, that is they were more likely to be display fear in an unfamiliar situation. In addition, in a study by Rosen, Adamson, and Bakeman (1992), females were more distressed than males by their mothers' fearful facial expressions.

By the time children begin to interact with one another, even before 2 years of age, they demonstrate a preference for interaction with members of their own sex (e.g., Legault & Strayer, 1990; Maccoby, 1988). Maccoby (1988, 1990) suggested that this may be partially due to the behavioral compatibility of members of the same sex. More specifically, she suggested that the phenomenon of sex-segregation may be due to females' avoidance of males. Thus, many females may find males' rough-and-tumble play aversive and seek to avoid it. Alternatively, many males may dislike females' style of interaction. In fact, there is strong evidence that males avoid the types of interaction in which females engage (for reviews, see Huston, 1983, 1987).

2 to 3 Years of Age

Sex differences have been found in the assertive, empathic, and fearful behaviors of children in the early preschool years. Specifically, research with young preschoolers, ages 2 and 3, has shown that both males and females form a mixed-gender dominance hierarchy based on physical toughness with females generally below males (Omark et al., 1980; Strayer, 1980; Strayer & Strayer, 1976, 1980). Dominance hierarchies are based on implicit rules in which only members who are close in physical toughness engage in rough-and-tumble play. Because universally males are known to be more physically and verbally assertive than females by this age and at all successive ages (for reviews, see Maccoby & Jacklin, 1974; Parke & Slaby, 1983), knowledge of and experience with the rules of the physical toughness dominance hierarchy most likely are far greater for males than females.

As for females, research with children 2 and 3 years of age continues to suggest that they may be relatively more sensitive that males to the distress of others and may also be more fearful than males. In a fascinating review of studies of young children, Hoffman (1977) found evidence that females were more empathic than males, when empathy was defined as vicariously experiencing the emotions of another. In addition, in a study by Dunham, Dunham, Tran, and Aktar (1991), 2-year-old females were found to use social referencing of mothers more than males in a situation in which a robot was unresponsive to them. However, when the robot was responsive, females and males engaged in equal amounts of social referencing of mothers. Finally, Bowlby (1969) found that 3-year-old females expressed more fears than males.

3 to 5 Years of Age

Much research demonstrates that the play of 3- to 5-year-old children differs dramatically for most females and males. Further, previous research has shown that the content of the play of preschool-age girls and boys frequently reflects the domains of empathy and assertion, respectively. Specifically, although there are many individual differences within members of each sex, generally girls have been found to play with dolls more than boys, often recreating situations of need in which through empathic responsiveness the needs can be satisfied. In contrast, young boys have been found to play with guns, cars, trains, and trucks more than girls, in which they tend to direct physical assertion toward the toys and one another, often pretending to be superheroes from other worlds (for reviews, see Huston, 1983, 1987; Paley, 1984). It is likely that these toys provide different stimulus properties that elicit specific types of behavior. For example, dolls are often babies that require empathy and care. In contrast, guns and transportation vehicles provide strong forward movements, akin to physical assertion. It is not surprising, therefore, to hear stories from parents in which boys who are required to play with dolls sometimes convert the dolls into guns with which they shoot one another, and in which girls who are given cars and trucks sometimes create accidents in which the larger truck has to help the smaller car to feel better.

The organization of females' and males' interaction also begins to diverge in the early preschool years with females appearing to enjoy extended dyadic interaction more than males. For example, 3- to 5-year-old females were found to smile more than males with a puppet in an experimental setting in which the content consisted of a puppet trying to make friends with the child (Benenson, 1993). However, the sex difference occurred only when there was one puppet, not when there were three puppets. When three puppets attempted to befriend the child, males and females enjoyed the interaction equally. Similarly, in a study by Parker (1986) in which a 2½-foot, stationary, extraterrestrial creature attempted to befriend 4- and 5-year-old children, females preferred interaction with the creature more than males.

Importantly, this result is modified by the content of the interaction. Thus, in a more naturalistic study of 4- and 5-year-old children in which groups of 6 male classmates and of 6 female classmates were videotaped playing together at their schools, females were found to engage in longer bouts of dyadic interaction than males (Benenson & Apostoleris, 1993). Not surprisingly, however, males engaged in more dyadic interaction involving rough-and-tumble play than females. Thus, it appears that the content of females' interactions allows longer bouts of dyadic play than the content of males' interactions.

Between 3 and 5 years, both the content and the organization of the relationships of females and males undergo a striking divergence. Cross-culturally, at this age, females have been found to be more fearful, more compliant, and more nurturant of others than males. Males, in turn, were found to roam farther from home, to be more involved in rough-and-tumble play, and to be more likely to respond to physical attack when provoked than females (Parke & Slaby, 1983; Wenger, 1989; Whiting & Edwards, 1988). Our own observations of children in nursery school indicate that boys are frequently engaged in play that involves physical assertion, which is aimed toward other boys either directly or indirectly through objects. In contrast, girls are more involved than boys in taking turns either playing being tired, sick, dead, or otherwise vulnerable, or caring for tired, sick, dead, and vulnerable peers or dolls. Furthermore, in our study of groups of either 6 girls or 6 boys playing together in an unstructured setting at their schools, we have found that by 5 years of age,

many boys are often absorbed in bouts of "war" in which they spontaneously organize themselves into two opposing teams and engage in continuous physical attacks upon one another. In contrast, many girls are
generally involved in games that involve more gentle forms of contact, in
discussions of who is friends with whom, and in playing being vulnerable or
being the protector of the vulnerable one (Benenson & Apostoleris, 1993;
Benenson & Del Bianco, 1994).

It appears that some girls may feel more afraid or vulnerable than boys
at age 3, but by age 5, many girls have become more able than boys to
nurture others who are vulnerable. In a small study in which 3-year-old girls
were found to be more upset than boys when faced with a hurt puppet, the
reverse was found for 5-year-old girls. In fact, most 5-year-old girls very
consciously knew what to say and do to soothe the puppet in a way that
boys did not (Benenson et al., 1992). Likewise, it is likely that boys who
once engaged in physically assertive behavior with one other child at age 3,
by age 5 have begun to limit their physical assertion to objects or to games
in which there are some rules and teams that serve to control the impact.

Furthermore, the organization of the interactions of many females and
males diverge in ways that will continue throughout middle childhood and
possibly into adolescence and adulthood. Girls have been found to exhibit
greater preference than boys for extended dyadic interaction by age three.
Interestingly, before age 5, girls have also been found to form larger social
networks than boys. However, the reverse has been found after this age:
After age 5 boys formed larger groups than girls (Benenson, 1994;
Freedman, 1974; Pitcher & Schultz, 1983; Weisfeld, Omark, & Cronin,
1980).

Middle Childhood

By middle childhood, it is well documented that males form groups more
than females and females interact in dyads and triads more than males
(Belle, 1989; Benenson, 1990; Sutton-Smith, 1979; Thorne, 1986). At this
age, females form "best friend" relationships, friendships that most probably allow the maximum exchange of mutual empathy. In contrast, at this
age, many boys interact in groups, groups that most likely promote the
expression of assertiveness but in ways that limit its potentially harmful
consequences. Furthermore, these groups promote strong bonds among
members, so that other groups can be successfully defeated and individuals
within the group are prevented from deviating from the group's rules. In
addition, at this age, generally girls appear to be more concerned than boys
with exclusion of a third party from dyadic relationships (Eder & Hallinan,
1978). In turn, many boys are more concerned than girls with excluding
others from the "in group" (Best, 1983).

The content of the relationships of females and males in middle childhood also differs in well-documented ways. Cross-cultural research has demonstrated that universally females are expected to be responsive to other's distress and to care for young children, whereas males are expected to be able to regulate the force of their assertive behavior (Wenger, 1989; Whiting & Edwards, 1988). Thus, many females' original pleasure in being emotionally soothed and initial sensitivity to the distress of others continue to be converted to caring for others. For many males, their early experience with their own physical assertion and their initial responsiveness to others' physical stimulation and provocation continue to be converted to controlled physical assertion and assertion that is less physical and more symbolic, that is more verbal and gestural.

By middle childhood, many children consciously have expectations for their same-sex peers that belong to the content areas of empathy and physical or symbolic assertion. For example, when 9- and 10-year-old children were asked to describe into a taperecorder every one of their same-sex classmates, it was found that girls were more concerned than boys with the degree of niceness and reciprocity of their same-sex classmates. In contrast, boys were more interested than girls in the physical fighting, relationships to authority, athletic abilities, sense of humor, strangeness, and goofiness of their same-sex classmates. The vast majority of girls did not care as much as boys did about other girls' amount of physical fighting, relationships with authority, athletic abilities, strangeness, goofiness, or sense of humor (Benenson, 1990).

Importantly, the content and organization of relationships are likely to be intertwined. It is quite likely that girls choose dyadic interaction because dyads allow greater expression of empathy. Boys, in turn, are likely to form groups, because groups facilitate controlled physical assertion. If one member of the group becomes aggressive, the others can bond together to prevent his dominance of others. Groups also can compete against one another using physically assertive types of behavior. However, it is also highly probable that the different social organizations in and of themselves perpetuate different contents in relationships. For example, best friend relationships require sensitivity to the individual needs of the other or mutual caring for their integrity. In contrast, groups demand objectivity, impartiality, fairness, and limits on the oppression of an individual for their maintenance. Thus, any person in a best friend relationship, regardless of gender, needs to attend to different concerns than a person involved in a group interaction, in order for that kind of relationship to be sustained.

Finally, the games of boys and girls in middle childhood reflect many of the gender differences found earlier (Sutton-Smith, 1979). Thus, small overall sex differences found very early in life can be seen vividly in the play of boys and girls in middle childhood. Boys' games involve larger groups, in which the boys go farther away from homes or schools, and that are based on physical assertion. Usually, the games involve teams—teams that determine who is toughest within the team and how each team can best win against the other team. Girl's games involve only one or two other girls, occur nearer to home or school, and involve competition between individuals rather than teams.

Adolescence and Young Adulthood

In adolescence and young adulthood, many females and males continue to express different contents in their relationships. In a variety of studies, Gilligan et al. (1988) showed females to be more concerned than males with care and sensitivity to feelings of distress in others. In contrast, males were found to be more concerned than females with justice, fairness, rules, and objectivity. It is likely that for many females experience with a best friend and with exchange of empathy are transformed into a global attitude of caring for and responding to the individual needs of others. Similarly, for many males experience in groups involving exchanges of assertiveness are transformed into a global concern with justice, fairness, and objectivity. Thus, it is likely that some of the gender differences that began in childhood develop into early adulthood.

In summary, there appears to be solid evidence that many females are more involved than males in mutual exchange of empathy and that many males are more involved than females in mutual exchange of assertiveness. From the first year of life, in general girls are more responsive than boys to others' efforts to soothe them and are also more sensitive to others' emotional distress. They may also be more sensitive to threats of external danger than boys. As many girls develop, they become increasingly experienced in and comfortable with sharing another's feelings. They may often become better able than boys to assuage feelings of distress in themselves and others. Because the dyad may allow the most intense expression of these feelings, girls may choose dyadic relationships over larger group interaction. In middle childhood, girls develop best friend relationships in which mutual responsiveness to another's feelings is shared. By adolescence, girls' interests in responding sensitively to others' feelings combined with their formation of best friend relationships may converge to lead them to be concerned with different aspects of life than many males. Females then form close relationships with other girls and women who enjoy responding sensitively to others' feelings, who are able to express their own vulnerabilities, and who emphasize the importance of mutual caring.

In turn, many boys begin life engaging in more physical assertion than girls. As they develop, many boys direct increasing attention to learning and following the rules that govern the expression of physical assertion, so they and others are not hurt and can forge close bonds. Thus, a stable, rigid, linear, dominance hierarchy is formed in which the rules state that physical assertion can occur only with another boy who is similar in strength. With time, dominance hierarchies based on dyadic relationships between members evolve into stable groups. Groups allow the expression and control of assertive behavior; if one boy becomes aggressive, the other members of the group can control him. Further, the games boys play reflect their interest in assertion. In middle childhood, boys who can abide by the rules and express assertive behavior are in the group; those boys who cannot are excluded from the group. By adolescence, many boys' interest in assertion combined with their group interaction may converge to lead them to be concerned with different aspects of life than girls. Males then form close relationships with other boys and men who can express physical or other forms of forceful assertion, who can follow the rules and not let assertive behavior cause harm, who are concerned with fairness, justice, impartiality, and objectivity, and who can share these feelings.

A REINTERPRETATION OF DEBORAH TANNEN'S WORK

In her compelling account of the differences between women and men, Tannen (1990) concluded that females are concerned with connection and males with status. However, the current framework provides an alternative interpretation of her findings—that in their relationships, many females relative to males are concerned with maximizing mutual empathy and many males relative to females are concerned with maximizing assertiveness.

Tannen presented strong anecdotal evidence that as compared with males, females prefer expression of feelings of hurt and vulnerability, accommodation to another's emotions of vulnerability, discussion of personal secrets, talk that is emotionally soothing; direct helpfulness; indirect as opposed to direct conflict; equality not superiority; physical closeness not distance; more eye contact; and being protected. Based on these findings, she concluded that females are more concerned with connection than males. However, her data can be more precisely explained by inferring that females are more interested than males in exchange of empathic responsiveness.

Likewise, Tannen presented anecdotal evidence that as compared to females, males prefer: not expressing their feelings; jokes that often put others down, discussion of sports, guns, cars, political power, talk that has impact; direct conflict; indirect as opposed to direct helpfulness; superiority over equality; physical distance from each other; lack of eye contact; and being the protector. Based on these findings, she concluded that males are more concerned with status than females. Again, however, her data can be explained more precisely by inferring that males are more concerned than females with exchange of assertiveness. Thus, instead of pitting connection against status, connection can be construed as occurring in different content areas for females and males—through mutual empathy for females and through mutual assertiveness for males.

In contrast to Tannen's interpretation, therefore, it is hypothesized that women and men are both equally concerned with connection and status, helpfulness and conflict, equality and superiority, physical closeness and distance, being protected and being the protector. The difference is that for many women and men, the content of the relationships in which they engage differs. For example, in contrast to many men, for many women, efforts are made to maximize responsiveness to emotional distress at the expense of exchange of forceful assertion. Thus, talk focuses on vulnerabilities as opposed to strengths; helpfulness is often provided through discussion of the emotional distress being endured; conflicts are frequently mediated by a third person who can provide empathy; superiority in responding to one's own and other's emotional distress is more important than superiority in assertiveness; hierarchies are based on ability to soothe others not upon forceful assertion; closeness and lots of eye contact occur in situations of responsiveness to another's expression of feelings but not in situations that require forceful exchange; protection is given and received in the domain of responsiveness to emotional distress. In contrast, for many men, talk focuses on asserting impact on others, in sports, with guns, sex, cars, political power, and assertive jokes, not on discussions of vulnerabilities; helpfulness often occurs through having impact on a problem, not through discussion of the emotional distress caused by the problem; conflicts are often resolved in a confrontational manner that has impact— they are not avoided; superiority in assertion is more important than superiority in ability to be responsive to others' emotional distress; hierarchies are formed often based on ability to have impact; physical closeness and lots of eye contact occur in times of physical assertion more than in times of responding to another's feelings; protection is received and provided by asserting impact more than through responsiveness to others' emotions of distress.

Tannen reported on Dorval's (1990) research with 8-year-old children through adult college students who were asked to discuss a serious problem in a chair facing a best friend of the same sex. In his videotapes of these conversations, Dorval found that the females of all ages discussed the problem in more depth, faced one another more directly, and engaged in much greater eye contact than males of all ages. Several researchers have found the same results with 3- to 5-year-old children using a puppet or extraterrestrial creature that attempted to befriend individual children (Benenson, 1993; Parker, 1986). Girls enjoyed the dyadic interaction more than boys and engaged in greater eye contact than boys with the puppet. Importantly, however, the content of the interaction in both these studies centered on discussion of personal aspects of the self. When the content consisted of more physically assertive behavior, males engaged in greater dyadic interaction (Benenson & Apostoleris, 1993).

However, Tannen interpreted Dorval's results to mean that females are more connected than males. But the content of his experiment required discussion of personal aspects of the self and mutual empathy. The same-sex pairs had to sit in chairs and discuss a serious event, one that would presumably engender emotional vulnerability and concern. Therefore, it is suggested that the females enjoyed the content of the interaction more than the males. If Dorval had asked the participants to engage in a conflict, then it is highly probably that the males would most likely have been more involved than the females. In that case, Tannen would have had to conclude that males are more connected than females, who would probably sit farther apart and face each other less directly than males do during a conflict.

Thus, events can be approached in terms either of exchange of empathy or assertiveness. It is suggested that connection to others occurs for many females through mutual empathy and for many males through mutual assertiveness. Because physical assertion can cause harm, it must be controlled more tightly than expression of empathy and either ended more quickly before harm results or redirected into more symbolic forms or toward third parties. Nevertheless, both females and males form strong connections to others of the same sex—whether these connections are forged on the battlefield, on the basketball court, at a business conference; or in a nursery or nursing home, at a "slumber party," or in teaching or providing psychotherapy.

IMPLICATIONS OF EMPATHY AND ASSERTION FOR EMOTIONAL DIFFICULTIES

Both empathy and assertiveness are integral parts of life. Given that many females are more experienced than males with empathy and that many males are more experienced than females with assertiveness, it is reasonable to expect that many members of each sex are likely to be less knowledgeable in the content area that is more familiar to the other sex. That some girls and women encounter difficulties in expression of assertion in relationships is well known (e.g., Lerner, 1988). Likewise, according to many clinicians and theoreticians, some males experience difficulties expressing and responding to others' feelings (e.g., Osherson, 1986).

However, even more serious difficulties may arise when males and females inappropriately express assertion or empathy, respectively. Specifically, it is well known that more males than females have emotional difficulties revolving around an inability to control their physical aggression. In fact, in a review of studies of precursors of emotional problems in men, Kohlberg, LaCrosse, and Ricks (1972) found that expression of unprovoked physical aggression and an inability to follow rules in boys in middle childhood were the two best predictors of a range of adult psychopathology in men. Likewise, some girls and women become overly engaged in empathic caring for others at the expense of responding sensitively to their own needs (e.g., Bowlby, 1969; Jordan et al., 1991). At the extreme, there are clinical and legal cases describing women who remain in relationships in which they care for men who physically destroy them.

In fact, it may be that sex differences in content of relationships may be most pronounced in times of stress. Thus, in an important study by Turner (1991), 4-year-old children in nursery school who had insecure attachments to mothers at 1 year of age were found to express difficulties in specific content areas based on their sex. Thus, males who were insecurely attached at 1 year of age were found to be overly aggressive with peers in nursery school. In contrast, females who were insecurely attached at 1 year of age were found to be unusually positive and responsive to others' demands in nursery school. Interestingly, for children who were securely attached in infancy, there were no apparent sex differences in interactional style at age 4. Thus, when females are stressed, they are likely to become more involved than males in responding in a compliant and cooperative fashion to others' emotional needs. Likewise, when males are stressed, they are likely to become more forceful and physically aggressive than females. Further empirical research on the developmental trajectories of individual females and males would likely result in better understanding of the reasons emotional difficulties are expressed in differing ways by children and adults of each sex.

Individual Differences Within Sex

Clearly, empathy and assertion are both necessary aspects of relationships. Kohut (1971) suggested that children's feeling that adults are mirroring their emotions and children's idealization of adults are both essential processes for socioemotional development. Kohut believes that is it most often mothers who mirror children's feelings through the process of empathy and most often fathers who children idealize through recognizing fathers' assertive ways of interaction. If children are more likely to identify with the parent of the same sex, then these sex differences will be transferred from generation to generation.

Nevertheless, there are many boys and men who are more empathic than some girls and women and many girls and women who are more assertive than some boys and men. The question then arises as to how to explain both the differences between the sexes and individual differences within each sex. Research by Money and Ehrhardt (1972) and Stoller (1985), in combination with the work of ethologists, object relational theorists, and more traditional psychoanalytic clinicians, suggests that both environmental and biological forces combine to create differences in these content domains.

Most clinicians believe that the parent to whom the child is closest exerts the greatest influence on the child's developing personality. Because women are usually more involved in responsiveness to emotions, girls and boys who are closer to their mothers are more likely to gain experience in this way of interaction. Because men are usually more involved in assertion, boys and girls who are closer to their fathers are more likely to be experts in this area. Although it would be expected that many children raised by fathers would be generally more involved in assertion and less involved in empathic responsiveness than children raised by mothers, it is unknown whether girls raised by fathers would be as involved in assertive behavior as boys. Similarly, although children raised by mothers would be expected to be generally more empathically responsive than children raised by fathers, it is an empirical question as to whether boys raised by mothers would be as involved in empathic responding and as uninvolved in assertive behavior as girls.

There is also evidence that sex hormones influence children's and adults' involvement in assertive versus empathic interactions. Researchers following a sample of genetic females who were exposed to excessive amounts of androgens prenatally found these girls to prefer assertive forms of behavior, such as rough-and-tumble play or play with guns and transportation toys, significantly more than control girls (Berenbaum, & Hines, 1992; Berenbaum & Snyder, 1995; Money & Ehrardt, 1972). Other researchers have linked the hormone oxytocin to types of emphatic behavior in infrahuman mammals (Insel, 1990). It is likely that individual differences in levels of prenatal sex hormones will be found to influence expression of assertive and empathic behaviors in all human beings.

In summary, it is suggested that assertiveness be considered a basis for relationships. The importance of both empathy and assertion to relationships can then be explored in further depth. It appears likely that children go through various developmental changes in which the exchange of empathy versus assertion comes to dominate their relationships. Analysis of these trajectories, the factors that lead to following one versus the other pathway, the overlap among the expressions of the two emotions and the dominance of one type of emotion over the other can all be investigated.

Creating false distinctions, in which males are considered to be concerned with agency or status and females with communion or connection, serves to undermine the ability to observe different types of relationships. It is too implausible to believe that a human being could not be concerned with agency, status, communion, or connection. Living demands all of these characteristics. The ability to relate to others has been shown to be essential to emotional well-being for both boys and girls. In fact, difficulties in peer relations are a better predictor for males than females of future maladjustment. More precise understanding of the ways in which females have difficulties forming fulfilling relationships is needed. The current perspective allows future study of relationships to include females and males and emphasizes the importance of the investigation of the feelings that are currently termed *empathy* and *assertion*.

ACKNOWLEDGMENTS

This chapter is based on a colloquium presented at Harvard University at the Graduate School of Education in April 1992. The author is grateful to David McClelland whose wisdom and encouragement served as the inspiration for this chapter.

REFERENCES

Bakan, D. (1966). *The duality of human existence*. Chicago: Rand McNally.
Belle, D. (1989). Gender differences in children's social networks and supports. In D. Belle (Ed.), *Children's social networks and social supports* (pp. 173–188). New York: Wiley.
Benenson, J. (1990). Gender differences in social networks. *Journal of Early Adolescence, 10*, 472–495.
Benenson, J. (1993). Greater preference among females than males for dyadic interaction in early childhood. *Child Development, 64*, 544–555.
Benenson, J., Pascal, S., Liroff, E., Samuels, H., D'Angelico, S., & Mattie, M. (1992). *Emotional soothing and physical impact as evidence of sex differences*. Unpublished data, University of Hartford, Hartford, CT.
Benenson, J. F. (1994). Four to six years: Changes in the social structures of girls and boys. *Merrill-Palmer Quarterly, 40*, 478–487.
Benenson, J. F., & Apostoleris, N. H. (1993). *Gender differences in group interaction in early childhood*. Video presentation at the Society for Research in Child Development, New Orleans, LA.
Benenson, J. F., & Del Bianco, R. (1994). *Gender differences in the expression of vulnerability*. Unpublished manuscript, McGill University, Montréal, Québec, Canada.
Berenbaum, S. A., & Hines, M. (1992). Early androgens are related to childhood sex-typed toy preferences. *Psychological Science, 3*, 203–206.
Berenbaum, S. A., & Snyder, E. (1995). Early hormonal influences on childhood sex-typed activity and playmate preferences: Implications for development of sexual orientation. *Developmental Psychology, 31*, 31–42.
Best, R. (1983). *We've all got scars*. Bloomington: Indiana University Press.

Block, J.H. (1973). Conceptions of sex role: Some cross-cultural and longitudinal perspectives. *American Psychologist, 28,* 512–526.

Bowlby, J. (1969). *Attachment.* New York: Basic Books.

Carlson, V., Cicchetti, D., Barnett, D., & Braunwald, K. (1989). Disorganized/disoriented attachment relationships in maltreated children. *Developmental Psychology, 25,* 525–531.

Chodorow, N.J. (1978). *The reproduction of mothering.* Berkeley: University of California Press.

Chodorow, N.J. (1989). *Feminism and psychanalytic theory.* New Haven, CT: Yale University Press.

Dorval, B. (Ed.). (1990). *Conversational coherence and its development.* Norwood, NJ: Ablex.

Dunham, P., Dunham, F., Tran, S., & Aktar, N. (1991). The nonreciprocating robot: Effects of verbal discourse, social play and social referencing at two years of age. *Child Development, 62,* 1489–1502.

Eder, D., & Hallinan, M. (1978). Sex differences in children's friendships. *American Sociological Review, 43,* 237–250.

Eichenbaum, L., & Orbach, S. (1988). *Between women.* New York: Viking.

Fast, I. (1984). *Gender identity.* Hillsdale, NJ: Lawrence Erlbaum Associates.

Freedman, D. G. (1974). *Human infancy.* Hillsdale, NJ: Lawrence Erlbaum Associates.

Gilligan, C. (1988). Exit-voice dilemmas in adolescent development. In C. Gilligan, J.V. Ward, J.M. Taylor, & B. Bardige (Eds.), *Mapping the moral domain* (pp. 141–157). Cambridge, MA: Harvard University Press.

Gilligan, C., Ward, J.V., Taylor, J.M., & Bardige, B. (Eds.). (1988). *Mapping the moral domain.* Cambridge, MA: Harvard University Press.

Gilligan, C., & Wiggins, G. (1988). The origins of morality in early childhood relationships. In C. Gilligan, J.V. Ward, J.M. Taylor, & B. Bardige (Eds.), *Mapping the moral domain* (pp. 111–140). Cambridge, MA: Harvard University Press.

Goldberg, S., & Lewis, M. (1969). Play behavior in the year-old infant: Early sex differences. *Child Development, 40,* 21–31.

Goy, R. (1980). Early hormonal influences on the development of sexual and sex-related behavior. In F. O. Schmitt (Ed.), *The neurosciences: Second study program* (pp. 196–206). New York: Rockefeller University Press.

Greenberg, J., & Mitchell, S. (1983). *Object relations in psychoanalytic theory.* Cambridge, MA: Harvard University Press.

Hall, J.A., & Halberstadt, A.G. (1980). Masculinity and femininity in children: Development of the Children's Personal Attributes Questionnaire. *Developmental Psychology, 16,* 270–280.

Haviland, J.J., & Malatesta, C.Z. (1981). The development of sex differences in nonverbal signals: Fallacies, facts and fantasies. In C. Mayo & N.M. Henley (Eds.), *Gender and nonverbal behavior* (pp. 183–208). New York: Springer-Verlag.

Hittelman, J.H., & Dickes, R. (1979). Sex differences in neonatal eye contact time. *Merrill-Palmer Quarterly, 25,* 171–184.

Hoffman, M. (1977). Sex differences in empathy and related behaviors. *Psychological Bulletin, 84,* 712–722.

Horney, K. (1926). The flight from womanhood. *International Journal of Psychoanalysis, 7,* 324–339.

Huston, A.C. (1983). Sex-typing. In P.H. Mussen (Series Ed.) & E.M. Hetherington (Vol. Ed.) *Handbook of Child Psychology: Vol. 4. Socialization, personality and social development* (pp. 387–468). New York: Wiley.

Huston, A.C. (1987). The development of sex-typing: Themes from recent research. In S. Chess & A. Thomas (Eds.), *Annual progress in child psychology and child development 1986* (pp. 168–186). New York: Brunner/Mazel.

Insel, T.R. (1990). Oxytocin and maternal behavior. In N.A. Krasnegor & R.S. Bridges (Eds.), *Mammalian parenting* (pp. 260–280). New York: Oxford University Press.

Johnston, D.K. (1988). Adolescents' solutions to dilemmas in fables: Two moral orientations—two problem solving strategies. In C. Gilligan, J.V. Ward, J.M. Taylor, & B. Bardige (Eds.), *Mapping the moral domain* (pp. 49–71). Cambridge, MA: Harvard University Press.

Jordan, J.V., Kaplan, A.G., Miller, J.B., Stiver, I.P., & Surrey, J.L. (1991). *Women's growth in connection.* New York: Guilford.

Kagan, J. (1971). *Change and continuity in infancy.* New York: Wiley.

Kohut, H. (1971). *The analysis of the self.* New York: International Universities Press.

Kohlberg, L., LaCrosse, J., & Ricks, D. (1972). The predictability of adult mental health from childhood behavior. In B. Woman (Ed.), *Manual of child psychopathology* (pp. 1217–1284). New York: McGraw-Hill.

Legault, F., & Strayer, F.F. (1990). The emergence of gender-segregation in preschool peer groups. In F.F. Strayer (Ed.), *Social interaction and behavioral development during early childhood* (pp. 73–76). Montreal: University of Quebec at Montreal.

Lerner, H.G. (1988). *Women in therapy.* New York: Harper & Row.

Lyons, N.P. (1988). Two perspectives: On self, relationships, and morality. In C. Gilligan, J.V. Ward, J.M. Taylor, & B. Bardige (Eds.), *Mapping the moral domain* (pp. 21–48). Cambridge, MA: Harvard University Press.

Maccoby, E.E. (1988). Gender as a social category. *Developmental Psychology, 45,* 513–520.

Maccoby, E.E. (1990). Gender and relationships. *American Psychologist, 45,* 513–520.

Maccoby, E.E., & Jacklin, C.N. (1974). *The psychology of sex differences.* Stanford: Stanford University Press.

MacDonald, K.B., & Parke, R.D. (1984). Bridging the gap: Parent-child play interaction and peer interactive competence. *Child Development, 55,* 1265–1277.

Mahler, M., Pine, F., & Bergman, A. (1975). *The psychological birth of the human infant.* New York: Basic Books.

Malatesta, C.Z., Culver, C., Tesman, J.R., & Shepard, B. (1989). The development of emotion expression during the first two years of life. *Monographs of the Society for Research in Child Development, 54,* 140.

McClelland, D. (1985). *Human motivation.* Oakland, NJ: Scott, Foresman.

Money, J., & Ehrhardt, A.A. (1972). *Man and woman boy and girl.* Baltimore: Johns Hopkins University Press.

Moss, H.A. (1967). Sex, age and state as determinants of mother-infant interaction. *Merrill-Palmer Quarterly, 13,* 19–36.

Omark, D.R., Strayer, F.F., & Freedman, D.G. (Eds.). (1980). *Dominance relations.* New York: Garland.

Osherson, S. (1986). *Finding our fathers.* New York: The Free Press.

Osofsky, J.D., O'Connell, E.J. (1977). Patterning of newborn behavior in an urban population. *Child Development, 48,* 532–536.

Paley, V. G. (1984). *Boys and girls: Superheroes in the doll corner.* Chicago: University of Chicago Press.

Parke, R.D., Macdonald, K.B., Burks, V.M., Bhavnagri, N., Barth, J.M., & Beitel, A. (1989). Family and peer systems: In search of the linkages. In K. Kreppner & R.M. Lerner (Eds.), *Family systems and life-span development* (pp. 65–92). Hillsdale, NJ: Lawrence Erlbaum Associates.

Parke, R.D., & Slaby, R.G. (1983). The development of aggression. In P.H. Mussen (Series Ed.) & E.M. Hetherington (Vol. Ed.) *Handbook of Child Psychology: Vol. 4. Socialization, personality and social development* (pp. 547–641). New York: Wiley.

Parker, J. (1986). Becoming friends: Conversational skills of friendship formation in young children. In J.M. Gottman & J.G. Parker (Eds.), *Conversations of friends* (pp. 103–138). New York: Cambridge University Press.

Parsons, T., Bales, R.F., & Shils, E.A. (1953). *Working papers in the theory of action*. New York: The Free Press.

Pitcher, E. G., & Schultz, L. H. (1983). *Boys and girls at play: The development of sex roles*. New York: Praeger.

Robinson, J. L., Kagan, J., Reznick, J. S., & Corley, R. (1992). The heritability of inhibited and uninhibited behavior: A twin study. *Developmental Psychology, 28*, 1030–1037.

Rosen, W. D., Adamson, L. B., & Bakeman, R. (1992). An experimental investigation of infant social referencing: Mother's messages and gender differences. *Developmental Psychology, 28*, 1172–1178.

Sagi, A., & Hoffman, M.L. (1976). Empathic distress in the newborn. *Developmental Psychology, 12*, 175–176.

Savin-Williams, R.C. (1976). An ethological study of dominance formation and maintenance in a group of human adolescents. *Child Development, 47*, 972–979.

Savin-Williams, R.C. (1979). Dominance hierarchies in groups of early adolescents. *Child Development, 50*, 923–935.

Simner, M.L. (1971). Newborn's response to the cry of another infant. *Developmental Psychology, 5*, 136–150.

Stoller, R. (1985). *Presentations of gender*. New Haven, Yale University Press.

Strayer, F. (1980). Child ethology and the study of preschool social relations. In H.C. Foot, A.J. Chapman, & J.R. Smith (Eds.), *Friendships and social relations in children* (pp. 235–265). New York: Wiley.

Strayer, F., & Strayer, J. (1976). An ethological analysis of social agonism and dominance relations among preschool children. *Child Development, 47*, 980–989.

Strayer, F.F., & Strayer, J. (1980). Preschool conflict and the assessment of social dominance. In D.R. Omark, F.F. Strayer, & D.G. Freedman, (Eds.), *Dominance relations* (pp. 137–157). New York: Garland.

Sutton-Smith, B. (1979). The play of girls. In C.B. Kopp & M. Kirkpatrick (Eds.), *Becoming female: Perspectives on development* New York: Plenum.

Tannen, D. (1990). *You just don't understand*. New York: Ballantine.

Thorne, B. (1986). Girls and boys together . . . but mostly apart: Gender arrangements in elementary schools. In W.W. Hartup & Z. Rubin (Eds.), *Relationships and development* (pp. 167–184). Hillsdale, NJ: Lawrence Erlbaum Associates.

Turner, P. (1991). Relations between attachment, gender and behavior with peers in preschool. *Child Development, 62*, 1475–1488.

Weisfeld, G. E., Omark, D. R., & Cronin, C. L. (1980). A longitudinal and cross-sectional study of dominance in boys. In D. R. Omark, F. F. Strayer, & D. G. Freedman (Eds.), *Dominance relations* (pp. 205–216). New York: Garland.

Wenger, M. (1989). Work, play, and social relationships among children in a Giriama community. In D. Belle (Ed.), *Children's social networks and social supports* (pp. 91–115). New York: Wiley.

Whiting, B.B., & Edwards, C. P. (1988). *Children of different worlds*. Cambridge, MA: Harvard University Press.

Zahn-Waxler, C., Radke-Yarrow, M., Wagner, E., & Chapman, M. (1992). Development of concern for others. *Developmental Psychology, 28*, 126–136.

Zahn-Waxler, C., Robinson, J., & Emde, R.N. (1992). The development of empathy in twins. *Developmental Psychology, 28*, 1038–1047.

11 Extending the Core Relationship Theme into Early Childhood

Lester Luborsky
University of Pennsylvania

Ellen Luborsky
*Riverdale Mental Health Center,
   New York*

Louis Diguer
Universite Laval

Kelly Schmidt
George Washington University

Dorothee Dengler
Ulm, Germany

Pam Schaffler
*Harvard School of Public
Health*

Jeff Faude
University of Pennsylvania

Margaret Morris
University of New Mexico

Helen Buchsbaum
Robert Emde
University of Colorado

Although fads in clinical concepts come and go, the concept of a central relationship pattern has remained vital. Eight decades ago, Freud (1912/1958) set forth observations about a new concept of a central relationship pattern—a person-specific, pervasive, long-lasting, "transference template" that guides the conduct of close relationships. Since then, psychodynamic psychotherapists have usually relied on this concept and its supporting observations. One of these observations was that this pervasive pattern has its origins very early in life. But just how early it starts and how pervasive it is in the early years needed to be found out.

THE CORE CONFLICTUAL RELATIONSHIP
THEME METHOD

In the late 1970s, the advent of a reliable operational measure of central relationship patterns in psychotherapy gave a new kind of backing to the view of a stable, distinctive, central relationship pattern for each person (L. Luborsky, 1976, 1977; L. Luborsky, Crits-Christoph, & Mellon, 1986; L. Luborsky et al., 1985). This first new measure, the Core Conflictual Relationship Theme Method (CCRT; L. Luborsky, 1976, 1977; L. Luborsky & Crits-Christoph, 1990), has shown some stability in midlife, with consistency over an approximately 1-year period of psychotherapy (Crits-Christoph & Luborsky, 1990). But, early-in-life consistency had not yet been examined.

The essence of the CCRT method is the extraction of the most pervasive themes in narratives about relationships. Each narrative is scored for each of three types of components: wishes, responses from others, and responses of self. Then these scores are summarized, with the CCRT defined as the combination of the most pervasive of each of the three types of components (following the model in Luborsky, in press).

If the CCRT method could be applied to very young children's narratives, the study would show whether, for children in this age group, a central relationship pattern was evident in their narratives about close relationships — primarily about children with their parents. We planned to determine the CCRT for children at age 3, then repeat the same scoring of the CCRT with the same children at age 5 to determine the consistency of the relationship patterns over time. Beyond the study of age 3 and age 5, an additional plan was to compare the relationship patterns with those of adult groups whose narratives have also been scored by the same standard CCRT categories.

BACKGROUND OF RELATED RESEARCH

Three distinct sources have been tapped so far for evaluating children's relationship patterns in their very early years: (a) clinical retrospection based on adults' narratives about their early childhood; (b) infancy research with direct observations of early relationships; and (c) narratives told by young children.

Clinical Retrospection.   The retrospection method has had a long history in clinical practice. The method relies on early memories for reconstructing scenes, usually traumatic ones, that may have prefigured the current relationship pattern. There is impressive clinical evidence that an early traumatic scene acts like a template so that later episodes contain replications of components of the earlier scene (Reiser, 1984). Tomkins' (1987) script theory similarly places emphasis on the replication of scenes, as illustrated in the case presentation by Carlson (1986). Such a concept of long-lasting consistency of relationship patterns is also suggested by the famous 30-year longitudinal study of a young child with a gastric fistula (Engel & Reichsman, 1956).

Infancy Research.   Research on infancy has mushroomed in the last two decades. Two methods that have been used increasingly are the study of the mother–infant exchange and of attachment patterns (see also Bretherton, chapter 1, this volume).

The microanalysis of the mother–infant exchange has revealed much about the structure of their interaction (Tronik, 1982). The gain in knowledge about the enduring meaning of the exchange for personality development has been examined by Stern (1985, 1989) and by Beebe and Lachmann (1988).

Dahl and Teller (1994) cited a dissertation (Davies, 1989) describing 12 three-year-olds with 10 interactions each with their mothers and 10 inter-actions with each of two other children. Similar frames (i.e., relationship patterns) were found in each child's interaction with their mother and with the other children; the frames were also different for each child.

A systematic comparison of developmental changes in coping styles (E. Luborsky, 1987) was based on videos of 30 mother–child pairs of children at age 1, with evidence of greater differentiation of coping styles at age 2.

Research based on attachment theory (Bowlby, 1969, 1973) has provided a means of examining different patterns of attachment (Ainsworth, Blehar, Waters, & Wall, 1978) at 1 year and more recently beyond 1 year. In linking Bowlby's (1969, 1973) concept of internal working models of relationships with attachment patterns, recent research has extended the age range of attachment research and has been able to explore the links between internal representations and behavior (Bretherton, chapter 1, this volume; Bretherton, Ridgeway, & Cassidy, 1990; Main, Kaplan, & Cassidy, 1985).

Important work on delineating relationship patterns is represented by Sroufe (1983) and by Sroufe and Fleeson (1986), who pointed out that continuity and coherence in attachment patterns remains evident in the early years and beyond (e.g., Edelstein, chapter 4, this volume).

Narratives Told by Young Children.   Very young children who are just becoming verbal can tell narratives but find it difficult to do so consistently unless they are given considerable structure and assistance. Providing these children with a set of interesting stimulus pictures is a technique for stimulating narratives, as in Bellak's (1954) Children's Apperception Test

(CAT) derived from Murray (1938). Even with the CAT it is difficult to elicit organized narratives before age 3 or 4. The procedure of Buchsbaum and Emde (1990), partly based on Bretherton, Prentiss, and Ridgeway (1990), begins with a story stem and a doll family. That beginning has the effect of extending to earlier ages the ability of children to provide coherent narratives consistently.

PROCEDURE

Subjects

In our own study, 26 children (age 3) were included. These children had been in an earlier study of normal development (Buchsbaum & Emde, 1990). The 26 children were from Denver or its vicinity; they were first born, were normal at birth, and 16 were female. The parents were White, middle-class, and married; 25 of the 26 were still married at the time of the study. Eighteen of the mothers had full-time jobs so that their children were in day care. Fourteen of the children had a younger sibling and the mothers of two of them were expecting a second child.

After their third birthday, these children were interviewed briefly in their home, and they told four narratives to provide preliminary practice. Seven to 10 days later, they were interviewed and videotaped in the laboratory by a different interviewer.

For the analyses that involve a comparison of age 3 with age 5 we restricted our sample to those 18 children who took part at both times.

A Doll Family Story Method

The basic data for each child consisted of 10 videotaped narratives told in the laboratory by each of 25 children from the Buchsbaum and Emde sample of 3-year olds. The duration of this session was 25 to 30 minutes. For each narrative, the experimenter presented a stimulus story stem peopled with a doll family—a father, mother, and two children of the same gender as the child—in which an upsetting event has happened.[1] The experimenter then conducted an inquiry about what would happen next after the event in the story stem. For example, one of these stimulus story

---

[1] At 36 months, the 10 story stem events were about: spilled juice, toilet, monster, car keys, argument, ice cream, naps, restraint of aggression, departure/reunion, couch, moral dilemma-Heinz. At 60 months, the story stems were about: ice cream, monster, sad, car keys, argument, nap, bicycle, clean room/new toy, departure/reunion, couch, and band-aid (6 of the 10 were the same).

stems is called the "lost key"; it is a story in which the experimenter describes that the keys to the family car were lost. The doll mother accuses the doll father of losing the keys; the doll father denies this. The child is then asked, "What happens next?" Like the lost key story, most of the other stimulus stories are conflictual in content. An example of the lost key story is given in Fig. 11.1, along with the scoring of the wishes in that story in Fig. 11.2.

Basically, the doll family story procedure is a guided and prompted method of eliciting narratives. A scene is set by the experimenter's stimulus story, and then at each stage of the child's narrative the child is prompted to explain what happened next. The procedure is much like that of the Thematic Apperception Test (TAT); Murray, 1938), but in the TAT, a pictorial scene is presented; the subject then creates a story about it. In contrast, the relationship episodes told for the Relationship Anecdotes Paradigm (RAP) interview (L. Luborsky, 1990b) or in psychotherapy (L. Luborsky & Crits-Christoph, 1990) are intended by the narrator to be about actual events. In Buchsbaum and Emde's (1990) method of guided narratives the child's presentations of what the dolls do or say appear to contain a variable mixture of depictions of real relationship events along with fantasies about these relationships.

Data Analyses

Transcripts of the narratives were made from videos of the interview and then CCRT-scored by the method in L. Luborsky (1990a). First, a specially trained text-preparation judge marked the transcript with the CCRT-scorable thought units and the type of component to be scored for each thought unit. Second, trained CCRT judges (EL, PS, KS, & MM) inferred tailor-made categories and then rated each thought unit for each of the Edition 2 standard categories listed (approximately 30 wishes, 30 responses from others, and 30 responses of self).

For the present analysis of results, only a single judge's scores for each child was used; the transcripts were apportioned for scoring among the three judges. The use of only one judge per case appeared justified by the moderately good level of agreement in scoring among judges, as is discussed later in the results section.

A Scored Narrative as an Example

To help explain the data analysis, we give the scored story told by 5-year-old Constance after the lost keys story stem, along with the nondirective promptings by the experimenter (Fig. 11.1). The first column on the left has the tailor-made scores, that is, the judge's own inferences about each

"Lost Car Keys" Story

E: Mom and Dad look for the car keys?

C: Un-huh. //And...and...and then Jane comes in to the room.// //And...and Jane says, "How about you talk about it." (Brings dolls together).//

E: And then what happens after Jane says that?

C: Well, //then Susan comes in (reaches for Susan, brings to other dolls)// //and they all sit down and sit there and talk about it.//

E: So, they all sit down and talk about it. What are they talking about?

C: Well, //they're two are having a little talk (moves Jane and Susan together)// and //they're two having a little talk (faces Mom and Dad).//

E: And they're talking about...what are they talking about?

C: Well, //they're talking about the car keys (touches Mom and Dad)//, and //they're talking about playing (touches Jane and Susan).//.

E: And they're talking about playing?

C: Like...like...like sharing and stuff.

Tailor-made	Top Standard Categories	Top Clusters
PRS: facilitates dialogue between parents	#7: am open #9: am helpful	1: helpful
W: *to help parents solve problem	#12: to help others #17: to avoid conflict	8: to acheive & help others 4: to be distant and avoid conflict
PRS: sisters discuss sharing PRO: parents talk about lost key	#7: am open #15: am independent #11: are open #18: are cooperative	1: helpful 5: self-controlled 8: understanding 6: helpful
W: *to open communication	#9: to be open #11: to be close to others	5: to be close & accepting

FIG. 11.1. The story told by Constance (113) at age 5, to the "Lost Car Keys" stem. *The ratings of these wishes is given in Fig. 11.2. The double slashes (//) in the story mark off each thought unit to be stored.

Child: Constance Age: 5

Ratings of Thought Units

Standard Category: Wishes	To help parents solve problems	To open Communication
1. TO BE UNDERSTOOD	1	1
2. TO BE ACCEPTED	1	1
3. TO BE RESPECTED	1	1
4. TO ACCEPT OTHERS	3	2
5. TO RESPECT OTHERS	3	3
6. TO HAVE TRUST	3	2
7. TO BE LIKED	1	1
8. TO BE OPENED UP TO	4	4
9. TO BE OPEN	1	1
10. TO BE DISTANT FROM OTHERS	1	1
11. TO BE OPEN TO OTHERS	4	4
12. TO HELP OTHERS	(5)	4
13. TO BE HELPED	1	1
14. TO NOT BE HURT	1	1
15. TO BE HURT	1	1
16. TO HURT OTHER	1	1
17. TO AVOID CONFLICT	[5]	5
18. TO OPPOSE OTHER	1	1
19. TO HAVE CONTROL OVER OTH.	1	1
20. TO BE CONTROLLED BY OTH.	1	1
21. TO HAVE SELF-CONTROL	1	1
22. TO ACHIEVE	1	1
23. TO BE INDEPENDENT	1	1
24. TO FEEL GOOD ABOUT MYSELF	1	2
25. TO BETTER MYSELF	1	1
26. TO BE GOOD	1	2
27. TO BE LIKE OTHER	1	1
28. TO BE MY OWN PERSON	1	1
29. TO NOT BE OBLIGATED	1	1
30. STABILITY	5	4
31. TO FEEL COMFORTABLE	4	3
32. TO FEEL HAPPY	4	3
33. TO BE PROTECTED	3	3

FIG. 11.2. A sample of the ratings by Judge MM on the standard categories of wishes for Child 113: Lost car keys story (given in Fig. 11.1).

underlined thought unit. The middle column contains the top (most frequent) standard categories, and the column on the right contains these top categories expressed in terms of clusters.

As shown in Fig. 11.2, each judge starts with the thought unit's tailor-made inferences and rates each one on all of the standard categories. The rating reflects the degree to which the judge believes the standard category is expressed in the thought unit. In this example, two of the thought units and their tailor-made inferences are named in the heading of the columns and the ratings from 1 to 5 (with 5 being the highest) for each of the 33 standard categories are given in each column.

One judge's ratings of the wishes in the story by Constance are given in Fig. 11.2. Constance is clearly a child of our psychotherapy era who believes in conflict resolution by means of talking things over. You will see that for the thought unit's tailor-made inference "to help parents solve problems," this judge gave a score of 5 to the standard category "to avoid conflict." Judges identified their top choice by putting a circle around a rating and their second choice by putting a square around it. The standard category ratings in each column were summed across the narratives, which allowed us to locate the most pervasive across-narratives standard categories as expressed in the form of clusters.

Can 3- and 5-Year-Olds Comply With the Narrative-Telling Task?

At the outset of the analysis of results, the narratives were scored for the degree to which the child complied with the request to tell a narrative. This information was useful to us in two ways: (a) we could limit our sample to children who provided narratives that were complete enough to score, and (b) for children included in our sample we would have an estimate of the degree to which the child was willing or able to comply with the request to tell narratives. We rated compliance by a 5-point well-defined scale (L. Luborsky, 1990a) where the scale points were defined as abbreviated here. Point 1: The child will not respond to any of the stimulus stories despite additional prompting. Point 2: The child may begin to engage in responding to the stimulus story in a superficial way, but there is not an attempt to develop it. Point 3: The child makes an initial attempt to actively deal with the stimulus story, but entirely breaks this off or is distracted from creating an ending or resolution. Point 4: The child directly engages the doll in the content of the child's story; the child needs prompting but tends to be responsive to this prompting. Point 5: The child becomes actively involved with the stimulus story, needs very little prompting, works effortfully and agreeably within the stimulus story format to find a satisfactory resolution or outcome.

At 3 years of age, 21 of the 25 children were able to comply sufficiently to be included in the sample. At age 5, all of the children complied sufficiently to be included. For the 18 children who were included at age 3 and at age 5, the average compliance rating for age 3 was 3.49 and for age 5 was 3.96, showing that, as a whole, the compliance at age 3 was fairly good and it improved only moderately by age 5.

We also found that at age 3 the ratings of compliance differed over the 10 stories. We used a repeated-measures analysis of variance for the mean ratings of the 10 stories. We found a significant difference across the 10 stories [$F(9,180) = 2.14$, $p < .05$, two-tailed].

Two stories at age 3 were of special interest because the children were markedly less compliant in completing them; they were the exclusion-departure story and the reunion story. The average rating of compliance for these two stories was compared with the average of the other eight stories using a paired t-test procedure. The means were significantly different [t (20) = 2.73, $p < .05$, two-tailed] and the difference was in the predicted direction, that is, lower compliance was evident for these two stories. These story themes of departure and reunion prompted more disruption in compliance with storytelling than did the other themes, although some of them were also conflictual. This inadvertent finding dovetails with the use of Ainsworth's Strange Situation in attachment research (Ainsworth et al., 1978). The departure–reunion sequence again seems to activate stress reactions.

Although both age groups could tell a story and adequately follow directions, an interesting shift was noted about how they handled a conflict element within a story. When a story stem was not how a child wanted it, 3-year-olds sometimes changed the original story line and looked for a solution there. The 5-year-olds did not change the story stem. Instead they were likely to have the main character do something else about the problem, including pretending or hiding their character's agenda.

RESULTS

Do the Judges Agree in Scoring the CCRT?

As noted earlier, the level of agreement among judges was generally satisfactory and supported our decision to rely on the scoring of only a single judge in later analyses. Three types of agreement were examined for the CCRT scoring of the children's narratives. First, agreement was based on scoring by two judges (JF and DD) with a subsample of 12 of the 25 children at age 3 (Dengler, 1990). The two judges exactly agreed in their composite CCRT scores in 75% of the items. Second, from the sample of the 18 children in the present study for whom we had data at both age 3 and at age 5, we used the 3-year-olds ($N = 10$) who were rated by two judges (EL and PS). These judges agreed on the wishes (W) of 7 of the 10 children; on the responses from other (RO) of 10 of the 10 children; on the responses of self (RS) of 9 of the 10 children. (Agreement is defined as a match between the two judges in identifying the same cluster of each child with the highest average sum of standard categories). Finally, a weighted kappa measure of agreement was also computed by assigning a 1.0 to those instances where the first choice of each component was a match between judges; other partial matches were assigned weights of .66 or .33. These weighted kappas for each CCRT component were: W = .30; RO = .56; RS = .54. The lower kappas, especially for the wishes, appear to be attributable to the very low variability. The kappas are therefore not as representative of the reliability as the agreement percentages.

How Pervasive Are the Clusters of CCRT Standard Categories Within Narratives at Age 3 and Narratives at Age 5?

Our interest is in which clusters of standard categories were most pervasive, that is, were repeated most often across each child's 10 narratives. Pervasiveness was scored for each of the three components that make up the central relationship pattern that is measured by the CCRT: W, RO, and RS.

Our judges rated the narratives for each scorable thought unit for every standard category, using the 1–5 scale, with a high rating indicating that the standard category was strongly reflected in that thought unit. In our analysis, we summed the ratings given to each thought unit for each of the 30 standard categories. The lists of standard categories were then simplified by cluster analysis to only eight clusters (Barber, Crits-Christoph, & Luborsky, 1990). Our tables of results reflect the frequency of highest and next highest cluster scores for each child — a cluster score is the mean of the sums for the standard categories within each cluster.

For each of the three components (W, RO, RS) just one or two cluster scores among the eight clusters had a high frequency. For example (Table 11.1), the wish "to be loved, understood" was presented in the narratives among the 18 children at age 3 as highest or next highest 10 times (28%); and 5 times at age 5 (42%). Similarly, the wish "to feel good and to be comfortable" was presented 15 times for the 18 children at age 3 (42%) and 12 times at age 5 (33%).

Among the RO component scores (Table 11.2), the most frequent in the narratives was "helpful" (both at age 3 with 15 [42%] and at age 5 with 16 [44%]) and "understands" (both with 16 [45%] at age 3 and age 5). The RS (Table 11.3) that were most frequent were in the cluster "self-confident" and in the cluster "helpful" (at age 3 the frequency of helpful" was 7 [19%] and at age 5 it was 16 [44%] — the increase at age 5 in their narratives of being "helpful" was one of the largest increases from age 3 to age 5).

Is There a Core Theme for Each Child?

For examining this question the most telling data were the frequency profiles of the eight clusters of the CCRT components for each child. Our reasoning was that the more each child's profile concentrated on just a few clusters, the more we can conclude that the concept of a core theme for each child is a cogent one. The data from the profiles, both at age 3 and at age 5, tended to be consistent with this concept of a core theme. A cogent illustration of this concentration can be seen in the rankings of each child's pervasiveness on each cluster. Most children had a high pervasiveness within their top two clusters, with the remaining six clusters having

TABLE 11.1
Comparison of Children at Ages 3 and 5 for the Number of Times Highest or Next Highest for Each Wish Cluster
($N = 18$)

	To Assert Self 1	To Oppose, Hurt Others 2	To be Controlled or Hurt 3	To Avoid Conflict 4	To be Close, Accept Others 5	To be Loved, Understood 6	To Feel Good, Comfortable 7	To Achieve, Help Others 8	Total
				Wish Cluster					
Age 3	4	0	0	5	1	27.7% 10	41.6% 15	1	36*
Age 5	5	0	0	2	2	41.6% 15	33.3% 12	0	36*

*Total is 36 because each of the 18 children has a highest and next most highest cluster.

297

TABLE 11.2

Comparison of Children at Ages 3 and 5 for the Number of Times Highest or Next Highest for Each Responses From Other (RO) Cluster (N = 18)

	RO Cluster								
	Strong 1	Controlling 2	Upset 3	Bad 4	Rejects, Opposes 5	Helpful 6	Likes Me 7	Understands 8	Total
Age 3	0	2	0	1	1	41.6% 15	1	44.4% 16	36
Age 5	0	2	0	0	0	44.6% 16	2	44.4% 16	36

*Total is 36 because each of the 18 children has a highest and next most highest cluster.

TABLE 11.3

Comparison of Children at Ages 3 and 5 for the Number of Times Highest or Next Highest for Each Responses of Self (RS) Cluster (N = 18)

	RS Cluster								
	Helpful 1	Unreceptive 2	Respected 3	Oppose, Hurt Others 4	Self-Confident 5	Helpless 6	Sad 7	Anxious, Ashamed 8	Total
Age 3	19.4% 7	1	3	5	38.8% 14	4	0	2	36*
Age 5	44.4% 16	1	6	3	27.7% 10	0	0	0	36*

*Total is 36 because each of the 18 children has a highest and next most highest cluster.

299

considerably less pervasiveness. The drop in mean pervasiveness from the top two to the remaining six was about one third. This drop was about the same at age 3 as at age 5 and about the same for W and RS, but the drop for RO was a ratio of about .40:.46.

Does Each Child's Profile of Clusters Remain From Age 3 to Age 5?

The profile of clusters does stay very similar from age 3 to age 5 (even though 4 of the 10 story stems were different at age 5 than age 3). The Spearman rank correlations between cluster scores at age 3 and 5 are high: W, .84 ($p < .01$); RO, .89 ($p < .01$); RS, .74 ($p < .05$). The components of the CCRT that have the most similarity from age 3 to age 5 are the Ws and ROs (the same W, 83.4%; the same RO, 94.5%; the same RS, 72.3%).

Here is an example of a child we have called John whose RO and RS remain consistent from age 3 to age 5. At age 3, the story stem is about spilled juice; in John's story he has the mother clean up the juice (RO) and John then says, "Yum, Yum" and eats the meal she provides (RS). At age 5, the story stem is about falling off the bike while going to get ice cream; John has the mother give the child a band-aid (RO) and then the child picks up his bike and rides off again (RS).

How Pervasive are the Combined Components of the CCRT Patterns?

We now look to see the pervasiveness of the combined patterns of the CCRT components, that is the W, RO, and RS together, rather than singly as we have so far. Specifically, it is each child's combination of their three top frequency clusters for the W, RO, and RS. The highest number that could be the same in this measure would be three — one for the same highest frequency cluster for the Ws, one for the same for the RO, and one for the same for the RS. As an example, for Robert: the W and the RO stayed the same from age 3 to age 5. At age 5, the most pervasive wish is still "to feel good and comfortable" and the most pervasive response from the doll parents is still "to be helpful." The one component that changed for Robert was the RS: At age 5 his most pervasive response of the doll child is to be "self-confident" and "assertive." Robert's sameness score would be 2.

The mean sameness of the highest clusters for the 18 children at age 3 and again at age 5 was 2.5. Sixty-one percent of the children had a score of 3. Twenty-eight percent had a score of 2 and 11% had a score of 1. We conclude, therefore, that there is considerable consistency in the highest clusters from age 3 to age 5.

The consistency over time is greatest for the W (10 children with the same wish), next for the RO (8 children), and next for the RS (3 children). This preponderance of consistency over time for the W happens to be similar to the finding for adult groups (L. Luborsky & Crits-Christoph, 1990) where wishes have been found to have more consistent pervasiveness than the responses over a mean time of 1 year.

How Positive and How Negative are the Relationship Patterns at Age 3 and Age 5?

Central relationship patterns can be classed as positive or negative, after Freud's usual practice of labeling the transference as positive or negative (e.g., Freud, 1912/1958). Positive or negative appears to imply that the person was achieving satisfaction of wishes (positive responses from others or of self) or was not achieving satisfaction of wishes (negative responses from others or of self). With this concept in mind, we classified the CCRT patterns of each child at age 3 and at age 5. Positive and negative responses from other and of self were counted for all scored thought units for each child (Table 11.4).

Our sample of relatively well-functioning Denver children showed very low percentages of negative responses and conversely very high percentages of positive responses, both at age 3 and at age 5 (Table 11.4). For example, the RO at age 3 were 31% negative, and at age 5, 29% negative. The RS at age 3 were 37% negative and 23% negative at age 5.

When we evaluate the level of these negative responses of the children as very low, we base this on our main experience with adult patients (L. Luborsky & Crits-Christoph, 1990). The adults' level of negative responses is very high—the Penn Depression Study sample and the Penn Outpatient Department patient sample (Luborsky, Crits-Christoph, Mintz, & Auerbach, 1988) were 72% and 73%, respectively (Table 11.4). These higher percentages of negative responses may be attributable to the fact that the groups we have studied are adults and adults tend to have more negative responses.

Another obvious explanation is that the adults were patients and patients may have a high percentage of negative responses. For evidence we have two unpublished papers on normal (German) adults. One of these papers is on normal college students (15 men and 15 women) at the University of Goettingen in Germany (Cierpka et al., 1992). In this sample (Table 11.4) 43% of the RS were negative for women, and 42% were negative for men. The other sample was 35 normal women from Ulm, Germany (Dahlbender, 1992); the negative RO were 57% and the negative RS were 48%. A likely implication of these studies is that the normal groups are less negative than the patients, but still much more negative than the present child sample.

TABLE 11.4
Positive and Negative CCRT Responses: Percentages

	Positive	Negative	Neutral
Denver nonclinical children ($N = 18$)			
RO Age 3	69	31	
RO Age 5	71	29	
RS Age 3	63	37	
RS Age 5	77	23	
Penn depression patients[a] ($N = 30$)			
RO, RS (combined)	21	72	7
Penn OPD patients[a] ($N = 20$)			
RO, RS	19	73	
Goettingen nonclinical[b] ($N = 30$)			
RS	35	43	21
Ulm nonclinical[c] ($N = 35$)			
RO	38	57	5
RS	47	48	9

[a]Luborsky and Crits-Christoph (1990, p. 225)
[b]Cierpka et al. (1992)
[c]Dahlbender (1992)

Are There Gender Differences in Central Relationship Patterns Between Boys and Girls at Ages 3 and 5?

The commonalties across the frequencies of the eight clusters for boys versus girls were much more impressive than the differences. This was true for all three CCRT components.

But remember that there were 11 girls and 7 boys, so percentages are needed to reveal the few differences. For example, under the wish "to be loved and understood" at age 3 there were two top or next-to-top frequency clusters for the boys (i.e., the total number of top or next-to-top clusters for the seven boys is 14, and 2 out of 14 would be 14%). By comparison, at age 3 for the girls there were eight top or next-to-top clusters (this would be 8 out of 22 = 36%, where 22 is the number of top or next-to-top for 11 girls).

The wish "to be loved and understood" was more frequent for girls, but it is hard to test for significance whether 36% for girls is significantly greater than the 14% for boys. At age 5, the comparable figures are 36% for boys and 45% for girls, but the figure for girls is probably not significantly larger.

The differences between boys versus girls in RO clusters were small; the differences in RS clusters were also small.

DISCUSSION AND CONCLUSIONS

Compliance with the Task.   Even the 3-year-olds were able to comply and tell moderately complete narratives when provided with story stems. The completeness of the narratives supported their use for deriving from them their central relationship themes.

Pervasiveness of the CCRT.   To return to our original questions: Is there a pervasive central relationship pattern in the narratives about close relationships at age 3, and if there is, does it continue at age 5? The answer to both questions is "yes," based both on (a) a high level of pervasiveness of CCRT components across each child's set of narratives at age 3, and (b) the number of these pervasive CCRT components that reappear at age 5 (with a high percentage of similar components at the two ages).

The two most pervasive clusters were the wish "to be loved and understood" and the wish "to feel good and comfortable." The two most pervasive RO were "helpful" and "understands"; the two most pervasive RS were "self-confident" and "helpful." The *combination* of the W, RO, and RS also showed high stability from age 3 to age 5.

The changes from age 3 to age 5 that were most impressive were (a) the wish "to be loved, understood," which increased slightly and (b) the RS of being "helpful," which increased markedly and may reflect greater maturity and responsibility.

These findings are new, and, as new findings tend to do, lead to harder-to-answer questions: Is the CCRT pattern at age 3 likely to continue to reappear at even later ages through adolescence and adulthood? To answer this question, we need to reevaluate these children at later times. Fortunately, we now have some data to help with this task: Buchsbaum and Emde have made available their videos of the doll family interviews of the same children at age 8, although not all could be located due to the migratory nature of U.S. society. It is these and related data for this age group that we analyze next. Waldinger, Guastella, Diguer, Luborsky, and Hauser (1995) are assessing the CCRT by interviews with adolescents at age

14 and then again at age 23 based on longitudinal data collected by Stuart Hauser, Gil Noam, Sally Powers, Alan Jacobson, and Joseph Allen.

Positive Versus Negative Quality of the CCRT Pattern.   Positive and negative are meaningful modifiers of the central relationship pattern. We found that both at age 3 and at age 5 the CCRTs were overwhelmingly positive. Inevitably, further research is needed to learn whether this really is a representative finding to be taken at face value as a characteristic of the developmental stage of this age group. Consistent with this finding, older people and people who are patients tend to have more negative responses.

To sum up the results about positive and negative responses in narratives, several factors must be taken into account:

1. Most of the CCRT research so far has been on adults who are patients. Both of these factors are associated with an increase in the number of negative responses.

2. The type of narratives the children told may have contributed to the positivity of their responses. These narratives are partly fictional rather than accounts of actual events, and fictional accounts may be particularly prone to idealization. In contrast, the narratives collected from adults are intended to be descriptions of actual events (L. Luborsky, 1990a).

3. The particular sample of children may have been especially healthy. We need, therefore, to study other groups of children. From such studies we may emerge with the conclusion that the preponderance of positive responses may be a typical developmental characteristic. We are told by Seligman, Kamaen, and Nolen-Hoeksema (1988) and Seligman (1991), for example, that children are more optimistic than adults in their style of explaining the causes of negative events.

4. We need to check our assumption about *these* relationship patterns that the normal adult groups are not unduly affected by differences in cultural backgrounds, such as between American versus German.

Gender Differences in CCRT Patterns.   Gender similarities clearly are more prominent than gender differences in the CCRT components. The only difference that may be noteworthy is an increase at age 3 for the girls in the wish "to be loved and understood," which may go along with the slight decrease at ages 3 and 5 in the wish "to feel good and comfortable." These gender differences may involve differences in relatedness to others, which is thought by some, for example, Gilligan (chapter 9, this volume), to be more characteristic of women than of men. A large and older body of research based on Witkin (1949) has shown similar differences, for example that females are more responsive to the "field" than males and among ways of showing this, females are more attentive to faces of other people.

WHAT IS NEXT IN THIS LINE OF RESEARCH?

We have found that the children at this early age already have a pervasive pattern in close relationships and one that is mostly positive. To get more perspective on this finding, a study should be done with data from the children that also includes narratives about actual events, which would allow for better comparisons with our adult data.

The vulnerabilities of each child in close relationships are likely to be located in each child's most pervasive central relationship pattern. When special stresses give rise to symptoms, they should appear as part of that pattern. We have begun to examine this premise for the few children who experienced special traumatic conditions, but the agenda is just at its beginning.

The CCRT patterns we have found at ages 3 and 5 may be similar to patterns described as "attachment patterns," or "internal working models" (Bretherton, chapter 1, this volume; Bretherton, Ridgeway, & Cassidy, 1990; Case, chapter 3, this volume; Fischer & Ayoub, chapter 7, this volume; Main et al., 1985) or "transference patterns." This last concept gets support from the work of Fried, Crits-Christoph, and Luborsky (1990), who showed that the relationship episodes to the therapist provide a CCRT that is much like the CCRT derived from the relationship episodes to other people. This parallel is an important one, perhaps even more important than many of the rest of the 22 facets of Freud's definition of transference. Our next broad agenda is to more systematically examine the relations among these differently labeled concepts. We will then be able to examine the overlap among different researchers' apparently different but probably similar conceptual models.

Our results may be linkable to Piagetian and to other "transformational psychologies." The themes we uncovered may be related to stages of development (Loevinger, 1976). Only longitudinal analysis will be able to differentiate core themes that remain across the life span from those that change over time (Noam, 1991, chapter 6, this volume).

ACKNOWLEDGMENTS

This chapter is partially supported by a Research Scientist Award (to Lester Luborsky) from The National Institute of Mental Health Research Scientist Award MH40710-22 and the National Institute on Drug Abuse: DA0785-23-24; partially supported by the Clinical Research Center Grant P50MH 45178 and Coordinating Center Grant 418-DA07090 (to Paul Crits-Christoph). It is also partially supported by the John D. and Catherine T.

MacArthur Foundation through its Research Network on Early Childhood Transitions and by NIMH grant MH22803 and Research Scientist Award 5K02MH36808 (to Robert Emde).

REFERENCES

Ainsworth, M., Blehar, M., Waters, E., & Wall, S. (1978). *Patterns of Attachment*. Hillside, NJ: Lawrence Erlbaum Associates.

Barber, J., Crits-Christoph, P., & Luborsky, L. (1990). A guide to CCRT standard categories and their classification. In L. Luborsky & P. Crits-Christoph, *Understanding transference—The CCRT method* (pp. 37-50). New York: Basic Books.

Beebe, B., & Lachmann, F. (1988). Mother-infant mutual influence and precursors of psychic structure. In A. Goldberg (Ed.), *Frontiers of self-psychology: Progress in self-psychology* (Vol. 3, pp. 3-26). Hillsdale, NJ: The Analytic Press.

Bellak, L. (1954). *The Thematic Appreciation Test and the Children's Appreciation Test in clinical use*. New York: Grune & Stratton.

Bowlby, J. (1969). *Attachment and loss, Vol. I: Attachment*. New York: Basic Books.

Bowlby, J. (1973). *Attachment and loss, Vol. II: Separation*. New York: Basic Books.

Bretherton, I., Prentiss, C., & Ridgeway, D. (1990). Family relationships as represented in a story-completion task of thirty-seven and fifty-four months of age. In J. Bretherton, & M.W. Watson (Eds.), *Children's perspectives on the family: New directions for child development* (Vol. 48, pp. 85-105). San Francisco: Jossey-Bass.

Bretherton, I., Ridgeway, D., & Cassidy, J. (1990). The role of internal working models in the attachment relationship—an attachment story completion task for 3-year-olds. In M. Greenberg, D. Cicchetti, & E.M. Cummings (Eds.), *Attachment during the pre-school years* (pp. [??]). Chicago: University of Chicago Press.

Buchsbaum, H., & Emde, R. (1990). Play narratives in 36-month-old children—early moral development and family relationship. In A.J. Solnit, P., Newbauer, S. Abrams, & A.S. Dowling (Eds.), *The psychoanalytic study of the child* (Vol. 45, pp. 129-155). New Haven, CT: Yale University Press.

Carlson, R. (1986). After analysis: A study of transference dreams following treatment. *Journal of Consulting and Clinical Psychology, 54*, 246-252.

Cierpka, M., Zander, B., Krannich, S., Reich, G., Ratzke, K., Homburg, H., Staats, H., & Seide, L. (1992, June). *Differences in conflictual relationship themes of male and female students*. Paper given to annual meeting of the Society for Psychotherapy Research, Berkeley, CA.

Crits-Christoph, P., & Luborsky, L. (1990). Changes in CCRT pervasiveness during psychotherapy. In L. Luborsky & P. Crits-Christoph (Eds.), *Understanding transference—The CCRT method* (pp. [??]). New York: Basic Books.

Dahlbender, R. (1992, June). *Intra- and inter-subjectivity in RAP interviews of young women*. Paper given at annual meeting of the Society for Psychotherapy Research, Berkeley, CA.

Dahl, H., & Tellar, V. (1994). The characteristics, identification, and application of frames. *Psychotherapy Research, 4*, 253-276.

Davies, J. (1989). *The development of emotional and interpersonal structures in three-year-old children*. Unpublished doctoral dissertation, Adelphi University, Derner Institute for Advanced Psychological Studies.

Dengler, D. (1990). Anwendung des Zentralen Beziehungskonfliktthemas auf narrative von dreijahrigen *und suche nach zusammenhängen mit der fähigkeit zur problemlosung* [Use of central relationship themes from narratives of 3-year-olds and a search for relationships with ability in problem solving]. Unpublished MD dissertation der Universitat Ulm.

Engel, G. Jr., Reichsman, F., (1956). Spontaneous and experimentally induced depression in an infant with gastric fistula: a contribution to the problem of depression. *Journal of the American Psychoanalytic Association, 4*, 428-452.

Freud, S. (1958). The dynamics of the transference. In J. Strachey (Ed. and Trans.), *The standard edition of the complete psychological works of Sigmund Freud* (Vol. 12, pp. 99-108). London: Hogarth Press. (Original work published 1912)

Fried, D., Crits-Christoph, P., & Luborsky, L. (1990). The parallel of narratives about the therapist with the CCRT for other people. In L. Luborsky & P. Crits-Christoph (Eds.), *Understanding transference — The CCRT method* (pp. 147-157). New York: Basic Books.

Loevinger, J. (1976). *Ego development.* San Francisco: Jossey-Bass.

Luborsky, E. (1987). *Stability and transformation of coping and affect from 12 to 23 months of age.* Unpublished doctoral thesis, New York University, New York.

Luborsky, L. (1976). Helping alliances in psychotherapy: The groundwork for a study of their relationship to its outcome. In J.L. Claghorn (Ed.), *Successful psychotherapy* (pp. 92-116). New York: Brunner/Mazel.

Luborsky, L. (1977). Measuring a pervasive psychic structure in psychotherapy: The core conflictual relationship theme. In N. Freedman & S. Grand (Eds.), *Communicative structures and psychic structures* (pp. 367-395). New York: Plenum Press.

Luborsky, L. (1990a). A guide to the CCRT method. In L. Luborsky & P. Crits-Christoph (Eds.), *Understanding transference — The CCRT method.* New York: Basic Books.

Luborsky, L. (1990b). The Relationship Anecdotes Paradigms (RAP) interview as a versatile source of narratives. In L. Luborsky & P. Crits-Christoph (Eds.), *Understanding transference — The CCRT method.* New York: Basic Books.

Luborsky, L. (in press) Core Conflictual Relationship Theme (CCRT) — A basic case formulation method. In T. Eells (Eds), *Handbook of psychotherapy case formulation.* New York: Guilford.

Luborsky, L., Crits-Christoph, P., Mintz, J., & Auerbach, A. (1988). *Who will benefit from psychotherapy? Predicting therapeutic outcomes.* New York: Basic Books.

Luborsky, L., & Crits-Christoph, P. (Eds.). (1990). *Understanding transference — the CCRT method* New York: Basic Books.

Luborsky, L., Crits-Christoph, P., & Mellon, J. (1986). The advent of objective measures of the transference concept. *Journal of Consulting and Clinical Psychology, 54*, 39-47.

Luborsky, L., Mellon, J., Alexander, K., van Ravenswaay, P., Childress, A., Levine, F., Cohen, K.D., Hole, A.V., Ming, S., Crits-Christoph, P., Levine, F.J., & Alexander, K. (1985). A verification of Freud's grandest clinical hypothesis: The transference. *Clinical Psychology Review, 5*, 231-246.

Main, M., Kaplan, N., & Cassidy, J. (1985). Security in infancy, childhood and adulthood: A move to the level of representation. In I. Bretherton & E. Walters (Eds.), *Growing points of attachment theory and research. Monographs of the Society for Research in Childhood Development, 50*, (1-2, Serial No. 209), 66-104.

Murray, H. (1938). *Explorations in personality. A clinical and experimental study of fifty men of college age.* Oxford: Oxford University Press.

Noam, G. (1991). Beyond Freud and Piaget: Biographical worlds — interpersonal self. In T. Wren (Ed.), *The moral domain* (pp. 360-399). Cambridge: MIT Press.

Reiser, M. (1984). *Mind, brain body: Toward a convergence of psychoanalysis and neurobiology.* New York: Basic Books.

Seligman, M.E.P. (1991). *Learned optimism.* New York: Pocket Books.

Seligman, M., Kamaen, L., & Nolen-Hoeksema, S. (1988). Explanatory style across the life span: Achievement and health. In E. Hetherington, R. Lerner, & M. Perlmutter (Eds.), *Child development in life-span perspective* (pp. 91-114). Hillsdale, NJ: Lawrence Erlbaum Associates.

Sroufe, L.A. (1983). Infant-caregiver attachment and patterns of adaptation in pre-school:

The roots of maladaptation and competence. In M. Perlmutter (Ed.), *Minnesota Symposium on Child Psychology Vol. 16: Development and policy concerning children with special needs* (pp. 41-81). Hillsdale, NJ: Lawrence Erlbaum Associates.

Sroufe, L., & Fleeson, J. (1986). Attachment and the construction of relationships. In W. Hartug & Z. Rubin (Eds.), *Relationships and development* (pp. 51071). New York: Cambridge University Press.

Stern, D. (1985). *The interpersonal world of the infant*. New York: Basic Books.

Stern, D. (1989). The representations of relational patterns: Development considerations. In A. Sameroff & R. Emde (Eds.), *Relationship disturbances in early childhood* (pp. 52-69). New York: Basic Books.

Tomkins, S. (1987). Script theory. In V. Arnoff, A.A. Rabin, & R. Zucker (Eds.). *The emergence of personality* (pp. 147-216). New York: Springer-Verlang.

Tronick, E. (1982). Affectivity and sharing. In E. Tronick (Ed.), *Social interchange in infancy* (pp. 1-8). Baltimore, MD: University Park Press.

Waldinger, R., Guastella, F., Diguer, L., Luborsky, L., & Hauser, S. (1995). *Ego development and relationship themes in adolescence*. Manuscript in preparation.

Witkin, H.A. (1949). Sex differences in perception. *Transactions of the New York Academy of Sciences, 12*, 22-26.

12

Relatedness and Self-Definition: A Dialectic Model of Personality Development

Sidney J. Blatt
Yale University

Rachel B. Blass
The Hebrew University of Jerusalem

Personality development can be viewed as evolving from a complex dialectic transaction between two fundamental developmental processes: (a) the development of increasingly stable, enduring, and mutually satisfying interpersonal relationships; and (b) the development of a differentiated, consolidated, stable, realistic, essentially positive, and integrated self-definition or identity (Blatt, 1990, 1991; Blatt & Blass, 1990, 1992; Blatt & Shichman, 1983). This view of personality development provides an opportunity to appreciate more fully the important role that interpersonal relationships play in personality development, from the infant's early dependence on his or her mother to the establishment of mature, mutually satisfying, reciprocal, intimate relationships in adulthood. Although most approaches to personality development agree that the individual comes into being through interaction with significant others throughout the life cycle, many theories of personality development usually focus primarily on only one of the two dimensions of this developmental process – either on identity or relatedness.

Most theoretical and empirical work in psychology have addressed primarily the development of the individual as a self-contained unit, striving toward individuation, differentiation, autonomy, identity, and achievement. In this approach, development is viewed as a process by which innate capacities find optimal expression in the attainment of various levels of the self as separate, independent, and functional. Developmental research usually focuses primarily on issues of separation-individuation and the establishment of an identity. Although relationships with others are seen as playing a significant role in this process, such as in learning, imitation, and internalization or interiorization (Piaget, 1945/1962), the establishment and maintenance of relationships are not viewed as developmental goals in their own right. Rather, it is disengagement from others that is seen as resulting in a concomitant enrichment of the self expressed in increasing autonomy, independence, and achievement, which are viewed as the hallmarks of development.

In contrast to these theories that emphasize primarily separation, individuation, and the development of identity, other formulations focus primarily on attachment and the development of relatedness, and attempt to understand personality development primarily from the perspective of the individual in interaction with others. In this approach, the self is viewed as being comprised of, and its integrity and continuity being maintained by, the gestalt of past and present interpersonal relationships. The individual is viewed as motivated primarily by the seeking of interpersonal contact and relatedness, and psychological development is defined primarily by the quality of this interpersonal relatedness. The emergence of dependence, care, affection, intimacy, mutuality, and reciprocity are considered the hallmarks of development; emphasis is on the individual's relationships with others rather than on the development of the sense of self. The autonomous and independent sense of sense of self that emerges in the course of development is viewed not as a goal in its own right, but as a necessary by-product in the process of development toward increasingly mature interpersonal relationships.

Although many developmental theories have focused primarily on either self or relatedness, others have stressed the simultaneous development of both of these processes. The development of a sense of self and the capacity for relatedness are both viewed as basic developmental dimensions. Freud, for example, throughout his work conceptualized human existence in terms of the fundamental polarity of individuation versus attachment. In *Civilization and its Discontents* Freud (1930) wrote:

> the development of the individual seems to . . . be a product of the interaction between two urges, the urge toward happiness, which we usually call "egotistic," and the urge toward union with others in the community, which we call "altruistic." . . . The[se] two urges, the one towards personal happiness and the other towards union with other human beings must struggle with each other in every individual; and so, also, the two processes of individual and of cultural development must stand in hostile opposition to each other and mutually dispute the ground. (pp. 140-141)

In this manuscript, Freud also distinguished between "The man who is predominantly erotic . . . [and] give[s] first preference to his emotional relationships to other people . . . [and] the narcissistic man, who inclines to be self-sufficient . . . [and] seek[s] his main satisfactions in his mental processes . . . " (pp. 83-84). Earlier, Freud (e.g., 1914, 1926) contrasted object with ego libido, as well as libidinal instincts in the service of attachment with aggressive instincts necessary for autonomy, mastery, and self-definition. And Freud, of course, is often quoted as having noted that the two major goals in life are to love and work. Loewald (1962, pp. 490-491), in an overview of Freud's vast contributions, noted how Freud recognized and insisted from the very beginning to the end that this fundamental polarity of "individuation and primary narcissistic union" is "inherent in human existence," and that Freud attempted to conceptualize this polarity in various formulations such as in "his dualistic conception of instincts, of human nature, and of life itself." Loewald also noted that this duality or polarity of individuation and primary unity with the object in the environment is a basic phenomena of human development that underlies the significance of separation and internalization as basic developmental processes.

Numerous other psychoanalytic theorists including Adler (1951), Rank (1929), and Horney (1945, 1950) articulated a similar distinction. Bowlby (1969, 1973, 1988) explored libido and aggression as emotional substrates of human personality development, expressed in striving for attachment and separation (see also Bretherton, chapter 1, this volume). Balint (1959), from an object relations perspective, discussed two fundamental tendencies: (a) one toward clinging or connectedness ("ocnophilic"), and (b) the other toward self-sufficiency ("philobatic"). Shor and Sanville (1978), based on Balint's formulations, discussed psychological development as an oscillation between "necessary connectedness" and "inevitable separations"—between "intimacy and autonomy."

A wide range of nonpsychoanalytic personality theorists, using a variety of terms, also discuss interpersonal relatedness and self-definition as two central processes in personality development. Angyal (1941, 1951) and Bakan (1966), for example, discussed surrender or communion as a fundamental desire for union in which the person seeks to merge or join with other people, society, and with the inanimate environment in order to achieve a greater sense of integration and synthesis. Surrender and communion refer to a stable dimension of personality organization directed toward interdependent relationships in which themes of dependency, mutuality, and unity define a basic dimension in life. Both Angyal and Bakan also discussed autonomy and agency, as a basic striving toward individuation—a seeking of separation from others and from an attachment to the physical environment, as well as a fuller differentiation within oneself. Autonomy and agency refer to a stable dimension of functioning that emphasizes separation, individuation, control, self-definition and autono-mous achievement—a striving for uniqueness and the expression of one's capacities and self-interest (Friedman & Booth-Kewley, 1987).

Research investigators in personality development have also made similar distinctions. Gilligan (1982) stressed the importance of including interper-sonal responsibility as well as an emphasis on investment in rights and principles of justice in formulations of moral development. McAdams (1980) discussed the importance of motives for affiliative or intimacy and achievement or power (McClelland, 1980, 1986; Winter, 1973). Wiggins (1991), an empirically based personality investigator, argued that com-munion and agency should serve as primary conceptual coordinates for the measurement of interpersonal behavior and as the fundamental coordinates of a trait language for describing personality functioning. He noted that the circumflex and the five factor models of personality are "derived from the meta-concepts of agency and communion" (p. 107). Although Wiggins commented that agency and communion do not, by themselves, capture the broad spectrum of individual differences that characterize human transac-tions, he concluded that they are "propaedeutic to the study of these additional determinants of interpersonal behavior" (p. 109).

Thus, there is considerable consensus, from a number of theoretical perspectives, that normal personality development and organization in-volves an integration of these two basic dimensions: the capacity for interpersonal relatedness and the development of self-definition (Stewart & Malley, 1987). Angyal (1951) and Bakan (1966) stressed that the major task in life is to achieve a compromise and balance between these two "auton-omous" forces so that both are represented fully in one's experiences. Increased autonomy, mastery, and a capacity to govern one's life and environment is best done not by force or violence, but by understanding and respect for laws and rules of the social matrix. Similarly, a loving relationship not only requires relinquishing one's autonomy and agency to some degree, but it also requires a capacity for mastery of one's environ-ment, resourcefulness, and self-reliance, without which a relationship is in danger of deteriorating into helpless dependency, exploitation, and posses-siveness. Angyal and Bakan emphasized the importance of both differen-tiation and integration in psychological development in the emergence of dimensions of relatedness and self-definition, and the constructive resolu-tion of these polarities. Kobassa (1982) discussed a blend of communion and agency, or intimacy and power, as central to the development of psychological well-being and hardiness. McAdams (1985) found that an integration of power and intimacy motivation in Thematic Apperception Test (TAT) stories was correlated with a capacity to portray constructive action scripts that are future oriented and high on generativity. Power and intimacy are integrated by establishing a clear sense of self and an intimate exchange with others. A mature identity for McAdams (1985) is based on a sense of "sameness and continuity which provided unity and purpose" (p. 28).

Many of these theoretical formulations describe how these two basic dimensions develop in parallel or how they interact. Modell (1968), for example, stated that "With the painful acceptance of the limitations of other persons and an acceptance of separateness, there is established a capacity for a more mature form of loving, that is, a love relationship that can be maintained in the face of privation and ambivalence" (p. 60). Bowlby (1969, 1973) considered the complimentary development of autonomy and connectedness (of attachment and separation) and Schafer (1968) discussed the importance of maintaining a balance between dependency and self-sufficiency for the attainment of optimal personal development. The relationship between these two dimensions, however, goes well beyond parallel processes or a simple interaction, but rather involves a complex dialectical process along two developmental lines in which progress in each line is essential for progress in the other (Blatt & Shichman, 1983). A dynamic tension exists between communion and agency (Bakan, 1966), between surrender and autonomy (Angyal, 1951). Personality development evolves through an oscillation between necessary connectedness and inevitable separateness in a dialectic spiral or helix that interweaves two fundamental dimensions of personality development—relatedness and self-definition (Shor & Sanville, 1978). The development of an increasingly differentiated, integrated, and mature sense of self is contingent on establishing satisfying interpersonal experiences, and, conversely, the development of increasingly mature and satisfying interpersonal relationships depends on the development of more mature self-definition and identity. In normal personality development, these two developmental processes evolve in an interactive, reciprocally balanced, mutually facilitating fashion from birth through senescence (Blatt & Shichman, 1983).

Klein (1976) stressed the importance of an integration of individuality and affiliation and its expression in the development of the concept of "we." As Klein noted:

> The terminology of subject and object has contributed to misleading conceptualizations of selfhood and especially to obscuring its We aspect. The traditional view of man as becoming gradually aware of himself as subject confronting others as objects may be applicable *morphologically* but it does not describe the dynamic whole. (pp. 178-179)

Klein was particularly interested in the establishment of identity as a "specifically human necessity" that involved two aspects: an autonomous distinction from others as a locus of action and decision (agency), and a "we-ness" as a necessary part of the self that transcends one's autonomous actions. Klein commented: One must feel "both separate and a part of an entity beyond itself. . . . Identity must always be defined as having aspects of both separateness and membership in a more encompassing entity, and as developing functions that reflect one's role in a relationship with a larger entity" (p. 177). Klein viewed psychoanalysis and much of psychology as being predominantly concerned with a concept of self as a separate, autonomous unit and as not addressing the importance of the development of a sense of "belonging to" or of "we-ness." Klein argued for the need in psychoanalysis to develop a theory of the "wego" to parallel its theory of the ego and to include in its developmental theory a concept of we that emerges from the dialectic interaction between the development of a sense of self as separate and autonomous as well as related to others.

Investigators, mainly in infant research, have begun to elaborate the conceptualization of this dialectic developmental process. Emde (1988), in discussing the dialectic between the development of a sense of self and of relatedness, believed that the emergence of this dual emphasis is reflective of an important theoretical development: "It is perhaps ironic that in our age, so preoccupied with narcissism and self, [that] we are beginning to see different aspect of psychology, a "we" psychology in addition to a "self" psychology. I draw our attention to the fact that this represents a profound change in our world view" (p. 36). The profound change of which Emde spoke involves an expansion of concepts of the self-system to include the we dimension. Emde discussed three dynamic aspects of the self-system: the experience of self, the experience of the other (e.g., attachment figure), and the experience of the self-with-other or we. This development of a mature sense of "we" emerges from a complex transaction of the two fundamental developmental lines.

The purpose of this chapter is to explore further the development of these two fundamental developmental lines — relatedness and self-definition (or individuality) — as well as their complex dialectic interaction leading to psychological maturity. We attempt to elucidate aspects of the complex relationship between these two developmental tasks of relatedness and self-definition by using Erikson's epigenetic psychosocial model to define major nodal points in the development of a sense of self and a capacity for relatedness, and to consider how these two developmental processes interact in a mutually facilitating dialectic interaction. A reformulation of Erikson's epigenetic psychosocial developmental model provides an opportunity to appreciate more fully the relative roles of self-definition and relatedness at various points in psychological development and how different aspects of these two fundamental developmental lines are eventually integrated later in the life cycle in a "we" system (Emde, 1988; Klein, 1976; Stern, 1985), or a sense of "self-in relation" (Gilligan, 1988, chapter 9, this volume; Surrey,

1985), or "ensembled individualism" (Sampson, 1985, 1988). We also seek to demonstrate how these formulations about personality development can facilitate the investigation of aspects of psychopathology and of the therapeutic process.

A MODEL OF THE DIALECTIC BETWEEN RELATEDNESS AND SELF-DEFINITION

Through a linear series of hierarchical stages, Erikson (1959, 1963, 1964, 1968, 1977, 1982) described the individual's progress from infantile dependency through stages of identification and socialization toward increasing individuation. Although Erikson stressed the importance of interpersonal relations for the facilitation of psychological development, his emphasis is consistently on the antecedents and consequences of the attainment of self-identity. Such statements as "true engagement with the other is the result and test of firm self delineation" (Erikson, 1968, p. 167) reflect the special status that Erikson assigned to the stage of identity formation and, in a broader sense, to the process of separation and individuation. Erikson's overriding emphasis on individuation, to what appears, at times, to be a neglect of the attachment task of development, has been discussed as a major limitation of Erikson's epigenetic model (Blatt & Shichman, 1983; Carlson, 1972; Franz & White 1985; Gilligan 1982; Surrey, 1985).

Although attachment or relatedness has not received sufficient consideration in much of personality theory and in Erikson's formulations because of his dominant interest in identity, it is important to note that Erikson's model is not exclusively an identity theory of personality development. Attachment is, in fact, embedded in his model. Segments of Erikson's formulations call attention to the important of issues of relatedness. In discussing identity formation in one of his later statements, Erikson (1982), for example, noted: "a mature sense of identity means a sense of being at one with oneself as one grows and develops; and it means, at the same time, a sense of affinity with a community's sense of being at one with its future as well as its history—or mythology" (pp. 27-28). This requires both individuation and connectedness, an integration of identity formation and interdependence, a continuity as well as a separation from one's past and one's environment, and a sense of the future and the capacity to establish new connections. As Erikson (1982) noted further:

Epigenetically speaking, of course, nobody can quite "know" who he or she "is" until promising partners in work and love have been encountered and tested. Yet, the basic patterns of identity must emerge from (1) the selective affirmation and repudiation of an individual's childhood identifications; and

(2) the way in which the social process of the times identifies young individuals—at best recognizing them as persons who had to become the way they are and who, being the way they are, can be trusted. (p. 72)

The importance of attachment tasks, however, is underplayed in Erikson because of his unidimensional linear schematization of psychological development that places identity consolidation as the central goal or result of normal development. Within such a context, attachment and interpersonal relatedness appear to play secondary roles, those of facilitating, and as by-products of, identity development. Thus, attachment tasks in the Erikson model are intermediary links in the process of development toward individuation. Mature relationships are what occurs in the attainment of individuation (Blatt & Blass, 1990). Clear emergence of an emphasis on attachment in Erikson's developmental process is also limited by the way he (1959) uses the terms *self* or *identity* to refer generally to the individual as a separate and autonomous agent. Relationships are not commonly emphasized in Erikson's concept of identity; rather, the emphasis is on the "integration of perceptions of oneself as separate and distinct from the other" (Mussen, Conger, & Kagan, 1979, p. 495).

Self-identity, however, emerges through an ongoing dialectic between the self as separate and the self as experienced in its attachments to objects. Recognition of the role of attachment in the development of identity, the understanding of the dialectic between the development of relatedness and of self-definition, and the postulation that these constitute two distinct but interactive lines of development are the basis for our modification of Erikson's psychosocial developmental model. In the following section, we propose a reformulation of Erikson's model with particular emphasis on these two developmental lines, as well as their eventual integration.

The inclusion of a developmental dimension of attachment and intimacy as an integral aspect of personality development, and as a complement to the more usual emphasis on individuation, self-definition, and identity that exists in Erikson's model, is consistent with the call by feminist theorists (e.g., Chodorow, 1978, 1989; Gilligan, 1982; Miller, 1976, 1984) to correct the frequent failure to give equal status to the development of interpersonal relatedness in most theories of personality development. The reformulation of this important theoretical model allows us to understand what has been missing in many formulations of personality development. Aspect of both attachment and separation, or relatedness and self-definition, are discussed in Erikson's formulations in the context of self-development. By overcoming the limitations of the linearity and unidimensionality of this model, we can appreciate more fully the complex and essential dialectic relationship of attachment and separation in the stages and processes of personality development.

The first step in this reformulation, based on the interpersonal psycho-analytic formulations of Sullivan (e.g., 1953), is to include in Erikson's model an additional stage of cooperation versus alienation occurring around the time of the initial resolution of the oedipal crisis and the development of cooperative peer play at the age of about 4 to 6 years, and to place this stage at the appropriate point in the developmental sequence, between phallic "initiative versus guilt" and the "industry versus inferiority" of latency (Blatt & Shichman 1983). Erikson's eight-stage linear developmental line can now be differentiated into two parallel developmental lines of relatedness and self-definition. One developmental line, relatedness, includes the stages of trust versus mistrust, cooperation versus alienation, and intimacy versus isolation. The other developmental line, self-definition, includes Erikson's stages of autonomy versus shame, initiative versus guilt, industry versus inferiority, identity versus role diffusion, generativity versus stagnation, and integrity versus despair.

As illustrated in Fig. 12.1, development along these two lines, relatedness and self-definition or attachment and separation evolve through a complex interactive process. The evolving capacities for autonomy, initiative, and industry in the individuality developmental line, develop in interaction with the development of a capacity for relatedness — to engage with and trust another, to cooperate and collaborate in activities with parents and peers (e.g., play), to develop a close friendship with a same-gender chum (Sullivan, 1953), and eventually to experience and express feelings of mutuality, intimacy, and reciprocity in a mature adult relationship. In normal development, there is a coordination between the evolving capacities along these two developmental lines of relatedness and self-definition. Erikson initially emphasized interpersonal relatedness in his discussion of trust versus mistrust, followed by autonomy versus shame and initiative versus guilt of the self-definition line. This is now followed by a shift back to the relatedness line, to the new additional stage of cooperation versus alienation, and then back to the self-definition line, with the stage of industry versus inferiority. The following stage — identity versus role diffusion — involves self-definition, but it is also a stage in which the central developmental task is the integration of development that has occurred along the two lines. This is followed by intimacy versus isolation, again clearly a stage of interpersonal relatedness, followed by another stage of self-definition, generativity versus stagnation. The process culminates in the stage of integrity versus despair with the ultimate integration between relatedness and self-definition (Blatt & Blass, 1990). Although these two developmental lines interact throughout the life cycle and are ultimately integrated later in development, they remain relatively independent of each other through the early developmental years.

It is important to note that these two fundamental developmental processes of relatedness and self-definition and the changes they undergo are clearly shaped by the nature of the individual's actual relationships and are also expressed in the relationships he or she subsequently develops. Psychoanalytic investigators, for example, note a major shift in the child, at about the age of 5, from a focus on a separate dyadic relationship with each parent alone, to a beginning appreciation of a triadic interpersonal structure and his or her role in a family system with contrasting and coordinating relationships with each parent, who also have a relationship with one another. As a consequent of this beginning awareness of triadic relationships, the child is increasingly able to consider interpersonal relationships in comparative terms. The child's thinking is no longer restricted to simple contrasts (e.g., pleasure–pain or issues of power, control, and autonomy) that exist in a dyadic relationship, but the child can begin to reflect upon and compare and contrast the type and quality of the relationship he or she has with each parent and that the parents have with each other. Thinking is no longer just immediate, direct, and literal. Rather, qualities of self and others can be varied and reconstructed in new and complex ways. Thinking is no longer restricted to reproductions of concrete past experiences, but the child can begin to anticipate and plan for activities and events never experienced directly before (Blatt, 1983, 1990). The child not only has his or her own point of view, but now can also begin to appreciate the perspective of others and eventually realize that he or she is a unique person among all others, with a different and unique perspective (Feffer, 1959, 1970; Inhelder & Piaget, 1959/1964; Laurendeau & Pinard, 1962, 1970; Piaget, 1937/1954, 1961/1969).

The development of triadic interpersonal structures described by psychoanalytic theorists in the internalizations of the oedipal phase in many ways

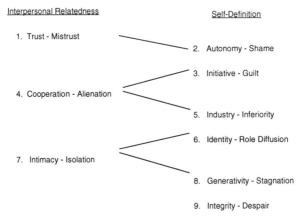

FIG. 12.1. The dialectic interaction of interpersonal relatedness and self-definition implicit in E. Erikson's psychosocial model.

corresponds to what occurs in cognitive development, of what Piaget (1937/1954) called operational thought with its capacity for reversibility, transformation, and conservation. Addressing primarily the coordination of the relationship among dimensions of inanimate objects, Piaget's and Werner's formulations of the development of concrete operational thought at about 6 years of age (Piaget, 1937/1954; Werner, 1948/1957; Werner & Kaplan, 1963) identify the emergence of a new cognitive schema in which the child is able to coordinate effectively the relationships among several dimensions. The child now understands the processes involved in the transformation of an object and has developed the capacity of appreciating reversibility and conservation. This is consistent with the psychoanalytic observations of a shift to triadic interpersonal relations in the oedipal phase (Blatt, 1983, 1990, 1995). The increased coordination and integration of aspects of individuality (or self-definition) and relatedness at age 5 or 6, with the beginning resolution of the oedipal crisis and the advent of concrete operational thought, is expressed in an emerging sense of "we." This sense of we becomes consolidated in peer relationships in latency with experiences of cooperation in the relatedness line and with experiences of industry and exploration in the self-definition line.

The coordination of the two developmental lines leading to the integration of concepts of self and of others in a concept of we, first expressed in concrete manifest terms at the beginning of operational thought at age 6 and consolidated during latency, occurs in more formal or abstract terms as the child begins to deal with complex internal psychological properties of the self and others in early adolescence, around the age of 11 or 12. The development of formal operational thought and the increased appreciation of internal psychological qualities, defines yet another level in the coordination and integration of concepts of self and other — of individuality and relatedness. Identity, although partly a stage in the development of self-definition, is also a cumulative, integrative stage in which the capacity to cooperate and share with others is coordinated with the capacity for sustained goal-directed, task-oriented, activity that has emerged from the development of autonomy, initiative, and industry. Identity involves a synthesis and integration of individuality and relatedness — the internality and intentionality that develops as part of individuality and self-definition as well as the capacity and desire to participate in a social group with an appreciation of what one has to contribute to, and gain from, participating in the collective, without losing one's individuality in the collective or the relationship. Thus, in this sense, Erikson's more advanced stage of identity versus role diffusion is a period of synthesis of mature integrated expression of individuality and relatedness (Blatt & Blass, 1990, 1992).

As Erikson described, the synthesis of these two developmental lines in an integrated self-identity in adolescence leads to more mature expression of relatedness in intimate relationships characterized by mutuality and reciprocity, as well as to fuller expression of individuality in generativity with sustained commitment to enduring values and goals. The integration of individuality and relatedness in an identity results in a capacity to establish a mutual and reciprocal relationship with another because one is now aware that he or she has something unique and special to offer and share with the other. This awareness partly derives from a sense of self-worth, pride, and competence that has previously evolved during the various earlier stages of the individuality developmental line as well as from an appreciation of the unique needs of the other. The capacity for intimacy also derives from a growing recognition of one's own needs and limitations, not only in what one has to offer the other, but also of the enrichment one can gain from the other and the pleasures in sharing and the advantages of reciprocity. Likewise, generativity, as formulated by Erikson, also involves extending beyond one's own self-interest and dedicating oneself to broader goals, values, and principles, including contributing to others and society. Thus, Erikson's stages of intimacy and generativity—the capacity to form a mutual and reciprocal relationship with another and to dedicate oneself to long-term principles and goals that extend beyond one's self-interest—are expressions of an integration of earlier developmental levels of individuality and relatedness that have been consolidated in a mature identity—in a "self-in-relation" (Gilligan, 1982, 1989; Surrey, 1985), an "ensembled individualism" (Sampson, 1985, 1988), or a full sense of "we." The later two stages of intimacy and generativity are mature expressions of a synthesis of the relatedness and self-definitional developmental lines. A further and more complete synthesis of relatedness and individuality ultimately occurs once again later in the life cycle, in the stage of integrity (Blatt & Blass, 1990). Integrity involves a more encompassing integration of the two developmental lines based on the gradual and natural convergence of intimacy and generativity as more mature and integrated expressions of each of the two developmental lines.

IMPLICATIONS FOR DIMENSIONS OF PERSONALITY DEVELOPMENT

Careful consideration of the two psychological developmental lines of relatedness and self-definition in our revision and elaboration of Erikson's model of psychosocial development enables us to appreciate more fully some of the details of the processes involved in the complex synergistic transaction of the two fundamental developmental lines of relatedness and self-definition.

Examination of Erikson's terms denoting the first three stages of the self-definition developmental line (autonomy, initiative, and industry), as well as the two later stages of integration (identity and integrity), reveals that he is actually describing the development of two fundamental aspects of the self: *an expressive mode of self* and *self-feeling*. Erikson contrasted (anal) autonomy with shame; (phallic) initiative with guilt; and (latency) industry with feelings of inferiority. These pairings are not a demarcation of polar opposites as in the juxtaposition of trust with mistrust at the oral stage or in intimacy with isolation in late adolescence, but the pairings are based on psychoanalytic psychosexual theory. The opposite of autonomy is not shame but a lack of autonomy; the opposite of shame is pride. The opposite of initiative is lack of initiative, and that of guilt is self-esteem. Finally, the opposite of industry is not inferiority but a lack of industriousness, whereas the opposite of inferiority is confidence. Thus, on one level Erikson is articulating behavioral expressions in the development of the self—autonomy, initiative, and industry—concepts that we refer to as an *expressive mode of self* (Blatt & Blass, 1990).

This expressive mode of self can be defined both from the perspective of the subject and/or the observer. In terms of the observer, the expressive mode of self is both an external behavioral manifestation of the self-experience (e.g., autonomy or initiative) and the individual's capacity to express him or herself under certain interpersonal conditions (e.g., an ability to act freely and efficiently in the absence of a guiding authoritative figure). Each term denotes a behavioral activity that can be defined as a continuum (e.g., autonomy can range from a low to a high degree of autonomy). The expressive mode of self at each of the stages corresponds to what Shapiro (1965) referred to as "a way of functioning, an attitude, and a frame of mind" (p. 11).

Erikson articulated yet another dimension in the development of self-definition in his counterposing a series of self-feelings with each of the behavioral expressive modes of self. He discussed shame in relation to efforts to achieve autonomy, guilt was associated with initiative, and feelings of inferiority with industry. We refer to these concepts as *self-feelings*—to experiences of the self in a broader sense, to the most basic feelings that one has regarding one's being (Blatt & Blass, 1990). These self-feelings refer to the experience of self that prevails during the individual's active expression—that is, the individual's attitudes toward such expression. Earlier in development, these self-feelings are experienced as polarities of shame and pride, guilt and self-esteem, and inferiority and confidence.[1]

In the later stages of the self-definition developmental line, at generativity

---

[1]Erikson (e.g., 1959, p. 113) referred to "self-feelings," but he seemed to assign them a different and much less prominent role in the developmental process.

and in the integrative stages of identity and integrity, the concepts denoting the expressive mode of self and self-feelings are closer to being opposites. Thus, generativity versus stagnation, identity versus role diffusion, and integrity versus despair reflect a greater integration of the two different expressions of the sense of self. This convergence of the two aspects of self, expressive mode and self-feeling, suggests that a fundamental change has taken place in the developmental process. It is no longer necessary to maintain the distinction between the two aspects of self when discussing the later stages in the self-definition developmental line. The terms to describe the development of the self in these later stages have become bipolar like the pairs of terms in the relatedness developmental line (i.e., trust–mistrust, cooperation–alienation, and intimacy–isolation) that have remained polar opposites throughout psychological development.

All three components of development — the quality of the attachment relationships, the expressive mode of self, and self-feelings — are internalized as the individual matures toward more complex levels of psychological development. Loewald (1980) defined internalization as "the process by which interactions within the original mother–child psychic matrix, and later between the growing individual and his environment, become transmuted into internal interaction constituting the individual psyche and creating, maintaining and developing an internal world" (p. 167). Our formulations of the dialectic developmental process now enable us to define more precisely what it is in the interaction that is transformed into internal processes and psychological structures. Internalizations in the relatedness developmental line are based on the quality of the relationship, both real and fantasized, between self and the object, expressed in a sense of trust, cooperation, mutuality, and intimacy that emerges in interaction with significant objects. In the self-definition developmental line, the expressive modes of self and the concomitant self-feelings that emerge within the relationship (Blass & Blatt, 1992) are internalized and become aspects of the self.

But a marked change occurs in the processes of personality development beginning in adolescence with the focus on the integration of the two developmental lines. Integration eventually replaces internalization as the central process through which psychological growth occurs. The increased emphasis on integration in adolescence indicates a fundamental shift in the mechanisms of psychological development from internalization to integration. Erikson (1968) noted this shift in his description of the identity stage in adolescence as involving "the integration of the identity elements ascribed . . . to the childhood stages" (p. 128). He noted that "Identity formation, finally, begins when the usefulness of identification ends. It arises from the selective repudiation and mutual assimilation of childhood identifications and their absorption in a new configuration . . . [into] a new, unique gestalt which is more than the sum of its parts" (pp. 158-159). The successful outcome of the establishment of this new configuration is an integrated sense of self-identity that contains dimensions of both self-definition and relatedness—"a self-in-relation." Thus, after identity formation, the relation between the two developmental lines becomes more intricate. Although generativity and intimacy can be assigned to the separateness and attachment lines respectively, the degree of integration that occurs in identify formation will have a major effect on the extent to which the capacity for generativity reflects both self-definition and attachment, and on the degree to which the capacity for intimacy is based on a loss of oneself within the relationship as well as an ongoing awareness of one's self-definition and the uniqueness that one has to contribute to a relationship. The degree of integration in identity formation will also influence the later consolidation and "emotional integration" (Erikson, 1968, p. 139) of the final stage of integrity.

Psychological development can now be defined as a process in which an individual, through close relationships with significant others, internalizes aspects of both the quality of relatedness, functional capacities experienced in the expressive mode of self, and conscious and unconscious attitudes and feelings about various expressions of self that existed in relationships with significant others at different stages of development (Blatt & Blass, 1990). As illustrated in Fig. 12.2, consolidation and integration of these internalizations at each developmental phase provide the basis for progression to the next developmental phase.

To illustrate this developmental process we describe briefly the specifics of the dialectic interaction between the two fundamental developmental lines within our extension of the Erikson model, assuming relatively optimal conditions for healthy development.

The initial development of trust in the relatedness developmental line enables the child to begin the process of self-definition, first in asserting a degree of autonomy and independence from significant, need-gratifying, others. If this expression of autonomy is accompanied by feelings of pride rather than shame, the expression of autonomy become more proactive rather than reactive as the child enters the stage of initiative. The feelings of trust and the experiences of autonomy and pride, together with biological/cognitive maturation, prompt expressions of "initiative" in interactions with significant others. Mother and father consciously and unconsciously communicate their feelings about the various expressions of the child's initiative. Some expressions of initiative are responded to positively, others are neither supported nor encouraged, and parents actively disapprove of others. The relative balance of these experiences, and how approval and disapproval are expressed by each of the parents about the child's behavioral modes of self-expression (i.e., initiative), determine the quality of self-

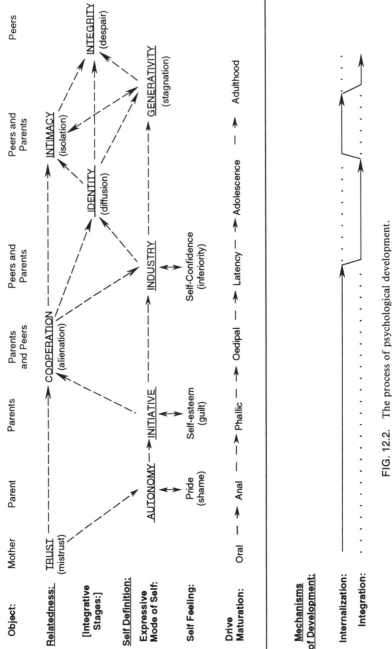

FIG. 12.2. The process of psychological development.

324

feelings (i.e., self-esteem) that are internalized. Internalizations that enhance the child's sense of self as a separate and functional individual with feelings of pride in his autonomy and a sense of self-esteem in being able to initiate activity in his or her own right, provides the child with the basis for establishing a new type of relatedness with his or her parents. If the parents have been appropriately responsive to the child's expressions of initiative (approving and supporting some while appropriately disapproving and setting limits on others), the child can begin to redefine his or her relatedness to both parents in terms of various efforts at initiative with one and/or both of them. These initiatives directed toward each of the parents contribute to establishing a new sense of relatedness in which experience of reciprocal sharing and cooperation gradually emerge, first with parents and later with peers.

Feelings of pride and self-esteem and experiences of a capacity for autonomy and initiative on the self-definition developmental line, along with experiences of trust and cooperation on the relatedness developmental line, contribute to the emergence of a more directed proactive capacity for industry and goal-directed activity. The expressive mode of self as industrious and the self-feeling of confidence eventually lead to the formation of an identity on the separateness developmental line as capable and functional. The experiences of trust in a powerful other and experiences of cooperation with parents and peers on the attachment developmental line contribute to the development of a sense of self in relation to others. Identity formation involves an integration and consolidation of the internalizations of various self-feelings, modes of self-expression, and qualities of relatedness that have emerged in earlier preadolescent developmental periods. Thus, identity is not only based on experiences of autonomy, initiative, and industry and on self feelings of pride, self-esteem, and confidence, but it also involves a sense of self in relation to others that has been established in earlier interpersonal experiences of trust and cooperation. This identity as a separate and capable individual who has positive and constructive relations with others, leads to more mature expressions of generativity and intimacy. These more mature expressions of self-definition and relatedness become more fully integrated later in adulthood leading to a sense of integrity.

Thus, active expression of new capacities attained at each developmental stage enables the individual to enter into new forms of interpersonal interaction. New forms of interaction are the consequence of both the activity of the caring agent and the active move of the individual toward the object (Blass & Blatt, 1992), one in which the individual strives for optimal levels of stimulation and opportunities for expression of newly found potential.[2] The new forms of interpersonal interaction created by the

---

[2]Such a view is consistent with studies by Stern (1977, 1983), Emde (1983), and others, and the formulations of Behrends and Blatt (1985), who stressed that the caring relationship is a reciprocal process in which both members of the dyad initiate and direct the interaction.

individual and his or her significant others open up the possibility for new forms of self-expression and new aspects of relationships that are then internalized in the formation of new psychological structures (see also Noam, chapter 6, this volume). This repeated developmental sequence, together with biologically determined maturation, contributes to the progressive evolvement of self-identity. We use the term *self-identity* as a superordinate concept to describe the gestalt of internalizations, which include the quality of the interpersonal relationships and the feelings toward the self acquired in these relationships.

IMPLICATIONS FOR PROCESSES OF PERSONALITY DEVELOPMENT

These reformulations and elaborations of the role of relatedness and self-definition in psychological development enable us to identify and appreciate more fully the important role of two basic mechanisms of psychological development — *internalization* and *integration* and their interplay throughout the life cycle.

Previously we presented the view (Behrends & Blatt, 1985; Blatt & Behrends, 1987) that certain basic mechanisms underlie the process of internalization at every developmental level and that these mechanisms instigate psychological growth throughout the life cycle. Two components of internalization are the establishment of a *gratifying involvement* and *experiences of incompatibility* with aspects of that gratifying involvement. Gratifying involvement refers to a relationship with a significant other in which the individual's stage-appropriate psychological needs are gratified. Thus, what constitutes a gratifying involvement changes with increasing maturation. In early infancy, for example, gratifying involvement refers to the mother's responding sufficiently and appropriately (a "good enough mother") to the infant's needs. In later years, gratifying involvement refers to relationships in which more mature needs are met, such as the need for autonomy and intimacy. Disruption of gratifying involvement ("an experienced incompatibility") occurs when the relationship no longer meets the needs of at least one of the participants, such as with object loss, deprivation of function, intrapsychic conflict, conflict between one's wishes and the demands and limitations of the environment, and maturational change (Behrends & Blatt, 1985). The establishment of a gratifying involvement is an essential precondition for internalization, but it is only with the disruption of this involvement that internalization takes place. The individual, in an attempt to preserve psychologically significant aspects of the relationship, gradually transforms those functions that the relationship had previously provided into his or her own enduring self-generative functions and characteristics (Behrends & Blatt, 1985).

Psychologically significant aspects of the relationship, gratifying elements as well as other distinguishing characteristics of the relationship, are internalized including conscious and unconscious feelings and attitudes experienced in the responses of significant others to behavioral modes of self that are expressed in the gratifying involvement. Gratifying aspects as well as additional nongratifying components of the relationship may be internalized. Thus, for example, hostile introjects (conscious and unconscious destructive elements in the relationship) may be internalized because they are intimately tied to some aspect of the relationship that was gratifying.

This formulation of internalization is applied and elaborated in our extension of Erikson's developmental model. This elaboration provides a context for the further study of the links between the internalization of behavioral modes of self-expression and the quality of relatedness, as well as between internalization and integration as processes of psychological development. Gratifying involvement with the object is an inherent component of the internalization process both on the attachment line and the separateness line (Blass & Blatt, 1992). On the attachment line, the gratifying interaction involves a sense of relatedness (e.g., trust, cooperation, or intimacy). Gratifying involvement on the separateness line is different and includes the object's reactions to the individual's expressions of his or her emerging sense of self as a separate, distinct, and functional entity. The individual internalizes his or her own expressions of functional capacities as well as the object's conscious and unconscious reactions to the individual's need for recognition and acceptance of the various elements of the expressive modes of self that occur in the relationship. Gratifying involvement in the self-definitional developmental line is based on the object's conscious and unconscious attitudes and feelings in response to the individual's phase specific expressive modes of self.

Gratifying involvement is experienced in both the quality of the attachment relationship and in the object's reactions to the individual's emerging expressions of a sense of self. As seen in the illustration presented above (p. 324), the acceptance of expressions of autonomy, initiative, and industry, and the sharing of experiences of trust, cooperation, mutuality, and intimacy determine the extent to which the relationship is experienced as gratifying.[3]

Although the internalization of the two aspects on the separation line (behavioral mode of expression and self-feelings) are interrelated, they also have a degree of independence: The self-feeling may affect the expressive

---

[3]This approach involves broadening of the concept of the "good enough mother" to include not only the mother as early caregiver, but all significant responses of caregivers not only to the individual's earliest self and relatedness needs, but to such needs throughout the life cycle.

mode of self, but the expressive mode is not completely dependent on the self-feeling. The internalization of these three aspects of psychological development (attachment, self-feeling, and expressive mode of self) provide the basis for the formation and consolidation of self-identity.

Innate biological forces are integral to the developmental processes of internalization. The oral, anal, phallic, oedipal, and latency periods, as well as the adolescent period with the resurgence of sexuality, involve powerful biological drives and needs that influence the interpersonal interactions in which the individual seeks expression, and through which internalization takes place. With the shift to integration at the stage of identity, the growing convergence of the developmental lines, and the consolidation of identity, the motivating forces become more psychological than biological. Colarusso and Nemiroff (1981), for example, viewed infancy and childhood as stimulated by the emergence of libidinal impulses and the appropriate frustration of these, whereas adult development is stimulated by psychological awareness. A similar view is proposed by Butler (1963) and Neugarten (1964), who called attention to a "decrease in ego energy" and a "shift in ego style" (Butler) and "increased interiority of the personality" (Neugarten) to describe the increased focus on internal psychological needs in the second half of the life cycle. This increased reflectivity and general shift from biological and concrete behavioral experiences to more internal psychological experiences is also consistent with Piaget's (1937/1954) observations of the development of formal operational thought in adolescence, in which the individual can now deal with abstract psychological dimensions such as values and attitudes.

We have focused on internalization and integration as the two primary mechanisms of psychological development, emphasizing the central role of integration in the later stages of identity and integrity. But internalization and integration are operative as the basic mechanisms of psychological development throughout the life cycle. An ongoing balance between the processes of internalization and integration is essential to normal development. Integration depends on the qualities of prior internalizations of aspects of self-definition and of increasingly mature relationships. But internalization without integration would also result in limited psychological development. The relative lack or failure of integration in preadolescence and adolescence would result in confusion that would be especially intense in the final adolescent phase—in identity formation. Integration of various internalizations is vital during this period. At adolescence and beyond, the major effect of deficient integration would be the emergence of a sense of meaninglessness, fragmentation, and a lack of purpose, partially expressed by *despair*, a term Erikson used to describe the negative outcome of the stage of integrity. In contrast, sufficient integration in adolescence and beyond creates a psychological context that enables the individual to develop coordinated, mutually facilitating, mature expressions of relatedness and self-definition, that enable him or her to cope effectively with the vicissitudes of later stages of the life cycle that begin with midlife crisis and continue throughout aging and senescence (see also Noam, chapter 6, this volume).

IMPLICATIONS FOR THE STUDY
OF PSYCHOPATHOLOGY

These formulations of a dialectic developmental relationship between relatedness and self-definition have important implications for understanding psychopathology because various forms of psychopathology can be understood as involving primarily either disruptions of experiences of relatedness or of self-definition.

Blatt (1974) delineated two primary types of depression on the basis of disruptions of relatedness or of self-definition. He distinguished an anaclitic or dependent depression derived primarily from disruptions of interpersonal relatedness in which there are feelings of loneliness and fears of abandonment, and an introjective or self-critical depression based primarily on disruptions of sense of self in which there are feelings of low self-esteem, worthlessness, failure, and guilt. These formulations of a dependent or interpersonal depression and a self-critical depression are congruent with Beck's (1983) formulations of sociotropic and autonomous types of depression and with the distinction by Arieti and Bemporad (1980) of a dominant other and a dominant goal type of depression (Blatt & Maroudas, 1992). Extensive research since the mid-1970s, using assessment procedures developed by Blatt and his colleagues (the Depressive Experiences Questionnaire [DEQ]; Blatt, D'Afflitti, & Quinlan, 1976, 1979) and by Beck and his colleagues (the Sociotropy and Autonomy Questionnaire [SAS]; Beck, Epstein, Harrison, & Emery, 1983), have demonstrated the validity of this distinction and its importance in understanding aspects of the onset, clinical course, and treatment of depression (Blatt & Homann, 1992; Blatt & Zuroff, 1992).

Subsequently, Blatt and Shichman (1983) extended these formulations about two types of depression to identify two primary configurations of psychopathology. They noted that several major forms of psychopathology, the infantile and the hysterical personality disorders, are "anaclitic" disorders that involve primary preoccupations about disruptions of interpersonal relatedness. The infantile personality is highly dependent and deeply concerned about the availability of caregivers. These patients tend to deny difficulties and avoid feelings of anger in order to maintain a dependent relationship. Hysterical personality disorders are also primarily preoccupied with issues of interpersonal relatedness, but at a somewhat more mature level in which they are concerned with the issues of being able to love as well as being loved. Their interpersonal difficulties involve concerns more about the reciprocity of relationships, in contrast to the more unidirectional concerns of the infantile personality in simply wishing to be cared for.

Blatt and Shichman (1983) also differentiated a number of clinical disorders as being primarily preoccupied with issues of self-definition. These "introjective" disorders, such as paranoia, obsessive compulsive disturbances, guilt-ridden depression, and phallic narcissism, are primarily preoccupied with issues of self-definition, ranging from paranoid patients' need to markedly differentiate themselves from others; to obsessive–compulsive patients' concerns about maintaining control, autonomy, and possessions; to preoccupations with issues of self-worth in guilt-ridden depression and phallic narcissism. Recent research (Levy et al., 1994; Ouimette, Klein, Anderson, Riso, and Lizardi, 1994) offer empirical support for these formulations. Using the Personality Disorders Examination (PDE; Loranger, 1988) to evaluate clinically different types of personality disorders in an inpatient sample, Levy and his colleagues found various types of personality disorders clustered around either anaclitic (relational) or introjective (self-definitional) issues, as measured by the DEQ (Blatt et al., 1976, 1979). Consistent with the theoretical formulations of Blatt and Shichman (1983), Levy et al. found that the Anaclitic dependence subscale of DEQ Factor I (Blatt, Zohar, Quinlan, Zuroff, & Mongrain, 1995) was significantly related to the number of criteria met for borderline, histrionic, and dependent personality disorders, and significantly and negatively correlated with the criteria for the schizoid personality disorder. Also consistent with theoretical expectations (Blatt & Shichman, 1983), Levy et al. found that DEQ self-criticism (Factor II) was significantly related to the number of criteria met for the schizoid, schizotypal, borderline, and narcissistic personality disorders. Ouimette et al. (1994), also using the Loranger (1988) PDE to assess personality disorders in outpatients, found that DEQ Dependency (Factor I) and the Sociotropy factor, as assessed by the PSI (Robins & Luten, 1991), a revision of the SAS, correlated significantly with dependent, histrionic, borderline, and dependent personality traits, and with a dependent personality disorder diagnosis. DEQ Self-criticism and Autonomy, in contrast, were significantly correlated with paranoid, narcissistic, obsessive–compulsive, schizoid, and passive-aggressive personality traits, and with a diagnosis of paranoid personality disorder. These findings suggest that it may be more effective to consider different forms of psychopathology, especially the various personality disorders, as disruptions of the normal developmental processes of relatedness and self-definition. Such an approach may also enable us to use dimensional measures to assess these processes of psychological disturbance, rather than the current method of considering different types of psychopathology in terms of symptoms and differences among various diagnostic categories defined by concepts of psychiatric disease (i.e., *DSM-III* and *DSM-IV*).

These findings suggest that the psychological processes of attachment and separation in the development of relatedness and self-definition in the dialectic model of personality development can facilitate our understanding of various forms of psychopathology as disruptions of these normal psychological processes. Even further, consideration of the various types of disruptions of the complex interweaving and integration of the quality of relatedness, expressive or functional modes of self, and self-feelings at various points in the developmental process, may allow for a refinement of the formulations of anaclitic and introjective forms of psychopathology. It is possible, for example, that some forms of introjective psychopathology could involve primarily an exaggerated emphasis on autonomy that derives from intense feelings of shame accompanied by defensive distancing from close interpersonal relationships, or from an exaggerated defensive sense of pride that makes one unable to accept realistic limitations as well as constructive criticisms from others. Consideration of the complex interplay among the quality of relatedness, modes of self-expression, and of self feelings at various points in the developmental process, as illustrated in Fig. 12.2, could facilitate a fuller appreciation of the subtle intricacies in the variations of feelings and behavior that are part of normal and disrupted psychological development. These distinctions may allow us to make further differentiations within the anaclitic and introjective types of psychopathology by identifying various developmental levels and dynamic organizations of adaptive and defensive functions within each of these two configurations of psychopathology.

These distinctions of the different dimensions of personality development may not only allow us to understand more fully the nature of different forms of psychopathology, but these formulations may facilitate the investigation of normal developmental processes. In a reanalysis of the data gathered as part of a study of mother–infant interaction of 36 mother-infant dyads when infants were 3 and 9 months of age (Feldman, 1993), for example, Feldman and Blatt (in press) found that a factor analysis of ratings of mother and infant behavior at both 3 and 9 months identified mother–infant dyadic play behavior (i.e., maternal imitation, dyadic reciprocity) and infant attention and initiation as two independent factors at both these times. These factors of infant behavior and mother–infant interaction identified at 3 and 9 months differentially predicted estimates of cognitive functioning and socioemotional behavior at 24 months of age. Consistent with the formulations of the role of relatedness and self-definition in personality development, infant play patterns at 3 months of age correlated significantly with the level of cognitive functioning at 24 months as assessed on the Stanford–Binet Intelligence Test, but not with estimates of socioemotional behavior. Ratings of mother–infant dyadic interaction patterns at 9 months, in contrast, correlated significantly with estimates of disruptions of socioemotional behavior at 24 months as assessed by the Achenbach Behavior Checklist, but not with estimates of intelligence. These findings suggest that one can identify precursors of the self-definitional developmental line in the infant's early attempts at assertion and initiative at 3 months, and precursors of the relatedness developmental line in the quality of the dyadic synchrony, bidirectionality, and reciprocity of the mother–infant interaction that emerges around 9 months of age.

IMPLICATIONS FOR UNDERSTANDING ASPECTS
OF THE THERAPEUTIC PROCESS

The differentiation of psychological disturbances as involving primarily a disruption of interpersonal relatedness or of self-definition has also contributed to further understanding of the therapeutic process in both short-term and more extended treatment. In one study (Blatt & Ford, 1994), seriously disturbed patients in long-term, intensive inpatient treatment were reliably classified as either anaclitic or introjective on the bases of clinical notes prepared at the beginning of treatment. Both anaclitic and introjective patients improved in a long-term, intensive, inpatient treatment program, but expressed this improvement in different ways. Introjective patients generally had significantly greater improvement than anaclitic patients and this improvement was expressed primarily in a reduction of manifest symptoms and by an increase in cognitive efficiency (increased IQ and diminished thought disorder as measured on the Rorschach). Improvement in anaclitic patients was generally more subtle and expressed primarily by improvement in their interpersonal relations with fellow patients and clinical staff and by a decrease in inappropriate, possibly autistic, representation of the human figure on the Rorschach.

Not only do anaclitic and introjective patients express therapeutic change in different ways, but they appear to be differentially responsive to different forms of therapeutic intervention. The Menninger Psychotherapy Research Project (e.g., Wallerstein, 1986) compared outpatients in psychotherapy and psychoanalysis. Despite numerous analyses of these data, no significant differences had been found between the outcome of these two types of treatment. In a reanalysis of this data, Blatt (1992) found that anaclitic patients had significantly greater improvement in psychotherapy than in psychoanalysis and that the reverse was true for introjective patients – they had significantly greater improvement in psychoanalysis than in psychotherapy. Thus, the distinction between these two types of patients, based on their primary preoccupation with issues of relatedness or self-definition, indicates that these two types of patients are differentially responsive to different types of therapeutic intervention and that they express their therapeutic gain in different ways (Blatt & Felsen, 1993).

The differentiation of concerns about relatedness and self-definition has also contributed to further understanding of the brief outpatient treatment of depression. The Treatment of Depression Collaborative Research Program (TDCRP), sponsored by the National Institute of Mental Health (NIMH), compared cognitive-behavior therapy (CBT), interpersonal therapy (IPT), imiprimine plus clinical management (IMI–CM), and placebo plus clinical management (PLA–CM) in the brief (16-session) outpatient treatment of depression. Minimal differences in therapeutic outcome were found between the four types of treatment evaluated in this project, except that IPT and IMI-CM appear to be somewhat more effective than CBT in treating severe depression. A significant treatment effect, however, was found in terms of personality attributes of the patients. Prior to beginning treatment, patients had been given the Dysfunctional Attitudes Scale (DAS; Weissman & Beck, 1978) which, as indicated by several independent factor analyses, identifies two primary factors of dysfunctional attitudes, need for approval and perfectionism (e.g., Cane, Olinger, Gotlib, & Kuiper, 1986; Imber et al., 1990). These two factors identified on the DAS correlate significantly with the two dimensions of depression as measured by the DEQ (Blatt et al., 1976, 1979) and the SAS (Beck et al., 1983). Although there were no significant interactions between these two pretreatment personality factors and outcome in the different types of treatment, the data revealed consistent indications that pretreatment perfectionism (or self-criticism) significantly impeded therapeutic response in all four types of treatment evaluated in this research project (Blatt, Quinlan, Pilkonis, & Shea, 1995).

SUMMARY

The theoretical formulations and research findings presented in this chapter indicate that relatedness and self-definition are central processes in personality development. The articulation of these two developmental lines have facilitated our understand of aspects of normal personality development, of various forms of psychopathology, and of the therapeutic process. These two developmental dimensions of relatedness and self-definition define a vital, lifelong, interactive developmental process that appears to capture a wide range of qualities that characterize normal as well as disrupted psychological processes. These two developmental dimensions may provide the basis for developing a theoretical model in which various forms of psychopathology can be considered as disruptions of normal developmental processes (Blatt, 1991, 1995; Blatt & Shichman, 1983), a theoretical model of psychopathology that may have etiologic as well as therapeutic implications.

REFERENCES

Adler, A. (1951). *The practice and theory of individual psychology* (P. Radin, Trans.). New York: Humanities Press.

Angyal, A. (1941). *Foundations for a science of personality*. New York: Viking.

Angyal, A. (1951). *Neurosis and treatment: A holistic theory* (E. Hanfmann & R. M. Jones, Eds.). New York: Wiley.

Arieti, S., & Bemporad, J. R. (1980). The psychological organization of depression. *American Journal of Psychiatry, 137*, 1360-1365.

Bakan, D. (1966). *The duality of human existence: An essay on psychology and religion*. Chicago: Rand McNally.

Balint, M. (1959). *Thrills and repression*. London: Hogarth Press.

Beck, A. T. (1983). Cognitive therapy of depression: New perspectives. In P. J. Clayton & J. E. Barrett (Eds.), *Treatment of depression: Old controversies and new approaches* (pp. 265-290). New York: Raven.

Beck, A. T., Epstein, N., Harrison, R. P., & Emery, G. (1983). *Development of the sociotropy-autonomy scale: A measure of personality factors in psychopathology*. Unpublished manuscript, University of Pennsylvania, University Park.

Behrends, R. S., & Blatt, S. J. (1985). Internalization and psychological development throughout the life cycle. *Psychoanalytic Study of the Child, 40*, 11-39.

Blass, R. B., & Blatt, S. J. (1992). Attachment and separateness: A theoretical context for the integration of self psychology with object relations theory. *The Psychoanalytic Study of the Child, 47*, 189-203.

Blatt, S. J. (1974). Levels of object representation in anaclitic and introjective depression. *Psychoanalytic Study of the Child, 24*, 107-157.

Blatt, S. J. (1983). Narcissism and egocentrism as concepts in individual and cultural development. *Psychoanalysis and Contemporary Thought, 6*, 291-303.

Blatt, S. J. (1990). Interpersonal relatedness and self-definition: Two personality configurations and their implication for psychopathology and psychotherapy. In J. L. Singer (Ed.), *Repression and dissociation: Implications for personality theory, psychopathology and health* (pp. 299-335). Chicago: University of Chicago Press.

Blatt, S. J. (1991). A cognitive morphology of psychopathology. *Journal of Nervous and Mental Disease, 179*, 449-458.

Blatt, S. J. (1992). The differential effect of psychotherapy and psychoanalysis on introjective patients: The Menninger Psychotherapy Research Project revisited. *Journal of the American Psychoanalytic Association, 40*, 691-724.

Blatt, S. J. (1995). Representational structures in psychopathology. In D. Cicchetti & S. Toth (Eds.). *Representation, emotion, and cognition in developmental psychopathology* (pp. 1-33). Rochester, NY: University of Rochester Press.

Blatt, S. J., & Behrends, R. S. (1987). Separation-individuation, internalization and the nature of therapeutic action. *International Journal of Psycho-analysis, 68*, 279-297.

Blatt, S. J., & Blass, R. (1990). Attachment and separateness: A dialectic model of the products and processes of psychological development. *The Psychoanalytic Study of the Child, 45*, 107-127.

Blatt, S. J., & Blass, R. B. (1992). Relatedness and self-definition. Two primary dimensions in personality development, psychopathology, and psychotherapy. In J. Barron, M. Eagle, & D. Wolitsky (Eds.), *The interface between psychoanalysis and psychology* (pp. 399-428). Washington, DC: The American Psychological Association.

Blatt, S. J., D'Afflitti, J. P., & Quinlan, D. M. (1976). Experiences of depression in normal young adults. *Journal of Abnormal Psychology, 85*, 383-389.

Blatt, S. J., D'Afflitti, J., & Quinlan, D. M. (1979). *Depressive experiences questionnaire.* Unpublished research manual, Yale University, New Haven, CT.

Blatt, S. J., & Felsen, I. (1993). "Different kinds of folks may need different kinds of strokes": The effect of patients' characteristics on therapeutic process and outcome. *Psychotherapy Research 3*, 245-259.

Blatt, S. J., & Ford, R. (1994). *Therapeutic change: An object relations perspective.* New York: Plenum.

Blatt, S. J., & Homann, E. (1992). Parent-child interaction in the etiology of dependent and self-critical depression. *Clinical Psychology Review, 12*, 47-91.

Blatt, S. J., & Maroudas, C. (1992). Convergence of psychoanalytic and cognitive behavioral theories of depression. *Psychoanalytic Psychology, 9*, 157-190.

Blatt, S. J., Quinlan, D. M., Pilkonis, P. A. & Shea, T. (1995). Impact of perfectionism and need for approval on the brief treatment of depression. *Journal of Consulting and Clinical Psychology, 63*, 125-132.

Blatt, S. J., & Shichman, S. (1983). Two primary configurations of psychopathology. *Psychoanalysis and Contemporary Thought, 6*, 187-254.

Blatt, S. J., Zohar, A. D., Quinlan, D. M., Zuroff, D. C., & Mongrain, M. (1995). Subscales within the dependency factor of the Depressive Experiences Questionnaire. *Journal of Personality Assessment, 64*, 319-339.

Blatt, S. J., & Zuroff, D. (1992). Interpersonal relatedness and self-definition: Two prototypes for depression. *Clinical Psychology Review, 12*, 527-562.

Bowlby, J. (1969). *Attachment and loss* (Vol. 1). New York: Basic Books.

Bowlby, J. (1973). *Attachment and loss, Vol. 2: Separation, anxiety, and anger.* New York: Basic Books.

Bowlby, J. (1988). Developmental psychology comes of age. *American Journal of Psychiatry, 145*, 1-10.

Butler, R. N. (1963). The life review. *Psychiatry, 26*, 65-79.

Cane, D. B., Olinger, L. J., Gotlib, I. H., & Kuiper, N. A. (1986). Factor structure of the Dysfunctional Attitude Scale in a student population. *Journal of Clinical Psychology, 42*, 307-309.

Carlson, R. (1972). Understanding women: Implications for personality theory and research. *Journal of Social Issues, 28*(2), 17-32.

Colarusso, C. A., & Nemiroff, R. A. (1981). *Adult development.* New York: Plenum Press.

Chodorow, N. (1978). *The reproduction of mothering: Psychoanalysis and the sociology of gender.* Berkeley: University of California Press.

Chodorow, N. (1989). *Feminism and psychoanalytic theory.* New Haven, CT: Yale University Press.

Emde, R. N. (1983). The prerepresentational self and its affective core. *The Psychoanalytic Study of the Child, 38*, 165-192.

Emde, R. N. (1988). Development terminable and interminable. *International Journal of Psycho-Analysis, 69*, 23-42.

Erikson, E. H. (1959). *Identity and the life cycle.* New York: International University Press.

Erikson, E. H. (1963). *Childhood and society* (2nd ed.). New York: Norton.

Erikson, E. H. (1964). *Insight and responsibility.* New York: Norton.

Erikson, E. H. (1968). *Identity, youth and crisis.* New York: Norton.

Erikson, E. H. (1977). *Toys and reasons*. New York: Norton.

Erikson, E. H. (1982). *The life cycle completed*. New York: Norton.

Feffer, M. (1959). The cognitive implications of role-taking behavior. *Journal of Personality, 27*, 152-168.

Feffer, M. (1970). Developmental analysis of interpersonal behavior. *Psychology Review, 77*, 177-214.

Feldman, R. (1993). *Rhythmicity and synchrony between mother and infant across the first year*. Unpublished doctoral dissertation, the Hebrew University of Jerusalem.

Feldman, R., & Blatt, S. J. (in press). Precursor of attachment and self definition in early mother-infant interaction. In J. M. Masling & R. F. Bornstein (Eds.), *Empirical studies of psychoanalytic theories, Vol. 6: Psychoanalysis as developmental psychology*. Washington, DC: APA Books.

Franz, C. E., & White, K. M. (1985). Individuation and attachment in personality development: Extending Erikson's theory. *Journal of Personality, 53*, 224-256.

Freud, S. (1914). On narcissism: An introduction. *The standard edition of the complete psychological works of Sigmund Freud, 14*, 73-102.

Freud, S. (1926). Inhibitions, symptoms and anxiety. *The standard edition of the complete works of Sigmund Freud, 20*, 87-174.

Freud, S. (1957). Civilization and its discontents. *The standard edition of the complete psychological works of Sigmund Freud, 21*, 64-145. London: Hogarth Press. (Original work published 1930).

Friedman, H. S., & Booth-Kewley, S. (1987). The disease-prone personality: A meta-analytic view of the construct. *American Psychologist, 42*, 539-555.

Gilligan, C. (1982). *In a different voice*. Cambridge, MA: Harvard University Press.

Gilligan, C. (1988). Adolescent development revisited. In C. Gilligan, J.V. Ward, & J. M. Taylor (Eds.), *Mapping the moral domain* (pp. vii-xxxviii). Cambridge, MA: Harvard University Press.

Gilligan, C. (1989). Remapping the moral domain. In C. Gilligan, J. V. Ward, & J. M. Taylor (Eds.), *Mapping the moral domain* (p. 3-19). Cambridge, MA: Harvard University Press.

Horney, K. (1945). *Our inner conflicts*. New York: Norton.

Horney, K. (1950). *Neurosis and human growth*. New York: Norton.

Imber, S. D., Pilkonis, P. A., Sotsky, S. M., Elkin, I., Watkins, J. T., Collins, J. F., Shea, M. T., Leber, W. R., & Glass, D. R. (1990). Mode-specific effects among three treatments for depression. *Journal of Consulting and Clinical Psychology, 58*, 352-259.

Inhelder, B., & Piaget, J. (1964). *The early growth of logic in the child: Classification of seriation*. New York: Harper & Row. (Original work published 1959)

Klein, G. S. (1976). *Psychoanalytic theory: An exploration of essentials*. New York: International Universities Press.

Kobassa, S. C. (1982). The hardy personality: Toward a social psychology of stress and health. In J. Suls & G. Sanders (Eds.), *Social psychology of health and illness*. Hillsdale, NJ: Lawrence Erlbaum Associates.

Laurendeau, M., & Pinard A. (1962). *Casual thinking in the child: A genetic and experimental approach*. New York: International Universities Press.

Larendeau, M., & Pinard, A. (1970). *The development of the concept of space in the child*. New York: International Universities Press.

Levy, K. N., Kolligan, J., Quinlan, D. M., Becker, D. F., Edell, W. S., & McGlashan, T. H. (1994). *Two configurations of psychopathology: A test of a theory and clinical implications*. Manuscript submitted for review.

Loewald, H. (1980). *Papers on psychoanalysis*. New Haven, CT: Yale University Press.

Loewald, H. W. (1962). Internalization, separation, mourning, and the superego. *Psychoan-*

alytic Quarterly, 31, 483-504.

Loranger, A. W. (1988). *Personality Disorder Examination* (PDE Manual). Yonkers, NY: D V Communications.

McAdams, D. P. (1980). A thematic coding system for the intimacy motive. *Journal of Research in Personality, 14*, 413-432.

McAdams, D. P. (1985). *Power, intimacy, and the life story: Personological inquiries into identity.* Homewood, IL: Dorsey.

McClelland, D. C. (1980). Motive dispositions: The merits of operant and respondent measures. In L. Wheeler (Ed.), *Review of personality and social psychology* (pp. 10–41). Beverly Hills, CA: Sage.

McClelland, D. C. (1986). Some reflections on the two psychologies of love. *Journal of Personality, 54*, 334-353.

Miller, J. B. (1976). *Toward a new psychology of women.* Boston, MA: Beacon Press.

Miller, J. B. (1984). *The development of women's sense of self* (Work in progress papers, No. 84-01). Wellesley, MA: Wellesley College, The Stone Center.

Modell, A. H. (1968). *Object love and reality.* New York: International Universities Press.

Mussen, P. H., Conger, J. F., & Kagan, J. (1979). *Child development and personality.* New York: Harper & Row.

Neugarten, B. L. (1964). *Personality in middle and later life.* New York: Atherton Press.

Ouimette, P.C., Klein, D. N., Anderson, R., Riso, L. P., & Lizardi, H. (1994). Relationship of sociotropy/autonomy and dependency/self-criticism to *DSM-III-R* personality disorders. *Journal of Abnormal Psychology, 103*, 743-749.

Piaget, J. (1954). *The construction of reality in the child* (M. Cook, Trans.). New York: Basic Books. (Original work published 1937).

Piaget, J. (1962). *Play, dreams and imitation in childhood.* New York: Basic Books. (Original work published 1945).

Piaget, J. (1969). *The child's conception of time* (A. J. Pomerans, Trans.). New York: Basic Books. (Original work published 1961).

Rank, O. (1929). *Truth and reality* (J. Taft, Trans.). New York: Knopf.

Robins, C. L. & Luten, A. G. (1991). Sociotropy and autonomy: Differential patterns of clinical presentation in unipolar depression. *Journal of Abnormal Psychology, 100*, 74–77.

Sampson, E. E. (1985). Redecentralization of identity: Toward a revised concept of personal and social order. *American Psychologist, 40*, 1203-1211.

Sampson, E. E. (1988). The debate on individualism: Indigenous psychologies of the individual and their role in personal and societal functioning. *American Psychologist, 43*, 15-22.

Schafer, R. (1968). *Aspects of internalization.* Madison, CT: International Universities Press.

Shapiro, D. (1965). *Neurotic styles.* New York: Basic Books.

Shor, J., & Sanville, J. (1978). *Illusions in loving: A psychoanalytic approach to intimacy and autonomy.* Los Angeles: Double Helix.

Stern, D. N. (1977). *The first relationship: infant and mother.* Cambridge, MA: Harvard University Press.

Stern, D. (1983). The early development of schemas of self, of other, and of various experiences of "self with other." In J. D. Lichtenberg & S. Kaplan (Eds.), *Reflections of self psychology* (pp. 49-84). Hillsdale, NJ: The Analytic Press.

Stern, D. N. (1985). *The interpersonal world of the infant.* New York: Basic Books.

Stewart, A. S., & Malley, J. E. (1987). Role combination in women in early adult years: Mitigating agency and communion. In F. Crosby (Ed.), *Spouse, parent, worker: On gender and multiple roles.* (pp. 44-62). New Haven, CT: Yale University Press.

Sullivan, H. S. (1953). *The theory of interpersonal psychiatry.* New York: Norton.

Surrey, J. L. (1985). *The "self-in-relation": A theory of women's development* (Work in progress, Papers, No. 2). Wellesley, MA: Wellesley College, the Stone Center.

Wallerstein, R. S. (1986). *Forty-two lives in treatment: A study of psychoanalysis and psychotherapy*. New York: Guilford.

Weissman, A. N., & Beck, A. T. (1978). *Development and validation of the Dysfunctional Attitude Scale: A preliminary investigation*. Paper presented at the meeting of the American Psychological Association, Toronto, Canada.

Werner, H. (1957). *Comparative psychology of mental development*. New York: International Universities Press. (Original work published, 1948)

Werner, H., & Kaplan, B. (1963). *Symbol formation: An organismic-developmental approach to language and the expression of thought*. New York: Wiley.

Wiggins, J. S. (1991). Agency and communion as conceptual coordinates for the understanding and measurement of interpersonal behavior. In W. W. Grove & D. Cicchetti (Eds.), *Thinking clearly about psychology, Vol. 2: Personality and psychotherapy* (pp. 89-113). Minneapolis: University of Minnesota Press.

Winter, D. (1973). *The power motive*. New York: The Free Press.

Author Index

Subject Index